FIRST EDITION

Voces de Aztlán

A Chicana/o History Reader, Vol. 2

EDITED BY

Juan Pablo Mercado, Ph.D.

SAN DIEGO

Bassim Hamadeh, CEO and Publisher
Amy Smith, Senior Project Editor
Casey Hands, Production Editor
Jess Estrella, Senior Graphic Designer
Kylie Bartolome, Licensing Coordinator
Susana Christie, Developmental Editor
Natalie Piccotti, Director of Marketing
Kassie Graves, Senior Vice President, Editorial
Jamie Giganti, Director of Academic Publishing

Cover image: Copyright © 2014 Depositphotos/fergregory.

Printed in the United States of America.

cognella® | ACADEMIC PUBLISHING
3970 Sorrento Valley Blvd., Ste. 500, San Diego, CA 92121

CONTENTS

INTRODUCTION

T he idea of developing this two-volume reader began during my first year of
teaching the undergraduate survey courses in United States history. I was
both excited and overwhelmed by the array of primary and secondary sources I
could assign my students. I realized, however, that the same could not be said for my
survey courses in Chicana/o history. There are, of course, foundational secondary
texts, including Rodolfo "Rudy" Acuña's *Occupied America*, Manuel Gonzales'
Mexicanos, and *Crucible of Struggle* by Zaragosa Vargas. There are even important
collections of primary sources including *Testimonio* by F. Arturo Rosales. However,
this project addresses the need for a collection of both primary and secondary
sources to be compiled in one book. Having a set of diverse and instructive primary
sources, coupled with important historical essays to contextualize them, provides
an important pedagogical tool for the classroom. This reader builds on the vital
work of previous Chicana/o historians and aims to contribute a diverse way to
teach and learn these critical but routinely distorted histories.

With the first edition of his seminal work, *Occupied America*, regarding the
history of Mexicans in the United States, Rudy Acuña provided dynamism,
excitement, and controversy within and outside the academy. The premise that
Chicanos were and remain a colonized people in the United States sparked an
energy among a group of activists and students ready to soak up a history that
was sorely lacking in most institutions of higher education. As an affirmation of
their historical agency, this new generation of Chicanos and Chicanas was now
equipped with academic evidence.

> History can either oppress or liberate a people. Generalizations
> and stereotypes about the Mexican have been circulated
> in the United States for over 124 years. Adjectives such as
> "treacherous," "lazy," "adulterous," and terms such as "meskin,"
> or "greaser," have become synonymous with "Mexican" in
> the minds of many Anglo-Americans. Little has been done to
> expose the false premises on which such cultural and racial

slurs have been based. Incomplete or biased analyses by historians have perpetuated factual errors and created myths … Mexicans—Chicanos—in the United States today are an oppressed people. They are citizens, but their citizenship is second-class at best. They are exploited and manipulated by those with more power … Awareness of their history—of their contributions and struggles, of the fact that they were not the "treacherous enemy" that Anglo-American histories have said they were—can restore pride and a sense of heritage to a people who have been oppressed for so long. In short, awareness can help them to liberate themselves …[1]

This collection of essays and primary sources is specifically designed for students of Chicana/o history. It is intended to provide evidence of historical agency and support the process of liberation that Acuña first wrote about in 1972.

The volume is organized chronologically into eight chapters and covers a broad range of topics and themes, mostly from twentieth century Chicana/o history. It begins with an examination of the late nineteenth century and the struggle to ward off land disposition and political and economic disenfranchisement. Chapter One also provides insight into the rise and expansion of Jim Crow as it was experienced by Native Americans and Mexican Americans in the Southwest. Chapter Two focuses on the Mexican Revolution and highlights the voices of those seeking to move beyond reform and, instead, advocate for a true social revolutionary movement. Chapter Three underscores the complexity of understanding the broader scope of American labor history during the progressive era while Chapter Four takes a closer look at the racialization process as it played out during the Great Depression. Chapter Five assesses a few of the watershed events of World War II, including soldiering, labor, and the experiences of Mexican American women on the home front. Chapter Six considers the experiences of Mexican American communities in the postwar period and posits the concept of conditional patriotism, while Chapter Seven surveys the major strands of *El Movimiento,* including the student movement, the farmworkers' movement, and the antiwar movement. The last chapter provides a deeper interrogation into cultural resistance in the post-movement period and offers a glimpse at potential opportunities for self-determination. All together, these sources provide an important opportunity to revise a broader history of the United States.

---

1 Rodolfo "Rudy" Acuña, *Occupied America: A History of Chicanos* (New York, NY.: Harper & Row, 1972), 1.

Encroachment and Resistance in the Southwest

Editor's Introduction

During the late nineteenth century, the United States was experiencing social, economic, and political shifts that all worked to dramatically transform the nation into a burgeoning capitalist regime. These shifts also produced a great deal of racialized violence along with economic subjugation. By the close of the nineteenth century, the opportunity and optimism of radical reconstruction in the moments just after the Civil War were met with an overt backlash attempting to replicate a system of racial and economic bondage. The promise of westward expansion and land speculation that advanced in this time was very much guided by a belief in white supremacy and the institutionalization of political disenfranchisement, economic suppression, and limited legal rights. This mindset was not sectional and in the southwestern part of the United States these circumstances were palpable.

The rise of Jim Crow and racialized violence also characterize this period of United States history. A combination of laws and customs sought to intentionally separate white and non-white peoples—specifically black from white, however the scheme grew to include most racialized groups. Moreover, the intensification of lynching became widespread throughout the South as this extralegal form of racialized violence was fueled by a deep racial antagonism, in part because of economic competition and white male sexual anxiety towards people of color. In the southwestern part of the country, where the population included more Mexican and indigenous people, similar racial animosity resulted in destructive outcomes. "Between 1850 and 1870, Los Angeles witnessed seventy-seven hangings by Anglo mobs, and most of their victims were Indians or Mexicans rightly or wrongly convicted of killing whites. The lynching of Mexicans ... became so common that the Spanish-speaking population cynically referred to American Democracy as

'Linchoncracia.'"[1] This term became synonymous for how Mexican Americans experienced exclusion and violence within American society and how the legal and social protections that were accorded to white Americans were not truly extended to all. In many instances, this had fatal repercussions.

David Correia's essay on Las Gorras Blancas deals with the legal and social attempt to normalize racial subjugation, yet he also works to demonstrate how race and class were connected in the case of land speculation in New Mexico. However, just as important to his study is the aspect of resistance to this attempted subjugation. He goes on to outline how a group of subsistence farmers came together to challenge the dispossession of land and commercial development in the Southwest. Figure 1.1 (at the end of this chapter) graphically illustrates the violent nature of this racialized violence in the region. The rise of lynching was not limited to the South nor to African Americans—its violence and destruction covered the expanse of the nation.

"Retribution Will Be Their Reward": New Mexico's Las Gorras Blancas and the Fight for the Las Vegas Land Grant Commons

Correia's essay focuses on the unique strategies of resistance developed by Las Gorras Blancas [White Caps] of New Mexico. Correia demonstrates that Las Gorras Blancas, in addition to challenging racial subjugation, also worked to dismantle an increasingly oppressive capitalistic transformation that was driving the westward expansion of the United States during the last decade of the nineteenth century. Las Gorras Blancas generated a wide-ranging social movement that sought to confront the destructive economic and environmental policies that directly impacted the working-class peoples of New Mexico. Guided by a philosophy of labor organizing and self-defense, this group of political and economic dissenters engaged in a sweeping form of resistance that drew on racial and class struggles.

THINGS TO LOOK FOR AS YOU READ..

- Economic changes for subsistence farmers in New Mexico
- How Las Gorras Blancas were economic actors in the region
- The tactics of resistance used by Las Gorras Blancas

---

1 Zaragosa Vargas, *Crucible of Struggle: A History of Mexican Americans from Colonial Times to the Present Era,* 2nd ed. (New York, NY.: Oxford University Press, 2017), 145.

"Retribution Will Be Their Reward"

New Mexico's Las Gorras Blancas and the Fight for the Las Vegas Land Grant Commons

David Correia

From February 1889 until the summer of 1891 a clandestine group of night riders known as Las Gorras Blancas (the White Caps) clashed with commercial ranchers, land speculators, and the Atchison, Topeka, and Santa Fe Railroad in the northwestern grasslands of New Mexico. The White Caps cut hundreds of miles of fences that enclosed thousands of acres of what commercial ranchers and land speculators considered among the best ranching lands in the territory. The fence-cutting campaign comprised nearly eighty separate attacks in an eighteen-month period. The midnight raids targeted the commercial ranchers and merchants, newly arrived following the U.S.-Mexican War (1846–48), and the timber and tie operators who fueled local railroad expansion. The targets were among the wealthiest and most politically powerful figures in New Mexico—ranchers, merchants, and politicians—who amassed great fortunes appropriating local common property resources.

At the center of the struggle was the commons of the Town of Las Vegas Land Grant, a community land grant created by Mexico before the area became U.S. territory. Mexico had distributed the Town of Las Vegas Land Grant to subsistence settlers in the 1830s and reserved the bulk of the more than five hundred thousand-acre grant for the collective management and use of land grant members. Both Spain and Mexico used common-property land tenure arrangements to populate the northern frontier of New Mexico. The difficulties of frontier settlement required a diverse subsistence strategy that included small, private agricultural plots augmented

David Correia, "'Retribution Will Be Their Reward': New Mexico's Las Gorras Blancas and the Fight for the Las Vegas Land Grant Commons," *Radical History Review*, Issue 108, pp. 49-72. Copyright © 2010 by Duke University Press. Reprinted with permission.

by a large commons for collective livestock grazing, fuel-wood collecting, and hunting. In addition, the subsistence communities that came to settle the dozens of community land grants in northern New Mexico served as a buffer between valuable mining regions in northern Mexico and the powerful Native societies to the north. After the U.S.-Mexican War, New Mexico and all its property claims fell under the authority of the United States, where land policies favored private-property land tenure and railroad-focused commercial expansion. For speculators and large ranchers, nowhere but in the former Mexican territories was it possible to acquire such vast acreages overnight. New Mexico's many large community property claims, often with hundreds of thousands of acres in common, became prime investment targets. Few common-property land-tenure arrangements survived the transfer to U.S. control and the onset of industrial development and commercial speculation.[1]

In the 1870s investment in railroad development linked the largest population center on the Town of Las Vegas Land Grant to national and international markets. With new transportation and communications connections, federal land administrators, investors, and speculators transformed Las Vegas into the military and economic center of the territory. The investors and speculators who followed the railroads into New Mexico undermined common-property land tenure, encouraged continued railroad expansion, expanded investment and credit for commercial and industrial development, and defended the interests of commercial elites through the application of repressive state authority. Las Gorras Blancas emerged out of the turmoil created by this economic upheaval. Over the course of eighteen months, the Mexican heirs to the Town of Las Vegas Land Grant organized in opposition to the waves of enclosure brought by railroad development and commercial speculation. Las Gorras Blancas orchestrated an organized pattern of widespread rural incendiarism. Fires that consumed the haystacks and barns of local elites frequently illuminated the night sky in Las Vegas and surrounding San Miguel County, and nearly every issue of local newspapers carried new reports of fences found cut and ranchers evicted by the White Caps. Local economic and political elites reacted to the "lawlessness" of the "White Cap Outrages," as the movement came to be described in the business-friendly press, through a reactionary campaign of rural repression. The press vilified suspected leaders. Local authorities harassed alleged members with frequent arrests.

For the first historians who examined Las Gorras Blancas, the movement provided an example of primitive social protest in action. These studies, following Eric Hobsbawm's call for historical attention to peasant resistance movements,[2] examined the cultural roots of insurgency in New Mexico but largely limited their explanation of the group's activities to kinship bonds and cultural tradition.[3] The first careful case study by Andrew

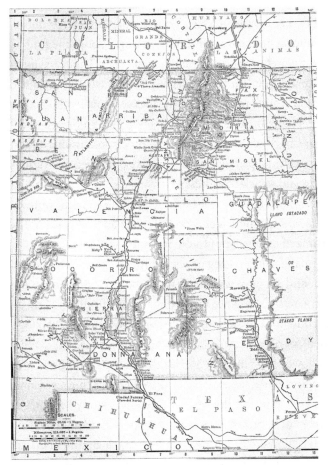

Figures 1.1.1 and 1.1.2 The Town of Las Vegas Land Grant encompassed more than 500,000 acres in San Miguel County surrounding Las Vegas, the main route of the Atchison, Topeka, and Santa Fe Railroad through New Mexico, as shown on this 1895 Rand McNally map of New Mexico and San Miguel County. Source: Rand McNally, "The New 11 x 14 Atlas of the World," 1895. Map courtesy of Pan Reitsch (copyright memoriallibrary. com)

Schlesinger defined the typical Hispano settler in New Mexico as prepolitical, primitive, and constrained by inherent cultural limitations: "He did not worry about the future," Schlesinger wrote, "as he did not regret the past; it would not change."[4] Though sympathetic to their plight and understanding of their tactics, Schlesinger nonetheless explained the mode of *mexicano* social protest similarly as did New Mexico's nineteenth-century elites: outsiders, labor agitators, and opportunists gave momentum to the movement, not new racial and class antagonisms born of the waves of property dispossession. Robert Rosenbaum took up Schlesinger's cultural pathologies argument and claimed that various and inherent cultural imperatives and social structures of Hispano agrarian communities in New Mexico offered a clue to the origins of resistance. The White Cap movement, he argued, while not entirely devoid of political or economic substance, was primarily a rural protest movement organized in defense of traditional lifeways.[5]

This preoccupation with Hispano culture rising up against Anglo enterprise reflected a tradition "among historians and social scientists writing about land issues in the Southwest [that] tended to characterize resistance by the poor Spanish-Indian-Mexican population as void of political content or consequence."[6] In contrast, more recent efforts have departed from cultural analyses of resistance. Anselmo Arellano situated the conflict in the political struggles that followed from the U.S.-Mexican War. Las Gorras Blancas in his view reflected a grassroots effort to defend existing Hispano political power against the changes wrought by elites and "political thieves."[7] In Arellano's study Las Gorras Blancas appear as one of a number of reformist organizations opposed to Anglo political authority. A recent article by Mary Romero has made the most explicit argument to date against the familiar "racialized ethnics" analysis of Las Gorras Blancas.[8] In addition, hers is the first to focus on political economy. She argues that the erasure of class struggle in the movement continues to bedevil a more nuanced and contingent understanding of "the cultures and traditions of the land grant descendants."[9] While the emphasis on racialized class relations among recent studies of Las Gorras Blancas resistance provides a necessary corrective to previous culturalist explanations, important blind spots still remain. Despite Romero's emphasis on new class relations and the transformation in landownership and tenure in nineteenth-century New Mexico, the various institutions and practices that constructed new financial networks and imposed capitalist wage relations remain underexamined and continue to escape close scrutiny. Lacking a detailed analysis of the political economy of social conflict in 1890s New Mexico, Las Gorras Blancas remains popularly and unfairly understood as a reformist peasant movement engaged in a desperate defense of rural traditions.

The purpose of this essay is to examine Las Gorras Blancas as first and foremost a broad social movement organized in opposition to the privatization of common property resources and the forced shift from subsistence to industrial production. My aim is to examine Las Gorras Blancas through a wider lens that draws into view not just cultural or racial conflict but also the regional patterns of resource-led, economic development in New Mexico. In doing this, I demonstrate that Las Gorras Blancas were powerful economic actors in the development of nineteenth-century New Mexico. As I show here, the campaign by Las Gorras Blancas against a new class of commercial ranchers and land speculators came on the heels of dramatic shifts in land tenure, rural and urban production, and political authority. Waves of enclosures squeezed communal property and thus threatened small-scale and subsistence production on the Las Vegas Land Grant. The enclosures captured and reserved a seemingly infinite reservoir of grazing, timber, and mining resources for newly arrived East Coast and European investors. As rural producers were thrown off the land, an emerging industrial workforce further transformed rural and urban production patterns in the territory. The emergence of Las Gorras Blancas came in response to transformative economic changes for Hispanic subsistence farmers in New Mexico.

New Mexico posed unique challenges to those seeking its resources. While the slow erosion in common-property land tenure established the conditions for increased investment in resource extraction and commercial speculation, it also fueled rural and urban discontent among land-grant heirs. The disruption of existing production patterns based on common-property land tenure, the imposition of private property, and the expansion of railroad development proved uneven, partial, and contested.[10] The White Caps met the diverse patterns and institutions that threatened common property land tenure with tactics and targets that evade simplistic explanations based solely on race or ethnicity. They cut fences and burned barns, but they also delivered a withering critique of political cronyism, commercial speculation, and industrial capitalism. They destroyed rail and telegraph lines, but they also organized the growing industrial workforce to oppose capitalist wage relations.

Despite the lack of political economy in previous analyses, the politics and actions attributed to Las Gorras Blancas reveal they had a sophisticated grasp of New Mexico's nineteenth-century political economy that developed into a radical social movement in opposition to the "land grabbers" and "political bossism" that served commercial interests. Their defense of common property relations galvanized a social movement that not only defended rural production but also targeted the technologies and institutions that made speculative investment possible—railroads, banks, and barbed wire fences—and for a time effectively muted the growing power of commercial interests and industrial firms over the Town of Las Vegas Land Grant. Their dual focus on rural and urban issues confounded territorial officials and rapidly expanded their political power among rural and urban working-class constituencies.

Though territorial officials ignored growing rural discontent in the years prior to Las Gorras Blancas, they understood its causes well. In October 1885 the New Mexico territorial governor Edmund Ross gave an early warning of potential problems to come.[11] In his annual report to the secretary of the interior, he chronicled a rather gloomy state of affairs for the territory. Among a long list of unresolved issues, Ross found most vexing the continued refusal of the United States to recognize common-property land titles in the territory. Despite treaty guarantees and decades of adjudication, millions of acres in scores of common-property Spanish and Mexican land grants lingered in legal limbo. The treaty that had ended the U.S.-Mexican War obligated the United States to honor the community-land grants in New Mexico that were based on Spanish and Mexican property law. The land grants, Ross told the secretary of the interior, were "unimpeachable" and "as perfect and conclusive as can be found anywhere." He found it inexcusable (a "serious embarrassment," he called it) that thirty years of federal adjudication had failed to resolve the issue.[12] According to Ross, "public robbers" capitalized on the uncertainty in property claims. Fraudulent homestead, timber-culture, and preemption claims "have been thus absorbed into great cattle ranches, merely for the purpose of getting control of water courses and springs, and thus keep out settlers and small herds, and in others the lands have been thus stolen for purely speculative purposes."[13]

The Ross report echoed previous warnings of land speculation and enclosures in New Mexico. Eight months prior to Ross's report, the General Land Office (GLO) concluded a four-year inquiry into corruption and land fraud in New Mexico. Its investigation, which included the careful scrutiny of nearly every private land claim in the territory, implicated commercial cattle ranchers, railroad companies, territorial politicians, and federal officials in a coordinated campaign of wide-ranging land fraud throughout the territory that had resulted in thousands of acres of illegal enclosures.[14] According to the report, while land speculation plagued the entire territory of New Mexico, a pattern of public corruption and intense speculation focused in particular on the Las Vegas Land Grant commons. The Las Vegas Land Grant was particularly appealing to land speculators and commercial cattle operators for its vast grasslands, timber reserves, and rail connections. Investigators from the GLO uncovered a conspiracy that included the San Miguel County district attorney Miguel Salazar, commercial ranchers, land speculators, and federal officials. Salazar colluded with public officials on behalf of a cabal of large cattle ranchers in a scheme to consolidate control of the Las Vegas commons.

Despite Ross's descriptions of bureaucratic malfeasance and the GLO's evidence of systemic fraud in the administration of public lands, their analyses stopped short of a broader consideration of the social impact of speculative investment and the erosion of rural land tenure. Despite the growing racial and class antagonisms that came with the capitalist transformation of New Mexico, territorial and federal officials, along with commercial operators, were unprepared for the challenge posed by Las Gorras Blancas, a challenge rooted in the antagonisms developing as a function of the capitalist transformation of New Mexico.

The Capitalist Transformation of New Mexico

By the time Las Gorras Blancas emerged in the late 1880s, forty years of global economic expansion had reached New Mexico and settled squarely on the Town of Las Vegas Land Grant. While land fraud likely exacerbated social conflict in 1880s San Miguel County, the emergence of a broad social movement in defense of common-property land-tenure arrangements reflected a broader set of social and economic shifts that came with commercial investment and land speculation in territorial New Mexico. While timber operators clear-cut the forests around Las Vegas, cattle operators flooded the open range with massive herds that turned New Mexico into a major livestock exporter. As railroad mileage increased, so, too, did commercial herds. Throughout this period homestead and timber-culture entries by commercial ranchers continued and further eroded common property claims to the Las Vegas Land Grant. Economic development in San Miguel County was thus a function of increased market access for New Mexico's resources fueled by new forms of credit. Between 1865 and 1900, fifteen hundred British companies blanketed the American West with venture capital.[15] In addition to railroad and cattle, mining investments contributed to the late nineteenth-century economic transformation in New Mexico and the intermountain West. Land speculators advertised investment opportunities in the "mountains of silver" found in New Mexico, and their exaggerations enticed European investment.[16] In the final forty years of the nineteenth century, British mining investments exceeded £77 million ($417 million) in the intermountain American West.[17] Between 1886 and 1900, twelve British mining companies invested £1.3 million ($6.3 million) in New Mexico.[18] The New Mexico Bureau of Immigration relentlessly advertised New Mexico's resource wealth, describing San Miguel County as possessing "the greatest and most varied natural resources [in the territory]." By the time of the Las Gorras Blancas raids, coalfield production exceeded 1 million tons in New Mexico, with values approaching $2 million.[19]

A series of closely related economic and technological changes paved the way for the large-scale exploitation of New Mexico's natural resources. The technical achievements of railroad development and barbed wire fencing established the necessary conditions for commercial ranching, industrial timber production, and expanded mining. These technologies of capital were funded by, and contributed to, the expansion of new financial institutions that made speculative investments possible on various common-property land grants. These factors overwhelmed common-property relations, supplanted subsistence production, and integrated places like Las Vegas into a network of global financial markets.

Railroads arrived in New Mexico in the late 1870s as though chased into the territory by a stampede of finance capital. By 1885, following a span of only five years, more than eleven hundred miles of track had been constructed in New Mexico.[20] The Atchison, Topeka, and Santa Fe Railroad bisected the Las Vegas Land Grant and concentrated speculative investment on the grant's nearly endless sea of grazing lands. The arrival of railroads enticed investment in large-scale commercial ranching accomplished through massive enclosures made possible by new barbed wire fencing technologies.

Until the second half of the nineteenth century, the lack of effective fencing materials and the cost of construction and maintenance bedeviled the western expansion of capitalist ranching. The smooth wire fences commonly used by prairie settlers proved ineffective on the large enclosures required in arid and semiarid western grasslands.[21] In the early 1870s Illinois-based merchants began to produce a variety of barbed wire fences for sale in the West. Barbed wire fencing served a variety of commercial ranching interests. The barbs limited damage by animals, thus reducing maintenance costs, and in less than a decade the technology—with its easy production methods, low capital investment, and minimal maintenance needs—had spread widely: by 1880 a million miles of barbed wire fenced the West.[22] Hundreds of miles of barbed wire crisscrossed northern New Mexico. By 1884 barbed wire fencing had produced wholesale enclosures throughout eastern and northern New Mexico.[23] The ubiquity of barbed wire closed off sheep trails and water holes throughout the upland north in New Mexico.

New transportation infrastructure and the ability to effectively and affordably enclose grazing lands spurred an increase in the circulation of finance capital in New Mexico, particularly in Las Vegas. While there were no banking institutions in New Mexico in 1870, by 1890 forty-six banks operated in the territory.[24] Newly opened territorial banks competed to fund speculative investments in land and cattle. Linked to finance capitalists in St. Louis, Chicago, and New York, New Mexico's nineteenth-century bankers absorbed huge capital investments from East Coast and European investors who sought to profit from New Mexico's resource bonanza. The first banks that opened in Las Vegas operated as a real estate syndicate. Speculators established banks, named themselves directors, and took out loans. Money poured into resource development: timber, mining, and cattle operations.[25]

The three banks that opened in Las Vegas between 1876 and 1890 financed the local economic expansion brought by the railroad.[26] The San Miguel National Bank of Las Vegas advanced loans for livestock investments at 18 percent interest rates.[27] Despite these high interest rates, the low cost of land and labor guaranteed huge profit margins. Through the loans large cattle operators in San Miguel County rapidly expanded herd sizes. The Scottish rancher Thomas Carson described early 1880s Las Vegas as "wide open. Real estate was moving freely, prices advancing, speculation rife; and infectious."[28] As competition for huge profits increased, competition fueled by easy access to credit and based on the free use of the commons, highly leveraged commercial ranchers fenced the commons in a scramble to protect their investments.

By 1889 New Mexico was fully integrated into national and international markets for investment and resource extraction. More than a decade of railroad development, the nearly complete enclosure of the common lands, and the expansion of credit markets had transformed property relations and land tenure on the Las Vegas Land Grant commons. Massive cattle herds owned by ranchers from Europe and the East Coast dominated the ranges around Las Vegas. The European cattle baron Wilson Waddingham consolidated over twelve thousand acres in fraudulent homestead claims along the Ute Creek and the Canadian River. By the 1880s Waddingham controlled nearly all important access points to springs and watercourses in huge swaths of San Miguel County.[29] As the number of cattle and ranchers increased, the competition for profits precipitated sell-offs by smaller ranchers and additional waves of enclosures. Established cattle operators and existing homesteaders fenced in more and more of the commons in a scramble to protect investments and property claims. "Seeing that it was quite hopeless to run cattle profitably on the open-range system," Carson fenced one hundred thousand acres in the 1890s in a pattern that played itself out across San Miguel County.[30] Despite increased freight and loan costs, investments in large herds remained profitable for the largest ranching operators as the massive enclosures kept production costs low.

The 1890 San Miguel tax assessment recorded the new economic disparity in the county.[31] Waddingham, who recorded no property claims in the county, owned 22,500 of the 149,655 cattle there. Two small, Anglo-dominated enclaves of newly arrived economic elites accounted for nearly half of all cattle grazing on the Las Vegas Land Grant—2,356 cattle per resident. One tax assessment precinct, dominated by large cattle operations and territorial elites, reported a herd that exceeded 40,000 head of cattle. Commercial operators overwhelmed subsistence producers, who averaged barely more than 16 head of cattle. This growing disparity produced sharp divisions in Las Vegas and fueled popular discontent among the heirs of the Mexican recipients of the Town of Las Vegas Land Grant.

The enclosures and commercial herds imposed a new commercial and industrial geography on a landscape previously organized around common-property land-tenure arrangements and subsistence production. New fences and railroads impeded access not only to water holes and grasslands but also to churches and schools. The social interruptions wrought by these transformations contributed to popular discontent among small-scale producers. As the commons slowly disappeared behind barbed wire fences, frustrated smallholders were increasingly forced into wage jobs with the railroad or local commercial ranchers.

Resistance and the Origins of Las Gorras Blancas

Las Gorras Blancas began cutting fences only after the collapse of legal efforts to defend common-property land tenure on the Las Vegas Land Grant commons. The legal struggle over the commons began in 1873 when a group of economic and political elites claimed all authority over the land grant, including the right to distribute land to new settlers. The U.S. Congress had confirmed the grant and its common property in 1860 to the Town of Las Vegas. Congress, however, failed to explain in the confirmation exactly who or what comprised the "Town of Las Vegas." While the 1873 attempt to seize the land grant failed, it had the effect of clouding common property legal claims for the grant. As a result of the uncertainty created by Congress, many settlers tried to protect farming and grazing plots by fencing in small portions of the grant. In the early 1880s a number of commercial cattle operators purchased recently fenced tracts of common lands and asserted private ownership.

This pattern continued until 1887 when three brothers—Jose, Francisco, and Pablo Padilla—each fenced in 160-acre sections of the grant commons. The Padillas feared that the expansion of commercial grazing threatened collective resource access to the commons. They argued in court that grazing by nonheirs on the grant commons created uncertainty over the legal ownership of the Las Vegas Land Grant. The unique threat to collective resource use prompted an unusual solution. Their status as land grant heirs, they claimed, gave them the legal right to fence the common lands on behalf of other grant members. The fences, they claimed, did not constitute a conversion to private lands but rather a defense against commercial enclosure. Legal opposition to the Padillas came from Philip Milhiser, the representative of an investment consortium that relied on enclosures and advocated the privatization of the land grant commons.

Milhiser v. Padilla pitted familiar enemies in the struggle for New Mexico land grants against each other. Milhiser represented the interests of the Las Vegas Land and Cattle Company, a cattle, timber, and real estate corporation. The Padillas represented local land grant members. Elisha Long, the chief justice of the New Mexico Supreme Court, heard the district court case. Long appointed a special master to referee the dispute and recommend a course of action. The July 1888 referee's report favored the right of the

Padillas to fence the commons. Despite the recommendation Long spent the next year in deliberation. It was during the limbo of Long's lengthy delay that a number of cattle operators erected massive enclosures on the grant commons. One cattle operator fenced in more than ten thousand acres.[32] In addition, speculators continued to make homestead and timber-culture claims to the Santa Fe Land Office for land around Las Vegas.[33] Long finally rendered his decision in November 1889. In it, he concluded that the land grant belonged to the Town of Las Vegas (despite ongoing uncertainty over who or what group represented the interests of the "Town of Las Vegas"). Most interesting, Long concluded that the Padillas' fences were allowable under the terms of the original Mexican grant. In doing so, Long stretched the definition of agricultural land—that portion set aside for settlement—to include also the common grazing land, leaving open the possibility for the legal privatization of common property.

Las Gorras Blancas activities began during Long's deliberations and, without a legal solution to the enclosures, increased through the summer and fall of 1889. By May, reports of fence cutting by huge parties of hooded horsemen swamped territorial and county officials. District Attorney Salazar, an important ally and accommodator of land speculators, moved swiftly in defense of commercial interests. In early summer, he brought twenty-six men to trial on charges of fence cutting and property damage, but the lack of witnesses to back up circumstantial evidence doomed his efforts. The first trial ended in an acquittal on all counts. Although Salazar did not know it then, it would be the closest he would ever come to a conviction against fence cutting on the Las Vegas commons.

Less than two months later, a series of dramatic attacks on the fences of prominent political leaders and wealthy ranchers announced the full arrival of Las Gorras Blancas. Night riders cut miles of barbed wire on a ranch along the Tecolote River owned by two wealthy Las Vegas merchants. The homes of the surveyor general and the captain of the militia burst into flames and burned to the ground. A former governor and two European ranchers found miles of fences cut and scores of fence posts destroyed.[34] In August, night riders destroyed miles of fences and posts and uprooted the crops of the county sheriff, Lorenzo Lopez. The sheriff, to the dismay of local business interests, complied with Las Gorras Blancas' demands and removed remaining wire and posts himself. Letters poured into the governor's office from commercial ranchers. "I have appealed to the sheriff of our county" wrote one rancher,

> but am doubtful if any efficient protection will be given me, as the so called White Caps have been doing about as they see fit in this county for nearly the year past ... about two weeks ago notice was

Figure 1.1.3. Juan José, Pablo, and Nicanor Herrera (from left to right). This photo is believed to have been taken during the period when they were union organizers in New Mexico. Source: Charles Siringo, *Cowboy Detective: A True Story of Twenty-two Years with a World-famous Detective Agency* (Chicago: W.B. Conkey Company, 1912).

> given to our sheriff that if he did not remove a fence which was
> around some land he claimed to own, it would be cut. I know you
> will be astonished when I say that he immediately removed the fence
> and brought the wire and the gates into town.[35]

In November, the railroad agent in nearby Rowe, New Mexico, stormed out of his house with a loaded shotgun ready to confront Las Gorras Blancas as they destroyed his fence. Amid a barrage of return fire, he fled back "into his house to save his life," and barely survived. The summer ended with White Cap attacks on the fences and property of the Indian agent and the county tax assessor.

Local officials scrambled to make sense of the group. Political leaders and local newspapers sought an explanation for the rise of Las Gorras Blancas in the rapid increase in Knights of Labor chapters, which suddenly seemed to pop up everywhere in San Miguel County. Where Knight chapters appeared, they noted, Las Gorras Blancas activities followed. The focus on the Knights of Labor as a front for Las Gorras Blancas activities drew attention to three brothers, Juan José, Pablo, and Nicanor Herrera. All three were prominent union members and Knights organizers in San Miguel County.

By the late 1880s the Knights had become one of the largest labor unions in the United States.[36] The union found success in the mid-1880s organizing the coal-mining and lumber camps of Colorado, Wyoming, and Utah. Juan José Herrera had spent years working in and organizing coal and lumber camps throughout the Rocky Mountain West. When the Herrera brothers first organized Knights of Labor chapters in New Mexico, only three Knight chapters existed. By the spring of 1890 they had organized twenty more. Nearly all operated under the Spanish name Los Caballeros del Trabajo.

Intense organizing efforts by Los Caballeros and expanded activities by Las Gorras Blancas dominated local politics in late 1889 and early 1890. Territorial and federal officials, convinced of Caballero/Las Gorras Blancas connections, began a campaign to stop both the epidemic in fence cutting and the increase in union organizing among land-grant members. Salazar pursued legal harassment as a strategy. He ordered the arrest of twenty-three people after an October grand jury relying on flimsy evidence had indicted forty-seven men, including the Herreras, on fence-cutting charges.[37] In the days following the arrests, crowds began to appear outside the Las Vegas jail. On December 11, 1889, the sheriff telegraphed the governor, Bradford Prince, pleading for "fifty rifles and ammunition for same. The kind you keep for the militia" to defend the jail from "a mob over one hundred strong."[38] Salazar responded by arresting Juan José and Nicanor Herrera. The arrests further inflamed supporters. "The three leaders of fence cutters just captured and in jail," a colleague of Salazar's cabled the governor; "large parties of their friends coming into town. Trouble expected."[39] The crowd swelled over a tense weekend, but the violence that Salazar expected never materialized. After three days in jail all suspected fence cutters were bailed out and welcomed into the arms of a crowd of over three hundred supporters and family members. With children holding the hands of the released men, nearly all members of various Caballeros chapters, their families, and supporters marched through the streets of Las Vegas in an impromptu parade waving American flags and singing the abolitionist and labor song "John Brown's Body."

The public expression of solidarity for the suspected fence cutters encouraged a new pattern of overtly political demonstrations by Las Gorras Blancas. In December 1889, and again in March and August 1890, large groups of masked night riders rode into Las Vegas and followed the December parade route into the plaza. There they posted and distributed copies of a handbill, titled "Nuestra plataforma" ("Our Platform"), describing their aims.[40] The manifesto identified the agents and tactics of economic exploitation, enumerated the potential consequences that motivated the group's actions, and described their political goals:

> Our purpose is to protect the rights of the people in general; and especially those of the helpless classes. ... We want no 'land grabbers' or obstructionists of any sort to interfere. We will watch them. ... If the old system should continue, death would be a relief to our sufferings. And for our rights our lives are the least we can pledge. ... If they persist in their usual methods retribution will be their reward.

The tactics of Las Gorras Blancas and the rhetoric of the manifesto suggested that the group was not a reformist movement but instead a direct threat to the newly emerging economic order. Salazar described "Nuestra plataforma" to the governor as "anarchical, revolutionary and communistic."[41]

In February the *Las Vegas Optic* newspaper advocated a compromise resolution to the fence cutting:

> While the Optic does not approve of the acts of those who have been engaged in the cutting of those unlawful fences on the grant, yet we do not wholly condemn their course but believe that it has been largely and usually those that have improperly taken the law into their own hands. ... Let us then unite ... and preserve and protect this great property from all further depredation, that it may be kept intact and held for the common benefit of all our citizens.[42]

Despite condemnations and pleas for compromise, Las Gorras Blancas attacks in early 1890 expanded to include new targets among the large timber and tie operators cutting trees on the grant commons for the railroad. On March 6, 1890, three hundred masked and armed night riders ripped up railroad ties and cut telegraph lines. In the attack they destroyed six thousand ties.[43] The escalation of attacks and increase in targets beyond merely fences frightened political and commercial elites, who again flooded the governor with letters demanding government protection and weapons to combat the White Caps. On March 29, the deputy sheriff who operated a ranch along the Upper Pecos River wrote a letter to the governor with a series of claims of violence and criminal activity by Las Gorras Blancas, including "robbing the stores in the small towns and threatening the lives of those who oppose them."[44] The deputy sheriff pleaded to the governor for "not less than one dozen rifles with ammunition" to defend the fences along the Pecos.

Despite increased concern among politically elite San Miguel residents, the White Caps continued to target wealthy cattle operators. In April they cut the fences of the probate judge Manuel C. de Baca, who promptly wrote to the governor and demanded that a militia be raised to put down the White Caps.[45]

Political pressure increased, but the April 1890 trial for suspected fence cutters arrested in December never happened. The charges were dismissed when the sheriff failed to locate the grand jury witnesses. A furious Salazar speculated that "those witnesses have been killed and disposed of by the white caps."[46] Repeating the scene of four months earlier, the defendants spilled out of the Las Vegas courthouse and into the arms of cheering supporters.[47] Meanwhile, attacks on the railroad continued. Groups of masked riders stopped teamsters hauling ties for the railroad and ordered them to charge more for their labor. In August 1890 railroad workers found a notice posted to a depot and section house that read, "to all section foreman and operators, you are advised to leave here at once otherwise you will not be able to do so." A number of employees quit work following the posting. The railroad pleaded with territorial officials for protection.[48] The attacks on the railroad corresponded with new attacks on wealthy ranchers. In July Waddingham found a note, written in Spanish, posted on some of the fences that enclosed his twelve-thousand-acre ranch:

Sir:

> This notice is with the object of requesting you to coil up your wire as soon as possible from the North and South sides. They are fences which are damaging the unhappy people and we request you further to coil up your wire as soon as you can to the agricultural land, and if you do not do it, you will suffer the consequences from us.
>
> Your Servants,
> The White Caps[49]

By August no rancher or timber and tie operator working on the land grant had escaped attention. The effect was a total shutdown of railroad construction and cattle operations that rippled through the local economy. "You will see," wrote one merchant in a letter to various U.S. senators, "that the R.R. Co. has ceased to buy any more ties in this Territory, cutting us short of an annual expenditure by [the Atchison, Topeka, and Santa Fe] of $100,000 annually."[50]

The secretary of the interior, James Noble, ordered Governor Prince to "enforce private rights" and put a stop to the "White Cap Outrages."[51] Noble was under constant pressure from various senators and a prominent Washington, D.C. attorney named Benjamin F. Butler, who had himself fenced four hundred thousand acres of land in New

Mexico.[52] Butler had sent an agent to New Mexico in June of 1890 to investigate White Cap activities.[53] The agent's 1890 report had alarmed Butler, who then spent the better part of a year lobbying federal officials to defend commercial interests. Butler's appeals for federal intervention relied on racialized arguments to suggest that only labor agitators could be responsible for the campaign of Las Gorras Blancas. "You must recollect," he told the secretary, "that these are Mexicans; that the Mexicans in New Mexico, with the exception of perhaps five per cent, are the most ignorant people on the face of the earth."[54]

But letters to the governor and to Secretary Noble from political opportunists and outraged commercial ranchers competed with others that blamed large ranching interests for unrest in the county. One writer reminded the governor that "many parties fenced in big tracts of land in the Las Vegas grant, shutting off water and wood from people settled on parcels of these lands long ago and thereby left without means of support."[55] The judge who had previously dismissed fence-cutting indictments located the origins of unrest in "the establishment of large landed estates, or baronial feudalism" in San Miguel County.[56]

In the early debate over the origins of White Cap activities, Governor Prince was initially unmoved by the demands from hard-liners like Butler. While he acknowledged that the problem of fence cutting posed a serious threat to resource extraction and railroad development in the county, he remained skeptical that the White Caps constituted any real menace. "While an unfortunate feeling exists [in Las Vegas] arising principally from the unsettled titles to land grants and the belief of a large body of people that they have rights in common in certain grants on which others have been fencing considerable areas," Prince wrote the secretary, "yet there is naturally much exaggeration about the matter and that every kind of wrong doing however committed is now very naturally attributed to the so-called 'White Caps.' "[57]

The national Knights of Labor and the three local Anglo-controlled Knights chapters, however, lobbied the governor to oppose Las Gorras Blancas. The tactics, particularly threats against workers who refused to follow Las Gorras Blancas demands, brought the Herreras into conflict with the local chapters and the national headquarters. In July, Juan José Herrera, representing local Caballeros chapters, offered to meet with the governor to discuss Los Caballeros. Herrera maintained that there were no formal links between Los Caballeros and Las Gorras Blancas, and he denied that he or any member of Los Caballeros played any role in Las Gorras Blancas activities. Prince traveled to Las Vegas in July 1890, where he spent nearly a month conferring with business interests. He made a speech to the Las Vegas Commercial Club, where one merchant took the opportunity to present the governor with a bill for damages done by the White Caps.[58] Prince finally met with Juan José and Nicanor Herrera in August, during the same week that Las Gorras Blancas posted the notices in train depot houses ordering section men, then making $1.40 per day, off the job.[59] Prince met with leaders of the Anglo-controlled Las Vegas assembly of the Knights the following day. The meetings convinced Prince that the Herreras were connected to Las Gorras Blancas. He encouraged the local Anglo Knights to write to the Knights of Labor national president Terrence Powderly: "The land grabbers fenced up our public domain, whatever they chose, without the shadow of a title, or if they purchased a tract of land with a title, they would fence in ten times as much as they bought," their letter began. "About this time a renewal of the commission of Brother J. J. Herrera came to hand, and as organization proceeded, so also did fence cutting. … Now who these fence cutters are we are not prepared to say. But the Mexican people who are being organized as K of L, are of the poorer class and consequently they are more ignorant."[60] The letter went on to ask Powderly to suspend new charters for Knight assemblies in New Mexico, particularly those organized by Herrera, until a resolution to White Cap resistance could be achieved.

After finding success in locating opposition to Las Gorras Blancas within the Anglo Knights of Labor chapter, the first group outside local business interests to publicly condemn the White Caps, the governor called a public meeting to find support for the establishment of "a committee to take steps to protect property and especially to obtain testimony on which the authorities could act."[61] The governor was convinced that "the name of the Knights of Labor has been used as a cloak for the dissemination of lawless ideas and the organization of a secret society generally known as White Cap."[62] He credited Juan José Herrera with organizing Caballeros chapters as a front for Las Gorras Blancas. "He has recently organized about 20 assemblies of Knights of Labor in San Miguel County, which are still unchartered; and it is generally believed that at the same time he has disseminated the ideas and created the secret organization which have resulted in the depredations in question. At all events the outrages have followed in his track in a very noticeable manner."[63]

Prince hoped the public meeting would serve as a forum to "devise means to stop the depredations and punish the wrong-doers."[64] Instead, angry land-grant heirs excoriated the governor and local business interests. Attendees denounced local business interests as "land grabbers" and praised "those who were defending the rights of the people against them."[65] Local residents, one after the other, complained bitterly about the enclosures and cattle operators who fenced the commons. The governor came away shocked. "More than one half of the people of that town," he wrote, "including many of those whom we would call the best citizens, sympathize with the fence cutting on the Las Vegas Grant, and this prevents that strong public sentiment which we ought to have as an aid in suppressing these outrages."[66] Despite the popular support and local anger

Prince found in Las Vegas, his report to the Interior Department recommended that the president either dispatch troops to New Mexico to restore order or hire Pinkerton detectives to infiltrate the White Caps. "There can be no doubt that there is a secret oath-bound organization in San Miguel County," Prince wrote to Noble. "It is believed to be confined entirely to natives of New Mexico and almost entirely to the most ignorant class. As nearly as can be ascertained a few active and educated men have arranged this organization, working on the idea that the common people are being deprived of their rights."[67]

As federal attention on Las Gorras Blancas increased in the fall of 1890, Juan José Herrera and others shifted from labor organizing to party politics when they joined the Partido del Pueblo Unido (The United People's Party), a political third party composed largely of reformists and union activists. The move by the chief organizers of Los Caballeros into party politics coincided with an abrupt end to White Cap activities. That the end of White Cap attacks would accompany the beginning of party activities stoked speculation that the Herreras were indeed behind Las Gorras Blancas activities. There was, however, another possible explanation for the end of fence cutting. By the fall of 1890 every single fence that had enclosed the Las Vegas Land Grant commons had been cut, and none had survived reconstruction. Initially, the strategic shift to party politics proved effective. During the fall elections the entire slate of Partido candidates was elected, including Juan José Herrera as the county's probate judge and Pablo Herrera as the county's representative to the territorial legislature.

Two events in February of 1891, however, unraveled the political momentum of the Partido and undermined the possibility that popular enthusiasm for Las Gorras Blancas and its aims would translate into radical change or even political reform. The first came at the close of the legislative session in February, when Pablo Herrera resigned from the legislature and left the party in disgust. One session convinced him that neither the legislature nor the Partido could be a vehicle for radical political and economic changes. "The time I spent in the penitentiary was more enjoyable than the time I spent here," he said in remarks to the entire legislature. "There is more honesty in the halls of the Territorial prison than in the halls of the legislature."[68] Returning to San Miguel County, he resumed the labor organizing that had first inspired grassroots opposition to resource extractive industrial development of the Las Vegas Land Grant commons. Territorial officials feared Pablo Herrera's organizing would lead to a revival of White Cap activities in the county. Not long after his return to Las Vegas, a deputy sheriff gunned him down as he walked unarmed along the street in front of the courthouse. There were no charges pending against Herrera at the time of the shooting. The deputy was not charged with any crime.

Herrera's violent death signaled the beginning of a broad backlash against Las Gorras Blancas, Los Caballeros, and the Partido. The climax came with a second shooting in late February, when unknown shooters raked the offices of Thomas Catron, a prominent territorial lawyer, politician, and land speculator, with gunfire. Prince used the shooting as a pretext to infiltrate the Partido and Los Caballeros. For the job he hired the Pinkerton National Detective Agency, a union-busting firm notorious for its use of labor spies and agents provocateurs.[69] The Pinkerton operative Charles Siringo spent the summer of 1891 investigating Los Caballeros and the Herrera brothers. Unfortunately for Prince, what Siringo lacked in counterintelligence skills he made up for in bluster and self-promotion. He publicized fantastic claims that he had infiltrated the White Caps, befriended Nicanor Herrera, joined various secret societies, and uncovered links between Las Gorras Blancas, the Knights of Labor, and the Partido. While Siringo's claims fanned the flames of anti-White Cap sentiment, particularly among conservative newspaper editors, Prince refused to pursue legal action. Siringo's evidence, more spin than substance, was based on a "partial confession" he claimed to have taken from Nicanor, along with endless unsubstantiated anecdotes and circumstantial evidence.[70] While Prince refused to pursue legal remedies, the U.S. attorney for the territory sought grand-jury indictments for fence cutters based on a separate and lengthy federal investigation. But like Siringo's investigation and previous criminal cases against local land-grant activists, the testimony before the grand jury was comprised of unsubstantiated claims by various settlers who themselves had fenced dubious homestead claims on the commons. The grand jury refused to make any indictments.[71]

Where territorial and federal officials failed, however, San Miguel's merchant and commercial class succeeded. A reactionary group called the United Protection Association aggressively defended commercial interests and painted antibusiness and antienclosure proponents as agitators and opponents of progress. In the wake of constant denunciations by conservative political leaders and business-friendly newspapers, the reaction covered the territory. Newspapers throughout the territory of New Mexico frequently editorialized against the Partido and Las Gorras Blancas. Under the weight of constant public attacks, the Partido del Pueblo Unido failed to translate support for Los Caballeros and Las Gorras Blancas into a political constituency.[72] The momentum that had propelled Las Gorras Blancas into a political movement dissolved in the face of the coordinated attacks by territorial officials and commercial interests. Following the assassination of Pablo Herrera and the erosion in political support for the Partido, commercial interests reestablished political and economic authority over the land grant. By the mid-1890s barbed wire fences had returned to the commons; investments in livestock and railroad development also again corresponded to pre-Gorras Blancas levels.

Conclusion

Resistance to range enclosures and the spread of capitalist ranching was not unique to New Mexico. From Texas to Montana, the GLO noted with astonishment the scale and scope of violent resistance to range enclosures throughout the American West.[73] The fence cutting that began in Las Vegas in 1889 was part of a series of localized agrarian protest movements, or White Capism, that stretched from Indiana to the western territories and states. The name came from the common use among night riders of white hoods, which they used to conceal their identity. The reactionary White Caps in Indiana, a forerunner to the early twentieth-century Ku Klux Klan, operated as moral enforcers of rural traditions amid dramatic social and economic changes.[74] The conservatism of the movement in Indiana gave way to more radical elements in the West. Fence cutting first erupted in Texas in 1883 where small ranchers, desperate for water during an extended drought, created local night-riding secret societies to cut the fences of large estates and return free access to water and grasslands. As the movement spread west, the iconic white hoods were often the only similarity between the more radical groups in places like New Mexico and the conservative White Caps in Indiana. In New Mexico, night-riding activities reflected local patterns of resistance to the social upheaval that followed the arrival of barbed wire fencing, railroad development, and large-scale, commercial ranching.

The fence cutters in New Mexico reflected similar antifencing sentiments as did those in Texas, but theirs also included an explicit challenge to the class of merchants and commercial ranchers and their newly emerging economic order founded on the coercive power of the barbed wire fence to establish durable private property rights. Las Gorras Blancas destroyed hundreds of miles of barbed wire fences, thousands of railroad ties and telegraph lines, and supported the organizing efforts of a new urban working class throughout the county. They developed a sophisticated critique of political economic changes that served as the foundation of an eighteen-month campaign against the commercial and industrial transformation of New Mexico. As a clandestine group of night-riding fence cutters, Las Gorras Blancas interrupted the commercial and industrial expansion that relied on range enclosures. These actions defended common-property land claims and subsistence production relations and challenged new industrial wage relations.

The focus of Las Gorras Blancas on both rural and urban organizing and direct action was a strategy rooted in the particular political economy of late nineteenth-century Las Vegas. Years of economic expansion by grazing and timber operators based on the large-scale exploitation of natural resources on the Las Vegas Land Grant had eroded access to water and range for subsistence producers. Between 1850 and 1890 increased investment in commercial grazing operations relied on unfettered access to the expansive resources on the Town of Las Vegas Land Grant. As competition over those resources increased following the arrival of the railroad, commercial speculators conspired with territorial authorities to privatize common property. The enclosures that followed railroad expansion expropriated subsistence grazing resources. By the time homestead entries on the Las Vegas Land Grant flooded the Santa Fe land office in the early 1880s, 5.2 million sheep grazed New Mexico's grasslands, three times the number prior to the arrival of the railroad.[75] When Las Gorras Blancas were at their peak, more than 1.3 million cattle turned New Mexico's rangelands into a factory of meat production.[76] The increase in sheep and cattle numbers in New Mexico reflected a transition from subsistence to capitalist meat production that placed enormous pressure on what had previously been a pastoral production economy. The enclosures turned rural smallholders into ranch hands and railroad workers.

Where Las Gorras Blancas reacted to the enclosures with organized political resistance based on union organizing and direct action, their absence in the mid-1890s opened the door for bandits and brigands, like the notorious Vicente Silva, to replace social protest with "a carnival of crime."[77] For conservative newspapers and territorial politicians the fact that many of the members of Los Caballeros became members of Silva's La Sociedad de Bandidos de Nuevo Mexico was final proof that Las Gorras Blancas was nothing but a criminal syndicate. "Gorras Blanco [sic], La Sociedad de Bandidos de Nueva Mejico [sic], and the Partido del Pueblo Unido are one and the same," wrote the prominent Las Vegas politician Miguel Otero.[78] These conclusions conveniently ignored the underlying violence of the enclosures and the political and economic focus of Las Gorras Blancas and Partido activities. The many local shills for industrial interests in industrializing New Mexico were content to connect the campaign of property damage conducted by Las Gorras Blancas to the random rural violence practiced by the Silva gang. Local conservative newspapers became particularly adept at playing a speculative game of connect-the-dots: "Commencing in fence-cutting, it progressed to barn-burning, and culminated in murder, while it also degenerated into larceny both petty and grand."[79] Critics of Las Gorras Blancas, such as Otero, ignored the political foundation and broad public support for the group's opposition to enclosures and were blind to the role played by federal and territorial efforts in undermining the Partido and Las Gorras Blancas. Political and economic elites blamed Las Gorras Blancas for the increase in rural violence and the rise of criminal gangs in an argument that self-servingly ignored the social and economic dislocations that followed the forced shift from subsistence to industrial production on the Las Vegas Land Grant and the waves of enclosures that followed.

Notes

The research for this essay was supported through a grant from the Office of the New Mexico State Historian. Previous versions have been greatly improved by comments from Estevan Rael-Galvez, Kay Matthews, Mark Schiller, and one anonymous reviewer. I thank Amy Chazkel, David Serlin, and the *RHR* editorial collective for organizing this special issue.

1. For a review of the patterns, tactics, and consequences of land speculation during the territorial adjudication of Spanish and Mexican property claims in New Mexico, see David Correia, "Making Destiny Manifest: United States Territorial Expansion and the Dispossession of Two Mexican Property Claims in New Mexico," *Journal of Historical Geography* 35 (2009): 87–103.

2. E. J. Hobsbawm, *Primitive Rebels: Studies in Archaic Forms of Social Movements in the Nineteenth and Twentieth Centuries* (New York: W. W. Norton, 1959).

3. Andrew Schlesinger, "Las Gorras Blancas, 1889–1891," *Journal of Mexican American History* 1 (1971): 87–143; Robert. W. Larson, "The White Caps of New Mexico: A Study of Ethnic Militancy in the Southwest," *Pacific Historical Review* 44 (1975): 171–85; Robert Rosenbaum, *Mexicano Resistance in the Southwest: "The Sacred Right of Self-Preservation"* (Austin: University of Texas Press, 1981).

4. Schlesinger, "Las Gorras Blancas," 90.

5. Rosenbaum, *Mexicano Resistance in the Southwest.*

6. Mary Romero, "Class Struggle and Resistance against the Transformation of Land Ownership and Usage in Northern New Mexico: The Case of Las Gorras Blancas," *Chicano-Latino Law Review* 26 (2006): 90.

7. Anselmo Arellano, "The People's Movement: Las Gorras Blancas," in *The Contested Homeland: A Chicano History of New Mexico*, ed. Erlinda Gonzales-Berry and David Maciel (Albuquerque: University of New Mexico Press, 2000), 60.

8. Romero, "Class Struggle and Resistance," 88.

9. Ibid., 109.

10. For analyses of identity, social, and political relations and political violence in New Mexico, see Ned Blackhawk, *Violence over the Land: Indians and Empires in the Early American West* (Cambridge, MA: Harvard University Press, 2006); and Andres Resendez, *Changing National Identities at the Frontier: Texas and New Mexico, 1800–1850* (Cambridge: Cambridge University Press, 2005). For a review of pre-nineteenth-century economic development in New Mexico, see Ross Frank, *From Settler to Citizen: New Mexican Economic Development and the Creation of Vecino Society, 1750–1820* (Berkeley: University of California Press, 2000).

11. *Report of the Governor of New Mexico to the Secretary of the Interior* (Washington, DC: Government Printing Office, 1885), in New Mexico State Records Center and Archive (NMSRCA), Santa Fe, New Mexico: Territorial Archives of New Mexico (TANM), microfilm roll 102: frames 279–84.

12. *Report of the Governor of New Mexico*, NMSRCA: TANM, 102:281.

13. Ibid., 102:283. The Timber Culture Act of 1873, the Homestead Act of 1862, and the Preemption Act of 1841 provided for the alienation and distribution of public lands in newly acquired territories. As Ross noted in his report, and as the General Land Office demonstrated (see note 16) in their 1885 investigation, federal officials routinely approved timber-culture, homestead and preemption claims within the boundaries of existing Spanish and Mexican land grants in New Mexico.

14. Letter from the Secretary of the Interior transmitting copies of reports upon the subject of fraudulent acquisition of titles to lands in New Mexico, March 3, 1885, Senate Report, 48th Congress, 2d sess., Ex. Doc. No. 106.

15. O. Winther, "Promoting the American West in England, 1856–1890," *Journal of Economic History* 16 (1956): 506–13.

16. C. Spence, "British Investment and the American Mining Frontier," *New Mexico Historical Review* 36 (1961): 121–37.

17. C. Spence, "When the Pound Sterling Went West: British Investments and the American Mineral Frontier," *Journal of Economic History* 16 (1956): 482–92. The conversion into dollars is derived from the average exchange rate from 1860 to 1900 of U.S. $5.42 = £ 1; see L.H. Officer, "Dollar-Pound Exchange Rate from 1791," Measuring Worth, 2010, www.measuringworth.org/exchangepound.

18. Spence, "British Investment and the American Mining Frontier," 137. The conversion is derived from the average exchange rate from 1886 to 1900 of $4.87 = £ 1.

19. G. L. Seligman, "The El Paso and Northeastern Railroad's Economic Impact on Central New Mexico," *New Mexico Historical Review* 61 (1986): 217–31. The figures are in nineteenth-century dollars.

20. David Myrick, *New Mexico's Railroads: An Historical Survey* (Albuquerque: University of New Mexico Press, 1990).

21. E. Hayter, "Barbed Wire Fencing—A Prairie Invention: Its Rise and Influence in the Western States," *Agricultural History* 13 (1939): 189–207.

22. Ibid., 191.

23. Ibid., 196. Hayter based his claims of wholesale enclosures on various newspaper reports from the period.

24. Ralph Edgel, "A Brief History of Banking in New Mexico," Report 39, Bureau of Business Research, University of New Mexico (1962), 6.

25. Larry Schweikart, "Early Banking in New Mexico from the Civil War to the Roaring Twenties," *New Mexico Historical Review* 63 (1988): 1–25.

26. Edgel, "Brief History of Banking in New Mexico," 7.

27. E. Rogers and S. B. Elkins, "Business in New Mexico's Early Banking Era, 1873–1875," *New Mexico Historical Review* 70 (1995): 67–76.

28. Quoted in L. Harrison, "Thomas Simpson Carson, New Mexico Rancher," *New Mexico Historical Review* 42 (1967): 127–43.

29. V. Westphall, *The Public Domain in New Mexico, 1854–1891* (Albuquerque: University of New Mexico Press, 1965).

30. Harrison, "Thomas Simpson Carson," 135.

31. San Miguel County Assessments, 1887–1890, NMSRCA.

32. August 12, 1890, letter from Territorial Governor L. Bradford Prince to Secretary of the Interior John Noble, NMSRCA: TANM, 121:640. As a territory, New Mexico's Supreme Court was part of the federal judiciary.

33. August 25, 1890, letter from San Miguel County Commission Chairman Stephen Booth to Prince, NMSRCA: TANM, 121:661.

34. June 26, 1890, report to Governor Prince, NMSRCA: Prince Papers, 121:580–81.

35. July 22, 1890, letter to Governor Prince, NMSRCA: Prince Papers, 121:586–87.

36. For the Knights of Labor, see Leon Fink, *Workingmen's Democracy: The Knights of Labor and American Politics* (Urbana: University of Illinois Press, 1983); Jason Kaufman, "Rise and Fall of a Nation of Joiners," *Journal of Interdisciplinary History* 31 (2001): 553–79. For the Knights in New Mexico, see Robert Larson, "The Knights of Labor and Native Protest in New Mexico," in *Labor in New Mexico: Unions, Strikes, and Social History*, ed. Robert Kern (Albuquerque: University of New Mexico Press, 1983), 31–52.

37. July 25, 1890, letter from Salazar to Prince, NMSRCA: TANM, 121:590.

38. December 11, 1899, telegram from Lorenzo Lopez to Prince, NMSRCA: TANM, 121:572–73.

39. December 13, 1889, telegram from E. W. Wynkoop to Prince, NMSRCA: TANM, 121:574

40. August 8, 1890, handbill, NMSRCA: Interior Department Territorial Papers, 8:625.

41. July 25, 1890, Salazar to Prince, NMSRCA: TANM, 121:591.

42. *Las Vegas Optic*, February 1, 1890, NMSRCA.

43. June 26, 1890, report to Governor Prince, NMSRCA: Prince Papers, 121:580–81.

44. March 29, 1890, letter from Deputy Sheriff Joseph Trumbly to Prince, NMSRCA: TANM, 121:575–76.

45. April 15, 1890, letter from C. de Baca to Prince, NMSRCA: Prince Papers, 121:577–78.

46. July 25, 1890, Salazar to Prince, NMSRCA: TANM, 121:591.

47. August 8, 1890, letter from John Martin, Frank Ogden, and J. B. Allen to Knights of Labor National President Terrence Powderly, NMSRCA: TANM, 121:621–23.

48. August 11, 1890, Atchison, Topeka, and Santa Fe Railway memo, NMSRCA: TANM, 121:628–29.

49. Undated notice, NMSRCA: TANM, 121:584.

50. August 3, 1890, letter from J. W. Barney to Senator P. B. Plumb, NMSRCA: Interior Department Territorial Papers, 8:601–4.

51. See July 23, 1890, letter from Prince to New Mexico Chief Justice O'Brien, and July 28, 1890, letter from Secretary Noble to Prince, NMSRCA: TANM, 121:589 and 607; and July 15, 1890, letter from Benjamin F. Butler to Noble, NMSRCA: Interior Department, 8:563.

52. Larson, "White Caps of New Mexico," 177.

53. July 9, 1890, letter from Butler to Noble, NMSRCA: Interior Department, 8:565.

54. July 21, 1890, letter from O. D. Bartlett to Butler, NMSRCA: Interior Department, 8:621.

55. July 21, 1890, letter from F. Leduc to Prince, NMSRCA: TANM, 121:594–95.

56. July 30, 1890, letter from Judge James O'Brien to Prince, NMSRCA: TANM, 121:614–15.

57. July 23, 1890, letter from Prince to Noble, NMSRCA: Interior Department, 8:582–83.

58. NMSRCA: Interior Department, 8:610.

59. August 12, 1890, letter from Prince to General Nelson Miles, NMSRCA: Interior Department, 8:614 and 634.

60. August 18, 1890, letter to Powderly, NMSRCA: TANM, 121:621–23.

61. August 12, 1890, letter from Prince to Noble, NMSRCA: TANM, 121:639–43.

62. Ibid.

63. Ibid.

64. August 20, 1890, letter from Prince to Noble, NMSRCA: Interior Department, 8:639–40.

65. Ibid.

66. Ibid.

67. Ibid.

68. Schlesinger, "Las Gorras Blancas, 1889–1891," 123.

69. Tobias Duran, "Francisco Chavez, Thomas B. Catron, and Organized Political Violence in Santa Fe in the 1890s," *New Mexico Historical Review* 59 (1984): 291–310.

70. Charles Siringo, *Cowboy Detective: A True Story of Twenty-Two Years with a World-Famous Detective Agency* (Chicago: W. B. Conkey, 1912).

71. December 15, 1891, letter from U.S. Attorney Eugene Fiske, NMSRCA: TANM, 121:671–72.

72. For a review of the broad political backlash against Las Gorras Blancas, Los Caballeros, and the Partido, see Anselmo Arellano, "Through Thick and Thin: Evolutionary Transitions of Las Vegas Grandes and Its Pobladores" (PhD diss., University of New Mexico, 1990).

73. Hayter, "Barbed Wire Fencing," 203.

74. Madeleine Noble, "The White Caps of Harrison and Crawford County, Indiana: A Study in the Violent Enforcement of Morality" (PhD diss., University of Michigan, 1973).

75. C. Raish and A. M. McSweeney, *Economic, Social, and Cultural Aspects of Livestock Ranching on the Espanola and Canjilon Ranger Districts of the Santa Fe and Carson National Forests: A Pilot Study* (Albuquerque: U.S. Forest Service, 2003).

76. C. W. Dahms and B. W. Geils, *An Assessment of Forest Ecosystem Health in the Southwest* (Washington, DC: U.S. Forest Service, 1997).

77. *Las Vegas Daily Optic*, April 12, 1894.

78. Miguel A. Otero, *My Life on the Frontier, 1882–1897* (Albuquerque: University of New Mexico Press, 1939).

79. *Las Vegas Daily Optic*, April 12, 1894.

READING 1.1   POST-READING COMPREHENSION QUESTIONS

• Summarize who Las Gorras Blancas were.

• Describe the strategies that Las Gorras Blancas used to resist.

• Paraphrase the saying that is synonymous with Las Gorras Blancas: "Cuando llegó el alambre, también llegó el hambre" [When the (barbed) wire arrived, so did hunger].

Cabinet Card Death Photograph of Navajo Frank Lynching (1882)

Frank Tafoya, or *Navajo Frank* as he was known, was arrested in New Mexico in the summer of 1882 for allegedly harassing a white man and his wife. While in jail, a mob of white men broke in, removed him from his cell, and hanged him in public. Historian Zaragosa Vargas notes that "Organized violence became a method of punishment for the region's non-white population, and there were frequent calls for the formation of vigilante committees to enforce swift punishment through lynchings and hangings."[1] Images like this of the hanging of Navajo Frank mark a period in United States history when a person's basic rights of a fair trial or due process were willfully ignored and justice was often met at the end of a dangling rope if you were not white. This image demonstrates more than just the death of a young indigenous man at the hands of a white mob—it explicitly draws us into a world of racialized violence where publicly accepted killings were a community event and the consequences for disrupting the racial order of the region often resulted in violence or death.

THINGS TO LOOK FOR AS YOU VIEW THE IMAGE..............................

- Where is the hanging taking place?
- Who is attending this hanging?
- The body language of the crowd

---

1 Vargas, *Crucible of Struggle,* 145.

Figure 1.1 Cabinet Card Death Photograph of Navajo Frank Lynching (1882)

Source: https://commons.wikimedia.org/wiki/File:Navajo_Frank_lynching_-_Deming,_New_Mexico,_1882_ (cropped).png

End-of-Chapter Critical Thinking Questions

Directions: Respond to each of the questions about the reading and the image. Refer to these sources to support your answers.

- In what ways were Las Gorras Blancas successful in challenging Anglo incursion?
- Identify and discuss the ways that this essay underscores the relationship between race and class.
- What sorts of messages do public hangings send to both white and non-white peoples of the community?

Further Readings

Cole, Stephanie, and Natalie J. Ring, eds. *The Folly of Jim Crow: Rethinking the Segregated South.* College Station, TX.: Texas A&M University Press, 2012.

Gonzales-Berry, Erlinda, and David Maciel ed. *The Contested Homeland: A Chicano History of New Mexico.* Albuquerque, NM.: University of New Mexico Press, 2000.

Gonzales-Day, Ken. *Lynching in the West, 1850–1935.* Durham, NC.: Duke University Press, 2006.

Deverell, William. *Whitewashed Adobe: The Rise of Los Angeles and the Remaking of Its Mexican Past.* Berkeley, CA.: University of California Press, 2004.

Feimster, Crystal Nicole. *Southern Horrors: Women and the Politics of Rape and Lynching.* Cambridge, MA.: Harvard University Press, 2011.

Haley, Sarah. *No Mercy Here: Gender, Punishment, and the Making of Jim Crow Modernity.* Chapel Hill, NC.: The University of North Carolina Press, 2016.

Kelman, Ari. *A Misplaced Massacre: Struggling over the Memory of Sand Creek.* Cambridge, MA.: Harvard University Press, 2013.

Limerick, Patricia Nelson. *The Legacy of Conquest: The Unbroken Past of the American West.* New York, NY.: W.W. Norton, 1987.

Montejano, David. *Anglos and Mexicans in the Making of Texas, 1836–1986.* Austin, TX.: University of Texas Press, 1987.

Painter, Nell Irvin. *Standing at Armageddon: The United States, 1877–1919.* New York, NY.: W.W. Norton, 1987.

Postel, Charles. *The Populist Vision.* New York, NY.: Oxford University Press, 2007.

Rosenbaum, Robert. *Mexicano Resistance in the Southwest: The Sacred Right of Self-Preservation.* Austin, TX.: University of Texas Press, 1981.

Saxton, Alexander. *The Indispensable Enemy: Labor and the Anti-Chinese Movement in California.* Berkeley, CA.: University of California Press, 1995.

Vargas, Zaragosa. *Crucible of Struggle: A History of Mexican Americans from Colonial Times to the Present Era.* 2nd ed. New York, NY.: Oxford University Press, 2017.

CHAPTER 2

The Mexican Revolution

....

Editor's Introduction

In this chapter, readers will learn how Mexicans responded to and resisted the circumstances wrought by years of social, political, and economic corruption. The Mexican Revolution can, in part, be characterized as a prolonged period of violence and national reconstruction resulting from the process of a popular uprising seeking to delegitimize the decades-old government of Porfirio Díaz. The *Porfiriato* saw Mexico make many significant gains with respect to its international economic standing as well as important domestic improvements. However, these improvements came at a perilous cost as Mexico experienced a significant disparity in wealth among its inhabitants. The Díaz regime installed the most efficient and centralized government machine the country had ever experienced.[1] This Díaz political machine was not concerned with the plight of the poor and working-class peoples of Mexico. Rather it sought to exploit natural resources, acquire huge properties, and manipulate domestic labor rights while repressing any form of opposition. Mexican resources were sold off to foreigners at the direction of the Díaz administration. Concurrently political participation and local autonomy were violently crushed.[2]

Fundamental to the Díaz political scheme was a comprehensive land policy that sought to displace indigenous landholdings and replace them with corrupt land speculators and large-scale ranches with the incentive to encourage foreign investment.[3] Issue of land and property routinely emerge as factors in revolutionary movements, and it is evident that in Mexico this was the case. The Mexican government was explicitly infringing on the livelihood of its people with the hopes

---

1 Thomas E. Skidmore and Peter H. Smith, *Modern Latin America*, 6th ed. (New York, NY.: Oxford University Press, 2005), 263.

2 Michael J. Gonzales. *The Mexican Revolution, 1910–1940* (Albuquerque, NM.: University of New Mexico Press, 2002), 59.

3 Skidmore and Smith, *Modern Latin America,* 261.

of a greater economic position on the global stage. The feelings of imbalance animated frustrations for many Mexicans, especially the laboring and working-class peoples of a nation who were being exploited for the gain of what seemed to be a handful of ultra-wealthy, detached elites. Human needs were being frustrated by underpaid work and poor living conditions, corrupt political and business interests, and a lack of self-determination.

The primary and secondary sources collected in this chapter all speak to the struggle towards a reimagined Mexico. In the reading by Manuel G. Gonzales, he provides a sweeping overview of the revolution while the three primary sources cover topics such as political autonomy, economic mobility, gender rights, and land acquisition. Moreover, all the sources allow us to examine and understand not only the frustrations of a nation but also a critical but rare first-hand perspective of the plan(s) to move beyond those frustrations and activate change.

The Great Migration 1900–1930

In this short excerpt from Manuel G. Gonzales' book *Mexicanos*, he provides insight into the early stages of the Mexican Revolution and details the rise of Porfirio Díaz and his endeavor to bring *order and progress* to the nation. That attempt, however, came at a significant cost to many of the Mexican people, especially its poor and indigenous. The author is also able to identify and discuss some of the most important agents of dissent to *El Porfiriato*.

THINGS TO LOOK FOR AS YOU READ...

- Roots of the Mexican Revolution
- Demands of the Revolution
- Goals of the Partido Liberal Mexicano (PLM) and *magonistas*

The Mexican Revolution

Manuel G. Gonzales

....

[...].

L et us look at Mexico first. Students of the Mexicano experience in this country have tended to accentuate the problems encountered in American society. There can be no denying that incoming Mexicans have faced severe problems, more than most immigrant groups, including racial prejudice and discrimination. Yet the fact remains that since the early 1900s, Mexicans have willingly entered the United States in huge numbers, and many have opted to remain in this alien environment, so far from the psychological security of their native villages and cities. Why have they come? Why do they continue to do so, albeit in diminishing numbers? An impartial observer must recognize, at the very least, that with all the problems they encounter, the United States still offers immigrants significant advantages over the Old Country. It would seem, life in Mexico is even more oppressive than life in the United States.

Certainly, this was the case in the first decades of the twentieth century, a period of Mexican history dominated by the Revolution, a conflict that in itself indicated enormous discontent among the populace. In contrast to a purely political uprising, a true revolution impacts every aspect of life—politics, economics, culture, society itself. The upheaval that Mexico experienced in 1910–1920 qualified in every respect; it was one of the few true revolutions of the twentieth century.[1]

Its origins were rather modest. It began as a protest movement initiated by Francisco I. Madero, a bespectacled intellectual and member of the landholding elite from the state of Coahuila, on November 20, 1910, after he lost a fraudulent election for the presidency to the incumbent, Porfirio Díaz (1830–1915). While

Manuel G. Gonzales, Selection from "The Great Migration: 1900-1930," *Mexicanos: A History of Mexicans in the United States*, pp. 130-137, 157-158. Copyright © 2019 by Indiana University Press. Reprinted with permission.

Madero's motives were almost completely political, the revolt quickly escalated into a full-fledged social revolution, so profound was popular dissatisfaction with the Porfiriato.

The roots of the 1910 cataclysm can be traced far back into Mexican history. Some scholars today find its genesis in the agrarian discontent already in evidence by the late eighteenth century. Popular disaffection increased throughout the following century as the peasant masses were gradually incorporated into world capitalist markets, a trend culminating during the late nineteenth century, a fateful period dominated by General Díaz. A partisan of liberalism and a lieutenant of Benito Juárez, Porfirio Díaz gained immense popularity early in his military career when he helped General Ignacio Zaragoza repel the French invasion at Puebla in 1862. The death ten years later of Juárez, by now a political rival, paved the way for the ascendancy of Díaz, who gained the presidency in 1876. Determined to end the chaos that marked the political life of the struggling republic—the presidency changed hands seventy-five times from 1821 to 1876—Díaz gradually consolidated his position, ultimately establishing a one-man dictatorship, which he maintained until his ouster in 1911.

The Porfiriato had popular support in the beginning. Mexico had paid dearly for the political and economic instability that prevailed after its independence in 1821. The loss of its northern territories to the United States in 1848 was only one, though undoubtedly the most catastrophic, of the setbacks encountered by the young nation. Corruption at all levels of government was rampant, years of weak and ineffectual leadership encouraged the breakdown of law and order, the economy was in shambles, and social problems abounded. Díaz was determined to resolve the most pressing of these problems, and Mexicans, tired of years of violence and insecurity, were sympathetic to these efforts. Still, divisions were typical. The Church, in particular, fought frantically to preserve its privileges against the "godless" liberals. Díaz was forced to impose his will over recalcitrants using strong-arm methods. Lacking a democratic tradition, many citizens were convinced that there were no viable alternatives to these measures. Moreover, Díaz's policies appeared to work reasonably well in the beginning.

The top priority of the new administration was to restore the power of the central government at the expense of the state legislatures, something that was accomplished by the 1880s. Díaz then turned to strengthening the economy. Mexico was rich in subsoil resources and cheap labor but lacked technological expertise and capital. Díaz sought to remedy the situation by turning to foreign entrepreneurs, especially British and even American investors, the latter not very popular given the recent war of conquest. Foreign capital, enticed by generous grants of land and favorable tax laws, poured into the country after the 1870s; and, as Mexico was inexorably incorporated into the global market under the aegis of capitalism, the economy did improve dramatically. The mining industry was revived, with copper now rivaling silver as the most valuable ore. Oil production began in 1901, and nine years later some thirteen million barrels were produced, mostly for export. A vast network of railroads was constructed linking the most strategic state capitals to one another and to American border towns, notably El Paso and Laredo, a crucial link to San Antonio. By 1892, Mexico had built 6,876 miles of railway; and by 1910, the figure reached 12,000 miles. After the turn of the century, the government also succeeded in establishing an iron and steel industry centered on the northern city of Monterrey. Díaz had promised order and progress, and even his enemies were forced to concede that he had been able to deliver the goods to a surprising extent by the last years of his presidency.

But by this time there were many dissidents who had come to question whether the impressive material gains warranted the immense sacrifices asked of the masses. No doubt Díaz had brought his people more security. However, it came at the expense of liberty. Moreover, while a small but powerful minority in Mexico, the Europeanized upper class, was able to share the material benefits of Díaz's reforms with foreign entrepreneurs, especially Wall Street bankers, the great majority of the citizenry found that its economic status had hardly improved at all or had even deteriorated, in part because Mexico's population soared during the Porfiriato from 8.7 million to 15 million inhabitants. The railroads themselves, as George J. Sanchez has argued, while helping to integrate formerly isolated villages into the larger community, also disrupted traditional patterns of life, causing deep discontent in peasant society.[2]

The most unfortunate victims of progress were Indians. At the end of the nineteenth century, the indigenous community in Mexico was still enormous; more than a third of its inhabitants were listed as Indians in official records, and some two million of them spoke native dialects exclusively. Díaz, who ironically was part Mixtec himself, was convinced by his advisors, above all his treasury secretary Jose Ives Limantour, that the native population was hopelessly backward and that their very existence posed a grave obstacle to modernization. *Ejidos,* Indian communal holdings, were rapidly divided under Díaz and the land redistributed, the chief beneficiaries being foreigners and the Mexican upper class, mostly whites. William Randolph Hearst and his mother Phoebe, for instance, acquired more than two and a half million acres. Luis Terrazas of Chihuahua, did even better, amassing lands totaling nearly five million acres by 1910, at a time when only 3 percent of the nation's population owned any land at all. Generally, Indians were reduced to working as peons on large haciendas, where they lived in squalor as virtual slaves, one of the most disruptive effects of the rapid incursions made by capitalism into Mexican agrarian society. Those who refused to cooperate were dealt with in severe fashion. Among the intransigents were Yaquis from Sonora who were shipped off to toil in the henequen haciendas of Yucatán after the turn of the century. Making matters worse, the alienation of ejido lands was accompanied by growing anti-Indian prejudice, the Mexican variation of the racism that increased everywhere in the Western world as the nineteenth century waned.

Ultimately, most scholars feel, the single most substantial cause of the coming upheaval was agrarian discontent. The economic crisis brought on by the widespread loss of land by the peasants was the key factor. Could the Mexican elites have nipped the revolutionary fervor in the bud, asks the historian Michael J. Gonzales, had they closed ranks more effectively against the masses? "Given the breadth and depth of the agrarian crisis," he concludes, "this seems doubtful."[3]

Serious resistance to the regime began to develop after the turn of the century. Anti-Díaz sentiment focused on the border states of the north, which became the seedbeds of rebellion. It was here that Ricardo Flores Magón (1873–1922), the most memorable precursor of the Revolution, got his start, as a cofounder of the Partido Liberal Mexicano (PLM) in 1901. Dedicated to overthrowing the Díaz regime, and ultimately the capitalist system, party leaders, including Ricardo and his brothers, were exiled to Texas within a few years. Headquartered first in Laredo and later in San Antonio, now becoming the center of exile politics, the *magonistas* initiated a series of rebellions in northern Mexico in 1906. Persecuted by the US government for violating neutrality laws, PLM leadership fled first to St. Louis, Missouri, then to Los Angeles in 1910. In the meantime, Ricardo Flores Magón had abandoned liberal ideas and had begun to espouse anarchism, a transition that can be traced in *Regeneración,* his influential newspaper founded in 1900. In 1911, magonistas attempted an invasion of Baja California from their base in the north, where Ricardo Flores Magón remained to direct operations. The uprising proved to be premature as the insurgents failed to arouse popular support among the masses. Crestfallen, the survivors retreated to the United States, where they suffered ongoing persecution by US authorities. During this period, the uncompromising opposition leader also worked to construct a working-class movement, based on anarchist principles, among the Mexicanos of the Southwest.

In February 1915, an attempt to overthrow US rule and reclaim the Southwest was initiated in southern Texas. The insurrection was announced in the mysterious *Plan de San Diego*—a document apparently drawn up in the Duval County town of San Diego—the origins of which remain obscure.[4] Mexicano insurgents, some from across the border, others US-born, numbered as many as five thousand individuals. Their leaders included Aniceto Pizaña and Luis de la Rosa. The 1915–1917 revolt, however, dissipated in the face of repression in Texas, during which hundreds of Mexicanos were killed, and the disavowal of the irredentist movement by President Venustiano Carranza of Mexico.[5]

While this bizarre episode seemed to be fueled by the loss of lands to aggressive Anglo entrepreneurs (made possible by the recent arrival of the railroad into South Texas), and leadership was provided by local Mexicano elements, the magonistas, despite their denials, were apparently implicated in the plot; the San Diego manifesto was vaguely anarchist in spirit. The US government, determined to eradicate the PLM, stepped up its efforts to prosecute party chiefs; Ricardo Flores Magón spent the last years of his life in a Kansas prison, where he died in 1922 under suspicious circumstances. The magonistas failed, mostly for the same reasons that all anarchist-inspired movements have died out—lack of organization and an unrealistic program. Its legacy, however, as recent scholarship has demonstrated, was profound.[6] It was Ricardo Flores Magón who first openly challenged the Díaz regime, exposing its vulnerabilities and laying the foundations for the Great Revolution of 1910.

Francisco Madero, scion of a wealthy hacendado family from Coahuila, was no friend of anarchism, but he was able to tap the discontent that the magonistas had accentuated when he launched the Revolution with his *Plan de San Luis Potosí,* issued in San Antonio in November 1910. The bulk of his support came from the middle class rather than the workers. While the bourgeoisie, which constituted a little less than 10 percent of the population, had fared relatively well under the Porfiriato, a financial debacle in 1907 had abruptly altered their prospects for the future, alienating them from the government. According to the historian Ramon Eduardo Ruiz: "One event, as so often happens, ignited the fuse of rebellion. The financial crisis of 1907, which marked the swan song of prosperity, revealed the flaws in Mexico's economic and social fabric and became the watershed of rebellion. Until the depression paralyzed mining, commerce, and industry, the people paid homage to the Mexican success story; with its onset, even disciples of the Old Regime began to listen to the disciples of change."[7]

The ease of his initial success must have surprised Madero. But taking over power was one thing; consolidating that power was an entirely different matter. Like Father Hidalgo before him, Madero unleashed forces he could not control. Ascending to the presidency on November 6, 1911, he was assassinated by counterrevolutionists three months later, the beginning of a lengthy period of intermittent civil strife, at times bordering on complete chaos. While political principles may have been paramount at the beginning, the rebellion soon deteriorated into a series of power struggles as one caudillo after another attempted to gain control of Mexico City, efforts that often resulted in political assassination. Emiliano Zapata, the most dedicated of the revolutionists, an Indian leader who fought for "land and liberty," was killed in 1919. The same fate befell Venustiano Carranza, the Coahuila strongman and architect of the famous 1917 Constitution, in 1920, and Pancho Villa, as much a bandit as he was a revolutionary, three years later. These executions were simply the tip of the iceberg. Between 1.5 and 2 million men, women, and children lost their lives during the Revolution.[8] This cataclysmic figure contradicts the common stereotype in the United States of the "cowardly" Mexican.

Despite the obstacles, many Mexicans were able to flee the country even during the periods of most intense violence. Some eight thousand refugees, for example, crossed the border from Piedras Negras, Coahuila, to Eagle Pass, Texas, in a single day in October 1913. And in one week in June 1916, almost five thousand Mexicans poured into El Paso. The numbers increased dramatically, however, once the violence abated.

The Revolution created as many problems as it resolved. Massive destruction, the result of pillage, looting, and burning, was everywhere, especially in the areas west and north of the capital, the Bajío. Mexico City was the objective of the various rebel armies and their leaders, most of whom swept down from the north—Madero and Carranza from Coahuila, Villa from Chihuahua, and Álvaro Obregón from Sonora—and it was in the Bajío that the heaviest fighting took place as government troops, the *federales,* moved north to defend the capital. These strife-torn states, which included Guanajuato, Michoacán, and Jalisco, were also among the most heavily populated in Mexico, and the destruction of their crops left the population on the verge of starvation.

Difficulty in acquiring land in an area where the hacienda system was so firmly entrenched also compounded peasant discontent. The end of the Revolution in 1920, with the triumph of Obregón, alleviated the situation somewhat, but it did not solve the basic problems. Agrarian reform, the most popular demand of the landless peasants, was enacted all too slowly by the triumphant Sonoran faction headed by Obregón and Plutarco Elías Calles. In the end, it was clear, there was not nearly enough arable land to meet the needs of the desperate rural population.[9]

Peasant disillusion with agrarian reform was partly responsible for the Cristero Rebellion that broke out in western Mexico in 1926–1929, but there were other factors that added to the crisis. The most immediate cause of Catholic dissatisfaction was the anticlerical legislation of the postrevolutionary period. The Catholic Church had made itself unpopular with the revolutionaries by its support of conservative elements during the conflict. A champion of the status quo, the Church found itself extremely vulnerable with the fall of the Porfiriato. President Calles, Obregón's successor, and the most anticlerical of Mexico's revolutionary presidents, was determined to weaken the institution through a series of tough measures, including the expulsion of foreign clergymen and the closing of parochial schools. The attempt to curtail clerical privileges produced an unanticipated reaction in the countryside. Government leaders had miscalculated the extent to which parish priests had won over the hearts and minds of the peasantry, generally the most conservative element in any society. Devoted to their priests, mestizos and Tarascan Indians (*purépechas*) in Jalisco, Michoacán, and Colima rallied to their defense.

Violence swept through the towns and villages of western Mexico as the government eschewed a policy of reconciliation and insisted on fighting to the bitter end. It is estimated that some eighty thousand lives were lost in this holy war. Peasants, many of them innocent bystanders, were driven off their small plots of land, their only means of survival. In Arandas, Jalisco, for example, thirteen hundred inhabitants fled north for fear of reprisals by government troops. The Mexican historian Jean Meyer estimates that as many as one-half million war refugees may have found their way into the United States.[10]

The years immediately after the revolutionary upheaval, the decade of the 1920s, witnessed the largest exodus from Mexico, particularly from the western states of Guanajuato, Jalisco, and Michoacán. Flight was facilitated by the reconstruction of the railroad lines, which had been largely destroyed during the years of heavy fighting. Altogether, during the Revolution and its aftermath, a million people, some of them political exiles representing every class of society, most of them starving peasants, moved north to seek a better life across the border.

In fact, large numbers of Mexicans had been entering the United States even before the Revolution. As Chicano historians have discovered recently, beginning in the 1880s, with the arrival of the railroad in the Southwest, many immigrants, mostly from the northern border states, had moved north from Mexico.[11] These early immigrants, like later arrivals, found economic conditions in the Old Country stultifying. Dissatisfied with the Porfiriato, some political malcontents preferred life abroad. After the turn of the century, the numbers of people moving north increased sharply. The historian Lawrence A. Cardoso believes that as many as a half million Mexicans entered the United States during the first decade of the twentieth century.[12]

While political exiles before the Revolution were almost exclusively liberal in their sentiments, those who came during the upheaval itself—when they made up about 10 percent of the total—and especially in the aftermath, tended to espouse conservative positions. Whatever their politics, though, these émigrés, mostly of urban and professional backgrounds, came to be the backbone of the small middle class that developed in the colonias of the Southwest. Their most popular destination was San Antonio, where they settled in the Mexicano barrio on the West Side. In these ethnic enclaves, as Arnoldo De León persuasively argues, these elites came to play an important role in preserving traditional culture:

> They promoted a Mexican past through the distribution of Mexican books, magazines, musical records, and Spanish-language

newspapers from Mexico City. They sponsored speaking engage-
ments and theatrical performances and editorialized or extolled
the virtues of *la patria* (Mexico, their native country). Meantime,
they formed their own clubs and held exclusive cultural activities.
They maintained a commitment to preserving Mexican nationalist
sentiments within the community of immigrants.[13]

[...].

Notes

1. For the great upheaval, see William H. Beezley and Colin M. MacLachlan, *Mexicans in Revolution, 1910–1946: An Introduction* (Lincoln: University of Nebraska Press, 2009), who argue for a new chronology and stress the role of the revolutionary leaders and their policies.
2. See Sánchez, *Becoming Mexican American: Ethnicity, Culture, and Identity in Chicano Los Angeles, 1900–1945* (New York: Oxford University Press, 1993), chap. 1.
3. Gonzales, *The Mexican Revolution, 1910–1940* (Albuquerque: University of New Mexico Press, 2002), p. 2.
4. For a copy of *El Plan de San Diego, see Testimonio: A Documentary History of the Mexican American Struggle for Civil Rights,* ed. F. Arturo Rosales (Houston, TX: Arte Público Press, 2000), pp. 63–65.
5. See Nicholas Villanueva, "No Place of Refuge: Mexicans, Anglos, and Violence in the Texas Borderland, 1900–1920" (PhD diss., Vanderbilt University, 2013).
6. See James A. Sandos, *Rebellion in the Borderlands: Anarchism and the Plan of San Diego, 1904–1923* (Norman: University of Oklahoma Press, 1992).
7. Ruiz, *Triumphs and Tragedy: A History of the Mexican People* (New York: W. W Norton, 1992), p. 311.
8. A modest estimate, according to Michael C. Meyer and William L. Sherman, *The Course of Mexican History* (New York: Oxford University Press, 1979), p. 552.
9. For life in a typical peasant community, see the classic study of a village in Michoacán by one of Mexico's greatest historians, Luis González, *San José de Gracia: Mexican Village in Transition,* trans. John Upton (Austin: University of Texas Press, 1974).
10. Meyer, *The Cristero Rebellion: The Mexican People between Church and State, 1926–1929,* trans. Richard Southern (New York: Cambridge University Press, 1976), p. 179. For *la Cristiada,* neglected by US historians until now, and its aftermath, see Julia G. Young, *Mexican Exodus: Emigrants, Exiles, and Refugees of the Cristero War* (New York: Oxford University Press, 2015).

11. Richard Griswold del Castillo and Arnoldo De León, *North to Aztlán: A History of Mexican Americans in the United States* (New York: Twayne Publishers, 1996), p. 23, see a significant rise of Mexican immigration after 1880; consequently, they believe there is a good deal of continuity in Mexican American history between the nineteenth and the twentieth centuries. This point of view is challenged by scholars who believe that an entirely new phase of that history is initiated at about 1900 with the beginning of mass immigration. See Gilbert G. González and Raúl Fernández, "Chicano History: Transcending Cultural Models," *Pacific Historical Review* 63 (Nov. 1994): 488–89.
12. Cardoso, *Mexican Emigration to the United States, 1897–1931* (Tucson: University of Arizona Press, 1980), p. 34.
13. De León, *Mexican Americans in Texas: A Brief History* (Arlington Heights, IL: Harlan Davidson, 1993), p. 71.

READING 2.1   POST-READING COMPREHENSION QUESTIONS

- Describe the experiences of indigenous Mexicans before the Revolution.

- Summarize the goals of the Partido Liberal Mexicano (PLM) and its leadership.

- Paraphrase the passage: "Díaz had promised order and progress, and even his enemies were forced to concede that he had been able to deliver the goods to a surprising extent by the last years of his presidency … But by this time there were many dissidents who had come to question whether the impressive material gains warranted the immense sacrifices asked of the masses."

The PLM Program, (1906)

The 1906 Partido Liberal Mexicano (PLM) Program was a revision of the political, economic, and social prospects of Mexico and its citizens. The Program was set up as an alternative to the *Porfiriato*—the period of almost three decades when Porfirio Díaz ruled the country. This political manifesto is critical to understanding some of the changes that many Mexicans fought and died for during the revolutionary period. The PLM was a transnational organization that operated both within and outside of Mexico. Its aim was to contribute to a worldwide effort to dismantle capitalism. The PLM used a two-pronged approach of propaganda and direct action, and the Program was crafted, in part with suggestions solicited from the Mexican public, to organize a broad base of support among Mexicans. The PLM platform proved to be significant in coalescing progressives and served as a model for the conceptualization of a refashioned Mexican society. Many of the points addressed in the PLM Program made their way into the Constitution of 1917.

THINGS TO LOOK FOR AS YOU READ

- Reforms regarding education
- Reforms regarding the Catholic clergy
- Reforms regarding land use

PLM Program, 1906

Ricardo Flores Magón

Constitutional Reforms

1. Reduction of the presidential term to four years.

    ...

4. Elimination of obligatory military service and the establishment of the national guard. Those who lend their services to the permanent army will do so freely and voluntarily. ...

5. To reform and put into effect constitutional articles 6 and 7 eliminating the restrictions that private life and public peace impose upon freedom of speech and freedom of the press. ...

6. Abolition of the death penalty, except for treason.

    ...

9. Elimination of military tribunals in time of peace.

The Improvement and Encouragement of Education

10. An increase in the number of primary schools on such a scale that they will more than take the place of those that will be closed because they belong to the clergy.

11. The obligation to provide overall secular teaching in all the schools of the republic, be they those of the government or private, declaring it to be the responsibility of their administrators if they don't comply with this principle.

Ricardo Flores Magon, "1906 PLM Program," *Dreams of Freedom: A Ricardo Flores Magón Reader*, ed. and trans. Chaz Bufe and Mitchell Cowen Verter, pp. 131-134. Copyright © 2005 by AK Press. Reprinted with permission.

12. Declaring instruction to be obligatory until 14 years of age, with the responsibility being the government's to provide protection, in whatever form possible, so poor children, because of their misery do not lose the benefits of education.

...

Restrictions On the Abuses of The Catholic Clergy

17. The churches will be considered as commercial establishments, remaining therefore obligated to keep books and to pay proportionate taxes.

18. Nationalization, in accord with the laws, of the real estate that the clergy owns in the power of third parties.

...

20. Elimination of the schools directed by the clergy.

Capital And Labor

21. To establish a maximum of eight hours work and a minimum wage in the following proportion: one peso overall in the country in areas where the average wage is less than that cited, and more than one peso in those regions in which the cost of living is high and in which this wage [one peso] isn't enough to save the worker from misery.

...

24. Absolute prohibition of the employment of children under 14 years of age.

25. To obligate owners of mines, factories, workshops, etc. to maintain their properties in good hygienic conditions and to make hazardous places as safe as possible for those working in them.

...

27. To obligate bosses to pay indemnities for work accidents.

28. To declare null and void the present debts owed by agricultural workers to their bosses.

...

31. To prohibit the bosses, under severe penalties, from paying for work in any than in cash ... and to eliminate company stores.

...

33. To make Sunday an obligatory day of rest.

Lands

34. The owners of lands are obligated to work productively all that they possess; whatever part of the lands that they leave unproductive will be recovered by the state, which will employ them in conformity with the following articles:

35. Mexicans living in foreign lands who ask for it will be repatriated at government expense and will be given lands to cultivate.

36. The state will give lands to whomever asks for them, with no other conditions than that they dedicate themselves to agricultural production and that they don't sell the lands.

37. So that these benefits are not taken advantage of solely by those few who have the necessary means to work the lands, but also by the poor who lack these means, the state will create or foment the creation of an agricultural bank that will give poor agricultural workers loans at low interest, repayable over time.

Taxes

...

40. To increase the taxes on speculation, luxury goods, and vices, and to lighten the taxes on articles of basic necessity. ***

...

47. Measures to eliminate or restrict speculation, pauperism and lack of articles of basic necessity.

48. Protection of the indigenous race.

...

50. Upon the triumph of the Liberal Party, the goods of those functionaries who were enriched under the present dictatorship will be confiscated, with the proceeds applied to the redistribution of the lands, especially restitution to the Yaqui, Maya, and other tribes communities, or individuals whose lands were confiscated. ...

51. The first national congress after the fall of the dictatorship will annul all of the changes to our constitution made by the government of Porfirio Díaz; it will reform our Magna Carta in the manner necessary to put into effect this program. ...

Special Clause

52. It will remain the responsibility of the Organizing Junta of the Partido Liberal Mexicano to address as quickly as possible the foreign governments, making it manifest to them, in the name of the party, that the Mexican people do not want any additional debts placed upon the country and that, therefore, it will not recognize any new debt that under any form or pretext the dictatorship has thrown upon the nation. ...

READING 2.2 **POST-READING COMPREHENSION QUESTIONS**

- Summarize how the constitutional reforms are organized.

- Describe how the platform addresses indigenous peoples.

- Paraphrase the "Special Clause" included at the end of the Program and consider its significance.

To Women, (1910)

"To Women" is a call to action for all Mexicans to advocate for the better treatment and reconfigured status of women within the social and political sphere of Mexico. Ricardo Flores Magón illustrates the historical trajectory of the subjugation of women and demands that a reimagined Mexico must include a new vision for all Mexicans, including Mexicanas. The letter was written by Magón and published in *Regeneración*, a political magazine he founded and that represented one current of discontent expressed by the Partido Liberal Mexicano (PLM). The PLM advocated for change as part of a broader group of Mexican radicals who struggled to end the Porfirio Díaz dictatorship in Mexico.

THINGS TO LOOK FOR AS YOU READ..

- The role women have in this transformation
- The role men have in this transformation
- The role society has in this transformation

To Women

Regeneración, September 24, 1910.

Ricardo Flores Magón

W omen comrades, the cataclysm is afoot, her eyes furious, her red hair blowing in the breeze, her nervous hands ready to knock upon all the doors in her country. Wait for her calmly. Although she carries death in her bosom, she is the announcement of life; she is the herald of hope. She will destroy and create at the same time; she will tear down and construct. Her fists are the formidable fists of the people in rebellion. She does not bring roses or kisses; she carries an axe and a torch.

Interrupting the millennial feast of the complacent, sedition raises its head and Balthasar's phrase changes with the times into a shaking fist, suspended above the head of the so-called managing class.

The cataclysm is afoot. Its torch will light the blaze that will consume privilege and injustice. Women comrades, do not fear this cataclysm. You constitute half of the human species, and whatever affects it affects you as an integral part of humanity. If men are slaves, you will be, too. Shackles do not recognize gender; the infamy that shames man disgraces you as well. You cannot separate yourselves from the degradation of oppression. The same claw that strangles men's necks strangles yours as well.

It is therefore necessary to be in solidarity in the great contest for freedom and happiness. Are you mothers? Are you wives? Are you sisters? Are you daughters? Your duty is to aid man: be with him when he vacillates—inspire him; fly to his side when he suffers to soothe his pain; and laugh and sing with him when triumph smiles. What if you do not understand politics? It is not a question of politics: it is a question of life and death. The chains of men are your own. Ay! Yours are perhaps heavier and blacker and more degrading. Are you a worker? Just because you are a woman, you are paid less than a man, and you are made to work more; you have to suffer the insolence of the foreman and the boss. If you are pretty as well, the bosses assault your virtue, they will surround you, they will embrace you until you surrender your heart to them, and if you give up, they will steal it from you with the cowardice that they steal the products of your labor from you.

Under the empire of social injustice where humanity rots, a woman's existence oscillates within the restricted field of her destiny, whose frontiers are lost in the blackness and fatigue or hunger and the shadows of matrimony or prostitution.

It is necessary to study, it is essential to see, it is indispensable to scrutinize page by page this somber book called life, this bitter briar patch that tears the flesh of the human heart in order to realize exactly how woman participates in this universal suffering.

The misfortune of woman is so ancient that its origin is lost in the shadow legend. In the infancy of humanity, the birth of a girl was considered to be a misfortune by the tribe. The woman worked the earth, fetched firewood from the forest and water from the stream, tended the herd, milked the cows and the goats, built the cottage, made fabric into clothing, cooked the food, and cared for the sick and the children. The dirtiest jobs were performed by the woman. If an ox died of fatigue, the woman took its place hauling the plough. When a war flared up between enemy tribes, the woman's owner changed, but she continued under the lash of her new master, to perform the tasks of a beast of burden.

Later, under the influence of Greek civilization, woman ascended a few steps in the regard of men. She was no longer the primitive clan's beast of burden, nor did she live a cloistered life as in Oriental societies. At that time, if she belonged to a free family, her role was that of producer of citizens for her country or of slaves, if she had the rank of a helot.

Christianity arrived after this, worsening the situation of woman with its contempt for the flesh. The Great Fathers of the Church focused their hatred against feminine graces. Saint Augustine, Saint Thomas, and other saints before whose images poor women kneel, called woman the daughter of the devil, a vessel of impurity, and condemned her to suffer the tortures of hell.

The condition of woman in this century varies according to her social class, but, despite the softening of customs, despite the progress of philosophy, woman continues to be subordinate to man by tradition and by law. Eternally treated as a minor, the law places her under the tutelage of her husband. She cannot vote or be elected, and she would have to be extremely fortunate to enter into civil contracts.

Throughout the ages, woman has been considered to be an inferior being to man, not just by the law, but also by custom, and this erroneous and unjust conception is responsible for the hardship she has suffered ever since humanity barely lifted itself above primitive fauna through its use of fire and the flint axe.

Humiliated, scorned, tied by strong bonds of tradition to the pillory of an irrational inferiority, familiarized by a priest with the affairs of heaven, but totally ignorant of the problems of Earth, woman finds herself suddenly swept up by the whirlwind of industrial activity that needs workers, cheap workers above all, that takes advantage of the fact that she is not educated like men are for the industrial struggle, that she is not organized with those of her class to fight with her brother workers against the rapacity of capital.

To this we owe the fact that women, who work more than men but earn less, are abused and abased and held in contempt today like they were yesterday—that theses are the bitter fruits she harvests for a life of sacrifice. A woman's salary is so paltry that frequently she must prostitute herself to be able to support her family when she cannot find a man who will marry her in the matrimonial market, which is another kind of prostitution sanctioned by the law and authorized by a public functionary. And marriage is nothing other than prostitution when a woman weds without love, but solely with the intent of finding a man to support her, that is, as she does in the majority of marriages, she sells her body for food, just like a fallen woman.

And what can be said about the immense army of women who did not find a spouse? The growing shortage of primary goods, the disturbing decrease in wages for human labor resulting from the perfection of machinery together will [sic] all of the more and more pressing demands the modern world creates, are incapacitating man economically from taking upon himself the burden of maintaining a family. Obligatory military service, which seizes a great number of strong young males from the bosom of society, further diminishes the masculine supply in the matrimonial marketplace. The emigration of workers, provoked by various economic and political reasons, reduces the number of men capable of entering into matrimony even further. Alcoholism, gambling, and other vices and illnesses reduce even more the quantity of marriage candidates. All this results in an extreme reduction in the number of men suitable for marriage and, as a consequence, the number of single women is alarming. As single women's financial situation is very stressful, prostitution increasingly expands its ranks and the human race degenerates further through the debasement of the flesh and spirit.

Women comrades: this is the dreadful scene that modern societies offer. In this scene, you see that men and women suffer equally from the tyranny of a political and social environment that is in complete disaccord with the development of civilization and the advances of philosophy. In your moments of worry, stop raising your beautiful eyes to heaven: that is where are those [sic] who have contributed most to making you eternal slaves. The remedy is here on Earth, and it is rebellion.

Make your husbands, your brothers, your fathers, your sons, and your male friends take up the rifle. Whoever refuses to raise a firearm against his oppressors, spit in his face.

The cataclysm is afoot. Jimenez and Acayucan, Palomas, Viesca, Las Vacas, and Valladollid are the first gusts of this formidable storm. It's a tragic paradox: freedom, which is life, can only be conquered by meting out death.

READING 2.3   POST-READING COMPREHENSION QUESTIONS

- Summarize at least three of the historical examples provided in the letter.
- Describe the impact of the revolution on the struggle for women's rights in Mexico.
- Paraphrase in your own words the line: "The remedy is here on Earth, and it is Rebellion."

The Plan de Ayala, (1911)

The Zapatistas initially backed the leadership of Francisco Madero. When the Porfirio Díaz administration was supplanted, however, one of the first orders of business was to neutralize the rebels from Morelos. As a response to the frustration of the aftermath of the takeover they crafted a plan to address what they understood as tyranny and oppression. Many of the grievances listed in the plan served as specific factors that led to a popular response among Mexicans and revealed the various elements of a social revolutionary movement.[1]

THINGS TO LOOK FOR AS YOU READ...

- Grievances against Francisco Madero
- Instances of economic monopolies
- Strategy of nationalization

---

1 According to historian Juan Gómez-Quiñones, social revolutionary movements can be understood as significant multifaceted progressive political struggles or linked struggles, demanding full political responses and accesses, combined with social historical contents and the articulations of invigorated ideological consciousness, strategy(ies), democracy(ies), and addressed to society, institutions, and the state with the expectation of resolution, both nationally and internationally.

The Plan de Ayala

Emiliano Zapata and Otilio Montaño, Translation by John Womack

....

Liberating Plan of the sons of the State of Morelos, affiliated with the Insurgent Army which defends the fulfillment of the Plan of San Luis, with the reforms which it has believed proper to add in benefit of the Mexican Fatherland.

We who undersign, constituted in a revolutionary junta to sustain and carry out the promises which the revolution of November 20, 1910, just past, made to the country, declare solemnly before the face of the civilized world which judges us and before the nation to which we belong and which we call [sic, love], propositions which we have formulated to end the tyranny which oppresses us and redeem the fatherland from the dictatorships which are imposed on us, which [propositions] are determined in the following plan:

1. Taking into consideration that the Mexican people led by Don Francisco I. Madero went to shed their blood to reconquer liberties and recover their rights which had been trampled on, and for a man to take possession of power, violating the sacred principles which he took an oath to defend under the slogan "Effective Suffrage and No Reelection," outraging thus the faith, the cause, the justice, and the liberties of the people: taking into consideration that that man to whom we refer is Don Francisco I. Madero, the same who initiated the above-cited revolution, who imposed his will and influence as a governing norm on the Provisional Government of the ex-President of the Republic Attorney Francisco L. de Barra [sic], causing with this deed repeated sheddings of blood and multiplicate misfortunes for the fatherland in a manner deceitful and ridiculous, having no intentions other than satisfying his personal ambitions, his boundless instincts as a tyrant, and his profound disrespect for the fulfillment of the preexisting laws emanating from the

immortal code of '57 [Constitution of 1857], written with the revolutionary blood of Ayutla;

Taking into account that the so-called Chief of the Liberating Revolution of Mexico, Don Francisco I. Madero, through lack of integrity and the highest weakness, did not carry to a happy end the revolution which gloriously he initiated with the help of God and the people, since he left standing most of the governing powers and corrupted elements of oppression of the dictatorial government of Porfirio Díaz, which are not nor can in any way be the representation of National Sovereignty, and which, for being most bitter adversaries of ours and of the principles which even now we defend, are provoking the discomfort of the country and opening new wounds in the bosom of the fatherland, to give it its own blood to drink; taking also into account that the aforementioned Sr. Francisco I. Madero, present President of the Republic, tries to avoid the fulfillment of the promises which he made to the Nation in the Plan of San Luis Potosí, being [sic, restricting] the above-cited promises to the agreements of Ciudad Juárez, by means of false promises and numerous intrigues against the Nation nullifying, pursuing, jailing, or killing revolutionary elements who helped him to occupy the high post of President of the Republic;

Taking into consideration that the so-often-repeated Francisco I. Madero has tried with the brute force of bayonets to shut up and to drown in blood the pueblos who ask, solicit, or demand from him the fulfillment of the promises of the revolution, calling them bandits and rebels, condemning them to a war of extermination without conceding or granting a single one of the guarantees which reason, justice, and the law prescribe; taking equally into consideration that the President of the Republic Francisco I. Madero has made of Effective Suffrage a bloody trick on the people, already against the will of the same people imposing Attorney José M. Pino Suáez in the Vice-Presidency of the Republic, or [imposing as] Governors of the States [men] designated by him, like the so-called General Ambrosio Figueroa, scourge and tyrant of the people of Morelos, or entering into scandalous cooperation with the científico party, feudal landlords, and oppressive bosses, enemies of the revolution proclaimed by him, so as to forge new chains and follow the pattern of a new dictatorship more shameful and more terrible than that of Porfirio Díaz, for it has been clear and patent that he has outraged the sovereignty of the States, trampling on the laws without any respect for lives or interests, as has happened in the State of Morelos, and others, leading them to the most horrendous anarchy which contemporary history registers.

For these considerations we declare the aforementioned Francisco I. Madero inept at realizing the promises of the revolution of which he was the author, because he has betrayed the principles with which he tricked the will of the people and was able to get into power: incapable of governing, because he has no respect for the law and justice of the pueblos, and a traitor to the fatherland, because he is humiliating in blood and fire, Mexicans who want liberties, so as to please the científicos, landlords, and bosses who enslave us, and from today on we begin to continue the revolution begun by him, until we achieve the overthrow of the dictatorial powers which exist.

2. Recognition is withdrawn from S. Francisco I. Madero as Chief of the Revolution and as President of the Republic, for the reasons which before were expressed, it being attempted to overthrow this official.

3. Recognized as Chief of the Liberating Revolution is the illustrious General Pascual Orozco, the second of the Leader Don Francisco I. Madero, and in case he does not accept this delicate post, recognition as Chief of the Revolution will go to General Don Emiliano Zapata.

4. The Revolutionary Junta of the State of Morelos manifests to the Nation under formal oath: that it makes its own the plan of San Luis Potosí, with the additions which are expressed below in benefit of the oppressed pueblos, and it will make itself the defender of the principles it defends until victory or death.

5. The Revolutionary Junta of the State of Morelos will admit no transactions or compromises until it achieves the overthrow of the dictatorial elements of Porfirio Díaz and Francisco I. Madero, for the nation is tired of false men and traitors who make promises like liberators and who on arriving in power forget them and constitute themselves tyrants.

6. As an additional part of the plan, we invoke, we give notice: that [regarding] the fields, timber, and water which the landlords, científicos, or bosses have usurped, the pueblos or citizens who have the titles corresponding to those properties will immediately enter into possession of that real estate of which they have been despoiled by the bad faith of our oppressors, maintain at any cost with arms in hand the mentioned possession; and the usurpers who consider themselves with a right to them [those properties] will deduce it before the special tribunals which will be established on the triumph of the revolution.

7. In virtue of the fact that the immense majority of Mexican pueblos and citizens are owners of no more than the land they walk on, suffering the horrors of poverty without being able to improve their social condition in any way or to dedicate themselves to Industry or Agriculture, because lands, timber, and water are monopolized in a few hands, for this cause there will be expropriated the third part of those monopolies from the powerful proprietors of them, with prior indemnization, in order that the pueblos and citizens of Mexico may obtain ejidos, colonies, and foundations for pueblos, or fields for sowing or laboring, and the Mexicans' lack of prosperity and well-being may improve in all and for all.

8. [Regarding] The landlords, científicos, or bosses who oppose the present plan directly or indirectly, their goods will be nationalized and the two-third parts which [otherwise would] belong to them will go for indemnizations of war, pensions for widows and orphans of the victims who succumb in the struggle for the present plan.

9. In order to execute the procedures regarding the properties aforementioned, the laws of disamortization and nationalization will be applied as they fit, for serving us as norm and example can be those laws put in force by the immortal Juárez on ecclesiastical properties, which punished the despots and conservatives who in every time have tried to impose on us the ignominious yoke of oppression and backwardness.

10. The insurgent military chiefs of the Republic who rose up with arms in hand at the voice of Don Francisco I. Madero to defend the plan of San Luis Potosí, and who oppose with armed force the present plan, will be judged traitors to the cause which they defended and to the fatherland, since at present many of them, to humor the tyrants, for a fistful of coins, or for bribes or connivance, are shedding the blood of their brothers who claim the fulfillment of the promises which Don Francisco I. Madero made to the nation.

11. The expenses of war will be taken in conformity with Article II of the Plan of San Luis Potosí, and all procedures employed in the revolution we undertake will be in conformity with the same instructions which the said plan determines.

12. Once triumphant the revolution which we carry into the path of reality, a Junta of the principal revolutionary chiefs from the different States will name or designate an interim President of the Republic, who will convoke elections for the organization of the federal powers.

13. The principal revolutionary chiefs of each State will designate in Junta the Governor of the State to which they belong, and this appointed official will convoke elections for the due organization of the public powers, the object being to avoid compulsory appointments which work the misfortune of the pueblos, like the so-well-known appointment of Ambrosio Figueroa in the State of Morelos and others who drive us to the precipice of bloody conflicts sustained by the caprice of the dictator Madero and the circle of científicos and landlords who have influenced him.

14. If President Madero and other dictatorial elements of the present and former regime want to avoid the immense misfortunes which afflict the fatherland, and [if they] possess true sentiments of love for it, let them make immediate renunciation of the posts they occupy and with that they will with something staunch the grave wounds which they have opened in the bosom of the fatherland, since, if they do not do so, on their heads will fall the blood and the anathema of our brothers.

15. Mexicans: consider that the cunning and bad faith of one man is shedding blood in a scandalous manner, because he is incapable of governing; consider that his system of government is choking the fatherland and trampling with the brute force of bayonets on our institutions; and thus, as we raised up our weapons to elevate him to power, we again raise them up against him for defaulting on his promises to the Mexican people and for having betrayed the revolution initiated by him, we are not personalists, we are partisans of principles and not of men!

Mexican People, support this plan with arms in hand and you will make the prosperity and well-being of the fatherland.

Ayala, November 25, 1911

Liberty, Justice and Law

Signed, General in Chief Emiliano Zapata; Generals Eufemio Zapata, Francisco Mendoza, Jesús Morales, Jesús Navarro, Otilio E. Montaño, José Trinidad Ruiz, Próculo Capistrán; Colonels ...; Captains ... [This] is a true copy taken from the original. Camp in the Mountains of Puebla, December 11, 1911. Signed General in Chief Emiliano Zapata.

READING 2.4   POST-READING COMPREHENSION QUESTIONS

- Summarize why the Plan is so intent on recovering the natural resources of Mexico, including land rights.

- Describe why the Zapatistas felt betrayed by Francisco Madero.

- Paraphrase point number 15 of the Plan.

End-of-Chapter Critical Thinking Questions

Directions: Respond to each of the questions about the readings. Refer to these sources to support your answers.

- Identify and discuss at least three specific issues that these sources outline for a reimagined Mexico.

- In what ways did Ricardo Flores Magón and the PLM establish themselves as the ideological vanguard of the Mexican revolution?

- Why was the recognition of land rights so central to Emiliano Zapata and his band of revolutionaries?

Further Readings

Gómez-Quiñones, Juan. *Sembradores: Ricardo Flores Magón y el Partido Liberal Mexicano: A Eulogy and Critique* (Monograph No. 5). Los Angeles, CA.: Chicano Studies Research Center, 1973.

Gonzales, Michael J. *The Mexican Revolution, 1910–1940.* Albuquerque, NM.: University of New Mexico Press, 2002.

Harris, Charles H., and Louis R. Sadler. *The Texas Rangers and the Mexican Revolution: The Bloodiest Decade, 1910–1920.* Albuquerque, NM.: University of New Mexico Press, 2004.

Hart, John Mason. *Revolutionary Mexico: The Coming and Process of the Mexican Revolution.* Berkeley & Los Angeles, CA.: University of California Press, 1997.

Horne, Gerald. *Black and Brown African Americans and the Mexican Revolution, 1910–1920.* New York, NY.: NYU Press, 2005.

Lomnitz, Claudio. *The Return of Comrade Ricardo Flores Magón.* Cambridge, MA.: The MIT Press, 2014.

MacLachlan, Colin M., and William H. Beezley. *El Gran Pueblo: A History of Greater Mexico.* 2nd ed. Upper Saddle River, NJ.: Prentice Hall, 1999.

Pérez, Emma. *The Decolonial Imaginary: Writing Chicanas into History.* Bloomington, IN.: Indiana University Press, 1999.

Poniatowska, Elena. *Las Soldaderas: Women of the Mexican Revolution.* El Paso, TX.: Cinco Punto Press, 2000.

CHAPTER 3

Mexican American Labor

....

Editor's Introduction

The progressive era was marked by a broad set of activists looking to respond to a myriad of issues ranging from economic inequalities to sexual and reproductive rights, environmental issues to vice and criminal prohibitions, and everything in between. Many of the reformers of the era had differing political and social visions for the nation, yet what bound them together was a desire to remake society in the United States. Adding to this pressure to create large scale change was the fact that the disparity between the economic elite and the American working class was growing exponentially during these years. Many American workers caught up in the groundswell of mass production and mass consumption found their standard of living steadily declining, and now more than ever sought to express their frustrations in the form of unionization and workplace strikes. "Mexicans became another group of workers exploited by employers. They were not only paid less than other workers besides blacks, but their wages never increased irrespective of work experience. During these years when waves of strikes swept the United States, the workers responded to their exploitation, abuse, and discrepancy in wages by striking."[1]

The formation of the American Federation of Labor (AF of L) was a critical step in the collective advocating for the rights of workers. However, because the AF of L represented a mostly privileged worker—skilled and in almost every case native born and white—this left a lot to be desired by many in the workforce. The Industrial Workers of the World (IWW or Wobblies) on the other hand wanted to create "One Big Union" that encompassed all workers of the world regardless of race, ethnicity, or country of origin. They viewed themselves as more than just a labor union but rather a revolutionary organization set on toppling the global

---

1 Vargas, *Crucible of Struggle,* 178.

capitalist regime. The IWW made it a point to recruit Mexican workers on both sides of the border and employed a more militant version of labor organizing.[2]

It is important to ask, where in fact do Mexicans fit in with the history of the American labor movement? It is true that Mexicans have participated and struggled for labor rights in this country for decades if not centuries but why, consistently, are they not understood as part of the broader national labor movement? We can go back to the late nineteenth century and think about how, in response to industrial development, land disposition, and oppressive working conditions Mexicans found the need to develop strategies of organization and resistance in the form of Las Gorras Blancas. There is also the example, across the Southwest, of Mexicans joining the Holy order of the Knights of Labor. This was another group that was intent on restructuring a destructive capitalist system based on economic exploitation and racial subjugation. These labor activists, along with the IWW, make up a compelling and essential part of the American labor movement—yet routinely the experiences and contributions of Mexican and Mexican American workers are not part of these histories. The two sources included in Chapter Three highlight the impact of labor organizing and the collective effort to better the living and working conditions of laborers through unionization, especially the role the IWW played in advocating for all, including Mexican, workers.

The Wheatland Riot

From Carey McWilliams' groundbreaking work *Factories in the Field*, the following chapter focuses on the history of migratory labor in California, the Wheatland Riot, and its aftermath. McWilliams points out the long and disturbing history of the violent suppression of migratory labor and union organizing in California. The chapter also weaves together the protest tactics of the IWW along with the forceful response on the part of the business owners and the state government.

THINGS TO LOOK FOR AS YOU READ...

- The relationship between violence and labor suppression
- Strategies of the IWW
- Living and working conditions in Wheatland

---

2 Vargas, *Crucible of Struggle,* 179.

The Wheatland Riot

Carey McWilliams

The erratic and violent development of agriculture in California has been paralleled by the sporadic turbulence which has characterized the history of farm labor in the State. The story of migratory labor is one of violence: harsh repression interrupted by occasional outbursts of indignation and protest. Nor is there much probability that the future will be one of peaceful adjustment to new social conditions; no one familiar with the dominant interests in California agriculture can have any illusions on this score. Violence, and more violence, is clearly indicated. It is indicated not only by the established patterns of industrialized agriculture, but, more explicitly, by the past record of violence in the industry. This record, it should be observed, stems from the early social behavior of the Californians. The history of the Vigilance Committees of 1850 and 1856 is well known and requires no repetition. While it is true that these early committees were organized to cope with crime, it is indisputable that they were largely representative of the "merchants and propertied" classes and that, at least in 1856, their activities were directed in part against organized labor. During the period when the vigilantes were in action, they completely usurped the functions of governmental officials, defied the Governor of the State, conducted their own trials, equipped and drilled an armed force, and operated in effect as an insurrectionary junta. The story of the vigilantes entered deeply into the consciousness of the merchants, business-men, and industrialists of California. They never forgot the experience and their successors have never hesitated to constitute themselves "vigilantes" whenever the occasion has demanded "action." In 1934 "vigilante committees" appeared in practically every city, town, and rural district in California during the "Red" hysteria of that year. The significance of this deeply rooted tradition of violence must constantly be kept in mind. Insurrection was once sanctioned—violence was once glorified in the historical annals of the State—these facts have been remembered. Hence present-day industrialists are quick to drape themselves in the cloak of the vigilante tradition. Mining camps throughout the West, in Montana, Idaho, and Nevada, quickly improvised Vigilance Committees, on the San Francisco pattern, when they were first faced with a strong labor movement. Vigilantism, as such, had its origin in California.

The eruptions of farm labor have been at infrequent intervals and, in every instance, they have been violently suppressed, each incident provoking a long chain of prosecutions in the courts. No tearful glorification of the occasional protests of farm labor, however, is to be found in the official histories. Whatever theoretical considerations may be entertained concerning the use of violence in labor disputes, it is evident that, from a historical point of view, migratory labor has made gains in California when it has been militant. It has been potentially militant for a great many years, but, when strong protest movements have occurred, they have, in each instance, been directed by a clearly class-conscious leadership. One of the earliest instances of the stirring of deep-seated unrest in migratory labor was the Wheatland Riot, which occurred on the ranch of a large hop grower named Durst, near Wheatland, California, on August 3, 1913. Wheatland, clearly marked as one of the most significant episodes in the history of migratory labor in the West, also forms an important chapter in the social history of California. In the lurid illumination which the fires of the riot cast forth, the ugly facts about the condition of farm labor in California were, for the first time, thoroughly exposed. The riot and the subsequent trial attracted national attention.[1] It resulted in two important public documents bearing on the subject of farm labor (Report on the Wheatland Riot, issued June 1, 1914, and the Section titled "The Seasonal Labor Problem in Agriculture," Vol. V, Reports of the United States Commission on Industrial Relations), and one of the first serious studies of migratory labor (*The Casual Laborer,* 1920, by Carleton H. Parker).

The Wheatland affair marked the culmination of several years of agitational and organizational work on the part of the Industrial Workers of the World. To see the affair in proper perspective, therefore, it is necessary to indicate something of the background of these activities.

In the years between the Chicago convention at which the I.W.W. was formed in 1905, and 1913, the wobblies had been active in the fields, along the highways, on the trains, and in the jungle camps, with their spectacular propaganda and vivid agitation. The roots of the I.W.W.—if the organization may be said to have had any roots—were to be found among the migratory workers of the West. Not only were these workers unmercifully

---

1 See *Harper's Weekly,* April 4, June 20, 1914; *The Outlook,* May 16, 1914; *Technical World,* August, 1914.

exploited—the conditions under which they worked making them highly susceptible to the inflammatory agitation of the wobblies—but they followed, in general, the routes pursued by the I.W.W. organizers. Organizers, coming from the timber camps of the Northwest, drifted south into the agricultural fields. Always on the move, the wobblies, themselves essentially migratory, moved naturally into the currents of farm labor. Their organizational techniques—job action, organizing on the job, low dues or no dues at all—were well adapted to the circumstances under which farm labor was employed. They moved with the workers and organized them, so to speak, in transit.

During the years 1905–1913, the wobblies had demonstrated considerable strength in California. They had, for example, conducted two sensational "free-speech" fights: in San Diego and in Fresno. The fight in Fresno was of particular importance, as Fresno has long been the nerve center of agricultural labor in California, located as it is in the heart of the San Joaquin Valley. In Fresno the wobblies fought for the right to maintain a headquarters, to distribute literature, and to hold public meetings. For six months, through one fall and winter in 1910, they battled the Fresno authorities. As often as they were crushed, they launched new campaigns, finally succeeding in winning a kind of tolerance for their activities. The courage and tenacity of the wobblies in Fresno attracted the attention of many migratory workers and made a deep impression throughout the State.

The San Diego fight was, if anything, even more sensational. Beginning in January, 1912, the San Diego authorities began to suppress wobbly meetings, the campaign culminating in a remarkable ordinance which outlawed free speech throughout the city (San Diego then had a population of about 40,000). The wobblies promptly sent out word for a "concentration" on San Diego, the idea being to crowd the jails and to raise such a fracas that the city fathers would despair of making arrests. Newspapers, at the time, carried scare headlines about "thousands" of workers converging on San Diego; in fact, only about 150 wobblies were involved. To cope with the situation, the authorities sponsored a local vigilance committee which established camps and posted armed guards along the highways leading to San Diego (one of the first California "border patrols"), turning back all transients. In San Diego itself the vigilantes rounded up all persons even remotely suspected of being wobblies and marched them, one night, to Sorrento. There the wobblies were made to mount an improvised platform, kiss the American flag and sing the national anthem, while hundreds of vigilantes stood about armed with revolvers, knives, clubs, blackjacks, and black snake whips. Then they were marched to San Onofre and driven into a cattle pen and systematically slugged and beaten. After a time, they were taken out of the pen and beaten with clubs and whips as, one at a time, they were made "to run the gantlet." One wobbly subsequently died in jail; scores received serious injuries. Not only was this performance sanctioned by the authorities, but the Merchants

Association and the Chamber of Commerce passed resolutions praising the vigilantes. Speaking on behalf of San Diego, the *San Diego Tribune,* in its issue of March 4, 1912, spoke of the wobblies as follows: "Hanging is none too good for them and they would be much better dead; for they are absolutely useless in the human economy; they are the waste material of creation and should be drained off into the sewer of oblivion there to rot in cold obstruction like any other excrement." When one local editor protested, the vigilantes attempted to lynch him. The facts, as I have given them, merely summarize the findings of Mr. Harris Weinstock who was appointed by Governor Hiram Johnson to investigate the incident.

After the San Diego free-speech fight, wobbly locals were established throughout California: in Fresno, Bakersfield, Los Angeles, San Diego, San Francisco and Sacramento. From these locals, camp delegates were sent into the fields to organize workers "on the job." Many "job strikes" were called and, frequently, they were successful. Largely because of the sensational character of their propaganda and the militancy of their free-speech fights, the wobblies built up a reputation in California out of all relation to their actual numerical strength. The I.W.W. had less than 5000 members in the State in 1913 and less than 8 per cent of the migratory farm workers were members. Nevertheless, the wobblies were a great influence. Whenever "labor trouble" occurred in the fields or in the construction camps, it was usually discovered that a "camp delegate" had been on the ground. The songs of the I.W.W. were frequently heard in the fields and in the jungle camps under the railroad bridges. To such an extent had this agitation permeated the mass of farm laborers that when the Wheatland incident occurred the I.W.W. was able to assume complete leadership of the workers. Conditions similar to those which existed on the Durst ranch in 1913 had existed in California for twenty years or longer, but militant action awaited the arrival of the wobblies.

1. The Riot

Immediately prior to August 3, 1913, some 2800 men, women and children were camped on a low, unshaded hill near the Durst hop ranch at Wheatland. Of this number, approximately 1500 were women and children. Over half the total number of workers in this miserable camp were aliens; at one of the subsequent mass meetings seven interpreters had to be used; and a field boss made note of twenty-seven nationalities represented in one working gang of 235 men on the ranch. Following the established practice of his fellow growers, Durst had advertised in newspapers throughout California and Nevada for workers. He had asked for 2700 workers when, as he subsequently admitted, he could only supply employment for about 1300. Within four days after his fanciful advertisements had appeared, this strange aggregation of workers had assembled. They came by every conceivable means of transportation; many of them had walked from near-by towns and cities. A great number had no blankets and slept on piles of straw thrown on tent floors. The tents, incidentally, were rented from Durst at seventy-five cents a week. Many slept in the fields. One group of 45 men, women and children slept packed closely together on a single pile of straw. There were nine outdoor toilets for 2800 people. The stench around the camp was nauseating, with children and women vomiting; dysentery was prevalent to an alarming degree. Between 200 and 300 children worked in the fields; and hundreds of children were seen around the camp "in an unspeakably filthy condition." The workers entered the fields at four o'clock in the morning, and by noon the heat was terrific, remaining, as it did, around 105 degrees. The water wells were "absolutely insufficient for the camp," with no means provided of bringing water to the fields. "Numerous instances of sickness and partial prostration among children from 5 to 10 years of age were mentioned in the testimony." One reason for Durst's chariness about providing water was that his cousin, Jim Durst, had a lemonade concession, selling lemonade to the workers at a nickel a glass. There was no organization for sanitation, no garbage disposal. Local Wheatland stores were forbidden to send delivery wagons to the camp, so that the workers were forced to buy what supplies they could afford from a "concession" store on the ranch.

The commission of inquiry which investigated the incident found that Durst had intentionally advertised for more workers than he needed in order to force wages down and that he purposely permitted the camp to remain in a filthy condition so that some of the workers would leave before the season was over, thereby forfeiting 10 per cent of their wages which he insisted on holding back. Carleton Parker stated that the amount paid, per hundred pounds of hops picked, fluctuated daily in relation to the number of workers on hand. Earnings varied between $1.00 and $.78 a day. Over half the workers were destitute and were forced to cash their checks each night. Throughout the season, at least a thousand workers, unable to secure employment, remained idle in the camp.

The foregoing is a very meager and abbreviated statement of the conditions which were found to have existed at the camp, on and prior to August third. Of the workers assembled, about a third came from California towns and cities; another third were "quasi-gypsies" from the Sierra foothills, with ramshackle wagons and carts; the remaining third were "hoboes," or their "California exemplars, the fruit tramps," with many foreigners among this group, including Japanese, Hindus, and Puerto Ricans. Of this strange assortment, about 100 men were I.W.W. "card men," i.e. they had, at one time or another, carried a wobbly card. Some of the wobblies had organized a loosely formed local in the camp in which some thirty workers had been enrolled. "It is a deeply suggestive fact," reads the official report, "that these thirty men, through their energy, technique and skill in organization, unified and dominated an unhomogeneous mass of 2,800 unskilled laborers" within two days. It was subsequently estimated that about 400 workers of those assembled knew, in a rough way, something of the philosophy of the I.W.W., and could sing some of its songs. Of the hundred card men, some had been in the San Diego fight, some had been soapboxers in Fresno. Among these men were Blackie Ford—an experienced I.W.W. organizer—and Herman Suhr.

Resentment had been steadily mounting in the camp for several days prior to August third. For the most part, the workers were indignant over living conditions; they were not primarily interested in wages. On August third, the wobblies called a mass meeting, Blackie Ford (he was unarmed) addressed the workers, and, among other remarks, told them to "knock the blocks off the scissor bills." He took a sick baby from its mother's arms and, holding it before the eyes of about 2000 workers, shouted: "It's for the kids we are doing this." The meeting had come to a close with the singing of "Mr. Block"—a wobbly song—when the sheriff and his posse arrived with the district attorney (who was, also, Durst's private attorney). The sheriff and a few of his men started through the crowd to arrest Ford. One deputy, on the fringe of the crowd, fired a shot in the air "to sober the mob," and, as he fired, the fighting started. The district attorney, a deputy sheriff, and two workers, a Puerto Rican and an English boy, were killed, and many more persons were injured, in the riot which followed. The posse, apparently astonished at the resistance they had encountered, fled the scene. Shocked beyond measure by reports of the riot, the State was immediately up in arms. The Governor dispatched four companies of the National Guard to Wheatland. The guardsmen marched to the workers' camp, surrounded it, and assisted the local officers in arresting about a hundred workers. Most of the workers had left the camp the night of August third, the "roads out of Wheatland being filled all that night with pickers leaving camp." The townspeople of Wheatland were so badly frightened by the incident that the National Guard remained on the scene for over a week.

Feeling that they had a revolutionary situation to cope with, the authorities were panicstricken and promptly launched a campaign of wild and irresponsible persecution. The Burns Detective Agency was called in and a hundred or more of its operatives were deputized. There followed one of the most amazing reigns of terror that California has ever witnessed. Wobblies were arrested literally in every part of the State. No one was ever able to make an accurate estimate of the number of arrests; many cases were subsequently reported of men being arrested and held by local authorities incommunicado for seventy and eighty days. The total number of arrests ran well into the hundreds. Private detectives seized Suhr in Arizona (he was not even present when the riot occurred) and, without legal formalities, loaded him into a box car and brought him back to

California. En route to Marysville, California, where the trial was held, Suhr was kept from consulting his attorney, being taken from hotel to hotel by night. Stool pigeons were placed with him to elicit confessions and he was beaten on an average of once a night with rubber bludgeons. It was several weeks after his "arrest" before his attorneys could even discover his whereabouts. Many other defendants were arrested and hurried from county to county in order to elude defense attorneys who were scurrying about trying to find their clients. So terrible was the treatment of these prisoners that one committed suicide and another went insane. An operative of the Burns Agency was, in fact, later convicted in Contra Costa County for a violent assault upon one of the men who was arrested but never tried. Eight months after the Wheatland riot occurred, Ford and Suhr were convicted of murder and sentenced to life imprisonment and this conviction was sustained on appeal,[2] the first California labor *cause célèbre*. During the trial sixty or more wobblies rented a house in Marysville, which they used as headquarters. Every day of the trial, they marched from this house to the courtroom. When Austin Lewis, the defense attorney, needed a witness, he merely scribbled the name and address of the witness on a card and handed it to one of these men. Sympathetic brakemen and conductors on the trains invariably honored the cards as passenger tickets and allowed wobblies to travel about the State hunting witnesses.

Wheatland was not a strike, but a spontaneous revolt. It stands out as one of the significant episodes in the long and turgid history of migratory labor in California. For the first time, the people of California were made to realize, even if vaguely, the plight of its thousands of migratory workers. It had been customary to assume the existence of these laborers, but never to recognize the fact of their existence. The deplorable conditions under which they lived and worked were, also, brought to light for the first time. Although the immediate public reaction was one of horror over the I.W.W. menace, so-called, the incident made an impression. It created an opportunity for effective investigation by the Commission on Immigration and Housing in California which, under the distinguished chairmanship of Simon J. Lubin, did much to improve living and housing conditions among migratory workers in the State. As the annual reports of this commission began to appear after 1914, the Californians were given some interesting facts about labor conditions in the State's most important industry. It was discovered, for example, that, in 1914, there were about 75,000 migratory farm laborers in the State; and that, when employed, these people worked on ranches "devoid of the accommodations given horses." Sample studies indicated that about a fourth of them were suffering from one type of sickness or another and that about an equal percentage were feebleminded.

---

2 *People v. Ford*, 25 Cal. App. 388.

2. Kelley's Army

Following the Wheatland affair, and during the winter of 1914, an incident occurred which, for the first time, threw considerable light on the question of what happened to 75,000 migratory farm laborers during the winter months. The number of unemployed in San Francisco that winter was unusually large and the city authorities soon discovered that "General Kelley," a gentleman of mysterious antecedents, had organized an army of the unemployed. About two thousand men had enrolled in the army and were living in abandoned warehouses and store buildings; quite a number were camped in tents in the Mission district. Kelley had his men organized into companies and squads and put them through regular military maneuvers. As the size of the army increased, Kelley became more outspoken in his demands upon the authorities for relief, or "charitable assistance," as it was then called. The officials, and the business interests of the city, soon became alarmed over the situation, and, seizing upon Kelley's desire to stage a "march on the capitol," they escorted his army to the ferries and sent them across the bay to Oakland. The Mayor of Oakland, not at all delighted by this visitation of "rainsoaked, sick, and coughing" men, hurriedly arranged for their transportation to Sacramento. In Sacramento, they organized a "camp" and were preparing to march on the capitol building, 1500 strong, when a rival "army," of eight hundred special deputy sheriffs, arrived with pick handles and drove them across the river, burned their blankets and equipment, and mounted an armed guard along the bridge to keep them out. In the process of ousting the army, the deputies were none too gentle. E. Guy Talbott, a local clergyman, states that many of Kelley's men "were beaten into insensibility and the most atrocious and barbarous methods were used." Within three weeks the Army, "rained on and starved out," melted away. For years afterwards, however, the story of Kelley's Army lingered in the social consciousness of the Californian as a grim portent of the days to come.

When the Industrial Relations Commission arrived in California in August, 1914, they took testimony both on the Wheatland affair and on the strange rise and fall of General Kelley's Army, and the connection between the two incidents was clearly indicated. "You can't analyze the Wheatland affair and the riot that took place," testified Carleton Parker, "or the problem of the unemployed in San Francisco last winter without bringing into the analysis the seasonal character of employment in California." Testifying further, he said: "The fact that San Francisco is said to have in winter thirty-five to forty thousand men lying up until the earlier season when the first agricultural demand for labor occurs, is explained by the fact that along in November and December, especially in November, agricultural work practically ceases. The State being fundamentally an agricultural State, the industrial life of the State not being of tremendous importance, and the fact that the State is geographically isolated, means that we have to nurse our own casual labor class through the winter." Witness after witness testified as to the instability of employment, the lack of co-ordination, and the refusal of the agricultural interests of the State to assume any measure of responsibility for the situation which they had created. It is interesting to note that one witness did suggest that if the growers continued to shirk their responsibility, it might be well for the State to condemn some of their holdings and settle the unemployed on the land so that they could earn a living. At about the same time, San Diego, faced with a serious unemployment problem, took over four thousand acres of "waste" land, and gave food and lodging to hundreds of unemployed, and paid them fifty cents a day, while they worked in improving and cultivating the tract. The experiment was quite successful and was continued until 1916, when, the demand for labor increasing, it was abandoned. August Vollmer, describing the operation of the plan in the *Christian Science Monitor,* advocated its extension throughout the State and claimed that there were approximately 11,000,000 acres of "waste" lands in the State that might be put to constructive social use in this manner.

The recognition of an acute social problem in migratory farm labor, a problem so serious as to shake the foundations of the State, which the Wheatland Riot and the appearance of General Kelley's Army had forced upon the people of California, was, unfortunately, destroyed by the World War. Both incidents passed into history. Even the beginning toward a solution of the problem, as indicated by the creation of the State Commission on Immigration and Housing, was soon nullified. Reactionary postwar administrations proceeded to undermine the work of the commission (Simon J. Lubin resigned in protest), and the blind chaos of former years once more prevailed.

Bibliography

"Marysville Strike," April 4, 1914, Inez Haynes Gilmore, *Harper's Weekly.*
"Porterhouse Heaven and the Hobo," Aug. 1914, Walter V. Woehlke, *Technical World.*
"San Diego I.W.W.," July 6, 1912, Walter V. Woehlke, *Outlook.*
"Wheatland Riots," May 16, 1914, Travers Clements, *Outlook.*
Casual Laborer and Other Essays (Chapter II: "Wheatland"), 1920, Carleton H. Parker.

READING 3.1 **POST-READING COMPREHENSION QUESTIONS**

- Summarize the events of the Wheatland Riot.

- Describe the reputation the Wobblies built up as a labor organization.

- Paraphrase the quote: "The story of migratory labor is one of violence: harsh repression interrupted by occasional outbursts of indignation and protest."

Industrial Workers of the World (1919)

The Industrial Workers of the World (IWW) was more than just a labor organization. It also sought to dismantle many of the oppressive political and social conditions that it felt were repressing people around the world. In an era when labor organizing was increasing, the IWW leadership understood that in many cases the labor gains that were made were only to be realized by a certain segment of the working class. This image highlights the motto of the IWW: "One Big Union." It also underscores the idea that the IWW was not merely looking to advocate for American workers but, rather, it was looking to support and harness the power of workers around the world. With industrial unionism as its foundation, the IWW introduced countless Mexicans to its radical ideas regarding unjust wages and increasing wealth inequality. The IWW was explicitly seeking to organize Mexicans into "One Big Union" as a strategy to help ensure fair wages and advocate for better working conditions.[1] In part, the approach of the IWW was not only to build a multiracial organization, but also to help shape a collective of class-conscious workers who understood that their strength would come in numbers against an oppressive and violent capitalist system, and that a global revolution was needed.

THINGS TO LOOK FOR AS YOU VIEW THE IMAGE..

- The motto of the IWW
- The message of the poster
- The imagery in the poster

---

1 Vargas, *Crucible of Struggle,* 179.

Figure 3.1 Industrial Workers of the World (1919).

Source: https://commons.wikimedia.org/wiki/File:Industrial_Workers_of_the_World.jpg.

End-of-Chapter Critical Thinking Questions

Directions: Respond to each of the questions about the reading and the image. Refer to these sources to support your answers.

- Assess and describe the significance of the IWW and its motto of "One Big Union."
- Evaluate and discuss the following quote: "Wheatland was not a strike, but a spontaneous revolt."

Further Readings

Andrews, Thomas G. *Killing for Coal: America's Deadliest Labor War.* Cambridge, MA.: Harvard University Press, 2008.

Cole, Peter, David M. Struthers, and Kenyon Zimmer. *Wobblies of the World: A Global History of the IWW.* London, UK.: Pluto Press, 2017.

Freeberg, Ernest. *Democracy's Prisoners: Eugene V. Debs, the Great War, and the Right to Dissent.* Cambridge, MA.: Harvard University Press, 2008.

Gómez-Quiñones, Juan. *Mexican American Labor, 1790–1990.* Albuquerque, NM.: University of New Mexico Press, 2004.

Green, James R. *Grass-Roots Socialism: Radical Movements in the Southwest, 1895–1943.* Baton Rouge, LA.: Louisiana State University Press, 1978.

McWilliams, Carey. *Factories in the Field: The Story of Migratory Farm Labor in California.* Berkeley, CA.: University of California Press, 2000.

Montgomery, David. *The Fall of the House of Labor: The Workplace, the State, and American Labor Activism, 1865–1925.* Cambridge, UK.: Cambridge University Press, 1988.

Rees, Jonathan. "Beyond Body Counts: A Centennial Rethinking of the Ludlow Massacre." *Labor: Studies in Working-Class History of the Americas* 11, no. 3 (2014): 107–115.

Ruíz, Vicki. *From Out of the Shadows: Mexican Women in Twentieth-Century America,* 10th anniversary ed. New York, NY.: Oxford University Press, 2008.

Tutino, John. *Mexico and Mexicans in the Making of the United States.* Austin, TX.: University of Texas Press, 2013.

Weber, Devra Anne. "Wobblies of the Partido Liberal Mexicano: Reenvisioning Internationalist and Transnational Movements through Mexican Lenses." *Pacific Historical Review* 85, no. 2 (2016): 188–226.

Whitten, Woodrow C. "The Wheatland Episode." *Pacific Historical Review* 17, no. 1 (1948): 37–42.

Wilkerson, Isabel. *The Warmth of Other Sons: The Epic Story of America's Great Migration.* New York, NY.: Vintage Books, 2010.

Zinn, Howard, Dana Frank, and Robin D.G. Kelley. *Three Strikes: Miners, Musicians, Salesgirls and the Fighting Spirit of Labor's Last Century.* Boston, MA.: Beacon Press, 2001.

CHAPTER 4

The Great Depression and Forced Deportation

....

Editor's Introduction

The first quarter of the twentieth century in the United States saw massive immigration from Europe as well as different parts of the world. However, these "new immigrants" were not only from Northern and Western Europe as had been the case in the past. Now they included Eastern and Southern European as well as Asian and Mexican immigrants. America was grappling with a so-called "race problem" and increasingly turned towards the budding pseudo-science of eugenics to reinforce nativism. This period was also marked by a rise in internal migration, where many Americans were looking to create cultural communities and gain economic opportunities by separating themselves from the long shadow cast by Jim Crow.

Perhaps the most iconic moment of this stage in United States history was the stock market crash in October of 1929. This singular event often gets blamed for the Great Depression and rightfully so. We can clearly see how a lack of banking regulation and reckless speculation on the part of large financial institutions led to this disaster. However, there were many other factors that led up to that economic crisis, including domestic overproduction and a lack of meaningful investment in the lives and security of workers. This was an era highlighted by scientific advancement in the workplace in terms of production and technology. Fordism and Taylorism were fully embraced, which produced a bulk of new commodities that flooded the consumer market. Yet this period also demonstrates an explicit divestment in the financial well-being of the worker and an all-out assault on labor unions. As a response to this financial crisis, it was clear that a scapegoat would be needed to help alleviate some of the political pressure on Herbert Hoover and galvanize his presidential administration. Unfortunately for some Americans, this political solution entailed rounding up and terrorizing close to one million people of Mexican descent living and working in the United States, regardless of citizenship status.

The sources included in this chapter underscore the significant ways in which the racialization process manifested itself in the United States during the first decades of the twentieth century. Natalia Molina powerfully explains how "... between 1879 and 1939, areas home to L.A.'s Chinese, Japanese, and Mexican populations were separately and serially targeted as 'rotten spots.' Armed with institutional power buttressed and legitimated by the language of 'scientific objectivity,' public health officials developed discourses that attributed the serious health problems confronting these minorities to purported deficiencies in the groups' biological capacities and cultural practices."[1] In an excerpt from his groundbreaking monograph *Becoming Mexican American*, George J. Sánchez provides a transnational history of Mexican Americans and specifically "... addresses the responses of Mexicans to economic crisis and the mass repatriation campaigns of the 1930s."[2] Lastly, figure 4.1 captures the chaos and uncertainty that characterized the highly disruptive effort of this massive forced deportation scheme of ethnic Mexicans from the United States.

Fit to Be Citizens? Public Health and Race in Los Angeles, 1879–1939

In the introduction to her groundbreaking work *Fit to be Citizens?* Molina leads us into an examination of how notions of race were used to mislead the public and disproportionately police certain groups. In particular, she states that by "[p]ortraying people of Chinese, Mexican, and Japanese ancestry in Los Angeles as threats to public health and civic well-being obscured the real causes of communicable disease and illness—inadequate medical care, exposure to raw sewage, and malnutrition."[3] Additionally, the author demonstrates irrefutably the link between racial assumptions and public health.

THINGS TO LOOK FOR AS YOU READ...

- The link between disease and race
- How social membership is marked
- The idea of racial hierarchy

---

1 Natalia Molina, *Fit to Be Citizens?: Public Health and Race in Los Angeles, 1879–1939* (Berkeley, CA.: University of California Press, 2006), 1.

2 George J. Sánchez, *Becoming Mexican American: Ethnicity, Culture and Identity in Chicano Los Angeles, 1900–1945* (New York, NY.: Oxford University Press, 1993), 210.

3 Molina. *Fit to Be Citizens?: Public Health and Race in Los Angeles, 1879–1939*, 2.

Introduction to *Fit to Be Citizens?*

Natalia Molina

ealth Officer Dr. Walter Lindley assured city residents in 1879 that Los Angeles had "everything that God could give" a city.[1] Among L.A.'s many virtues, the doctor emphasized "the health giving sun [present] almost every day in the year ... the ocean breeze just properly tempered by hills and orange groves ... pure water pouring down from a mountain stream [and] ... the most equable temperature in the civilized world."[2] Such healthful abundance, however, did not lessen the need for the services of the city's chief health officer and his fledgling department. In stressing the importance of improving sanitary conditions in Los Angeles, he called for the construction of a municipal sewer system and appealed to the city council to eradicate Chinatown, "that rotten spot [that pollutes] the air we breathe and poisons the water we drink."[3]

And so began what became a long tradition among city health officials of tracing any blemish on the pristine image of Los Angeles—including all forms of disease and any manner of disorder—to the city's marginalized communities. As the chapters that follow will show, between 1879 and 1939, areas home to L.A.'s Chinese, Japanese, and Mexican populations were separately and serially targeted as "rotten spots." Armed with institutional power buttressed and legitimated by the language of "scientific objectivity," public health officials developed discourses that attributed the serious health problems confronting these minorities to purported deficiencies in the groups' biological capacities and cultural practices. Thus, from the start, Los Angeles health officials' efforts to promote the reputation of the city as modern and healthful were interwoven with their role as local arbiters of the meanings of race and racial identities.

Portraying people of Chinese, Mexican, and Japanese ancestry in Los Angeles as threats to public health and civic well-being obscured the real causes of communicable disease and illness—inadequate medical care, exposure to raw sewage, and malnutrition. Misled by their own racial assumptions, health officials betrayed their institution's mission. They devoted inordinate attention and disproportionate effort toward policing racial groups while neglecting the dangers posed by the incidence of communicable disease among the rest of the city's residents. Issues of race, class, and gender were considered in all aspects of health officials' work, from identifying and defining problems, to developing preventative health care programs, to handling disease outbreaks. Disease itself was defined as much by sociocultural beliefs in the inherent uncleanliness of immigrants and nonwhites as by biological explanations. Such definitions effectively stigmatized entire populations of already-marginalized groups in the city.

Perhaps most important in the long term was the public health department's gatekeeper role. Indeed, health and hygiene norms increasingly became standards for "Americanness," and health officers helped determine who was considered part of the body politic. They had the power to restrict people's sense of social membership and shape their relationship to the nation-state. As the historian Suellen Hoy argues, "[C]leanliness became something more than a way to prevent epidemics and make cities livable—it became a route to citizenship, to becoming American. It was, in fact, confrontation with racial and cultural outsiders that transformed cleanliness from a public health concern into a moral and patriotic one."[4] It was health officers, for example, who had responsibility for deciding who was healthy enough to work or attend public school. Public health ordinances dictated where Chinese fruit and vegetable vendors could establish businesses and even prescribed the architectural style of the produce markets. They determined when Mexican railroad laborers could leave their work camps and where Japanese residents could seek institutionalized health care. They approached these communities, which they considered a "menace,"[5] with the attitude that they needed to "safeguard the public" against them.[6]

City and county public health officials in Los Angeles consistently failed to distinguish between U.S.-born and foreign-born individuals in the Chinese, Japanese, and Mexican communities (even *Californios,* those Mexicans who had lived in California when it was still Mexico), thus marking all members of these groups as permanently "foreign."[7] Suspended indefinitely in this "not-yet-American" state, Japanese, Chinese, and Mexican residents of Los Angeles were excluded from the benefits of full social participation in the life of their city. Social membership is usually equated with citizenship status, but it is important also to investigate how those who are not citizens negotiate a sense of national identity, calibrating notions of citizenship and democracy in the process.[8] By shifting the focus to the local level, one can see the ways in which social membership is negotiated every day.[9] In this study, examining local institutions, particularly those whose mission was to promote public health, is crucial to demonstrating how institutional policies affected a sense of social membership. As an institution, the department of public health regulated immigrants' everyday life practices. Moreover, the city and county health departments' official standards, guidelines, and recommendations were routinely evoked by the city council and others to prevent Chinese, Japanese, and Mexican residents from bargaining freely over wages and working conditions; from owning land or accumulating other assets that might appreciate in value and be passed on to subsequent generations; and even from moving freely about the city in search of housing, employment, and business opportunities.[10]

The growth of Los Angeles and the increasing national recognition of public health as a prominent profession in the nation and important institution in the city were closely entwined. Just as demographic growth and increased immigration warranted the attention of government legislators and private investors, so too they demanded the attention of health officials. Sanitation and good health were central to the image of Los Angeles, and public health officials remained thoroughly committed to promoting the reputation of the burgeoning city. The many connections between the health departments and the broader municipal infrastructure challenge the idea of public health as being driven by pure principles of "scientific objectivity."[11] Overarching social and political issues of the time played essential roles in the development of the city and county health departments, determining where clinics were established and what types of programs were offered to whom.

Health officials not only incorporated their racially charged visions into policies and ordinances that targeted ethnic communities but also helped shape the ways mainstream populations perceived ethnic peoples. Moreover, people operating at various levels of power, in and out of government, routinely appropriated public health discourses to advance goals of their own, including the shaping of racial categories and meanings.[12] "Experts" from the fields of public health, public service, law, and social work reinforced each other's ideas, thereby increasing the legitimacy that the general public accorded to their claims. The process by which public health as an institution and a discourse evolved into a key site of racialization in late-nineteenth- through mid-twentieth-century Los Angeles—how it came to exert an influence that extended far beyond the realm of health—is the central question this book addresses.[13]

Refining the Racial Hierarchy

In 1875, the Southern Pacific Railroad extended its line from San Francisco to Los Angeles. Additional connections to railroad lines during the 1880s made Los Angeles the terminus of two cross-continental railroads. Each new link precipitated another, larger jump in the size of the city. Census data place the total population of the city in 1880 at slightly over eleven thousand. By 1900, Los Angeles claimed a population of more than one hundred thousand within city limits and an additional seventy thousand residents in the county.[14] But in Los Angeles, unlike comparable cities in the Midwest and East, population density grew only modestly. As a result, the city and county developed into a sprawling metropolis with a much higher ratio of land per capita than was common elsewhere.[15]

If L.A.'s geographical limits seemed infinitely expandable, its social boundaries did not. The city and surrounding county were the site of persistent struggles between the white elite and the racially diverse remainder of the population.[16] Sparring matches over politics, civil rights, housing, employment, and the distribution of city and county services occurred regularly, increasing social polarization throughout the city. These conditions made having a stake in assigning L.A.'s ethnic groups their proper place in the city's racial order especially important. Public and private discussions of the need for maintaining a high standard of public health were laced with references to the perils presented by the city's immigrant minorities. Health officials recorded their racial concerns in quarterly and annual reports, in internal memos, in their correspondence with other health and government officials, and in the press. The multiethnic population of Los Angeles preoccupied public health officials because of a widespread perception that immigrants threatened the health of the nation in both a real and a metaphorical sense.

From the late nineteenth to the early twentieth century, Americans across the country struggled to adapt to the broad changes that accompanied industrialization. Large numbers of people moved from rural to urban areas, and major sites of labor shifted from the fields to the factories. The composition of immigration changed as well. In most cities, southern European newcomers replaced earlier Irish and German populations as the largest immigrant groups.[17] Public dissatisfaction and calls for reforms in various arenas, from business to social welfare programs, accompanied these sociopolitical and cultural transformations. As the country embarked on a "search for order" that would calm growing fears of chaos,[18] public health, which emerged as a field toward the end of the nineteenth century, seemed an ideal solution.[19] With its promise of "scientific objectivity" and its embodiment of many of the values championed by the Progressives, it was an institution well suited to the era.[20]

On the East Coast and in the Midwest, health workers and social reformers directed their efforts at the newly arriving white immigrants from southern Europe, whom they attempted to assimilate into American culture. In Los Angeles, the situation was more complicated. Los Angeles health officials dealt only infrequently with the city's ethnic white (southern and eastern European) immigrants. Their main concerns, instead, were the health issues posed by Chinese, Japanese, and Mexican residents. Asians and Mexicans were not easily classified into racial categories. They were neither white nor black. What position should they occupy in the racial order? The highest levels of government determined legal citizenship, but institutions, such as public health departments, determined who had access to social membership. Public health officials were able to inject new concepts and ideas into delineation processes that are usually informal and carried out at a much lower level (such as a city or even a neighborhood), marking some people as worthy, capable, and deserving members of society and others as correspondingly unworthy and incapable of participation. What degree of social membership and/or legal citizenship should be extended to which groups? Public health officials, with their standards and guidelines, programs and policies, helped answer and institutionalize responses to these questions. I argue that by examining public health as a site of racialization, we will see how public health workers at the local level contributed to the construction of racial categories. In Los Angeles County, the earliest interactions between public health officials and Mexican and Japanese immigrants reveal how race relations in this area differed from those in the rest of the nation.

Developing a Regional Racial Lexicon

In the country as a whole, race was commonly perceived in dichotomous terms as the categories of "white" and "black." The general public identified other major "races" as Slavs, Hebrews, and Mediterraneans. Los Angeles had its share of these groups, but they were rarely mentioned as racially distinct. The black/white imagery that dominated conceptions of race elsewhere gave way in Los Angeles to a notion of race as a graded continuum shading from white, at the top, downward through various forms of "nonwhite," represented by the city's Chinese, Japanese, and Mexican populations. In Los Angeles, people "saw" race differently. The numerically small size of the African American population, combined with the fact that Asians and then, later, Mexicans were highly sought after as laborers, displaced the prejudices usually reserved for African Americans onto these three groups (table 4.1.1).[21]

The history of the development of the nonwhite category in contrast to the widely accepted black-white paradigm highlights the fluidity of racial understandings and the many ways in which racial categories evolved. In the wake of the major changes nationwide brought about by large-scale immigration and industrialization, the notion of "an unquestioned hegemony of a unified race of 'white persons'" broke down.[22] Poor

Table 4.1.1 Population of Los Angeles Broken Down by Race, 1880–1940.

Year	White in County	White in City	Negroes in County	Negroes in City	Japanese in County	Japanese in City	Chinese[a] in County	Chinese[a] in City	Mexicans[a] in County	Mexicans[a] in City	Total Population (County)	Total Population (City)
1880	31,707	10,379	188	102	1	1	1,169	604	1,721 (FB)	N/A	33,381	11,183
1890	95,033	47,205	6,421[b]	1,258	36	26	4,424	1,871	1,293 (FB)	498 (FB)	101,454	50,395
1900	163,975	98,082	2,841	2,131	204	150	3,209	2,111	1,613 (FB)	817 (FB)	170,298	102,479
1910	483,478	305,307	9,424	5,101	8,461	4,238	2,602	1,954	11,793 (FB)	5,632 (FB)	504,131	319,198
1920	894,507	546,864	18,738	15,579	19,911	11,618	2,591	2,062	33,644	21,598 (FB)	936,455	576,673
1930	1,949,882	1,073,584	46,425	38,894	35,390	21,081	3,572	3,009	167,024	97,116	2,190,738	1,238,048
1940	2,660,042	1,406,430	75,209	63,774	36,866	23,321	997	4,736	59,260	36,840 (FB)	2,765,569	1,504,277

Sources: U.S. Census Office, *Statistics of the Population of the United States at the Tenth Census* (Washington, DC: Government Printing Office, 1883); *Report on the Population of the United States at the Eleventh Census: 1890* (Washington, DC: Government Printing Office, 1895); *Abstract of the Twelfth Census of the United States* (Washington, DC: Government Printing Office, 1904); *Thirteenth Census of the United States* (Washington, DC: Government Printing Office, 1913); *Fourteenth Census of the United States Taken in the Year 1920* (Washington, DC: Government Printing Office, 1923); *Fifteenth Census of the United States: 1930* (Washington, DC: Government Printing Office, 1933); *Sixteenth Census of the United States: 1940* (Washington, DC: Government Printing Office, 1943).

[a] From 1890–1920, Mexicans were legally considered white. The values entered for these years for Los Angeles City reflect the numbers of foreign-born (FB) Mexicans, not the native born of Mexican origin. In 1930, the census classified Mexicans for the first time as a nonwhite group; the figure represents all people of Mexican origin, foreign and native born. In 1940, the figure once again reflects only foreign-born Mexicans.

[b] In 1890, the census included Negro, Chinese, Japanese, and Indian in one category.

and ethnic whites continually needed to define themselves against the "other," most often African Americans, in order to establish their racial privilege.[23] The fervor with which whites guarded their racial privilege is not surprising. Whites' position at the top of the racial order resulted in heightened access to institutionalized power.[24] By definition, racialized populations, since they were constructed in structural opposition to whites, had limited access to institutional power.

The ambiguity that resulted from retooling racial categories also meant that people who were neither white nor black had no clearly defined position in the racial hierarchy. The "nonwhite" category helped stabilize the new racial order. Like whiteness, nonwhiteness was neither a monolithic nor a static category; it incorporated degrees of access to privilege, and its composition changed in response to national factors (e.g., labor needs, immigration laws, and economic cycles) and more regional pressures (e.g., the presence or absence of other marginalized populations). The racial ordering within the category of "nonwhite" also was affected by the process of racialization itself. As Tomás Almaguer has shown, in nineteenth-century California, groups were racialized in relation to one another, falling into different places along a graded continuum that began with whites, who were followed by Mexicans, African Americans, Asians, and, finally, Native Americans.[25] As Claire Jean Kim has pointed out, the racial order is not a "single-scale hierarchy (A over B over C), but a field structured by at least two axes: that of superior/inferior and that of insider/foreigner. Blacks and whites constitute the major anchors (bottom and top respectively) of this order, and incoming immigrants and other groups get positioned relative to these two loci."[26] In Los Angeles, Mexicans were positioned above the city's Chinese and Japanese residents in many respects. For example, until the Depression, health officials extended Americanization programs to Mexicans.[27] Asians, meanwhile, remained labeled as outsiders, a threatening "yellow peril," simultaneously inferior and alien.

Mexicans' higher status relative to Asians, however, did not enhance their position vis-à-vis the city's white population. They continued to be regarded as subordinate, foreign, and disease ridden. This racialized view had significant and direct consequences for public health in Los Angeles and equally important indirect effects on the city's social structure. During the 1916 typhus epidemic and the 1924 plague, for instance, public health officials focused on "reforming" Mexicans, whom they "knew" to be naturally dirty and inherently too ignorant to rectify their unsanitary living conditions. Because medical discourse had the power to naturalize racial categories, it also had the effect of naturalizing societal inequalities. Rather than addressing the structural inequality that produced the unhealthy environments that hosted virulent diseases, public health departments consistently identified the root problem as racialized people who were in need of reform. By shaping racial categories and infusing them with meaning, health officials helped define racialized people's place in society.

Defining the Meaning of *Mexican*

Throughout this book, I focus primarily on Mexicans because, by 1930, they were the largest immigrant group in Los Angeles. Beginning in the early 1900s and continuing through World War II, health officials in Los Angeles were more involved with Mexicans than with any other ethnic groups. Throughout the first half of the century, city and county health officials in Los Angeles tracked Mexican communities more consistently than they did the Chinese or Japanese populations (especially after a series of federal laws, culminating in the Immigration Act of 1924, severely restricted immigration from Asia).

Examining the connections between the experiences of the city's Chinese, Japanese, and Mexican residents demonstrates how immigrants were racialized in relation to one another, a process that often resulted in the institutionalization of a racial hierarchy. How the health officials came to view and treat Mexicans, however, was directly tied to their assumptions about and experiences with L.A.'s Asian residents. Indeed, from 1869 until 1920, the Los Angeles City Health Department used only two racial categories: "Chinese" and "the rest of the population."[28] As chapters 1 and 2 will make clear, in important ways, "Mexican" was a category constructed from what it was not: not white, not Chinese, not Japanese. Thus, in 1924, for example, what it meant to be "Mexican" in Los Angeles was determined in part by what it meant to be "Japanese." The relational nature of L.A.'s racial categories makes it imperative to include the public health experiences of the "Chinese" and "Japanese" in this study, even though the city and county health departments' policies and programs addressed these groups only intermittently.[29] A comparative examination of all three groups clarifies how racialization projects can differ in their intent, application, and impact, depending on the specific group targeted.[30]

Despite Mexicans' centuries-long history in the Southwest, L.A.'s city and county departments of health overlooked them until the early 1900s. Health officials subscribed to the then-popular belief that Mexicans, like Native Americans, were a race that eventually would fade away.[31] They essentially dismissed the city's Mexican residents as transients. By the early 1900s, however, officials realized that the number of Mexicans in Los Angeles was not diminishing but growing. Starting in the 1910s, Mexicans began to fill a manual labor void created by the exclusion of Asians. First, Chinese laborers were forced out, through the 1882 Chinese Exclusion Act (and repeated ten-year extensions of its provisions); later, Japanese workers faced a similar form of exclusion through the 1907–8 Gentlemen's Agreement and state laws passed in 1913 and 1920 restricting land ownership by "aliens."[32] As the number of Mexicans in Los Angeles increased, so too did concerns about how this group's presence might affect the economic, social, and physical landscape of the city.[33] Until the 1930s, labor shortages shielded Mexicans from some of the worst discriminatory practices leveled against the city's Asian communities.

City and county health departments' reports and policies indicate that Mexican women occupied a central place in public health officials' response to immigration. During the first decades of the twentieth century, L.A.'s resident Mexican population consisted mainly of single males. Mexican women immigrated in low numbers in the early twentieth century.[34] Nonetheless, an examination of institutional records and discourses reveals department-sponsored prenatal, birthing, and well-baby programs that targeted Mexican women and children. Public health officials viewed Mexicans and their "backward" culture as antithetical to their efforts to make Los Angeles a "modern" city. They launched Americanization programs in hopes that assimilation would eliminate Mexicans as an obstacle to progress. Mexican women and children may have seemed the best vehicles for achieving this goal. Officials considered Mexican women malleable and influential within their families, and they may have thought that infants, being too young to have absorbed their birth culture, stood a chance of being successfully Americanized.[35] In addition, they wished to stem the threat of unwanted births and alleged bad parenting.[36] Thus, although Mexican women were considered "*socially* peripheral" and represented only a small portion of the population, they were "*symbolically* central" because, unless they could be won over, Mexicans as a group would continue to threaten health officials' construction of Los Angeles as a bastion of health.[37]

In the early decades of the twentieth century, health officials' efforts to Americanize Mexicans sometimes consisted of little more than rhetoric. Still, even half-hearted assimilation programs indicated a possibility that this group, although not classified as white, might be capable of blending into American culture. No similar possibilities existed for Asians. Neither city nor county departments developed any significant health care programs for the Japanese and Chinese communities. Instead, members of these groups, recognizing that meeting institutionally defined standards for health and cleanliness was a precondition for social membership, often used their own funds to hire public health nurses to work with their communities.

When the U.S. economy collapsed and the Great Depression began, attitudes toward Mexicans shifted rapidly. In Los Angeles, with jobs scarce, white residents and government agencies increasingly regarded Mexicans as an economic burden, and the idea that Mexicans' social inferiority arose from their biological inferiority returned. Buttressed by ideologically defined medical standards, the inferiority of Mexicans soon became "indisputable." Assimilation programs were replaced with repatriation drives. Now public health discourses—especially the notions that Mexicans were disease carriers and an exceptionally fertile people—were mobilized to legitimize the removal of the same population that only a few years earlier had been deemed an essential source of cheap labor.

Beginning in 1930, many of the changes in health departments' programs and discourses with respect to Mexicans involved applying assumptions, terms, and actions once reserved for the city's Chinese and Japanese residents to this population. Now it was Mexicans who were deemed "aliens" and targeted for deportation. Thus, in the course of less than fifty years, three entirely different populations were assigned the lowest position in L.A.'s racial hierarchy: a powerful example of how rapidly racism can be repackaged, re-energized, and relegitimized.

Challenging Racialization: Responses to Public Health Discourses

Public health policies and discourse played an important role in shaping and promoting images of Asians and Mexicans as non-normative. Even today, stereotypes of the overly fertile Mexican woman, the unclean Mexican man, the wily Asian vendor, and the germ-spreading Chinese launderer persist.[38] Yet analyses of Chinese launderers' protests over restrictive ordinances and Mexicans' appeals to the Los Angeles City Council for public housing, for example, reveal that from the start these groups were not passive targets of discrimination. They appropriated legal and medical discourses to challenge dominant assumptions, made gains for their communities, and participated in defining the racial order.[39] As the chapters that follow will show, Chinese, Japanese, and Mexicans fought back in court, petitioned the city council, stalled the enforcement of city legislation, resisted through refusals to attend health clinics, utilized alternative health practices, refused to let housing inspectors into their homes, and wrote letters to state and national officials protesting unfair treatment. Sometimes they succeeded in having their demands met. Other times they did not. At the very least, they brought their concerns into the public forum.

Central Themes and Organization of the Book

In the chapters that follow, I examine the role of public health as a key site of racialization by tracing several interrelated themes. Chapters 1, 2, and 3 highlight the importance of looking at racialization from a comparative perspective. The book as a whole is concerned primarily with Mexicans, but examining the experiences of nonwhite groups in Los Angeles in relation to one another, as well as in relation to the dominant white population, reveals the ways in which racial logic assumed different forms during the same historical moment. The evidence these chapters provide regarding public health's role in the development of a regional racial lexicon also contributes to the main theme of chapter 4, namely, how powerful the idea of scientific objectivity became when it was harnessed to the institution of public health. Chapter 5 demonstrates how Mexican American activists appropriated the language of public health to make civil rights demands. Cumulatively, all five chapters confirm not only that race is best understood as a subjective, social construction but also that racialization is a dynamic, ongoing process.

In chapter 1, I argue that as a fledgling institution, public health in Los Angeles had a dual mission: promoting and preserving the biological health of the citizens *and* promoting and preserving the economic and cultural health of the city. Public health officials' commitment to making Los Angeles a "modern" (meaning sanitary and healthful) metropolis influenced the way they perceived and treated the city's nonwhite residents. The chapter assesses some of these booster narratives, focusing on public health departments' prominent role in projecting an image of Los Angeles as a healthy "Eden" where people lived carefree lives, surrounded by economic prosperity. Health officials often seemed just as concerned as the chamber of commerce that this idyllic image of Los Angeles reach its intended audience (white, financially secure Easterners and Midwesterners) without being marred by any reference to the presence of ethnic communities in the city.

Chapter 1 shows that public health discourses (often embedded in media narratives and newspaper photographs, as well as in policies and guidelines) characterized the Chinese in Los Angeles as dirty and unhygienic, disease carriers who, as launderers and produce vendors, threatened the health of citizens. City officials, including members of the city council, then used these stereotypes to justify developing legislation that undermined Chinese entrepreneurs' economic viability. By tracing the early interactions between Chinese communities and health officials, I demonstrate that health officials, far from embodying "scientific objectivity," had a history of racializing space and immigrant groups before Mexicans made their mark on the urban landscape beginning in the 1910s. The same public health discourses—and often the same public health officials as well—that racialized the Chinese later racialized Mexicans.

Chapter 2 focuses on the formative years of the Los Angeles County Health Department, when health officials nationwide first began to take stock of the country's large-scale health issues. I argue that as one of the early and primary contacts with Mexican and Japanese residents, public health officials helped establish a regional racial lexicon that categorized and ranked county residents as white, Mexican, Japanese, or other. The health department's records, including correspondence, testify to the far-reaching influence that county officials had in shaping what local, state, and national leaders, as well as the general public, knew about ethnic communities in Los Angeles.

Chapter 2's analysis of the county's response in 1916 to an outbreak of typhus fever in the Mexican labor camps run by the railroad companies reveals an important source of the stereotype of Mexicans as dirty and disease ridden. Under the guise of protecting the health of all residents, officials gained the authority to closely inspect the bodies as well as the living quarters of Mexican railroad workers and their families, force them to undergo delousing "baths," and quarantine anyone even *suspected* of being infected by typhus.

The 1920s were an important period of growth for the Los Angeles County Health Department. In chapter 3, I analyze the public health policies of the decade and trace the increase in services to Mexicans. The department introduced a system of health care centers, placing the largest center in Belvedere, a predominantly Mexican area. The chapter also examines county health programs directed at women and children (such as well-baby clinics) and these programs' underlying tenets. The department used well-baby clinics to intensify the programs it directed at Mexican mothers. Tropes of Americanization and citizenship permeated the program lessons directed at Mexican mothers. Health officials preached that embracing the benefits of a hygienic and healthy lifestyle was the first step on the road to assimilation—for Mexicans. No such possibility was extended to the Japanese, then the county's second-largest ethnic group. Because the racially coded language of public health constructed the Japanese as a threat to white Americans, this group was viewed as permanently ineligible for either legal or social participation in the community at large.

I contrast these proactive steps toward improving Mexican communities with the treatment of Japanese communities, showing how the Japanese continued to be marginalized. Local politicians, connecting Japanese birth rates to discussions of "yellow peril," fanned fears and resulted in calls from the general (white) public for increased immigration restrictions.

Chapter 4 examines city and county public health policies directed at Mexicans during the Depression. The health departments played a key role in the repatriation programs that gained popularity as the economy continued to worsen. Public health discourses appropriated by various government officials legitimated local efforts to force the city's Mexican residents to return to Mexico. The Americanization efforts of the 1920s were abandoned as health officials in the 1930s adopted racial assumptions emphasizing more immutable biological traits that rendered Mexicans unassimilable. Chapter 4 also assesses changes in attitudes and actions regarding the Chinese. Whereas in the 1910s zoning laws had circumscribed the location of Chinese laundries and produce markets, in the 1930s citizens used public health ordinances to drive Chinese launderers out of business.

Chapter 5 recounts Mexican Americans' demands in the late 1930s for better health and housing conditions in Los Angeles. Despite twenty years of county health programs and services, Mexicans' health and housing conditions languished in comparison to those of whites. In their appeals for change, Mexican Americans described the same dismal conditions in their neighborhoods that health inspectors had reported for decades. They, however, rejected inspectors' claims that they were to blame for their poor living conditions. Turning the tables, they indicted the city and county for perpetuating these conditions and for undercutting Mexican American communities' chances to thrive.

Encouraged by newly created New Deal programs, Mexican Americans, both as individuals and as members of labor and civil rights organizations, demanded that the city build public housing. This quest for better housing, which Mexican Americans saw as a way to improve overall health conditions in their communities, also signaled a major demographic shift. Mexican communities no longer consisted primarily of sojourners or seasonal laborers, typically single men who rented rooms while they were working in the area and who returned to Mexico for part of the year. In contrast to the 1910s, when the first waves of Mexican immigrants had arrived, the Mexican population in Los Angeles in the 1930s included a large proportion of family units and second-generation Mexican Americans.[40] Permanent housing, and single-family dwellings in particular, had become essential. Mexican Americans' demands for public housing marked their desire to be recognized as citizens, deserving of the same rights as all other Americans.

Notes

1. Lindley was the first head of the city's public health department. He delivered the inaugural "Los Angeles City Annual Health Officer's Report, November 13, 1879" (not the same as the Annual Health Reports, which started in 1889), Los Angeles City Archives (Untitled) Records, LACA; quote from 14:997.
2. Ibid., p. 3.
3. Ibid.
4. Suellen Hoy, *Chasing Dirt: The American Pursuit of Cleanliness* (New York: Oxford University Press, 1995), 87.
5. John Pomeroy to B of S, February 17, 1916, B of S/R.
6. John Pomeroy to B of S, December 17, 1918, B of S/R.
7. Health department reports confirm that health officials overwhelmingly regarded all Asians and Mexicans as foreigners and immigrants, no matter how long they or their families had lived in the United States.

8. The anthropologist Renato Rosaldo introduced the concept of "cultural citizenship" to refer to the practices immigrants engage in to claim space in society that leads to forms of empowerment through cultural representations or political involvement. Renato Rosaldo, *Culture and Truth: The Remaking of Social Analysis* (Boston: Beacon Press, 1989). Others, such as Aihwa Ong, have built on Rosaldo's definition but also shown the limits of this interpretation. Ong argues that by focusing only on the agency of the individual one neglects how the political economy constrains actors. Aihwa Ong, "Cultural Citizenship as Subject-Making: Immigrants Negotiate Racial and Cultural Boundaries in the United States," *Current Anthropology* 37, no. 5 (1996): 737–63, and *Flexible Citizenship: The Cultural Logics of Transnationality* (Durham, NC: Duke University Press, 1999).

9. James Holston, ed., *Cities and Citizenship* (Durham, NC: Duke University Press, 1999).

10. Such practices led to an ideological control of space that resulted in de facto racial segregation in certain parts of the city. For an insightful analysis of the uses of social control of space in Los Angeles, see Raúl Villa, *Barrio-Logos: Space and Place in Urban Chicano Literature and Culture* (Austin: University of Texas Press, 2000).

11. For studies that examine race and municipal politics in the United States, see Nayan Shah, *Contagious Divides: Epidemics and Race in San Francisco's Chinatown* (Berkeley: University of California Press, 2001); William Deverell, *Whitewashed Adobe: The Rise of Los Angeles and the Remaking of Its Mexican Past* (Berkeley: University of California Press, 2004), ch. 5; Tera Hunter, *To 'Joy My Freedom: Southern Black Women's Lives and Labors after the Civil War* (Cambridge, MA: Harvard University Press, 1997); Keith Wailoo, *Dying in the City of the Blues: Sickle Cell Anemia and the Politics of Race and Health* (Chapel Hill: University of North Carolina Press, 2001).

12. Michel Foucault's work has been instrumental in examinations of the role institutions play in "the subjugation of bodies and control of populations." As he pointed out, power is a dispersed and decentered force that is difficult to grasp and possess fully. Michel Foucault, *The History of Sexuality,* vol. 1, *An Introduction,* trans. Robert Hurley (New York: Random House, 1976), 137–40.

13. The following works also examine medicine within a U.S. paradigm during this same period and have furthered my understanding of the racialization process: Alexandra Stern, *Eugenic Nation: Faults and Frontiers of Better Breeding in Modern America* (Berkeley: University of California Press, 2005); Charles L. Briggs and Clara Mantini-Briggs, *Stories in the Time of Cholera: Racial Profiling during a Medical Nightmare* (Berkeley: University of California Press, 2003); Laura Briggs, *Reproducing Empire: Race, Sex, Science, and U.S. Imperialism in Puerto Rico* (Berkeley: University of California Press, 2002); Shah, *Contagious Divides;* Alan Kraut, *Silent Travelers: Germs, Genes, and the "Immigrant Menace"* (New York: Basic Books, 1994). These works have been very helpful to my understanding of the development of public health in the United States: John Duffy, *The Sanitarians: A History of American Public Health* (Urbana: University of Illinois Press, 1990); Judith Walzer Leavitt and Ronald L. Numbers, *Sickness and Health in America: Readings in the*

History of Medicine and Public Health (Madison: University of Wisconsin Press, 1978); Judith Walzer Leavitt, *The Healthiest City: Milwaukee and the Politics of Health Reform* (Princeton, NJ: Princeton University Press, 1982); Charles Rosenberg, *The Cholera Years: The United States in 1832, 1849, and 1866* (Chicago: University of Chicago Press, 1962); Nancy Tomes, *The Gospel of Germs: Men, Women, and the Microbe in American Life* (Cambridge, MA: Harvard University Press, 1998).

14. In 1900, L.A.'s total population was 102,479. See U.S. Census Office, *United States Census of Population, 1900* (Washington, DC: Government Printing Office, 1901–3), 1:796–803. The same year, Los Angeles eclipsed Chicago as the nation's fastest-growing city. Just ten years later, L.A.'s population increased by another 211 percent. See Janet Abu-Lughod, *New York, Chicago, Los Angeles: America's Global Cities* (Minneapolis: University of Minnesota Press, 1999), 5–15.

15. By 1930, New York reported a central city population per square mile of 23,179; Chicago, 16,723; and Boston, 17,795. Los Angeles, in comparison, had a central city population per square mile of only 2,812 in 1930. Robert M. Fogelson, *The Fragmented Metropolis: Los Angeles, 1850–1930* (Berkeley: University of California Press, 1967), 143.

16. I use the term *white* because health officials consistently used "white" as a racial category. In 1900, foreign-born residents totaled 19,964, compared to 82,515 native born. Forty-one percent, or 8,266, of the foreign born were English speaking, including immigrants from England, Canada, Ireland, Wales, and Australia. The non-English-speaking foreign born were German, Chinese, French, Italian, Mexican, Slavic, and Japanese (in descending order from highest to lowest percentage). U.S. Census Office, *United States Census of Population, 1900,* 1:796–803. For histories of Los Angeles that trace the city's socioeconomic development, see Fogelson, *Fragmented Metropolis;* Abu-Lughod, *New York, Chicago.*

17. Oscar Handlin, *The Uprooted: The Epic Story of the Great Migrations That Made the American People* (Boston: Little, Brown, 1973); John Higham, *Strangers in the Land: Patterns of American Nativism, 1860–1925* (New Brunswick, NJ: Rutgers University Press, 1955).

18. Robert Wiebe identified the search for order as a goal unifying various reform initiatives. See Robert Wiebe, *The Search for Order, 1877–1920* (New York: Hill and Wang, 1967). For alternative interpretations of the Progressive Era, see Gabriel Kolko, *The Triumph of Conservatism: A Re-Interpretation of American History, 1900–1916* (New York: Free Press of Glencoe, 1963); Richard Hofstadter, *The Age of Reform: From Bryan to F.D.R.* (New York: Knopf, 1955); Samuel P. Hays, *The Response to Industrialism, 1885–1914* (Chicago: University of Chicago Press, 1995). Daniel Rodgers's classic essay challenges using the term *Progressivism* as a central organizing principle in American history. Daniel Rodgers, "In Search of Progressivism," *Reviews in American History* 10, no. 4 (1982): 113–32.

19. Breakthroughs in bacteriology at the end of the nineteenth century drastically changed the development of the field. New discoveries in microbiology provided scientific explanations about how infectious and contagious diseases spread. This new information helped launch

campaigns to battle disease and promote public health. Tomes, *Gospel of Germs;* Duffy, *Sanitarians;* Hoy, *Chasing Dirt.*

20. According to James Whorton, "Progressivism combined confidence in science with an expansive social optimism and sense of progress." James C. Whorton, *Crusaders for Fitness: The History of the American Health Reformers* (Princeton, NJ: Princeton University Press, 1982), 140.

21. In 1910, the city's African American population was 7,599 (2 percent of the total) and was confined mainly to the segregated areas of Central Avenue. See U.S. Census Office, *Thirteenth Census of the United States Taken in the Year 1910* (Washington, DC: Government Printing Office, 1913), 180. African Americans did not, of course, escape racism on the West Coast. My point here is simply that in the presence of other racialized groups, discrimination against African Americans took different forms than those prevalent in the South. For a history of African Americans in early-twentieth-century Los Angeles, see Josh Sides, *L.A. City Limits: African American in Los Angeles from the Great Depression to the Present* (Berkeley: University of California Press, 2003); Lawrence B. de Graaf, "Recognition, Racism, and Reflections on the Writing of Western Black History," *Pacific Historical Review* 44 (1975): 22–47.

22. Matthew Frye Jacobson, *Whiteness of a Different Color: European Immigrants and the Alchemy of Race* (Cambridge, MA: Harvard University Press, 1998), 42.

23. David Roediger, *The Wages of Whiteness: Race and the Making of the American Working Class* (London: Verso Press, 1991).

24. George Lipsitz, *The Possessive Investment in Whiteness: How White People Profit from Identity Politics* (Philadelphia: Temple University Press, 1998). For studies of whiteness, see Eric Avila, *Popular Culture in the Age of White Flight: Fear and Fantasy in Suburban Los Angeles* (Berkeley: University of California Press, 2004); Deverell, *Whitewashed Adobe;* Neil Foley, *The White Scourge: Mexicans, Blacks and Poor Whites in Texas Cotton Culture* (Berkeley: University of California Press, 1997); Thomas A. Guglielmo, *White on Arrival: Italians, Race, Color, and Power in Chicago, 1890–1945* (New York: Oxford University Press, 2003); Ian Haney-Lopez, *White by Law: The Legal Construction of Race* (New York: New York University Press, 1996); Jacobson, *Whiteness.*

25. Almaguer emphasizes the importance of region and historical period in understanding how we think of bodies as racialized. He argues that the small population of African Americans in California, coupled with the diverse populations of natives and immigrants, resulted in a racially stratified hierarchy among Mexicans, Asians, Native Americans, and whites that defied binary racialization. My study demonstrates how these categories continued to be negotiated in the twentieth century, as the Native American population was drastically reduced, as Asians faced severe immigration restrictions, and as the perception of Mexicans as *Californios* gave way to the view that Mexicans were immigrants. Tomás Almaguer, *Racial Fault Lines: The Historical Origins of White Supremacy* (Berkeley: University of California Press, 1994).

26. Claire Jean Kim, *Bitter Fruit: The Politics of Black-Korean Conflict in New York City* (New Haven, CT: Yale University Press, 2000), 10.

27. I do not mean to suggest that health officials extended the notion of Americanization to Mexicans as easily or comprehensively as they did to European immigrants. Health officials publicly chastised Mexicans for their "unclean living habits" even while engaging in rhetoric that advocated Americanization. At various historical moments, health officials also suggested limiting immigration from Mexico, thereby completely denying Mexicans the opportunity to become Americans.

28. After 1920, the city health department expanded its categories to include "Mexican," "Japanese," and "Negro"; the county department used "white," "Mexican," "Japanese," and "other" to keep track of the populations under its jurisdiction.

29. Since public health departments at the city, county, state, and national levels focused on Japanese and Chinese communities inconsistently, there are few records available. The limited source material makes it difficult to analyze these groups' experiences in any depth. There are, however, ample primary sources that show how racialization projects *differed* for Mexican, Chinese, and Japanese communities.

30. In their highly influential study, Omi and Winant define racialization as a "sociohistorical process by which racial categories are created, inhabited, transformed, and destroyed." Michael Omi and Howard Winant, *Racial Formation in the United States from the 1960s to the 1980s* (New York: Routledge, 1986), 56. They emphasize the historically specific and socially constructed nature of racial categories by drawing attention to "*projects* in which human bodies and social structures are represented and organized" (55–56, emphasis in the original).

31. For a history of Manifest Destiny, see Reginald Horsman, *Race and Manifest Destiny: The Origins of American Racial Anglo-Saxonism* (Cambridge, MA: Harvard University Press, 1981). Martha Menchaca has examined legal discrimination against Mexicans from 1848 through 1947. She argues that Mexicans often were considered akin to Indians. U.S. officials classified lighter-skinned Mexicans as white and darker-skinned Mexicans as Indian. See Martha Menchaca, "Chicano Indianism: A Historical Account of Racial Repression in the United States," *American Ethnologist* 20, no. 3 (1993): 583–603.

32. The Chinese Exclusion Act provided for an absolute moratorium on the immigration of Chinese workers (a category defined so broadly that it included nearly anyone who attempted to emigrate from China) for a ten-year period (a provision that was renewed in 1892, made permanent in 1902, and not rescinded until 1943). The 1882 act also denied the possibility of U.S. citizenship to resident Chinese aliens. The Gentlemen's Agreement was a treaty forged between the United States and Japan in 1907 (with an additional provision appended in 1908 to strengthen the agreement) to quell increasing tensions, especially in San Francisco, over the immigration of Japanese workers. The Japanese government agreed to deny passports to laborers bound for the United States, and President Theodore Roosevelt promised to persuade San Francisco city officials to rescind a blatantly

discriminatory law aimed at Asian schoolchildren in the city. Chapters 1 and 2 provide further information about the early-twentieth-century legal and social experiences of the Chinese and Japanese in the United States.

33. For many Mexicans it was the lure of employment that spurred migration (Los Angeles employers in the early twentieth century sought laborers to build railroad lines, plant and harvest agricultural crops, and work in low-wage jobs in the city's newly developing industries), but for others it was the start of the Mexican Revolution in 1910 that prompted emigration. Devra Weber examines Mexico's transformation to a capitalist society that left over 96 percent of Mexican families landless and thus forced to seek a new life in the United States. Devra Weber, *Dark Sweat, White Gold: California Farm Workers, Cotton, and the New Deal* (Berkeley: University of California Press, 1994), 48–53.

34. George Sánchez, *Becoming Mexican American: Ethnicity, Culture, and Identity in Chicano Los Angeles, 1900–1945* (New York: Oxford University Press, 1993), 41. For studies of Mexican women in the early twentieth century, see Vicki Ruiz, *Cannery Women, Cannery Lives: Mexican Women, Unionization, and the California Food Processing Industry, 1930–1950* (Albuquerque: University of New Mexico Press, 1987), and *From out of the Shadows: Mexican Women in Twentieth-Century America* (New York: Oxford University Press, 1998); George Sánchez, " 'Go after the Women': Americanization and the Mexican Immigrant Woman, 1915–1929," in *A Multi-Cultural Reader in U.S. Women's History,* ed. Ellen DuBois and Vicki Ruiz (New York: Routledge, 1990), 284–97. Histories of Mexican women in the nineteenth century are scarce. Notable exceptions are Miroslava Chávez-García, *Negotiating Conquest: Gender and Power in California, 1770s to 1880s* (Tucson: University of Arizona Press, 2004); Antonia Castañeda, "Engendering the History of Alta California, 1769–1848: Gender, Sexuality, and the Family," in *Contested Eden: California before the Gold Rush,* ed. Ramón Gutiérrez and Roberto Orsi (Berkeley: University of California Press, 1998), 230–59; Deena J. González, *Refusing the Favor: The Spanish-Mexican Women of Santa Fe, 1820–1880* (New York: Oxford University Press, 1999).

35. Ruiz, *From out of the Shadows,* ch. 3, "Confronting America"; George Sánchez, " 'Go after the Women.' "

36. On the pervasiveness of the eugenics movement in California, see Stern, *Eugenic Nation.*

37. I am drawing on the terminology used by Peter Stallybrass and Allon White in *The Politics and Poetics of Transgression* (Ithaca, NY: Cornell University Press, 1986), 23.

38. Roderick Ferguson's unique study of how racial and sexual difference is produced and how these standards in turn serve as the justification for marginalizing nonheteronormative black bodies is very insightful. Ferguson argues that much of the work of professional sociology in the twentieth century revolved around this discourse of normativity. Roderick Ferguson, *Aberrations in Black: Toward a Queer of Color Critique* (Minneapolis: University of Minnesota Press, 2004).

39. The historian Alan Kraut argues that public health historians usually write history as if power flowed in one direction with only immigrants being affected, "medicine and hygiene being merely aspects of newcomers' acculturation." Kraut, *Silent Travelers,* 278 n. 5. The following works examine how racialized groups protested medical discourses and processes that constructed them as non-normative: Paul Farmer, *AIDS and Accusation: Haiti and the Geography of Blame* (Berkeley: University of California Press, 1992); Shah, *Contagious Divides;* Briggs and Mantini-Briggs, *Stories;* John McKiernan-Gonzalez, "Fevered Measures: Race, Contagious Disease and Community Formation on the Texas-Mexico Border, 1880–1923" (PhD diss., University of Michigan, 2002); Alexandra Stern, "Buildings, Boundaries, and Blood: Medicalization and Nation-Building on the U.S.-Mexican Border, 1910–1930," *Hispanic American Historical Review* 79, no. 1 (1999): 41–81.

40. George Sánchez, *Becoming Mexican American,* 224–25.

Bibliography

Los Angeles City Archives.

Abu-Lughod, Janet. *New York, Chicago, Los Angeles: America's Global Cities.* Minneapolis: University of Minnesota Press, 1999.

Almaguer, Tomás. *Racial Fault Lines: The Historical Origins of White Supremacy.* Berkeley: University of California Press, 1994.

Avila, Eric. *Popular Culture in the Age of White Flight: Fear and Fantasy in Suburban Los Angeles.* Berkeley: University of California Press, 2004.

Briggs, Charles L., and Clara Mantini-Briggs. *Stories in the Time of Cholera: Racial Profiling during a Medical Nightmare.* Berkeley: University of California Press, 2003.

Briggs, Laura. *Reproducing Empire: Race, Sex, Science, and U.S. Imperialism in Puerto Rico.* Berkeley: University of California Press, 2002.

Castañeda, Antonia. "Engendering the History of Alta California, 1769–1848: Gender, Sexuality, and the Family." In *Contested Eden: California before the Gold Rush,* edited by Ramón Gutiérrez and Roberto Orsi, 230–59. Berkeley: University of California Press, 1998.

Chávez-García, Miroslava. *Negotiating Conquest: Gender and Power in California, 1770s to 1880s.* Tucson: University of Arizona Press, 2004.

de Graaf, Lawrence B. "Recognition, Racism, and Reflections on the Writing of Western Black History." *Pacific Historical Review* 44 (1975): 22–47.

Deverell, William. *Whitewashed Adobe: The Rise of Los Angeles and the Remaking of Its Mexican Past.* Berkeley: University of California Press, 2004.

Duffy, John. *The Sanitarians: A History of American Public Health.* Urbana: University of Illinois Press, 1990.

Farmer, Paul. *AIDS and Accusation: Haiti and the Geography of Blame.* Berkeley: University of California Press, 1992.

Ferguson, Roderick. *Aberrations in Black: Toward a Queer of Color Critique.* Minneapolis: University of Minnesota Press, 2004.

Fogelson, Robert M. *The Fragmented Metropolis: Los Angeles, 1850–1930.* Berkeley: University of California Press, 1967.

———. *The White Scourge: Mexicans, Blacks and Poor Whites in Texas Cotton Culture.* Berkeley: University of California Press, 1997.

Foucault, Michel. *The History of Sexuality.* Vol. 1. *An Introduction.* Translated by Robert Hurley. New York: Random House, 1976.

González, Deena J. *Refusing the Favor: The Spanish-Mexican Women of Santa Fe, 1820–1880.* New York: Oxford University Press, 1999.

Guglielmo, Thomas A. *White on Arrival: Italians, Race, Color, and Power in Chicago, 1890–1945.* New York: Oxford University Press, 2003.

Handlin, Oscar. *The Uprooted: The Epic Story of the Great Migrations That Made the American People.* Boston: Little, Brown, 1973.

Haney-Lopez, Ian. *White by Law: The Legal Construction of Race.* New York: New York University Press, 1996.

Hays, Samuel P. *The Response to Industrialism, 1885–1914.* Chicago: University of Chicago Press, 1995.

Higham, John. *Strangers in the Land: Patterns of American Nativism, 1860–1925.* New Brunswick, NJ: Rutgers University Press, 1955.

Hofstadter, Richard. *The Age of Reform: From Bryan to F.D.R.* New York: Knopf, 1955.

Holston, James, ed. *Cities and Citizenship.* Durham, NC: Duke University Press, 1999.

Horsman, Reginald. *Race and Manifest Destiny: The Origins of American Racial Anglo-Saxonism.* Cambridge, MA: Harvard University Press, 1981.

Hoy, Suellen. *Chasing Dirt: The American Pursuit of Cleanliness.* New York: Oxford University Press, 1995.

Hunter, Tera. *To 'Joy My Freedom: Southern Black Women's Lives and Labors after the Civil War.* Cambridge, MA: Harvard University Press, 1997.

Jacobson, Matthew Frye. *Whiteness of a Different Color: European Immigrants and the Alchemy of Race.* Cambridge, MA: Harvard University Press, 1998.

Kim, Claire Jean. *Bitter Fruit: The Politics of Black-Korean Conflict in New York City.* New Haven, CT: Yale University Press, 2000.

Kolko, Gabriel. *The Triumph of Conservatism: A Re-Interpretation of American History, 1900–1916.* New York: Free Press of Glencoe, 1963.

Kraut, Alan. *Silent Travelers: Germs, Genes, and the "Immigrant Menace."* New York: Basic Books, 1994.

Leavitt, Judith Walzer. *The Healthiest City: Milwaukee and the Politics of Health Reform*. Princeton, NJ: Princeton University Press, 1982.

Leavitt, Judith Walzer, and Ronald L. Numbers. *Sickness and Health in America: Readings in the History of Medicine and Public Health*. Madison: University of Wisconsin Press, 1978.

Lipsitz, George. *The Possessive Investment in Whiteness: How White People Profit from Identity Politics*. Philadelphia: Temple University Press, 1998.

McKiernan-Gonzalez, John. "Fevered Measures: Race, Contagious Disease and Community Formation on the Texas-Mexico Border, 1880–1923." PhD diss., University of Michigan, 2002.

Menchaca, Martha. "Chicano Indianism: A Historical Account of Racial Repression in the United States." *American Ethnologist* 20, no. 3 (1993): 583–603.

Omi, Michael, and Howard Winant. *Racial Formation in the United States from the 1960s to the 1980s*. New York: Routledge, 1986.

Ong, Aihwa. "Cultural Citizenship as Subject-Making: Immigrants Negotiate Racial and Cultural Boundaries in the United States." *Current Anthropology* 37, no. 5 (1996): 737–63.

———. *Flexible Citizenship: The Cultural Logics of Transnationality*. Durham, NC: Duke University Press, 1999.

Rodgers, Daniel. "In Search of Progressivism." *Reviews in American History* 10, no. 4 (1982): 113–32.

Roediger, David. *The Wages of Whiteness: Race and the Making of the American Working Class*. London: Verso, 1991.

Rosaldo, Renato. *Culture and Truth: The Remaking of Social Analysis*. Boston: Beacon Press, 1989.

Rosenberg, Charles. *The Cholera Years: The United States in 1832, 1849, and 1866*. Chicago: University of Chicago Press, 1962.

Ruiz, Vicki. *Cannery Women, Cannery Lives: Mexican Women, Unionization, and the California Food Processing Industry, 1930–1950*. Albuquerque: University of New Mexico Press, 1987.

———. *From out of the Shadows: Mexican Women in Twentieth-Century America*. New York: Oxford University Press, 1998.

Saldívar-Hull, Sonia. Sánchez, George. *Becoming Mexican American: Ethnicity, Culture, and Identity in Chicano Los Angeles, 1900–1945*. New York: Oxford University Press, 1993.

———. "'Go after the Women': Americanization and the Mexican Immigrant Woman, 1915–1929." In *A Multi-Cultural Reader in U.S. Women's History*, edited by Ellen DuBois and Vicki Ruiz, 284–97. New York: Routledge, 1990.

Shah, Nayan. *Contagious Divides: Epidemics and Race in San Francisco's Chinatown*. Berkeley: University of California Press, 2001.

Sides, Josh. *L.A. City Limits: African American Los Angeles from the Great Depression to the Present*. Berkeley: University of California Press, 2003.

Stallybrass, Peter, and Allon White. *The Politics and Poetics of Transgression*. Ithaca, NY: Cornell University Press, 1986.

Stern, Alexandra. "Buildings, Boundaries, and Blood: Medicalization and Nation-Building on the U.S.-Mexican Border, 1910–1930." *Hispanic American Historical Review* 79, no. 1 (1999): 41–81.

_____. *Eugenic Nation: Faults and Frontiers of Better Breeding in Modern America*. Berkeley: University of California Press, 2005.

Tomes, Nancy. *The Gospel of Germs: Men, Women, and the Microbe in American Life*. Cambridge, MA: Harvard University Press, 1998.

Villa, Raúl. *Barrio-Logos: Space and Place in Urban Chicano Literature and Culture*. Austin: University of Texas Press, 2000.

Wailoo, Keith. *Dying in the City of the Blues: Sickle Cell Anemia and the Politics of Race and Health*. Chapel Hill: University of North Carolina Press, 2001.

Weber, Devra. *Dark Sweat, White Gold: California Farm Workers, Cotton, and the New Deal*. Berkeley: University of California Press, 1994.

Whorton, James C. *Crusaders for Fitness: The History of the American Health Reformers*. Princeton, NJ: Princeton University Press, 1982.

Wiebe, Robert. *The Search for Order, 1877–1920*. New York: Hill and Wang, 1967.

READING 4.1   POST-READING COMPREHENSION QUESTIONS

- Summarize how Molina organizes the book.

- Describe why it is important to examine the connections between Chinese, Japanese, and Mexicans.

- Paraphrase the line: "Public health policies and discourse played an important role in shaping and promoting images of Asians and Mexicans as non-normative."

Where Is Home? The Dilemma of Repatriation

A significant number of the American working class experienced economic struggles during the 1920s and 1930s, and combined with the influx of migration, this spurred heightened racial antagonism. In 1924 the Johnson-Reed Act was passed and created a racial quota system as a means of restricting immigration and citizenship in the United States. With an increasingly dire set of economic circumstances brought on by the Great Depression, coupled with a growing sense of nativism and racial resentment, the conditions were ripe for scapegoating. Undoubtedly, many American citizens of Mexican descent bore the brunt of this reality. The chapter by George Sanchez titled "Where is Home?: The Dilemma of Repatriation" assesses these events and provides a truly groundbreaking method of analysis of an often-obscured aspect of Mexican immigration history.

THINGS TO LOOK FOR AS YOU READ...

- The reasons for forced deportation
- The strategies used for mass deportation
- The role of the Mexican government in the deportation process

Where Is Home?

The Dilemma of Repatriation

George J. Sanchez

E very morning at the crack of dawn in 1931, María Olazabál watched at her kitchen window as hundreds of Mexican men and women ventured out in search of work. As entire industries collapsed during the Great Depression, Mexican workers were among the first to feel the effects of unemployment. Desperation rapidly overcame the Belvedere barrio. Night after night, Mrs. Olazabál saw workers return to their homes exhausted and empty-handed with little strength or money to feed their families. "The power and gas companies are shutting down the services to these people because they cannot pay, and it is frightening to see the misery endured by people ready and willing to work," she complained in a letter to *La Opinión*. As a recent resident of Belvedere, she was grateful that her husband was still making ends meet as a grocer.[1]

Concerned about the poverty around her, Mrs. Olazabál decided to help the less fortunate in her community. With the assistance of a few other Mexican women along North Rowan Avenue, Olazabál organized a group that made and sold tamales at cost to the barrio's unemployed. Though the women preferred to give the food away, they could not afford to do so; besides, they felt direct charity might hurt the pride of their compatriots. Olazabál boasted of the quality of the service, assuring her customers that the tamales were "made with total cleanliness." To link themselves with their friends and neighbors, the group called itself the Cooperative Society of Unemployed Mexican Ladies.[2]

María Olazabál was one of hundreds of Mexican immigrants in Los Angeles who aided those left stranded without jobs during the 1930s. During the Depression, many were forced to make difficult adjustments regarding their future in the city, caught in economic circumstances beyond their control. While Mexicans attempted to cushion the deprivation in the barrios, county officials and local businessmen, largely focusing on those without jobs and on welfare, developed campaigns to rid southern California of Mexicans. They believed the hard times made it imperative that the scarce jobs and resources be reserved for American citizens.

This chapter addresses the responses of Mexicans to economic crisis and the mass repatriation campaigns of the 1930s. Their responses reflected fundamental changes in Chicano cultural development in the city. Faced with limited choices, Mexicans made crucial family and individual decisions shaped in part by governmental policy in the United States and Mexico. Though the impact of outside forces was clearly significant, their personal choices eventually had a powerful effect on group ethnic identity. Approximately one-third of the Mexican community in Los Angeles returned to Mexico during the decade.[3] The majority who stayed in Los Angeles became ambivalent Americans, full of contradictory feelings about their place in American society.

After a period of phenomenal industrial growth since the turn of the century, Los Angeles, with its rapidly increasing population, found itself ill-prepared for the economic bust. A week before the stock market collapse in October 1929, city officials, brokers, and bankers had attended ground-breaking ceremonies for a new stock exchange building on Spring Street. Despite an emergency conference on unemployment in mid-December 1929, most officials felt that the next decade would bring continued prosperity to the area.[4]

But by 1930, most city residents realized the widespread economic depression had deep roots and the nation would not easily recover. Many lost their jobs; thousands of families found themselves without income. Nationally, unemployment rose to four million by January 1930, to five million by September, and to eight million by the spring of 1931. By 1933, one-third of the work force in the United States—15 million people—were out of work, a fivefold increase from 1929.[5]

In Los Angeles, the census of 1930, conducted in April, reported that 50,918 city residents were unemployed, or just under 10 percent of all gainful workers. Especially hard-hit were the skilled building trades—electricians, stone masons, and tile layers. Though, proportionally, Los Angeles had fewer unemployed than industrial cities such as Cleveland, Buffalo, and Detroit, by the end of 1930 one out of every five Angelenos could not find work. One study showed unemployment in Los Angeles peaking at 41.6 percent in 1933.[6] Even those with jobs severely felt the impact of the Great Depression. Wages fell by one-third in the United States, as both wages and hours were cut. In Los Angeles County, average wages declined 38 percent between 1926 and 1932.[7]

Because of their seasonal employment in agricultural work, Mexicans were among the first in Los Angeles to experience the consequences of the Depression. Agriculture was one of the earliest casualties of the economic crisis. Although agricultural employment in the city proper mirrored the overall employment picture, farm work in the San Joaquin Valley and Imperial Valley declined even before the stock market crash. The value of California farm products dropped precipitously from $750 million in 1929 to $372 million in 1932, with wages falling from 35 cents an hour in 1928 to 14 cents in 1933. Agriculture could no longer absorb urban workers who increasingly needed to supplement their low wages from unskilled industrial jobs. This development caused Mexican workers to depend even more heavily on wages earned in urban Los Angeles.[8]

Finding work in the city, however, became more and more difficult. By April 1930, one of every seven Mexican laborers was unemployed, a figure almost twice as high as that of any other ethnic group in Los Angeles. Moreover, as Anglo Americans found themselves without work—particularly after several months of unemployment—they began to exert pressure on city employers to hire only "citizens" for work that had normally or occasionally been limited to Mexicans.[9] By February 1931, *La Opinión* reported that laundries, factories, stores, and construction companies regularly replaced Mexican workers with Americans. Ethnic background, rather than strict definitions of citizenship, seemed to prevail in determining this form of discrimination. An ex-sergeant in the United States Army, born in the U.S., described how he was denied jobs because he was Chicano:

> During the last three months, I have been getting up very early;
> I dress up and go downtown or uptown to the construction sites
> where the supervisors know me and always have given me a job.
> Soon the supervisors come out and tell the people that are waiting
> to get a job to line up on one side, all the white people, and on the
> other side the ones that are not. Because I am of dark complexion
> I stay with the people of my race and of course, do not get hired
> because the supervisor has the order to hire only the "white people"
> and that is what he does.[10]

In August 1931, the California state legislature enacted a law making it illegal for any company doing business with the government to employ "aliens" on public jobs. The Alien Labor Act was a form of legislative discrimination that displaced many Mexican workers from construction sites, highways, schools, government office buildings, and other public works projects. The Mexican consul in Los Angeles estimated that this law immediately excluded more than 900 Mexicans from work in the city alone.[11]

Many Mexican families were forced to turn to public and private charities for help in surviving unemployment and economic deprivation. Yet here, too, discrimination became the norm. During the 1920s, Mexicans constituted about one-fourth of all city residents who received some form of public assistance. Erratic employment opportunities for men, coupled with dangerous work conditions that often left unemployed women in charge of large families, placed Mexicans among the groups in Los Angeles most likely to need periodic economic assistance. But during the Great Depression more Anglo American residents also found themselves in difficult circumstances. The result was increasing pressure on public officials to give preference in welfare allocations to American-born heads of households. By 1931 public works projects financed by local monies likewise barred employment of aliens.[12]

As unemployment climbed, almost all new relief was allocated for Anglo laborers who had lost their jobs. In Los Angeles County, the number of welfare cases jumped from 18,650 in the fiscal year 1928–29 to 25,913 in 1929–30, and to 42,124 in 1930–31. Expenditures skyrocketed from $1,690,450 in 1928–29 to $2,469,520 in 1929–30, and to $4,209,729 in 1930–31. Yet the percentage of Mexicans on relief steadily decreased from 21.5 percent in 1928–29 to 15.8 percent in 1929–30, and to 12.5 percent in 1930–31, despite widespread impoverishment in the Mexican community. The role of the federal government in public assistance was minimal during this period, and, thus, local officials determined this inequitable allocation of resources.[13]

Of the private groups dispensing assistance, the Catholic Welfare Bureau was the largest in the city, and handled most of the needy Mexican families unable to receive aid elsewhere. The bureau's unemployment relief steadily grew from $63,719 distributed among 3,211 -families in 1928–29 to $112,883 among 9,172 families in 1930–31. The bureau's funds, however, came largely from Los Angeles' Community Chest, which had been founded in 1924 to coordinate relief efforts among religious groups in the city. In better times, the Chest raised substantial funds from private sources. During the Depression, however, these resources evaporated, and the Chest grew" utterly dependent on public funds. Between 1929 and 1932 roughly 94 percent of its monies came from either the city or county. As a consequence the Catholic Welfare Department was subject to the same financial pressures regarding the distribution of its funds; thus it too began to discriminate among ethnic groups. In 1931, for example, food allowances for "American" families were reduced by 10 percent, while allocations for Mexican families were cut by 25 percent.[14]

Many Mexican residents of Los Angeles responded to the worsening economic conditions and growing pattern of discrimination by returning to Mexico. Although most of the early repatriates came from Texas border towns, during the winter of 1929–30 a sizable group of Los Angeles residents departed for their homeland. This first group was usually not destitute; many returned with automobiles and furniture accumulated by hard years of work and saving in the United States. A number of early returnees were single male white-collar workers who had never intended to stay permanently in Los Angeles. As office and sales clerks they had enjoyed modest economic success in the 1920s, and left the United States when the possibilities for making extra income vanished. As one resident of Los Angeles in this period remembered, the average Mexican always had it in his heart to return to Mexico. With economic opportunities dwindling in the U.S. and Mexico calling, many decided simply to head back.[15]

This group of early repatriates resembled those identified by Manuel Gamio in his classic study of Mexican immigrants in 1927. He discovered a great deal of movement back to Mexico with returnees bringing with them a host of consumer items, from agricultural tools to phonographs.[16] In fact, Gamio's investigators interviewed many southern California residents who had been enticed back to Mexico by their government's promise of agricultural land. These individuals left the United States with hopes of turning their small savings into larger enterprises in Mexico. Though ready to acknowledge the economic benefits of their stay, they also often deeply resented their treatment by American employers and local officials. José Castillo, for example, planning to return to Acámbaro, Guanajuato, never liked the customs in the United States, and expressed his desire to see his grandchildren raised as "good Mexicans."[17]

As the winter of 1930 approached, an increasing number of Mexican residents of Los Angeles decided to head south. All along the border consular officials reported large caravans of returnees from throughout the Southwest and Midwest. Some 2700 repatriates crossed through Nuevo Laredo during the first half of December, while 800 more were counted leaving through Laredo and Nogales on a single day in early January, 1931. By the end of 1930, nearly 10,000 Mexicans had crossed the border. But while hundreds had left Los Angeles, they were quickly replaced by new arrivals who had fled California's small rural towns expecting to find better public relief in a larger city.[18]

The growing financial burden of local relief led many officials in Los Angeles to look for scapegoats. Resentment and suspicion of "alien" Mexicans on relief increased as limited resources for the unemployed grew more scarce. President Hoover's attitude encouraged such feelings. While Food Administrator during World War I he had enthusiastically recruited Mexican farm workers to maintain wartime production, but in 1930 Hoover denounced Mexicans as one of the causes of the economic depression—"they took jobs away from American citizens"—and he initiated plans to deport them. Thus, a host of factors coalesced during this crisis which culminated in the depopulation of the Mexican community in Los Angeles by as much as 30 percent between 1930 and 1935.

Several historians have described the Mexican repatriation/deportation programs of the 1930s. In the first book-length study on this subject, Abraham Hoffman focused on Los Angeles County officials' role in sponsoring trains that returned Mexicans to the border from 1931 to 1934. Another perspective on repatriation is provided by Francisco Balderrama. Utilizing Mexican consulate records, he chronicled the role of the consulate office in Los Angeles, demonstrating how Mexican officials in the United States encouraged repatriation efforts while consistently fighting against abuses in the processes of deportation and repatriation of Mexicans. Finally, in another study, Mercedes Carreras de Velasco described the role of various branches of the Mexican federal government in repatriation efforts, particularly concentrating on the attempt to promote agricultural cooperative communities among the returnees. These studies and other evidence from the period provide insight into how the actual planning, coordination, and implementation of repatriation campaigns were conducted in Los Angeles and throughout the nation.[19]

What historians of repatriation have not yet examined is how the loss of thousands of family members, friends, and neighbors affected the social identity of those individuals who stayed in the United States. Moreover, we know little about repatriation's impact on the cultural development and adaptation of Mexican American communities. The departure of nearly a third of all Mexicans from Los Angeles had profound consequences among Chicanos.

To understand the emotional and psychological impact of the repatriation period, one must first examine which groups encouraged repatriation in Los Angeles. Communications between local officials, the business community, and federal authorities in the Labor Department who were responsible for immigration control set activities in motion. In late 1930 newly appointed Secretary of Labor William Doak began his work with a promise to rid the country of the "four hundred thousand illegal aliens" he believed were taking jobs away from American citizens. In a desperate attempt to rescue the Republican party from responsibility for the economic crisis, Doak charged the Immigration Bureau (which at the time was under the Department of Labor) to ferret out these "thousands." However, the task could really not be accomplished solely by federal authorities because the tiny Border Patrol, founded in 1924, was largely responsible for administering border checkpoints, while few other federal officials were assigned immigration responsibilities. Los Angeles, for example, had only thirty-five immigration agents assigned to it in 1931.[20]

Los Angeles officials were more than willing to aid in the effort. Charles P. Visel, newly appointed head of the Los Angeles Citizens Committee on Coordination of Unemployment Relief, devised a scheme in January 1931 to publicize a visit to the city by the regional immigration director in order to frighten local "aliens" into returning to their native country. In coordination with Secretary Doak and Colonel Arthur Woods, national coordinator of the President's Emergency Committee for Employment, Visel sent out a publicity release on January 26 to all newspapers in the city, especially the foreign-language press, which emphasized the upcoming campaign to rid the city of all deportable aliens. This plan eventually included a high-profile sweep of the Plaza district on February 26, 1931, in which four hundred individuals were detained, yet only seventeen people—eleven Mexicans, five Chinese, and one Japanese—were taken into custody.[21]

Fewer than 300 Mexican aliens were actually deported by federal authorities during this entire campaign.[22] The scare was successful, however, in encouraging Mexicans of varying legal status—including American-born citizens of Mexican descent—to contemplate leaving. As far as Mexicans' legal status was concerned, the laws were relatively new, contradictory, and largely intended for European immigrants expected to enter the country at designated seaports. In addition, various exemptions had been granted Mexican laborers which further complicated the issue. The net effect of the confusion was the rampant abuse of authority by those charged with implementing the law and the widespread distrust of American officials by Mexicans in Los Angeles.

The scare tactics were so effective in alarming the Mexican population that local businessmen began to worry about losing an abundant, reliable supply of cheap labor beyond the immediate crisis. The Los Angeles Chamber of Commerce, chaired by George Clements, pulled back from their initial support of repatriation and called on political officials to restore calm in the Mexican community. The ties between local urban industrialists and rural landowners in the San Joaquin Valley and Imperial Valley were strong, so despite widespread unemployment in the city, the business community was adamant about protecting the large pool of Mexican workers. What business leaders wanted was an orderly program that would lessen the burden on local welfare agencies without disturbing the availability of Mexican workers needed to complete the harvest at minimal wages.[23]

Meanwhile, welfare officials had begun discussing strategies for reducing the relief rolls as early as the fall of 1930. Much of this dialogue occurred among Los Angeles County' officials, since the county administered a large percentage of welfare relief in the region, particularly among Mexicans. By January 1931, welfare directors had approached the County' Board of Supervisors with a plan to pay the train passage to the border of those Mexican residents on relief. Officials estimated that oneway train fares were far less expensive than maintaining Mexicans on relief rolls.[24] The plan was adopted by the end of the month, and the first trainload of county-sponsored repatriates left Los Angeles on March 23, 1931.

Paradoxically, the Mexican government's representative in Los Angeles was crucial to the success of repatriation efforts. Along with local Mexican businessmen, Consul Rafael de la Colina had protested against the Immigration Bureau's efforts to scare Mexicans out of the city with threats of deportation. In his view, however, voluntary repatriation was another matter entirely. By late 1930, the consular staff had received frequent inquiries from disenchanted, unemployed barrio residents wanting assistance to return to Mexico. On January' 29, when local officials briefed Colina about their evolving plans to launch a repatriation campaign, the consul argued that the proposed program should be extended to Mexicans outside the county' as well as to those who did not receive welfare benefits. On March 8, 1931, when plans for county sponsorship of repatriation trains was announced, *La Opinión* called the deal a "great victory" for Colina. A month after the program began, he appeared before the Los Angeles Chamber of Commerce to allay fears that continued movement back to Mexico would hurt local industry. He argued that repatriation was the "only alternative for many unemployed Mexicans?"[25]

The consulate's strong advocacy of repatriation was motivated by the growing economic misery of Mexican immigrants in Los Angeles. Also underlying his support was the Mexican government's long-standing desire to see immigrants return to Mexico, particularly after they had acquired experience in the American labor force. The presence of so large an emigrant community across the border had rankled Mexican officials since the revolution. Mexican officials viewed the mass immigration as international mutiny amidst growing nationalistic fervor. They also sincerely believed the migration had been a labor drain that had depopulated the northern states. "México llama a sus hijos"—or "Mexico calls out to her children"—was the headline one southern California resident remembered from a flyer encouraging repatriation put out by the Mexican consulate office.[26]

In 1931, many destitute Mexicans in Los Angeles also began to believe that a return to their homeland would be prudent. But long spells of unemployment and debt left many Mexican residents unable even to pay the costs of transportation. During the winter of 1930–31, the Mexican consulate responded by arranging a reduced rate for Mexican repatriates to El Paso via the Southern Pacific railroad. Requests for additional help, however, continued to pour into the consulate offices. County plans to use relief funds to pay for passage to the border were welcomed by those who had organized more informal programs. In addition, welfare committees set up by the consulate office began to divert a significant percentage of their funds toward repatriation. One historian estimates that as many as 1500 individuals who left Los Angeles in April and May of 1931 had their passage paid for by the Comité de Beneficencia Mexicana in Los Angeles.[27]

Compared with those who left the city before formal deportation and repatriation campaigns began, Mexicans who departed after 1931 were more likely to be low-paid blue-collar workers.[28] They were destitute, unemployed for many weeks or months, and usually on relief. In fact, what often distinguished those who decided to go to Mexico from other working-class Mexican immigrants who did not, even within their extended families, was whether or not members of the family were employed and had been forced to go on relief. The Bureau of County Welfare had little trouble finding willing participants during its first year of organized repatriation; as many as three to five thousand residents on relief had requested county aid for transportation back to Mexico. Heads of families who had planned on waiting out the economic downturn now realized that their decision had simply allowed precious resources to dwindle. This was their chance to start anew in their native land, even if their return was prompted by desperate circumstances.[29]

Unlike the earlier group of repatriates who had exhibited some measure of optimism, these returnees were deeply troubled. They had brought back little to show for the years of hard work in the north. One observer noted that "the majority of the men were very quiet and pensive" on the trains, while "most of the women and children were crying."[30] Moreover, they resented their treatment in the United States, feeling that they deserved more than an unfriendly send-off after many years of toil. Some had lived in the city for over a decade and had developed close attachments to neighbors and neighborhoods in East Los Angeles. Moreover, they were anxious about the uncertainty of their future. To ease their anxiety, the only Mexican American student at Occidental College in 1931 remembered dressing in Mexican costume, singing songs in Spanish (particularly the farewell song, "Las Golondrinas"), and expressing gratitude to the departees for their role in building this country from the train platform. A few Anglo American church officials and parishioners also organized collections of food and clothing for the repatriates.[31]

Many, if not most, experienced little improvement in their status once back in Mexico. While early repatriates had brought resources with them that could be put to good use in starting over, later returnees often found themselves unable to translate their American experience into tangible economic results in Mexico. As one woman who repatriated to Mexico City said:

> How can we do anything? We are so poor. Surely many have learned useful skills there, but what good does that do here when they come back without anything, no fools, no work, nothing at all, not even to eat. What help can *repatriados* like that be?[32]

In fact, people returned to places where they had familial and other ties rather than to areas with greater economic possibilities. Despite government attempts to encourage repatriates to settle in agricultural colonies, Mexican officials estimated that fewer than 5 percent did so. Approximately 15 percent settled in large urban centers such as Mexico City and Guadalajara, but the economic opportunities there were also limited. The majority, probably close to 80 percent, went home to familiar villages, often returning to the place of their birth.[33]

The response of repatriates to their native villages varied tremendously. Paul Taylor discovered that many returnees to Arandas, Jalisco, easily reintegrated themselves into the community's life, quickly abandoning customs and dress that they had acquired in the United States. Many felt quite positive about their experience in the north and wanted to return when economic conditions improved, though Taylor surmised that this attitude may have resulted from the fact that Arandas produced very light-skinned individuals with few Indian features—many of whom might have remained immune from the worst of American prejudice.

James Gilbert, a sociology student at the University of Southern California, traveled throughout central Mexico in 1934 interviewing over 100 repatriates. He took a much broader sample than Taylor, and uncovered greater problems of adjustment, particularly among those who had returned with few resources. Most had difficulties obtaining employment or land to resume agricultural endeavors, and the single colony he investigated was fraught with environmental and economic difficulties.[34]

Within a repatriated family, it became clear that different members had very distinct adjustment problems. Women often had to readjust to more austere housekeeping conditions. "Here it is harder," said one woman who was living in a small village with her husband. "Cooking is more difficult. There we had gas ranges, but not here, and we used flour while here it is *maíz*." One young girl had to accustom herself to waking up at 4 a.m. in order to prepare corn tortillas for the family meals for the day, even though she herself refused to eat any not made of flour nor to use the tortilla as a replacement for a spoon. Another complained that the lack of running water forced her to bathe "in a little tub of water in the middle of the patio exposed to the four winds." Restrictive mores were particularly oppressive to young women, one of whom complained that she never went to dances or went out with boys because of local customs. "If you do, everyone starts talking, and you are regarded as a lost person. They won't have anything to do with you."[35]

Older children also had difficulty adapting to their new surroundings, having grown up accustomed to amenities in the United States. One woman who repatriated back to a family ranch from southern California at age seven remembered laughing at the first adults she encountered wearing huarache sandals, large sombreros, and white cotton pants she called "pajamas," only to find herself crying months later when her own clothes and that of her siblings ran thin and they had to begin dressing like other Mexicans. This same girl, however, taught other Mexican youngsters at the ranch how to dance the tango and play American baseball and basketball, earning the nickname "La Norteña" in the process. Many others did not know' how to read or write Spanish, so they were held back in school. Often children who had been born and raised in the United States dreamed of returning long after their parents had already decided to remain in Mexico.[36]

The most successfully adjusted repatriates were usually those who had spent the least amount of time in the United States and had been most isolated within barrios. For them, life in Mexico consisted of familiar surroundings. Not surprisingly, the most skilled and the most Americanized repatriates—the very' people the Mexican government hoped would bring progress to the villages—became the most discontented. They looked for the first opportunity to return to the United States, and often felt like social outcasts in their native land. Those that gave up "American ways" had an easier time of adjustment, yet failed to distinguish themselves in a way that would bring progress to the entire community.[37]

One significant exception to this pattern—but one totally unintended by the Mexican government—was the emergence of agrarian radicalism in certain areas of the central plateau due, in part, to the influence of repatriates. A study of *agraristas* in Lagos de Moreno, Jalisco, revealed that many of the early leaders of that region's agrarian movement were repatriates who returned from the United States with growing families; they demanded communal farm lands promised by the Mexican government as part of its post-revolution land redistribution policy. They had enjoyed higher wages while in the north and some had been involved in unions; in Mexico, they refused to return to sharecropping or debt peonage. In addition, some individuals, because of their exposure to other religious beliefs in the United States, tended to oppose priests who hindered agrarian reform. Some had gained basic literacy skills in the United States, a talent which catapulted them into leadership positions among the villagers. As one of these *agraristas* explained: "You see, there is precisely something about the United States which awakens me. ... We saw in the United States that progress comes from work ... and we remembered that here, the rich men don't work, they just exploit the poor."[38]

In Mexico City, a different form of political protest emerged among the repatriate community. In late 1932, the newly formed La Unión de Repartriados Mexicanos (the Union of Mexican Repatriates) pressured the Mexican government to halt repatriation efforts until the promises they made to the returnees were fufilled. They asked Mexican officials to recognize the "painful reality" of the repatriates' economic condition. They demanded, moreover, a stop to the "deception" by the National Committee on Repatriation which seduced potential repatriates with "a thousand promises of improvement and aid to all Mexicans who returned to their native country." On April 19, 1933, La Unión sent a letter to *La Opinión* in Los Angeles asking the newspaper to print the enclosed photographs of their condition and publish the news that "they had returned only to die of hunger and to inspire pity at the doors of charitable organizations, where they receive only one meal a day."[39]

This was not the first news to reach Los Angeles that repatriates were suffering in Mexico. As early as November 1931, *La Opinión* published a report from Aguascalientes that repatriates—some originating in Los Angeles—had been abandoned without money or help, often unable to find family or friends after years of separation. Other reports confirmed the problems experienced by the repatriates. A group considering repatriation from Anaheim, California, for example, was warned by a former resident who had returned to Abasolo, Guanajuato, that "the situation in our Mexico was distressing because there was no job openings." In the spring of 1932, Mexican consulates throughout the United States warned those considering repatriation to forgo expectations of locating a job in Mexico and to come only if they could not find work in the United States. In early 1933, a tragic story of a repatriate from California who resettled in Morelia, Michoacán, circulated throughout the Los Angeles Mexican community: despondent over his family's economic misery, he killed his wife and his four children with a hammer and then committed suicide.[40]

Increasingly, a large number of repatriates began to consider returning to the United States.[41] Los Angeles County officials, for example, received a letter in May 1934 from a former resident whose family had been repatriated in 1932 through the county-sponsored program. Pablo Guerrero wrote from the border city of Mexicali, Baja California, to request legal U.S. immigrant status for he and his family; ironically, all five children were born in the United States and, therefore, were legal citizens of the nation.

> I worked in the U.S. of A. since 1904 with different companies. I registered in the world war in Johnson, Arizona, Cochise Co. I have never given my services to the Mexican government nor to Mexican capital. I have worked all of my life, since I was 19 years of age in the U.S. of A., and that is why I wish to return to the country where I am entitled to live with my children so that they be educated in the schools of your country and not in Mexico.[42]

Most repatriates, including Pablo Guerrero, found county officials unsympathetic. In fact, United States federal authorities at the border were instructed to turn back any

Mexican who had been repatriated under the sponsorship of a charitable organization or government agency and who requested reentry. The stamp of "L.A. County Charities" on the back of a voluntary departure card precluded immigrants' return to the United States. Many were forced to reenter this country illegally, risking capture even if their families included American-born children.[43]

Instead of reconsidering their plans, county officials continued to promote repatriation long after it was clear that the situation in Mexico was, in many ways, worse than in the United States. The county program became more difficult to implement by mid-1933 as fewer Mexicans were willing to consider repatriation as an alternative to their economic woes. Evidence of this slowdown was reflected in fewer and fewer county-sponsored repatriation trains. Until April 1933, Los Angeles County had organized shipments of repatriates at approximately two month intervals. After this time, there was an abrupt decline in the number of departures. For example, the shipment in early August, 1933, contained only 453 people as compared with an average of 908 people in the thirteen previous shipments. The subsequent train in December 1933 contained even fewer repatriates. A six-month hiatus followed before the next, and final, county-sponsored train left Los Angeles.[44]

There were a number of reasons which account for the decline of interest in repatriation among Los Angeles Mexicans. First, and probably most important, many of those inclined to return to Mexico had already done so by mid-1933. After four years of economic depression and more than two years of continued encouragement by local American and Mexican officials to repatriate, the Mexican community in Los Angeles had lost thousands of individuals whose commitment to stay in the United States, both in economic and psychological terms, was relatively weak. The single male migrants to the city were among the first to leave, since they had fewer familial obligations and generally had not invested in real estate. Recent migrants to the city, including newcomers from both Mexico and rural California, were less well established in Los Angeles and likely had greater difficulty securing jobs in the midst of the Great Depression. Those that remained in the city in 1933 tended to be members of a family unit, to be property owners, and to be residents in the city for at least a decade.[45]

Second, the dismal reports about conditions of repatriates in Mexico that circulated by word of mouth and in the Spanish-language press undoubtedly discouraged further repatriation. Moreover, by 1932 the Mexican consulate in Los Angeles no longer encouraged repatriation except under the most exceptional circumstances. The departure of Consul Rafael de la Colina in March 1932, a staunch proponent of repatriation, no doubt also diminished the call for return to Mexico. Joaquín Terrazas, Colina's immediate successor, reported to *La Opinión* in May that Mexican nationals should stay in the United States even if they had poorly paid jobs. The economic situation in Mexico was so difficult, he reported, that repatriates should have little expectation of finding work in their native land. Consul Alejandro Martínez, who replaced Terrazas the following January, went so far as to tell a federal official that "there is no agreement between the United States and the Mexican Government" concerning repatriation, and that Mexican nationals who desire to return may do so "but the Mexican Government feels as long as they voluntarily left Mexico the government is under no obligation to help them return." According to a Los Angeles official, the Mexican government was increasingly reluctant to support repatriation because local communities in Mexico complained about the burdens which destitute repatriates created for their towns and cities.[46]

The third reason interest in repatriation had waned was the inauguration of President Franklin D. Roosevelt in March 1933. This change in administration brought about a transformation in the Mexican community's outlook toward their future in this country. Immediately after Roosevelt assumed the presidency, *La Opinión,* which generally focused on Mexican politics, told its readers not to be alarmed by the immediate fiscal crisis: "The confidence and solidarity of the North American people in this emergency situation are admirable." Much of the praise centered on the federal controls that Roosevelt promised for revitalization and the presidential theme of cooperation among the population during times of crisis. When compared with the disastrous policies of Herbert Hoover, Roosevelt's early presidency appeared to Mexicans to foreshadow not only economic recovery but a reduction in racial discrimination as well.[47]

In very practical terms, the policies of the Roosevelt administration rearranged the distribution of relief for Mexicans in Los Angeles. Federal assistance to the state and county contained provisions which prohibited discrimination in the allocation of direct relief on the basis of legal status, while raising the level of public assistance for all. Moreover, federal relief funds could not be used to transport aliens out of the county. On the other hand, the Federal Civil Works Program welcomed only American citizens or aliens who had taken out their first papers for naturalization. Nevertheless, not only did Mexican residents of Los Angeles now have greater possibilities for direct relief, they were motivated to file for naturalization because of the new provisions of work relief (see Table 4.2.1). The possibility of surviving the economic crisis in Los Angeles increased substantially with the Democratic administration in Washington.[48]

Los Angeles County officials who had committed themselves to a policy of repatriating or deporting Mexican aliens looked askance at these developments. Largely in the hands of the Republican party, government agencies in southern California resisted the federal intervention of the New Deal program on many different levels. Since most relief in California before 1933 had been distributed by private agencies, new federal

Table 4.2.1 Applications for Naturalization by Three-Year Intervals

Years	Number	Percent
1904–6	1	0.06
1907–9	4	0.23
1910–12	3	0.17
1913–15	25	1.44
1916–18	66	3.79
1919–21	206	11.84
1922–24	152	8.74
1925–27	279	16.04
1928–30	249	14.31
1931–33	192	11.03
1934–36	374	21.49
1937–39	189	10.86
Total	1,740	100.00

Source: Declarations of Intention and Petitions for Naturalization, National Archives, Laguna Niguel, California.

rules demanding that government funds be handled by public agencies created great turmoil. At both city and county levels, the establishment of public control ushered in mismanagement, unnecessary bureaucracy, and blatant political patronage. Lorena Hickok, an unofficial observer of relief efforts for Harry Hopkins, Roosevelt's administrator of relief, wrote in the fall of 1934 that relief in California was "the damnedest mess ... a wretchedly inefficient business."[49]

Local officials, bent on solving Los Angeles' economic woes in their own way, doubled efforts to entice Mexicans to leave. Earl Jensen, Superintendent of Charities, admitted to an "intensive recruiting drive on the part of the Welfare and Unemployment Relief Districts" to get Mexicans to sign up for the December 1933 trip which netted only 120 relief cases, or 412 individuals. The failure of that effort hastened officials to offer other incentives to repatriate, such as a modest cash allowance for families once they disembarked from the train in Mexico. Although this incentive produced a slight increase in the number of Mexicans departing, it largely failed.[50]

This third phase of repatriation produced the most overt examples of abuse and manipulation, and certainly increased the level of racial discrimination by local officials against Mexicans. Growing resentment against repatriation by Mexican Americans created conflict between them and local officials determined to continue the movement of Mexicans from southern California. This conflict occurred on a day-to-day basis, especially between county social workers and Mexican families seeking relief dispensation. John Anson Ford, who was elected onto the County Board of Supervisors in December 1934, remembered that during his tenure welfare officials, though lacking the legal authority to do so, pressured Mexican nationals to return to Mexico, trying to convince them that they had to go back. A longtime Mexican resident recollected that as a little girl she picked up margarine, peanut butter, other groceries, and clothes from a county warehouse. Her father, after being pressured to give up his Mexican citizenship, decided to return to Mexico rather than continue to suffer the uncertainties of poverty and county welfare.[51]

Señor Natividad Castañeda, like most others who left during this third phase of repatriation, entered the depression decade as a skilled worker, proud of his craft and able to earn good wages during more prosperous economic times. He, and others like him, had arrived in the city before 1923, and had been in the United States for much longer. By 1933, tens of thousands of Mexicans had lived in the United States for over two decades, many having arrived as adolescents and young adults. They had often bought property east of the river in Brooklyn Heights or Belvedere, married, and decided to raise their families in Los Angeles. In many ways, repatriates of this third phase closely resembled those who refused to return to Mexico during the Great Depression. What often set them apart, however, was a particular misfortune that made family survival extremely precarious and forced them to reevaluate their previous decisions. Castañeda's family, for example, finally agreed to repatriation only after the mother fell ill and died of tuberculosis, and the family home was foreclosed by the state.[52]

Pressure to repatriate and harassment in allocating relief was combined with the manipulation of the welfare system to serve the interests of local employers. For example, after the El Monte Berry strike of 1933 was settled, the County Charities Department investigated the predominantly Mexican work force to determine who would soon be out of work. They then placed an undercover agent among the workers and his task was to persuade people to return to Mexico, thus ridding the county of potential Mexican troublemakers and welfare relief recipients.[53] Local efforts could be hampered by federal guidelines, however, because accepting federal funds bound officials to distributing aid to all the unemployed, including strikers. The federal government's increased relief to Mexicans actually strengthened their bargaining power as field laborers, because the amount received in aid in 1933 was approximately the same amount per month as wages earned by agricultural workers. In fact, income from federal assistance programs created more security than seasonal farm labor.[54]

This situation angered local businessmen, as the comments of Los Angeles Chamber of Commerce President Clements suggest:

> The Mexican on relief is being unionized and is being used to foment strikes among the few still loyal Mexican workers. The Mexican casual labor is lost to the California farmer unless immediate action is taken to get him off relief.[55]

By 1935, farm owners, in fact, working in concert with the Los Angeles Chamber of Commerce, were instrumental in changing state and federal allocation of resources. In May, the California Relief Administration and the WPA agreed to drop workers from their relief rolls if they refused agricultural work. From August to October, 75,000 workers were denied relief in order to force them to work in California fields and processing plants. In addition, relief recipients in the Belvedere barrio, along with Mexicans from throughout Los Angeles, were sent out to work in agriculture. Between 1935 and the beginning of World War II, relief rolls in southern California were expanded or contracted depending on the seasonal labor needs of agricultural interests in the state.[56]

The maltreatment of Chicanos on relief, particularly the pressure put on residents by county officials to repatriate, deeply affected those Mexicans who stayed in the city. Many Chicanos recall vivid memories of the Great Depression. Antonio Soto, for example, interviewed during the 1970s, remembered that Mexicans in the 1930s were indiscriminately picked up and sent back to Mexico. "Even if they were citizens they had no rights and were treated like animals and put in cattle cars."[57] Mexicans who stayed behind also retain memories of relatives, neighbors, and fellow workers who departed under questionable circumstances. Those who remained in the United States realized that they, too, might have easily been deported or repatriated had it not been for the benevolence of a trusting neighbor, a child's extra income, or the family vegetable garden in the back yard.

By 1935, the Mexican community of Los Angeles had been substantially transformed by the effects of depression, deportation, and repatriation. First, a profound demographic shift resulted from the loss of one-third of the Mexican residents of the city, and, consequently, the internal composition of the Mexican population was altered. The departure of young, single, Mexican-born men who had greatly influenced the environment in the central Plaza area made more prominent the role of family units in the evolving culture of Chicanos in Los Angeles. Since housing around the Plaza area was geared primarily toward single men, during the Depression movement into East Los Angeles by the Mexican community accelerated. In addition, the return to Mexico by clerks and other low-level white-collar workers contributed even more to the homogenous profile of Mexicans as a low blue-collar work force.

Perhaps most important for the future of the Chicano community, the net effect of the repatriation of single men and young Mexican families was to quicken the demographic shift toward second-generation dominance. For the Mexican-origin population in California as a whole in 1930, the ratio of native-born to foreign-born was 91 percent. By 1940, however, the native-born now dominated by a ratio of 164 percent. The midwestern states, also sites of widespread repatriation, witnessed a similar shift.[58] Within the span of five years, what had been largely an immigrant community before the Depression became one dominated by the children of immigrants. This generational shift had profound implications on Mexican American ethnic leadership and cultural identity in Los Angeles.

The major outcome of repatriation was to silence the Mexican immigrant generation in Los Angeles and make them less visible. As construction on the new Union Train Terminal alongside the Placita in 1934 began, the presence of the Mexican immigrant community diminished further in the downtown area. Reminders of a vibrant Mexican immigrant life disappeared for the larger Anglo American population. The ethnic diversity which had in the past so profoundly marked the city was now becoming more segmented as movement of Mexicans into East Los Angeles gained momentum. Increased residential segregation, decreasing inter-ethnic contact, and concerted efforts on the part of local officials to rid Los Angeles of its Mexican population resulted in Chicanos becoming an "invisible minority."

Nothing epitomized the redefined status of Mexicans in Los Angeles better than the movement to restore the Los Angeles Plaza area, including Olvera Street and the city's oldest standing structure, Avila House. In 1926, Christine Sterling, a San Francisco-born woman of English descent, approached Harry Chandler, publisher of the Los Angeles *Times,* with the idea of rejuvenating the site of the city's founding. Two years later when the Avila House was scheduled for demolition, Sterling had gathered enough support to bring her "Plaza Beautiful" campaign to fruition. In addition to raising $30,000 for the restoration, a much larger program for the incorporation of the Plaza—involving some of the leading citizens of the city—was set in motion over the next few years. These citizens hoped to make the Plaza a major tourist attraction, featuring Olvera Street as a "picturesque Mexican market place."[59]

Ironically, restoration was completed at the very moment when thousands of Mexicans were being prodded to repatriate. The lesson was clear: Mexicans were to be assigned a place in the mythic past of Los Angeles—one that could be relegated to a quaint section of a city destined to delight tourists and antiquarians. Real Mexicans were out of sight and increasingly out of mind. Physically farther away from the center of power, Mexican immigrants remained close enough to provide the cheap labor essential to industry' and agriculture. Repatriation removed many, but others continued their struggle for survival east of the river. Their children, however, made it much harder for the Anglo American community to designate Mexicans as relics of the past. These young people, born and educated in the United States, demanded to be included in the city's future as Mexican Americans.

Notes

1. *La Opinión,* 30 and 31 Jan. 1931; Los Angeles City Directories, 1927–35, show that the Olazábal family was new to Belvedere in 1931, and that Mr. Olazábal was able to remain employed as a grocer through the most difficult years of the Depression.
2. *La Opinión,* 30 and 31 Jan. 1931.
3. The exact number of Mexicans who returned to their native land from Los Angeles in this period is difficult to know. Official estimates from organized train departures number below 14,000, but at least as many probably left Los Angeles on their own or with the help of private organizations. Carey McWilliams probably has the highest estimate of 75,000 in *Factories in the Field: The Story of Migratory Farm Labor in California* (Santa Barbara: Peregrine Smith, 1935), 125. More reasonable is the estimate arrived at by Matt Meier and Feliciano Rivera (taken apparently from other figures used by McWilliams in the 1930s) of 35,000 in *The Chicanos: A History of Mexican Americans* (New York: Hill and Wang, 1972), 161. Since most historians estimate the overall Mexican heritage population of Los Angeles in 1930 to be about 100,000, close to one-third left the city during these years.
4. John D. Weaver, *L.A.: El Pueblo Grande* (Los Angeles: Ward Ritchie Press, 1973), 76; Leonard J. ¡Leader, "Los Angeles and the Great Depression" (Ph.D. diss., University of California, Los Angeles, 1972), 1–4.
5. Frances Fox Piven and Richard A. Cloward, *Regulating the Poor: The Functions of Public Welfare* (New York: Vintage, 1971), 49.
6. Leader, "Great Depression," 4–11; William H. Mullins, *The Depression and the Urban West Coast, 1929–1933: Los Angeles, San Francisco, Seattle, and Portland* (Bloomington: Indiana Univ. Press, 1991), 127.
7. Francisco Enrique Balderrama, "En Defensa de la Raza: The Los Angeles Mexican Consulate and Colonia Mexicana during the Great Depression" (Ph.D. diss., University of California, Los Angeles, 1978), 25; Mullins, *The Depression and the Urban West Coast,* 52.
8. Leader, "Great Depression," 6; Gerald Nash, *The American West in the Twentieth Century* (Englewood Cliffs: Prentice-Hall, 1973), 137; Mark Reisler, *By the Sweat of Their Brow: Mexican Immigration in the United States, 1900–1940* (Westport, Conn.: Greenwood, 1976), 228–33.

9. Leader, "Great Depression," 6–7, 9; Jacqueline Rorabeck Kasun, *Some Social Aspects of Business Cycles in the Los Angeles Area, 1920–1950* (Los Angeles: Haynes Foundation, 1954), 32.

10. *La Opinión,* 8 Feb. 1931.

11. Robin Fitzgerald Scott, "The Mexican-American in the Los Angeles Area, 1920–1950: From Acquiescence to Activity" (Ph.D diss., University of Southern California, 1971), 116–17; *La Opinión,* 14 Aug. 1931.

12. *Los Angeles Times,* 13 Jan. 1931; *Los Angeles Daily News,* 17 April 1931; Leader, "Great Depression," pp. 29–30; Scott, "Acquiescence," 13.

13. California, State Relief Administration, *Review of the Activities of the State Relief Administration of California: 1933–1935* (San Francisco: State Printing Office, 1936), 349; California, *Report and Recommendations of the California State Unemployment Commission* (San Francisco: State Printing Office, 1932), 371.

14. Leader, "Great Depression," 32–38; California, *Report and Recommendations,* 371–74. For the fullest account of relief distribution in Los Angeles during this period, see Mullin, *The Depression and the Urban West Coast,* 27–36, 62–71, 98, 126.

15. Analysis of naturalization records by linking individuals to Los Angeles city directories; see note 28 below for further description. Abraham Hoffman, *Unwanted Mexican Americans in the Great Depression: Repatriation Pressures, 1929–1939* (Tucson: Univ. of Arizona Press, 1974), 36–37; interview with Carlos Munatones, conducted by Christine Valenciana, 4 Aug. 1971, OH 748, Oral History Program, California State University at Fullerton.

16. Manuel Gamio, *Mexican Immigration to the United States: A Study of Human Migration and Adjustment* (1930; rpt., New York: Dover, 1971), Appendix V, pp. 224–29.

17. Interview with José Castillo, Biographies and Case Histories II folder, Z-R5, Manuel Gamio collection, Bancroft Library, University of California, Berkeley.

18. Hoffman, *Unwanted,* 36–37, and Appendix D, 174–75.

19. ibid.; Balderrama, "Defensa," and *In Defense of La Raza: The Los Angeles Mexican Consulate and the Mexican Community, 1929 to 1936* (Tucson: Univ. of Arizona Press, 1982), especially Chap. 2; Mercedes Carreras de Velasco, *Los Mexicanos que devolvió la crisis, 1929–1932* (México, D.F.: Secretaría de Relaciones Exteriores, 1974). For contemporary studies, see James Carl Gilbert, "A Field Study in Mexico of the Mexican Repatriation Movement" (Master's thesis, Univ. of Southern California, 1934); and Paul S. Taylor, *A Spanish-Mexican Peasant Community: Arandas in Jalisco, Mexico,* Ibero-Americana, 4 (Berkeley: Univ. of California Press, 1933).

20. Hoffman, *Unwanted,* 39–41, 63.

21. Ibid., 43–63; *La Opinión,* 27 and 28 Feb. 1931.

22. Hoffman, *Unwanted,* 64–65.

23. Ibid., 68–71.

24. Carey McWilliams, "Getting Rid of the Mexican," *American Mercury* 28 (1933), 322–24.

25. Balderrama, *Defense,* 17–22; *La Opinión,* 6 Feb. and 8 March 1931.

26. Interview with María Bustos Jefferson, conducted by Christine Valenciana, 11 Sept. 1971, OH 1300, Oral History Program, California State University at Fullerton. See Chapter 5 for a full description of the reasons behind the advocacy for repatriation by the Mexican consulate.

27. Hoffman, *Unwanted,* 84–87; Balderrama, *Defense,* 42.

28. I created a subsample of individuals from my larger group who were living in Los Angeles in 1927–28 at which time they took out first or second papers for naturalization. Linking this information to Los Angeles city directories, I was able to locate 171 of these individuals and their families. Over the next ten years, 62, or 36 percent, disappeared from the directories, apparently moving out of the city. Although I currently have no way of telling whether, in fact, these individuals returned to Mexico, the numbers do suggest that a substantial proportion of even these Mexicans were affected by the repatriation campaign.

29. Hoffman, *Unwanted,* 88. For an example of a family struggling over whether or not to return to Mexico in 1931, see interview with Mrs. Carmen Landeros, conducted by Christine Valenciana, 7 Aug. 1971, OH 745, Oral History Program, California State University at Fullerton.

30. Lucas Lucio, organizer of three repatriation trips, in Balderrama, *Defense,* 28. See also interview with Allen A. Hunter, conducted by Christine Valenciana, 22 Aug. 1971, OH 744, Oral History Program, California State University at Fullerton.

31. Interview with María Bustos Jefferson and interview with Allen A. Hunter, Oral History Program, California State University at Fullerton.

32. Interview record No. 17 (in Spanish) from Gilbert, "Field Study," 146.

33. Emory Bogardus, *The Mexican in the United States* (Los Angeles: Univ. of Southern California Press, 1934), 91. Even the small percentage that settled in agricultural colonies differed with the Mexican government over where those colonies should be located. Most repatriates organized themselves for agriculture endeavors in the northern states, while Mexican government officials wanted colonies set up in the tropical and depopulated south; see Carreras de Velasco, *Devolvió,* 117.

34. Taylor, *Arandas,* Gilbert, "Field Study."

35. Gilbert, "Field Study," 137–42; Bogardus, *Mexican in the United States,* 93–94; interview with Theresa Martinez Southard, conducted by Christine Valenciana, 1 Sept. 1971, OH 753, Oral History Program, California State University at Fullerton.

36. Gilbert, "Field Study," 137–42; Bogardus, *Mexican in the United States,* 93–94; interview with Theresa Martinez Southard.

37. Gilbert, "Field Study," 136–37.

38. Ann L. Craig, *The First Agraristas: An Oral History of a Mexican Agrarian Reform Movement* (Berkeley: Univ. of California Press, 1983), 92–94, 178–82, 211.

39. *La Opinión,* 11, 19, 20 Feb. and 29 April 1933.

40. *La Opinión,* 2 Nov. 1931, 6 and 20 March, 28 May 1932, 19 Jan. 1933.

41. Gilbert found that the majority of repatriates he interviewed in 1934 wanted to return to the United States, for example. "Field Study," 164.

42. Pablo Guerrero, Letter to Los Angeles County, 28 May 1934, Box 4E, 40.31/340.39, Los Angeles County Board of Supervisors files.

43. See Hoffman, *Unwanted,* 91.

44. Ibid., 105–9, 172–73.

45. Evaluation of the characteristics of a sample of 171 individuals present in the city during 1927–28, and their movement out of the city over the next decade. The initial sample is taken from naturalization records, and compared with Los Angeles city directories for the period 1927 through 1935.

46. *La Opinión,* 11 April and 28 May 1932; undated report on Mexican immigrants by DcCourcey to Phillip J. Robinson, 6, Federal Writers Project collection, National Archives, Washington, D.C.; Earl E. Jensen, Superintendent of Charities, Letter to Los Angeles Board of Supervisors, 15 Feb. 1934, p. 3, Board of Supervisors Minutes, vol. 196, p. 233. Paul Taylor also notes the role of adverse reports from Mexico leading to a sharp decline in repatriation in *Mexican Labor in the United States: Migration Statistics, TV* (Berkeley: Univ. of California Press, 1934), 24.

47. *La Opinión,* 11 March 1933.

48. Jensen to Board of Supervisors, 2; Hoffman, *Unwanted,* 105, 108; Analysis of Naturalization documents, National Archives, Laguna Niguel, California.

49. William R. Brock, *Welfare, Democracy, and the New Deal* (Cambridge, Eng.: Cambridge Univ. Press, 1988), 152–54, 238–43, 339.

50. Although 172 relief cases, totaling 664 individuals, left on this April 1934 train, this effort still failed to raise the number of interested families to pre-New Deal levels. Jensen to Board of Supervisors, 15 Feb. 1934; Hoffman, *Unwanted,* 107–9.

51. Interview with John Anson Ford, conducted by Christine Valenciana, 4 Sept. 1971, OH 759, Oral History Program, California State University at Fullerton; "Repatriation of the 1930s: Mrs. Emilia Castañeda de Valencia," interviewed by Christine Valenciana, 8 Sept. 1971, California State University, Fullerton, Oral History Program: Mexican American Project, 12–13; 16–17. See also Albert Camarillo, *Chicanos in California: A History of Mexican Americans in California* (San Francisco: Boyd and Fraser, 1984), 49–51.

52. "Mrs. Emilia Castañeda de Valencia," 1, 6–7, 11; Analysis of Naturalization records, National Archives, Laguna Niguel, and Los Angeles city directories.

53. G. A. Clements, Memorandum to A. G. Arnoll, 20 July 1933, MS 118, Geo. P. Clements Papers, Department of Special Collections, University of California, Los Angeles; Ronald W. Lopez, "The El Monte Berry Strike of 1933," *Aztlán* 1 (1970), 109–10.

54. Donald L. Zelman, "Mexican Migrants and Relief in Depression California: Grower Reaction to Public Relief Policies as They Affected Mexican Migration," *Journal of Mexican-American History* 5 (1975), 6.

55. Quoted in Zelman, "Grower Reaction," 9.

56. Ibid., 9–13.

57. Porfirio J. Miranda, "Perceptions of Locus of Control among Three Multi-Generation Chicano/Mexican Families" (Ph.D. diss., University of California, Los Angeles, 1978), 215.

58. José Hernandez Alvarez, "A Demographic Profile of the Mexican Immigration to the United States, 1910–1950," *Journal of Inter-American Affairs* 25 (1983), 479.

59. W. W. Robinson, *Los Angeles from the Days of the Pueblo: A Brief History and a Guide to the Plaza Area* (San Francisco: California Historical Society, 1981), 95–102. The painting of a mural by socialist David Alfaro Siqueros produced such an uproar when completed that city officials had it whitewashed rather than depict a historic past not in tune with tourism and promotion.

READING 4.2   POST-READING COMPREHENSION QUESTIONS

- Summarize the principal reasons why Mexicans were constructed as scapegoats for the Great Depression.

- Describe some of the strategies used to target ethnic Mexicans as a result of the Great Depression.

- Paraphrase the passage discussing the "sweep" of the Plaza district in 1931: "Fewer than 300 Mexican aliens were actually deported by federal authorities during the entire campaign. The scare was successful, however, in encouraging Mexicans of varying legal status—including American-born citizens of Mexican descent—to contemplate leaving."

Hundreds of Mexicans at a Los Angeles Train Station Awaiting Deportation

Figure 4.1 provides an important vantage point of a highly disruptive period of United States history for Mexican Americans. This dizzying image captures hundreds of ethnic Mexicans—many of whom were American Citizens—in a train station in Los Angeles preparing to be deported to Mexico. Due to the high levels of unemployment and economic uncertainty stemming from the Great Depression, ethnic Mexicans were roundly blamed as a major reason for these dire circumstances. The question must be asked, why were Mexicans targeted and viewed as scapegoats for the Great Depression? Historian Vicki L. Ruiz offers her insights: "Mexicans were the only immigrants targeted for removal. Proximity to the Mexican border, the physical distinctiveness of mestizos, and easily identifiable barrios influenced immigration and social welfare officials to focus their efforts solely on the Mexican people. People whom they viewed as both foreign usurpers of American jobs and as unworthy burdens on the relief rolls."[1] Without the historical context, this image might be viewed as just another day at the station; regular folks standing in line waiting for their train. However, what this image proves to be is another critical example of how dangerous and erroneous notions of race are used to label certain groups in the United States as unworthy, and un-American. Those notions in turn have devastating consequences.

THINGS TO LOOK FOR AS YOU VIEW THE IMAGE

- The number of people in the image
- The body language of the people in the image
- How the people are dressed

---

1 Vicki L. Ruiz, *From Out of the Shadows: Mexican Women in Twentieth-Century America* (New York, NY.: Oxford University Press, 2008), 29.

Figure 4.1 Hundreds of Mexicans at a Los Angeles Train Station Awaiting Deportation

Source: https://commons.wikimedia.org/wiki/File:Hundreds_of_Mexicans_at_a_Los_Angeles_train_station_awaiting_deportation.jpg.

End-of-Chapter Critical Thinking Questions

Directions: Respond to each of the questions about the readings and the image. Refer to these sources to support your answers.

- How can we learn about the racialization process by examining public health?
- Describe the major circumstances of Mexican repatriation/forced deportation during the 1930s.
- Explain why it is so important to have these particular circumstances of United States history taught in public schools.

Further Readings

Balderrama, Francisco E., and Raymond Rodriguez. *Decade of Betrayal: Mexican Repatriation in the 1930s*. Rev. ed. Albuquerque, NM.: University of New Mexico Press, 2006.

Enciso, Fernando Saúl Alanís, Russ Davidson, and Mark Overmyer-Velázquez. *They Should Stay There: The Story of Mexican Migration and Repatriation during the Great Depression*. Chapel Hill, NC.: University of North Carolina Press, 2017.

Gates Jr., Henry Louis, and Gene Andrew Jarrett. *The New Negro: Readings on Race, Representation, and African American Culture, 1892–1938*. Princeton, N.J.: Princeton University Press, 2007.

García, Mario T. *Desert Immigrants: The Mexicans of El Paso, 1880–1920*. New Haven, CT.: Yale University Press, 1981.

Garza, Melita M. *They Came to Toil: Newspaper Representations of Mexicans and Immigrants in the Great Depression*. Austin, TX.: University of Texas Press, 2018.

Katznelson, Ira. *Fear Itself: The New Deal and the Origins of Our Time*. New York, NY.: Liveright Publishing Corporation, 2013.

Kelley, Robin D.G. *Hammer and Hoe: Alabama Communists During the Great Depression*. 25th Anniversary ed. Chapel Hill, NC.: The University of North Carolina Press, 2015.

McKay, Claude. *Home to Harlem*. Chatham, NJ.: Chatham Bookseller, 1973.

Molina, Natalia. *Fit to Be Citizens?: Public Health and Race in Los Angeles, 1879–1939*. Berkeley, CA.: University of California Press, 2006.

Ngai, Mae. *Impossible Subjects: Illegal Aliens and the Making of Modern America*. Princeton, NJ.: Princeton University Press, 2004.

Sanchez, George J., *Becoming Mexican American: Ethnicity, Culture and Identity in Chicano Los Angeles, 1900–1945*. New York, NY.: Oxford University Press, 1993.

Weber, Devra. *Dark Sweat, White Gold: California Farm Workers, Cotton, and the New Deal*. Berkeley, CA.: University of California Press, 1994.

CHAPTER 5

Mexican Americans and WWII

....

Editor's Introduction[1]

International circumstances in the decade following the 1930s propelled the United States into a global military conflict that would irrevocably transform the nation and the world on a scale hardly imagined before. The domestic mobilization in response to conditions in Europe, the Pacific, and Africa reshaped the economic and social landscape of the United States. The remaking of the economy was multifaceted, spurred specifically by the federal government and private enterprise. Investments in the military, particularly on the West Coast, resulted in one of the nation's largest internal migrations in history. African Americans from the South and Mexican Americans from the Southwest flocked to the West Coast to fill military jobs and drastically changed the social and ethnic make-up of the region.

The years leading up to the war also marked a period of expanded governmental programs and policies designed to improve a faltering economy and develop modern social welfare policies. The United States federal government sought to take a more active role in the economic and social realms of the country by creating jobs and offering assistance. Yet, many of the radical programs of this period failed to realize their objectives and often excluded its most vulnerable citizens from meaningful employment and federal benefits. While World War II is often referred to as the "Last Good War," the events surrounding it highlight both the obvious and subtle contradictions of United States democracy and inconsistent notions of citizenship.

The combination of primary and secondary sources included in this chapter deal with the themes of civil liberties, war time directives, notions of citizenship, and labor rights. It is evident that even in moments when people are deemed legal citizens by every measure of the law, economic, social, and political factors can still

---

1 A version of this introduction appears in "The Great Wall of Los Angeles," *Judy Baca, SPARC and A Chicana Mural Movement: Reconstructing U.S. History Through Public Art*, by Juan Pablo Mercado (Ph.D. diss., University of California, LA, 2018).

render certain peoples as non-citizens. During World War II close to one million African Americans enlisted in the armed forces yet could not use the same bathroom as white soldiers—they served in a Jim Crow military. Many Mexican Americans, who served courageously and died for the United States, were denied proper burials at home because it could have "offended" white patrons. Japanese Americans were "evacuated" from their homes, stripped of their property, forced into internment camps, and unjustly denied their lawful citizenship rights.[2] All of the sources in Chapter Five serve to complicate the perception of World War II as the "Last Good War."

Eulogio V. Frausto

This is a photo of Eulogio V. Frausto, a young Mexican American G.I. who entered the American Armed forces exactly one month after the bombing of Pearl Harbor. In this photo you begin to sense some of the pride and willingness that young enlisted Mexican American men felt to be part of the war effort. Many understood this as an obligation to help defend the United States but also wanted to be part of a broader world-wide struggle to combat fascism. There were, however, several important reasons why Mexican Americans were so involved in the war effort. Many of the Mexican communities in the Southwest tended to have large populations of draft-age Mexican American males. Most of these young men did not have jobs that were considered essential to the war effort, thus making them eligible for the draft. When World War II started there were approximately 2.7 million Mexicans living in the United States; around one-third of these were draft age males, and estimates show that close to half a million Mexican Americans served in the armed forces.[3] For those men who were living in the United States without proper residency documents, they were "encouraged" to enlist by legislation that promised citizenship in exchange for military service.[4] Because Mexican Americans generally did not have the opportunity for economic mobility that most Anglos had, the military provided them with this chance for upward movement. World War II also presented Mexican Americans with an apparent opportunity to gain social and cultural acceptance from the country. In the minds of many it was a way to assert—through

2 Ronald Takaki, *A Different Mirror: A History of Multicultural America* (Boston, New York, and London: Back Bay Books/Little, Brown and Company, 2008); Carlos Sandoval, *American Experience: A Class Apart* [DVD] (PBS, 2009); Mae M. Ngai, *Impossible Subjects: Illegal Aliens and the Making of Modern America* (Princeton, NJ.: Princeton University Press, 2005).
3 Rodolfo 'Rudy" Acuña, *Occupied America: A History of Chicanos*, 2nd ed. (New York, NY.: Harper & Row, 1981), 323.
4 Matt S. Meier and Feliciano Ribera, *Mexican Americans/American Mexicans: From Conquistadors to Chicanos* (New York, NY.: Hill and Wang, 1993), 160.

soldiering—that they were in fact American.[5] This image can serve as an important reminder of the service and opportunities realized by hundreds of thousands of young Mexican American soldiers.

ENTERED AMERICAN FORCES JAN. 7, 1942
MAY GOD SEE THAT HE RETURN AFTER PERFORMING
HIS DUTY

THINGS TO LOOK FOR AS YOU VIEW THE IMAGE...................................

- The body language of the soldier
- The significance of the two flags behind the soldier
- The inscription at the bottom of the photo

---

5 A version of this discussion appears in Juan Pablo Mercado, "Re-envisioning the Mexican American Experience in World War II: A Local History of Sacramento & the Mexican American WWII Generation" (2011). *Master's Projects* 192, 39–40.

Figure 5.1 Eulogio V. Frausto

LULAC Editorial, "World War II and Mexican Americans"

Roughly 500,000 Mexican American men served in the armed forces during World War II. They displayed valor and courage in the face of uncertain circumstances and proved capable of their task. Twelve Mexican American soldiers earned the Congressional Medal of Honor, the highest percentage of any ethnic group fighting in the war. Yet upon their return home they were routinely discriminated against and subjugated into a role of second-class citizenship. This editorial, which expressed the resentment and frustration to those circumstances, was published by the League of United Latin American Citizens (LULAC), an advocacy group that sought assimilation into American society.

THINGS TO LOOK FOR AS YOU READ..

- Historical context
- Notions of patriotism
- The impact of whiteness

LULAC Editorial

"World War II and Mexican Americans"

" We do not serve Mexicans here." "You will have to get out as no Mexicans are allowed." "Your uniform and service ribbons mean nothing here. We still do not allow Mexicans."

These, and many other stronger-worded ones, are the embarrassing and humiliating retorts given our returning veterans of Latin American descent and their families. They may be worded differently, and whereas some are toned with hate and loathness while others are toned with sympathy and remorse, still the implication remains that these so-called "Mexicans" are considered unworthy of equality, regardless of birthright or service. This situation is ironic indeed, in view of the fact that these same "Mexicans" have just finished helping this country to defeat countries to the east and west who would impose upon the world a superior people, a superior culture.

Why this hate, this prejudice, this tendency to discriminate against a people whose only fault seems to be that they are heirs of a culture older than any known "American Culture," to find themselves a part of a land and people they have helped to build and to defend, to find themselves a part of a minority group whose acquired passive nature keeps them boldly demanding those rights and privileges which are rightfully theirs? Can it be the result of difference in race, nationality, language, loyalty, intelligence or ability?

There is no difference in race. Latin Americans, or so-called "Mexicans," are Caucasian or white. There are only three races: the Caucasian, the Negroid, and the Mongoloid. Racial characteristics placed the Latin American among the white. Who dares contradict nature? There is no difference in nationality. These "Mexicans" were born and bred in this country and are just as American as Jones or Smith. In fact, the ancestors of these "Mexicans" were here before those of Jones or Smith decided to take up abode. Difference in language? No. These "Mexicans" speak English. Accented, perhaps, in some cases, but English all over the United States seems to be accented. That these "Mexicans" can speak Spanish is not a detriment, it is an asset. After all there are not too many people in this country who can boast a knowledge of the most widely spoken languages in the world. Difference in loyalty? How can that be when all revere the same stars and stripes, when they don the same service uniforms for the same principles? Difference in intelligence and ability? Impossible ...

We could go on and on naming erroneously imagined differences to be used as a basis for this hate and find each one false. This condition is not a case of difference; it is a case of ignorance. Yes, ignorance. Odd indeed to find this banal state of mind in a country of such enlightenment and progress. But then, ignorance is like a disease that is contagious, but contagious only for those who wish to suffer from it. Ignorance, bigotry, prejudice, an intolerance all down through the centuries have tried to crush intelligence with cruelty, reason with brutality, and spirituality with madness. This quartet of banalities constitutes the curse of the world. Ignorance is the parent of the other three.

Yes, ignorant broods hate and all its resultant actions of jealousy, misunderstandings, erroneous opinions, and premeditated feelings of discord and confusion. In this particular case of unjustified failure to foment a fraternal feeling between two groups of Americans, it is an ignorance of facts that poisons the atmosphere. And ignorance of the cultural contributions of Americans of Latin American descent to the still young American culture: an ignorance of the blood, sweat, and efforts given to this country for its betterment; an ignorance of the sufferings withstood and the lives given to preserve this country free and independent through its various periods of strife and conflict; and finally, an ignorance of a sense of appreciation for a long, profitable, and loyal association with a group of Americans whose voice cries out in desperate supplication:

> We have proved ourselves true and loyal Americans by every
> trial and test that has confronted us; now give us social,
> political, and economic equality and the opportunity to
> practice and enjoy that equality. We ask for it not as a favor,
> but as a delegated right guaranteed by our Constitution, and
> as a reward for faithful service.

Source: LULAC, editorial, "World War II and Mexican Americans," LULAC News, Vol. 12, October 1945, pp. 5–6.

- -

READING 5.1   POST-READING COMPREHENSION QUESTIONS

- Summarize the conditions that Mexican American veterans were facing.

- Describe the arguments LULAC used to challenge those conditions.

- Paraphrase the quote: "These 'Mexicans' were born and bred in this country and are just as American as Jones or Smith. In fact, the ancestors of these 'Mexicans' were here before those of Jones or Smith decided to take abode."

Guest Worker Programs

The brief essay titled "Guest Worker Programs" focuses on the recruited labor of Mexicans in the United States during World War II and for some twenty years afterwards. The essay details the circumstances of the purported labor shortage during the war period, but also goes on to assess the coercive labor conditions that allowed for this bi-national agreement to continue until well after the end of the war.

THINGS TO LOOK FOR AS YOU READ

- Definition of the American working class
- The connection between race and labor
- The idea of disposability

Guest Worker Programs

Juan Pablo Mercado and Alvaro Huerta

G uest worker programs in the United States continue to be highly debated components of "comprehensive immigration reform." Contemporary anxieties resulting from Mexican immigration to the United States have a distinct historical footing in the 1940s when a steady stream of temporary Mexican workers arrived, mainly in the Southwest United States, as part of an institutionalized guest worker program. The U.S.–Mexico Bracero Program (*brazo* is the Spanish word for arm and the term *bracero* usually refers to a manual laborer) established a fluid network of people and jobs throughout the Southwest. This flow of people, spurred by a putative wartime labor shortage, resulted in the largest guest worker program of its time, encompassing close to 4.5 million workers. Briefly examining the initial period of the Bracero Program in California contextualizes the trajectory of contemporary guest worker programs in the United States. Surveying the Bracero Program also reveals the extent to which people of Mexican origin, working and living in the United States, are not included in conventional notions of the American working class. Moreover, guest worker programs extend ideas about a cheap, controllable, and disposable labor force that underscore the inequalities of the U.S. labor sector.

During World War II, many Mexican Americans pledged their loyalty to the United States by serving in the military and contributing to the victory of the allied forces; however, just as important to this effort was the manual labor provided by Mexican contract workers on the home front. Braceros played an essential part in filling the labor need in railroad and canning and food-packing industries, but their efforts were mostly utilized in the agricultural sector. Mexican workers were eager and willing to help out in the war effort and proved to be indispensable at their jobs.

Juan Pablo Mercado and Alvaro Huerta, "Guest Worker Programs," *People of Color in the United States: Contemporary Issues in Education, Work, Communities, Health, and Immigration,* vol. 4: Immigration and Migration, ed. Kofi Lomotey, et al., pp. 156-161. Copyright © 2016 by ABC-CLIO. Reprinted with permission.

Figures 5.2.1 A seasonal guest worker hauls flats of strawberries to a field truck during the harvest at Patterson Farm in China Grove, North Carolina. Historically, guest worker programs in the United States, such as the Bracero Program between the United States and Mexico during the mid-1900s, have exploited immigrant laborers for the benefit of U.S. businesses and consumers. (Davis Turner/MCT via Getty Images)

Mexico also gained financially in the form of remittances sent back by these workers. However, the experiences of the braceros were also filled with racism, discrimination, exploitation, and manipulation mostly at the hands of misguided politicians, corrupt businessmen, and unscrupulous farmers.

With half a million Mexicans Americans serving in the armed forces, braceros served in a different capacity; it was their labor that played a crucial part in helping the United States to victory. The Bracero Program began in 1942 and ended 22 years later in 1964. The initial period of the program that encompassed World War II lasted from the summer of 1942 to the winter of 1945, Although this period was significant with respect to the American war effort, it was rather small in scale and only imported fewer than a quarter of a million Mexican laborers during this period. Relatively speaking, the number was small considering that almost 4.5 million Mexicans were recruited during the span of the program.

According to scholar-activist Ernesto Galarza, the prevailing sentiment among growers was that the Mexican laborers would make up a versatile labor force that could be easily moved to many different locations in cases where local labor needs fell short and crop production would be threatened. The Mexican workers would serve as "shock troops" used only in cases of emergencies as protection against the loss of valuable crop production. Yet, because the case for a "real emergency" could be made almost endlessly in California's harvests, the advantages of a cheap, controllable, and surplus labor force were obvious. While what constituted a real emergency was almost boundless, what was clear was that braceros filled an important role in the wartime economy and were seen as an economic boon by California's agribusiness. Flexibility and controlled mobility amounted to the best kind of crop insurance, and contract laborers were in fact the answer to many of the commercial farmers' needs.

The burden of World War II proved to be especially significant in California due to its vital agricultural sector—yet, domestic war policy disrupted a key segment of agricultural production in 1942. The United States required food for its troops, food for domestic consumption, and provisions for its allies. This meant that maximum farm production was essential to the war effort. However, in 1942, President Franklin D. Roosevelt signed Executive Order 9066 and authorized the forced displacement and relocation of all Japanese Americans in the United States. The manner in which American citizens of Japanese descent were dehumanized by the United States underscores the central relationship between race and civil rights. Japanese Americans were "evacuated" from their homes, stripped of their property, forced into internment camps, and unjustly denied their lawful citizenship rights due to unfounded racial and political anxieties. This had two major repercussions for the agricultural sector: first, the removing of Japanese field workers; and second, the displacement of Japanese farm families whose labor contributed significantly to the agriculture industry. As the Japanese immigrants and Japanese Americans were abruptly removed and forced into internment camps all throughout the Southwest, the farm labor shortage intensified.

Originally, Mexico was not enthusiastic about sending its young men to the United States as laborers. However, as U.S. authorities continued to pressure Mexico, they eventually conceded. The two governments entered into a preliminary agreement in 1942. Dubbed the Emergency Labor Program, this agreement would oversee the recruitment of braceros. However, there were still fresh memories in Mexico surrounding the repatriation, or mass expulsion, of both Mexican and American citizens to Mexico during the Great Depression. The implications of this economic collapse led to a sizable displacement of agricultural labor, and although the Great Depression affected everyone, it presented particular challenges to Mexican immigrants and Mexican Americans who were situated in a subordinate position in the economy. Compounding the problem of the economic depression was a prevailing notion that by removing immigrant workers and replacing them with Anglo workers the nation would resolve its economic problems. This was an especially contradictory notion considering that the United States had actively recruited Mexican workers only a few years before the Depression and subsequently was attempting to remove the wrongfully branded "scapegoat" labor force. It was understandable why the Mexican government proceeded with caution when entering into such an agreement with the United States. However, after a series of negotiations both countries crafted an agreement that would be mutually satisfying.

Mexico and the United States agreed to a contract that would "ensure" the rights of all the contract laborers. The major points of the agreement stipulated that Mexican workers would not displace domestic workers. They would also be exempt from military service, Also, the contract included detailed regulations regarding transportation, housing, and wages for the braceros. Yet, most important, the negotiations stipulated that discrimination in all forms would not be tolerated. It took almost a year of negotiations, but, in 1943, the U.S. Congress approved Public Law 45. This law propelled the federal government to the role of labor contractor and started the "administered migration" of Mexican laborers into the American Southwest.

In Northern California, braceros were received with enthusiasm. Festivals were organized with bands, parades, and big public gatherings. Mexican national holidays were celebrated with free barbeques at the expense of the local growers and citizens. In Sacramento, California, the Spreckels Sugar Company along with several of the local growers, all joined up to sponsor a celebration for the Mexican workers. Local Mexican Americans were hired to recruit female dancers and singers to provide entertainment for the farm workers. The braceros enjoyed food, music, and dancing—all in the hopes of building good will between the Sugar Company, the local farmers, and the braceros.

The good will and the embracing of braceros were clearly linked to the enthusiasm of large commercial farmers to manipulate the conditions of the guest worker program. A central reason why these large farmers pushed for imported contract labor was control. Braceros were not able to negotiate their wages or working conditions. They were also not able to select what employer they wanted to work for. Moreover, they were not able to quit their contracts. Despite the goodwill, however, incidents of rampant discrimination on the part of Anglo farm owners highlighted the belief that Mexican workers were inherently unskilled, inferior, and not deserving of equal legal or civil protections as workers in the United States. Because of widespread notions of inferiority coupled with unfair working conditions, it did not take long before braceros became highly sought-after in many farming jobs, becoming the backbone of the agricultural labor force in the Southwest.

The Bracero Program—which sought to address the temporary labor shortage of World War II—lasted over two decades and reflected explicit notions of racial inferiority commonplace to the U.S. labor force. Because Mexican workers did not have the same labor rights as American workers, it became more evident that the Bracero Program was part of a larger process of racialization and coercive working conditions taking place in the United States. Historian Natalia Molina notes that in the 1940s the term "wetback" grew more common in the United States in connection to the Bracero Program. As this term became more popular in usage, it served to group all people of Mexican descent together and fostered an impression of lawbreakers, seeking to criminalize all Mexicans. In this context, the racialization process refers to the way that both Mexican Americans and braceros were subject to prejudicial assumptions and harsh working conditions based on their status as nonwhite people living and working in the United States.

For instance, in Northern California local business and citizen groups often met to discuss the farm labor shortage throughout the region. Yet, they discussed the circumstances in very racialized terms. Essentially, the local farmers were concerned with ways to "recruit" Mexicans as farm laborers with the assistance of the local law enforcement. The local community worked alongside local law enforcement to impose so-called "greaser laws." These were usually some sort of vagrancy or loitering ordinances that were arbitrarily enforced and aimed at targeting Mexican men for petty misdemeanors. The strategy consisted of taking men into the custody of local law enforcement, issuing a large fine for the alleged infraction, and then parceling the men out as convict labor. These men were explicitly used as a controllable labor force in the agricultural sector. From a *Sacramento Bee* report highlighting this process and praising the manner in which farm laborers were being sought to fill labor shortages, the following excerpt was taken:

> The committee, under the chairmanship of Roy C. Donnally, man-
> ager of the United States Employment Service office in Sacramento,
> agreed wonderful strides so far have been made by various branches
> of the law enforcement agencies in making men available for farm
> labor. Donnally said the committee generally felt the perseverance
> of the local agencies in cleaning up the west end of the city will go
> a long way in helping the labor shortage. (*Sacramento Bee,* June
> 11, 1942)

Not surprisingly, the west end of the city consisted of a majority Mexican population. This was an example of harassment and entrapment by local businessmen and local law enforcement officials to secure a cheap and disposable labor force. These common practices of racialization and manipulation of workers, when understood in tandem with the Bracero Program, reveal a broad based and systematic process of regulating Mexicans for the purpose of social and economic control.

There is no doubt that U.S. employers coveted Mexican contract laborers during the Bracero Program. There is also no doubt that discrimination of these workers was essential for maintaining economic and social control. Contract labor was the desired mechanism to suppress wages, maintain poor working conditions, and limit mobility to a subjugated labor force: *braceros.* The history of the Bracero Program demonstrates how workers had no legal standing in the society in which they worked; moreover, so-called "greaser laws" furthered the criminalization and racialization of American workers of Mexican descent. Guest worker programs can have many positive results for employers and, to a limited extent, workers; however, it is critical to understand the historical circumstances of these programs and ensure that past injustices are not repeated in contemporary immigration policies.

Juan Pablo Mercado

See also: Immigration Reform; and see section on Perspectives and Debate: Should the U.S. Congress Adopt a Guest Worker Program?

Further Reading

Acuña, Rodolfo. 1981. *Occupied America: A History of Chicanos,* 2nd ed. New York: Harper & Row.

Barrera, Mario. 1979. *Race and Class in the Southwest: A Theory of Racial Inequality.* Notre Dame and London: University of Notre Dame Press.

Calavita, Kitty. 1992. *Inside the State: The Bracero Program, Immigration, and the INS.* New York: Routledge.

Galarza, Ernesto. 1964, *Merchants of Labor: The Mexican Bracero Story.* San Jose; The Rosicrucian Press.

Gõmez-Quiñones. 1994. *Mexican American Labor, 1790–1990.* Albuquerque: University of New Mexico Press.

Lorey, David E. 1999. *The U.S.-Mexican Border in the Twentieth Century: A History of Economic and Social Transformation.* Wilmington: Scholarly Resources Inc.

Meier, Matt, and Feliciano Rivera. 1993. *Mexican Americans/American Mexicans: From Conquistadors to Chicanos. New* York: Hill and Wang.

Molina, Natalia. 2014. *How Race Is Made in America: Immigration, Citizenship, and the Historical Power of Racial Scripts.* Berkeley and Los Angeles: University of California Press.

Ngai, Mae M. 2004. *Impossible Subjects: Illegal Aliens and the Making of Modern America*. Princeton and Oxford: Princeton University Press. Reading 5.1 Post-Reading Comprehension Questions

READING 5.2   POST-READING COMPREHENSION QUESTIONS

- Summarize the main arguments in this short interrogation of the Bracero Program.

- Describe why this program lasted as long as it did, 1942–1964.

- Paraphrase the quote: "… [T]he perseverance of the local agencies in cleaning up the west end of the city will go a long way in helping the labor shortage."

The Pachuca Panic

World War II provided a very important opportunity for women across the country and women of color, in particular were pushed into the wartime economy. Many Mexican American women experienced increasingly changing attitudes toward their traditional role in society and at home. The focus of Elizabeth Escobedo's noteworthy chapter on Mexican American women during the World War II period demonstrates how "[t]he controversial 'pachuca' figure represents one of the best examples of second-generation daughters becoming both a part and a symbol of shifting gender and racial ideologies on the World War II home front."[1]

THINGS TO LOOK FOR AS YOU READ...

- Pachuca identity
- Media representation
- Notions of citizenship

---

1 Elizabeth R. Escobedo, *From Coveralls to Zoot Suits* (Chapel Hill, NC.: University of North Carolina Press, 2013), 9.

The Pachuca Panic

Elizabeth R. Escobedo

O n 9 June 1943, twenty-two-year-old Amelia Venegas left her East Los Angeles home, baby in arms, to buy milk at a local market. Concerned by news of recent skirmishes between Euro-American servicemen and Mexican American zoot suiters on city streets, the young mother impulsively grabbed a pair of brass knuckles she had found months earlier on a local sidewalk. With wartime emotions at heightened levels, a woman left alone while her navy husband fought overseas could never be too careful.

Yet for all of her precautions, trouble would soon befall Mrs. Venegas. As she and her baby witnessed police officers harassing a group of zoot suiters, Venegas felt a sense of injustice rise within her. Unable to contain her emotions, the Mexican American woman cursed the law enforcement officials for their hostile treatment of the young men. "They should leave the zoot suiters alone," Venegas later explained vehemently to reporters. Unmoved by her verbal denunciations, the officers immediately arrested Venegas for disturbing the peace and, upon finding the brass knuckles on her person, charged the young mother for carrying a concealed weapon.[1]

As newspapers got wind of the story, the Venegas incident seemed to confirm the then widely held belief that a Mexican American gang menace was overtaking Los Angeles. Venegas appeared never to have before been in trouble with the law, and yet the *Los Angeles Times* featured a photograph of her baring her teeth and shaking a threatening fist at the camera. Not only did the press deem Venegas a "pachuco" girl—a label suggesting gang affiliation—but her protests on behalf of zoot suiters—a much despised youth population—also made her a perfect target for a sensationalist media campaign.[2]

Elizabeth R. Escobedo, "The Pachuca Panic," *From Coveralls to Zoot Suits: The Lives of Mexican American Women on the World War II Home Front,* pp. 17-44, 159-166. Copyright © 2015 by University of North Carolina Press. Reprinted with permission.

Although a public relations nightmare for the young mother, the experience of Amelia Venegas illuminates much more than just an example of the press's sensationalist depictions of Mexican youths as dangerous wartime hoodlums. The Venegas story also sheds light on the changes taking place in the lives of Mexican American women in Los Angeles during World War II. Not simply victims of a press hungry for scandal, many second-generation Mexican American women did in fact adopt a new youth subculture that rejected aspects of both traditional Mexican and mainstream American culture. Known both as female "zoot suiters" and "pachucas," these young women blatantly rebelled against social conventions. They not only donned the controversial zoot suit, or a modification of the attire, but often kept company with fellow zoot-clad youth on city streets.[3]

More than just a fashion rebel, the wartime pachuca represented an important symbolic site on which debates regarding the changing social landscape of the war years unfolded. Using style and behavior as a way to challenge ideas of respectability and to assert a distinctive identity, pachucas defied mainstream notions of proper feminine decorum as well as static, traditional definitions of Mexican femininity. As women's social roles broadened more generally, and the Mexican family struggled to maintain a hold on its daughters, the pachuca came to represent a female figure whose dangerous sexuality demanded restraint.

All the more dangerous was how pachucas seemingly mixed their blatant sexuality with a politicized identity of Mexican American womanhood. Pachucas not only embraced a persona that celebrated cultural difference, but many of the young women also felt no qualms in expressing discontent with their second-class citizenship. In struggling with the question of how to occupy both their neighborhood and their nation, pachucas often rejected the wartime vision of Americans of all races and creeds embracing a single, common culture. Rather, the young women created an affirming identity that accentuated their status as racialized outsiders.

The struggles over the meaning of the pachuca often took place in the courts, where reformers and Mexican parents tried to make sense of what they found to be a troublesome, delinquent personality. Utilizing oral interviews and over 250 Los Angeles County Superior Court Juvenile Division case files of Mexican American women (excluding dependency cases) between the years 1939 and 1945, this chapter explores the communal, familial, and individual dilemmas created by the emergence of the wartime pachuca.[4] Immigrant parents blamed Americanization for their daughters' experimentations with zoot culture; reformers conceptualized the pachuca "problem" as a cultural pathology, a condition intrinsic to distinctive Mexican family patterns. At stake were the reformers' larger project of cultural assimilation and the ability of the Mexican community to improve its image in U.S. society. Pachucas threatened both visions.

Over time, the notorious pachuca persona came to reveal the contradictions of the wartime environment, embodying both the new social opportunities available to young Mexican American women and a stigma in terms of female reputation and community status. On the one hand, pachucas posed a significant challenge to both their second-class citizenship in U.S. society and the patriarchal attitudes that defined the Mexican family and community. Yet, because of their perceived—and, at times, very real—association with juvenile delinquency and gang activity, the pachuca label also eventually came to identify any Mexican American woman who, like Amelia Venegas, seemingly defied social norms. In an effort to keep the gender and racial status quo in check, the Los Angeles populace—Euro-American and Mexican alike—embarked on a campaign to contain and stigmatize the young second-generation women who flew in the face of convention and adopted aspects of the defiant public persona.

Prior to the summer of 1942, the L.A. populace relatively ignored Mexican American women who adorned zoot suits, instead focusing almost entirely on their male counterparts. Mexican American men who adopted the zoot style—or "drapes," as the attire was often called in Los Angeles barrios—typically wore a fingertip jacket; trousers with wide knees that tapered at the ankle; heavy, thick-soled shoes; and hair in a duck-tail cut.[5] Although it is difficult to pinpoint the exact origins of the apparel, according to historian Eduardo Pagán, the zoot suit most likely originated among African American jazz artists and aficionados of the late 1930s, who no doubt increased the popularity of the style in the cities they toured. Indeed, Mexican American youths in Los Angeles gravitated with enthusiasm toward swing jazz during the war years, and thus it is not altogether surprising that the clothing and dance styles once associated with black urban subculture became just as popular among similarly marginalized populations.[6]

The zoot suit represented a spectacular style that was at once fashionable and defiant. Amid patriotic appeals for conformity and austerity, the conspicuous clothing came to signify the second generation's dissatisfaction with the hardship and segregation that defined their daily lives.[7] Although young Mexican Americans had begun experimenting with mass consumer culture in the 1920s and 1930s, it was not unusual for blacks and Mexicans to have restricted access to recreational facilities, including public parks and swimming pools, movie theaters, and restaurants, particularly in working-class Los Angeles neighborhoods with large nonwhite populations.[8] But the greater job mobility and better wages made possible by the Second World War afforded the second-generation both the motivation and the opportunity to challenge their relegation to the social periphery. With more money in their pockets, and a desire for recognition, Mexican American

Figures 5.3.1 A Mexican American youth in a zoot suit, 1944. Los Angeles Public Library Photo Collection.

youths increasingly ventured outside of their communities to frequent public spaces on the streets and in the dance halls, all-night cafeterias, and nightclubs of downtown Los Angeles, often dressed to the nines in zoot attire.[9]

As assertive, zoot-clad youth challenged segregation conspicuously and in greater number, city officials and law enforcement increasingly identified their dress and behavior as evidence of criminal tendencies. In cities nationwide, wartime rates of juvenile delinquency escalated among teenagers of all backgrounds—a phenomenon largely attributed to the recruitment of parents and older siblings into war work and the armed services, conditions that made it increasingly difficult to monitor the behavior of the nation's youth.[10] But in the diverse, urban metropolis of Los Angeles, authorities frequently cast the growing crisis of juvenile delinquency as an attendant "race problem," warning of a Mexican American gang crime wave taking over the city.[11]

Launching an all-out "war on crime," the Los Angeles Police Department (LAPD) engaged systematically in selective law enforcement during the World War II era, heavily patrolling Mexican neighborhoods and pursuing curfew and vagrancy violations in barrios with more vigor than in white sections of the city. Consequently, wartime arrest rates of Mexican American youths in Los Angeles swelled. As historian Ed Escobar notes, however, only small fractions of these arrests ever resulted in actual criminal prosecutions. Rather than documenting any notable increases in criminality among Mexican Americans, the high number of arrests bespeak the LAPD's adoption of more stringent police control mechanisms against youths of color.[12]

By August of 1942, the Los Angeles populace began to recognize young Mexican American *women* as an integral element of the gang menace allegedly plaguing city streets. After a young Mexican man named José Díaz was found dead near a Los Angeles water pit popularly known as the Sleepy Lagoon, police rounded up hundreds of second-generation youths of Mexican descent in connection with the now-infamous case. Despite a glaring lack of evidence, twenty-two young men connected with an L.A. neighborhood known as Thirty-eighth Street—all but one of Mexican ancestry—were arrested, charged with murder and assault, and tried. After months of court proceedings plagued by bigotry, the so-called zoot suit murder case came to an end with seventeen of the defendants convicted of charges varying from murder in the first degree to assault.[13] Two years later, after tireless efforts by the Sleepy Lagoon Defense Committee (SLDC)—a diverse coalition of Mexican Americans, progressive whites, Jews, and African Americans—the defendants won acquittal upon appeal.[14] In the meantime, however, the case helped solidify the connection between delinquency and Mexican American youth.

During the initial round up of suspects in the murder of Díaz, law enforcement officials investigated ten young women, ranging in age from thirteen to twenty-one years old, most of whom bore Spanish surnames.[15] This presence and involvement of young women of color in the scandal provided one of the biggest shocks to the wartime populace. As the *Los Angeles Evening Herald and Express* stated, "Particularly disturbing in one of the new outbreaks was the participation of several girls. It was hoped that the prevalent delinquency might be confined to the boys who stand accused."[16] To readers, the notion of youthful Mexican American women participating in street life alongside male counterparts likely suggested a flagrant violation of conventional gender expectations that equated respectable femininity with submissiveness and domesticity.

The treatment of the young women involved in the Sleepy Lagoon case illuminates the extent to which law enforcement officials perceived Mexican girl gang activity to be a danger to wartime Los Angeles. Initially, police booked three of the women from Thirty-eighth Street—Frances Silva, Dora Barrios, and Lorena Encinas—on suspicion of murder, holding them in the county jail in connection with the L.A. County grand jury's investigation.[17] Although these particular charges were later dropped, all of the young women undergoing investigation were eventually held as material witnesses for the prosecution's case against the young men and/or had their cases turned over to the juvenile court for disposition. Those called upon to testify declined to answer the prosecution's questions, refusing to implicate their companions. Court authorities and the press, however, simply rendered the girls' lack of cooperation as evidence of a well-organized gang mind-set.[18] Even when the court failed to find any of the young women guilty of involvement in the Díaz murder, authorities refused to let the girls' disreputable behavior go unpunished. The Los Angeles Juvenile Court charged eight young women—Bertha Aguilar, Dora Barrios, Lorena Encinas, Josephine Gonzáles, Juanita Gonzáles, Frances Silva, Lupe Ynostroza, and Betty Nuñez Zeiss—with the crime of rioting, declaring the girls wards of the state under the Department of Institutions.[19]

Most of the young women involved in the Sleepy Lagoon case eventually found themselves sentenced to placement at the Ventura School for Girls,[20] a California correctional facility, infamous at the time for its draconian discipline. The reformatory, whose picturesque location and academic name masked a repressive atmosphere, typically housed girls with long histories of delinquency, sexual promiscuity, and unsatisfactory stays at other reform institutions. These young women were on average paroled from the Ventura School after stays of sixteen months, but they remained wards of the California Youth Authority until they reached twenty-one years of age.[21]

Prior to the fateful night at Sleepy Lagoon, the term "pachuca" had not yet entered the lexicon of judicial discourse at the Juvenile Division of the Los Angeles County Superior Court. Juvenile court case files of Mexican American women living in Los Angeles between the years 1939 and 1945 reveal that not until immediately after L.A.

Figures 5.3.2 Dora Barrios, Frances Silva, and Lorena Encinas—arrested during the Sleepy Lagoon investigation, 1942. Los Angeles Public Library Photo Collection.

newspapers broke the story of Díaz's death did juvenile authorities pinpoint female zoot suiters as a manifestation of wartime female delinquency. Subsequently, juvenile officials began to use the words "pachuco-type" and "pachuca" to describe a number of young women of Mexican descent brought before the court.[22]

Figures 5.3.3 Young women under investigation for connection with the Sleepy Lagoon case stand in a lineup after the 1942 police dragnet. *Left to right:* Betty Nuñez Zeiss, Ann Kalustian, Frances Silva, unknown, Lorena Encinas, Dora Barrios, Josefina "Josephine" Gonzáles, and Juanita "Jenny" Gonzales. Los Angeles Public Library Photo Collection.

In utilizing the labels "pachuca" and "pachuco-type," juvenile authorities mirrored terminology recently adopted by Los Angeles newspapers and local officials. Originally a term associated with Mexicans involved in vice trafficking in and around El Paso, the word "pachuco" expanded beyond its original meaning amid the anti-Mexican sentiment of the Sleepy Lagoon trial. Major newspapers in Los Angeles began using the term after the Office of War Information (OWI), in an effort to preserve friendly relations between the United States and Mexico, asked editors to cease making specific reference to Mexicans in their coverage of juvenile delinquency. Most agreed to comply, but in searching for nouns alternative to "Mexican," reporters simply substituted labels like "zoot suiter" and "pachuca/o," value-laden terms that continued to conjure up images of criminality specific to Mexicans.[23]

According to legal records and contemporary observers, a pachuca could typically be identified by her controversial clothing, company, and behavior. Young Mexican American women often modified men's zoot attire to consist of a fingertip coat and cardigan or V-neck sweater; a skirt to the knee or above in length, a style that was, for the time, considered relatively short; and bobby socks pulled high toward the knee, with huarache sandals. The style varied from individual to individual, however, as some young women wore their skirts with saddle shoes or platform heels; others preferred wearing pants and thus adorned the zoot suit in its entirety. Many Mexican American women further emphasized their zoot look with dark lipstick, plucked eyebrows, and hair lifted high into a pompadour.[24] One juvenile authority described the "typical pachuco look" of a young Mexican American woman: "neat appearing, but ... with high pompadour, plucked eyebrows, short skirts, black socks. She likes to decorate herself with jewelry and trinkets."[25]

The company a Mexican American woman might keep with zoot suiters, jitterbugging in dance halls or loitering on street corners after dark, also served as identifying characteristics. Most young women labeled "pachucas" by the juvenile court were not charged with crimes committed against others. Rather, authorities brought them before the court because they lacked adequate supervision, roamed neighborhoods, and stayed out late with companions deemed "undesirable"—allegations based largely upon assumptions of pathological, unrestrained sexual behavior. The probation officer of fifteen-year-old Amalia Cervantes recounted such concerns in a 1944 report to the court: "Father stated that minor ... wants to be like a pachuco. ... [She not only] wears heavy, vulgar make-up to school and in her home, [but] is quite impudent and defiant, stays out to 2 and 3 o'clock in the morning, continually necks and pets with boys on her front porch until all hours."[26]

But among the young women themselves, the label "pachuca" often remained a contested term. Many Mexican American women who played with the pachuca look, or associated with zoot-suited teens, did not necessarily self-identify as a pachuca.[27] Irene

Figures 5.3.4 Young Mexican American women in Los Angeles, 1943. Note that the woman on the far left dons aspects of the zoot style, including high pompadour, dark lipstick, V-neck sweater, and high socks. Los Angeles Public Library Photo Collection.

Malagon, a young woman who frequently wore a fingertip jacket and a high pompadour during the 1940s, in later years definitively denied ever being a pachuca because she associated the figure with young women who fought and belonged to gangs. "I couldn't belong to a gang," Malagon stated.[28] Others took great pride in the notorious pachuca persona as a badge of rebellion. According to the case file of thirteen-year-old Isabel Ramos, on more than one occasion the teen told her mother she was "a Pachuco, and w[ould] do as she please[d]."[29]

Court officials were not alone in their disdain for women deemed zoot suiters. In fact, almost nothing proved more disruptive to Mexican families than the pachuca phenomenon. While few immigrant parents looked favorably upon sons who sported zoot attire, the behavior of young women proved especially unnerving. For the Mexican immigrant generation, women occupying the public arena under most circumstances—let alone in questionable attire and with disreputable company—spelled trouble. Mexican parents typically subscribed to a double standard in sexual relations, closely cloistering daughters until marriage, while allowing sons the freedom to do as they pleased. Such strict rules traced back to the Catholic Church and social customs in Mexico, where virginity was highly valued and a family's reputation usually depended on the chastity of its women.[30]

But as the wartime environment created conditions in which familial control over daughters loosened, more and more Mexican American women utilized the zoot attire and persona as a means to experiment with their social and sexual roles and assert new claims to public life. Some used their new status as wartime wage-earners to push for the privilege to socialize with peers outside of the watchful eyes of immigrant parents and to buy the latest fads in cosmetics and zoot suit styles. During the summer of 1942, seventeen-year-old Ida Escobedo started her first job—making incendiary bombs—at a small defense factory in Los Angeles. Entering the workforce in order to earn money for the family while her brothers fought overseas, Escobedo also had dreams of buying a tailor-made fingertip coat and matching skirt. The opportunity arrived when her mother gave her extra money to buy a dress to wear for her high school graduation. Well aware of the fact that her mother "didn't approve of [zoot] clothes or anything about it," she and her sister nevertheless went to a men's clothing store and purchased a "good looking" fingertip coat that she proudly flaunted at her graduation ceremony. "My mother just about died," Escobedo remembered. "She was ashamed of me."[31] By strategically creating a visual display that tested social propriety, those Mexican American women who experimented with zoot clothing and makeup often did so as a way to declare autonomy and claims to public life. Like Escobedo, many second-generation Mexican American women took pride in their zoot appearance and public identity, welcoming the opportunity to be noticed and to assert some element of control over their lives.

Figures 5.3.5 Mexican American and African American youths jitterbug at Club Los Pachucos, a dance hall and youth club begun by Los Angeles civic leaders to help combat juvenile delinquency during the war years, 13 November 1943. The zoot style of the female jitterbugs includes a blouse, sweater, or fingertip coat; a full skirt that falls at or above the knee; and huarache sandals with midcalf bobby socks. © Bettmann/CORBIS.

Other so-called pachucas skirted notions of propriety altogether by entering public life for their own self-interest, completely outside the context of wartime necessity, wage labor, and familial needs. One thirteen-year-old, Alma Galvan, habitually ran away from her father's home in Pasadena and on one occasion spent over a week living hand to mouth, sleeping in cars and on the back porches of houses with other wayward Mexican American girlfriends. Although Alma resorted to drastic measures, her meanderings about the city allowed her, at least until she was picked up by the authorities, the opportunity for autonomy and to engage in her favorite hobby—dancing with " 'pachuco' boys"—without parental interference.[32]

At a time when official rhetoric stressed the importance of wartime sacrifice, the acts of performance and self-indulgence engaged in by women with alleged pachuca tendencies suggested to some a striking disregard for the gravity of war. Some of the young women simply liked to jitterbug in dance halls. Others engaged in fistfights and frequented street corners after dark. Yet no matter how moderate or extreme their behavior, when men left daily to join the fight abroad and news of boys dying overseas dominated the airwaves, the contrast between sacrificing one's life for patriotic ideals and parading the streets in an effort to turn heads and find a late-night thrill grew ever more stark. Consequently, members of both the Mexican population and the Los Angeles general public grew increasingly concerned with the highly visible, public nature of pachuca activities.

Among fellow Mexican American women, the pachuca persona triggered decidedly mixed emotions and responses. Many Mexican American women condemned those who adopted aspects of the pachuca style and/or persona, claiming that the clothing was "stupid" and that those who chose to wear zoot styles meant "trouble" and "were asking for whatever they got."[33] Others admired or empathized with pachucas, recognizing the persistent racial discrimination of the time and insisting that the young women did not deserve the negative attention they received. As Teresa Pallan explained, "To me they were just people who dressed a certain way. ... They weren't violent criminals in my eyes."[34] Noemi Hernández recalled how her mother associated pachucas with "lower-class people," but to Hernández, the short skirts, huarache sandals, and high pompadours worn by pachucas were "just a fad." "I used to like it and I started emulating [them]," Hernández said.[35]

If second-generation Mexican Americans held differing opinions about pachucas, the immigrant generation tended to be more united in their condemnation of the young women. In a story detailing the alleged origins of Mexican youth gangs, *La Opinión*, the Spanish-language daily, bemoaned the scandalous appearance of pachucas, including their so-called painted faces and short skirts. The newspaper also likened the young women to prostitutes, asserting that their male companions served as pimps. And although referring to male zoot suiters as "pachucos," the newspaper deemed their female counterparts "las malinches," a reference to the woman (La Malinche) historically known as the archetype traitor of the Mexican people. According to both history and myth, La Malinche was the Christian Indian woman who aided the Spaniards in their conquest of the Aztecs by serving as a mistress to conquistador Hernán Cortés. The editors of *La Opinion* found this a fitting analogy to describe the wartime pachuca. Like Malinche, the young women publicly betrayed proper female behavior with their supposed sexual laxity, behavior that brought shame to the Mexican people.[36]

Major newspapers in Los Angeles exhibited a similar fixation with the presumed uncontrolled sexuality of second-generation youth. In 1943, for instance, the *Los Angeles Evening Herald and Express*—a Hearst newspaper well known for its lurid reporting—broke an exposé on the alleged promiscuity and delinquency of barrio women. Emphasizing the participation of "sexy-looking" zoot girls in "weird" sexual activity, the article stated that pachucas "have been quick to admit the free relationships that some have with members of boy gangs" and insinuated that these girls were infected with venereal disease by using the euphemism "not particularly clean." The reporter made further charges of sexual degeneracy and violent behavior, stating that a "gang girl gives herself freely, if she likes the boy. If she doesn't she knifes him or has other girls in her gang attack him."[37] Given earlier damning coverage of the female suspects in the Sleepy Lagoon murder trial, newspapers like the *Los Angeles Evening Herald and Express* helped shape perceptions of second-generation daughters as a significant threat to social stability.

Of course some young Mexican American women did, in fact, engage in sexual activity and a gang lifestyle during the war years. Evidence from juvenile case files suggests that many of the young women considered pachucas by the court desired sexual autonomy and engaged in sexual activity, often within the context of steady relationships with Mexican American men.[38] Even the names chosen by the young women to identify their peer group toyed with images of sexual familiarity and innuendo. Newspaper and court case file references to the "Cherríes" and the "Black Widows" indicate that this generation of young women wished to play up their sexuality in a manner markedly different from that of their mothers.[39] For these young women of color, sex offered an opportunity to experience a sense of excitement and pleasure in the context of lives typically defined by discrimination, poverty, and severe social restrictions.[40]

Yet most Mexican American young women simply adopted aspects of the pachuca persona in a spirit of adventure and independence, not delinquency.[41] As one thirteen-year-old of German and Mexican descent reportedly explained to the court, "The girl in Pachuco clothes is just as good as any other girl, except that the Pachuco girls have a bad reputation."[42] In fact, according to contemporary accounts, only a very small percentage of Mexican American girls demonstrated delinquent behavior during the war years. In 1942, for instance, one observer estimated that a mere 0.6 percent of the girls of the Mexican community necessitated "the attention of juvenile authorities."[43] Although youth gangs certainly existed in wartime Los Angeles, and a small number included Mexican American women, not every youthful social gathering represented a gang meeting, nor was every youth in a zoot suit a criminal.[44] But the uneasy wartime populace failed to distinguish delinquent pachucas from any Mexican American woman who rebelled against social conventions or adopted aspects of the pachuca look.

To Euro-American and Mexican communities, young women deemed pachucas represented a dangerous example of the increasing public role of *all* women during World War II. With more women entering the workforce than ever before, an anxious U.S. society feared that women with newfound freedoms would be unwilling to return to domestic life once the war ended. They might be encouraged to enter the public sphere as a wartime necessity but were simultaneously expected to maintain their femininity and sexual purity. Whether so-called pachucas actually retained "proper" sexual standards or not, their relatively short skirts, bold makeup, and more pronounced presence suggested a tainted sexual reputation, and they sounded alarms.[45]

As a woman of color, the pachuca figure also triggered both Euro-American and Mexican fears of miscegenation. The war years ushered in a time of heightened fears of unbridled sexuality, with authorities warning that the disruption of conventional family patterns and an increased lack of parental supervision could easily lead to a rise in sex delinquency. The press fed such anxieties with stories of sexually promiscuous "victory girls," women who allegedly enjoyed dressing in alluring clothing and loitering around military bases and transit depots, looking to proposition servicemen. Understanding women's sexual activity outside the marital sphere as immoral, military and public health officials characterized victory girls as "amateur" prostitutes, warning that they were tainted by venereal disease and thereby represented a significant health threat.[46]

Media coverage equating pachucas with prostitutes and emphasizing the sexual delinquency of second-generation women mirrored condemnations of so-called V-girls.[47] But as women of color, Mexican American women were subject to additional anxieties about their sexuality, anxieties that at times focused on fears of sexual encounters across the color line. Since California's antimiscegenation statute did not consider sex between whites and Mexicans to be interracial, and thus unlawful, some did worry that, without legal deterrents, sexual relations between the two communities could easily occur.[48] Indeed, in the wake of the Zoot Suit Riots, a *Newsweek* reporter surmised that male zoot suiters had attacked servicemen who tried to steal their girls, since "a sailor with a pocketful of money has always been fair game for loose women, and the girls of the Los Angeles Mexican quarter were no exception."[49] By likening the companions of zoot suiters to allegedly loose victory girls, major Los Angeles newspapers and, on this occasion, a national newsmagazine, attempted to limit social mixing between the two groups, with hopes that Euro-American servicemen and Mexican Americans would not engage in sexual relationships. Pachucos may have proved troublesome as members of a minority group asserting a more public role in urban life, but the sexual power of those considered to be pachuca posed an additional danger to the white social order.

Mexican parents expressed similar concerns over the prospect of second-generation daughters having sexual relations with white men, but they worried simultaneously that their daughters would become intimately involved with pachucos. Apprehensions only grew as wartime work and leisure conditions increased opportunities for "trouble." In 1944, all too aware of the changing circumstances, the parents of thirteen-year-old Sandra

Garza became so troubled by her association with local pachucos that they placed her on a train bound for Mexico to live with her aunt.[50] Similarly, the parents of fifteen-year-old Consuela Corral tried to keep their teenage daughter home in the evenings by locking her in the bedroom. Ever determined, Consuela escaped by way of the window, meeting her pachuco friends on a nearby street corner.[51]

To many Mexican parents, a daughter's experimentation with the pachuca identity ultimately represented the corrupting influence of American sexual patterns on Mexican culture. As historian Vicki Ruiz observes, the Mexican immigrant community typically believed white women were morally lax in their dealings with men. Euro-American parents generally did not submit their daughters to chaperonage and, to the Mexican immigrant generation, seemed much more carefree in their attitudes about dating. Moreover, U.S. consumer culture, with its promotion of cosmetics and fashion, seemed to reinforce notions of loose American sexual mores.[52] As one Mexican mother described her daughter's impending adolescence during the 1940s, there would be "none of this running around all night with one boy, the way those American girls up on Tenth do. There is a lot to be said for the Mexican way of keeping an eye on your girls."[53] Mexican parents feared that adoption of American sexual attitudes, seemingly emblematic of the pachuca identity, might persuade daughters to abandon their traditional values and bring disgrace upon their families.

Aurora Preciado, a native of Mexico, expressed these concerns when she reported her fourteen-year-old daughter Cecelia to the Los Angeles Juvenile Court authorities in 1945. A devout Catholic, this Mexican mother had worried for some time about her daughter's desire to wear a high pompadour and to come and go as she pleased, both day and night, with a group of pachuco boys and girls from the neighborhood. Despite numerous parental remonstrations, Cecelia simply refused to stay home after dinner and even stopped attending mass with her family. Instead, the young teen preferred dressing in the pachuca style and frequenting American movie theaters and dance halls with her peers. To Mrs. Preciado, such behavior suggested involvement in immoral activities; her fears only seemed to be confirmed when she found contraceptives in Cecelia's bureau. This traditional Mexican mother attempted to see her daughter "do right" by filing a petition with the juvenile authorities in hopes that court action might "scare" the girl into submission. Cecelia, on the other hand, insisted to juvenile authorities that—in spite of their pachuco attire—her friends were not "bad" girls but young women who simply desired a little liberty from parental restrictions.[54]

To parents like Mrs. Preciado, their daughters' flagrant violation of gender expectations not only represented pachuca behavior but symbolized the flagging authority of the family to police sexuality. Like their Euro-American female counterparts, Mexican

American women enjoyed leisure activities with the opposite sex, and thus rejected chaperonage. Moreover, they crossed geographic barriers by physically leaving urban barrios to frequent traditionally white public venues. Aghast Mexican parents thus watched in fear as daughters applied dark lipstick, teased their hair, and adorned zoot attire, all in preparation for a night of jitterbugging in one of the many ballrooms in downtown and greater Los Angeles. Because women were considered the purveyors of cultural values within the Mexican community, mothers like Mrs. Preciado feared that a daughter's interest in the pachuca subculture represented a threat to Mexican customs and traditions.

But while parents fretted about their children's loss of cultural ties to Mexico, the larger Los Angeles populace typically characterized pachuquismo as a distinctly Mexican identity—anything but evidence of Americanization. According to a fact-finding report by Adele Calhoun, branch assistant of the Division of Immigration and Housing in Los Angeles, "The idea that a child born in this country of Mexican parents is an American, is only technically true. In spirit and tradition and culture he is still more Mexican than American. ... Emotionally [Mexican youth] are somewhat more tensed up and unrestrained than the average American, and this condition, coupled with ignorance, of course lends itself to gangster trends."[55] Community leaders similarly warned that the pachuco phenomenon could possibly be tied to a fifth column movement of right-wing Sinarquistas in Mexico, while the press displayed coverage of crimes committed by Spanish-surnamed zoot suiters directly alongside stories of overseas Japanese atrocities. Because the zoot style failed to conform to standards deemed properly "American," Mexican American youths—like their Japanese American counterparts on the West Coast—came to represent yet another foreign enemy on the wartime home front.[56]

At the heart of the matter was the fear that beneath the outwardly flashy appearance of the zoot suiter lay a militant racial consciousness. Reports to the juvenile court frequently commented on the "race conscious" nature of pachucas and their propensity to stir up racial antagonism between minority groups and whites. Concerns over the behavior of Eva Flores, a fifteen-year-old Mexican American woman first brought before the juvenile court in 1942, reflect the heightened anxieties surrounding race relations during the war years. Between 1942 and 1944, Flores found herself before the juvenile court for various crimes, including intoxication, fighting, failing to return home at night, and petty theft. The young teen's behavior, in addition to her style of dress—a "pachuco" coat, pants, and high socks—raised significant concern among officials.

However, not until Eva's commitment to the county-run reformatory El Retiro School for Girls did Los Angeles Juvenile Court authorities connect her choice of attire to something even more troublesome—a politicized identity that threatened racialized norms. According to Superintendent Adelaide Williams, El Retiro had historically prided itself on easily assimilating minority female delinquents into the reform school's diverse population—that is, until Eva Flores arrived. Eva completely disrupted the feeling of racial harmony at the Los Angeles reformatory by "causing dissatisfaction among the Mexican and Negro girls." As Williams explained, "She managed to speak a Spanish word here, a message to another there, talked her pachucoa [sic] slang to still another and almost before we knew it, she had developed a race feeling on campus." Williams further lamented the fact that, for the first time, young pachuca women stood together, talked in groups, and organized among themselves. "She simply was 'dynamite' on the campus and in the short time we had her, [Eva] had all the Mexican and Negro girls surly, impudent and race conscious," Williams told probation officials.[57] Ironically, even as Mexican parents feared the potential of the pachuca to undermine Mexican culture, in the eyes of reformers, those young women who adopted "pachuca" tendencies came to stand for a new kind of politicized and defiant Mexican identity.

Several court records, in fact, show pachucas in trouble with authorities for their involvement in "racial disturbances." Teresa Quiñones, a young woman caught "terrorizing a group of white girls," complained that she threw rocks at her junior high school peers because "they are down on the Mexicans."[58] Similarly, Gloria Magaña admitted that she and a group of "Mexican girls" had been involved in a fight with "American girls" at Garfield High School after being called "dirty Mexicans."[59] While these so-called pachucas expressed discontent with their treatment as second-class citizens, reformers lamented the appearance of "racial feelings," worrying that in magnifying difference and stirring up antagonism, pachucas threatened the wartime vision of a unified American nation.

To best understand reformers' fears, it is important to consider notions of racial liberalism developing in intellectual circles during the war years. One of the most influential works, *The Negro Problem,* written by social scientist Gunnar Myrdal and published in 1944, developed an optimistic thesis about the ability of the United States to overcome racial hierarchies due to the power of the "American Creed." Myrdal based this creed on the idea that the United States "has a national experience of uniting racial and cultural diversities and a national theory, if not a consistent practice, of freedom and equality for all."[60] According to Myrdal, institutional structures like the church, school, trade union, and state all served to Americanize blacks and whites, allowing them to shed attachments to "caste" distinctions and to create a new, universal national culture based on sameness, not difference. Racial subjects, in essence, would inevitably become transformed into national subjects.[61]

Myrdal came to his conclusions during the late 1930s and early 1940s when the culture-based concept of "ethnicity" was just coming into favor among social scientists as a way to explain what scholar Nikhil Singh calls a "difference *different* from 'race'." [62] With the egalitarian vision of the New Deal, and the rise of antifascism during World War II, social scientists worked to refashion the race concept, exchanging biological under-standings of race for cultural and environmental explanations of difference. Immigrant populations living in the United States now found themselves grouped under the umbrella category of "ethnicity," a term that served to advance the notion that assimilation had eroded any and all "Old World" ethnic differences in favor of a common Americanism. As Singh points out, the idea that immigrant difference could gradually be incorporated into a "normative nationality" ultimately became the template for Myrdal and other social scientists interested in solving the race "problem" in the United States. Assimilation, it seemed, would be a logical solution to the dilemma of racism. [63]

Yet as the behavior of Eva Flores and her cohorts at the El Retiro School for Girls suggest, many so-called pachucas refused to fit the mold of ethnic immigrants who accepted a common Americanism. Wartime reformers may have hailed the ethnicity model of "Americans All" as a cure-all to social tensions, but the paradigm remained fundamentally flawed in its inability to appreciate the extent to which the historical experiences of racialized minority groups differed from those of white European ethnics, a difference that many Mexican American women remained all too aware of. Rather, the paradigm solidified whiteness as the normative American condition and rendered any hint of racial discontent or difference as deviant and un-American. Thus, as these youths failed to integrate easily into mainstream society, reformers increasingly feared that their wards represented not simply young women engaged in delinquent behavior but, even more problematic, young women of color engaged in delinquent behavior with a dangerously political thrust.

In fact, the persona created by pachucas did take on a degree of political meaning, as the young women outwardly challenged the vision of American commonality by embracing a womanhood that emphasized cultural difference. To be sure, some Mexican American women chose to wear zoot suits for the simple reason that they liked the style or as a way to take part in peer-group socializing. Thus wearing a zoot suit was not necessarily an inherently political act. But certainly few zoot-suited youths were completely oblivious to the implications of their controversial choices in appearance and behavior, particularly given the conservative context of the times. [64]

Participating in one of America's favorite consumer pastimes—beauty culture—sec-ond-generation daughters utilized the zoot subculture to create new, unique styles that did not attempt to look "white" or to conceal their Mexican ethnicity. Prior to the pachuca phenomenon, Mexican American women, like many other daughters of immigrant parents, often used makeup to look more "American" and to express their new sense of national identity and personal freedom in the United States. Cosmetic companies actively promoted white mainstream ideals of beauty and femininity to the Spanish-speaking public, and, as Vicki Ruiz points out, the popularity of bleach creams and hair dyes attests to the influence of American beauty culture on many barrio consumers.[65]

But the style of the pachuca meant an adoption of beauty rituals that largely defied white emulation. In fact, Mexican American women interested in the zoot look consistently reappropriated cosmetics and beauty advice in order to fashion a racial identity that challenged the vision of mainstream U.S. beauty ideals. During World War II, cosmetic companies and the federal government typically promoted the wearing of makeup as an affirmation of American ideals and a way for women to help maintain both national morale and femininity when engaging in "men's work."[66] But the beauty standards these companies had in mind dictated that hair would be arranged and makeup applied with subtlety and discretion. The wartime pachuca wanted neither. Pachucas seemed to parody the understated updos and subtle makeup of everyday women and Hollywood starlets, using dark red lipstick and affixing "rat" accessories into their hair in order to lift their tresses into an especially high bouffant. They also rejected the practical buns and braids of their more traditional Mexican mothers.[67] Embracing a flashy and ostentatious style, their shared adoption of exaggerated pompadours, generous makeup, and shorter skirts visibly signified a sense of belonging to a distinctly Mexican American subculture.

For thirteen-year-old Isabel Ramos, a self-proclaimed "pachuco girl," participation in the zoot subculture was a means of fitting in on her own terms, a way to feel that she could make her life better. Ever since she befriended a group of pachucos, Ramos took great pride in applying makeup and hemming up her skirt "half way between her knees and waist" before meeting fellow Mexican American teens on L.A. streets. Looking for any opportunity to escape the impoverished conditions and strict upbringing of her home life, she indulged in a defiant appearance that sparked recognition and acceptance among her peer group.[68] Similarly, Maria, another young Mexican American woman who adorned zoot attire during the war, did so because she never felt acceptance in U.S. society. As Maria stated: "I felt good dressing like that. I think it's because ... you felt like people were kind of looking down on you. You didn't feel like you belonged ... so we formed our own little group."[69] Whether or not it was their intention, by subverting mainstream consumer culture and visibly expressing discontent, women who wore the zoot style participated in a racialized, collective identity that helped them to escape their feelings about being outsiders in the United States by claiming an affirming identity *as* outsiders in the United States.

Even when confined to juvenile detention centers, Mexican American women often continued to engage rebelliously in the performative aspects of their public identities.

Figures 5.3.6 A Mexican American woman identified as Josie poses in her zoot suit while waiting for the Red Car in Los Angeles, 1945. In addition to a narrow fingertip coat, her zoot look includes high hair and plucked brows, dark lipstick, big earrings, and exposed knees. Los Angeles Public Library Photo Collection.

Numerous court case files suggest the dismay of probation officers as they troubled over Mexican American women's insistence on altering the uniforms of various reform institutions to resemble pachuca attire. Young Mexican American women still pulled up their skirts to lengths unacceptably short for the time and styled their hair in exaggerated pompadours; some creatively used cleaning cloths, instead of the typical "rat" hair accessory, to keep the high do in place. Although wards of the court, they continued to use aesthetics defiantly as a means of public presentation and group consciousness.[70]

The collective stylistic and behavioral nonconformity of pachucas caused the most concern among juvenile authorities. In a 1944 study of the state-run Ventura School for Girls, Nan Allan, the reformatory's superintendent, explained to a California investigative committee that while juvenile women of Mexican descent made up approximately 20 percent of the inmate population at the Ventura School, it would be unwise to increase these numbers since it was "hard [for Mexican American women] to assimilate ... with the kind that we have here." To substantiate her opinion, Allan referred to difficulties caused by the young Mexican American women who were sent to the Ventura School after testifying at the Sleepy Lagoon trial in Los Angeles. According to Allan, "They were a particularly difficult group to handle because they were so nationally conscious." Karl Holton, head of the California Youth Authority, agreed with Allan, stating that "pachuca gangs ... have very much of a chip on their shoulder, as far a [sic] persecution is concerned. They feel that they have been discriminated against, and that they haven't gotten a square deal, and they are looking for trouble all the time, and they usually find it."[71]

In a period of heightened American consensus, some Mexican American women made a bold decision to engage in an oppositional culture considered threatening by the larger public. California juvenile authorities strongly believed that the "nationally conscious" style and behavior of pachucas represented an attachment to a culture other than that of the United States. Rather than conform to the "American Creed," they instead desired to "speak a Spanish word," "to arrange ... clothing in a gang fashion," and to insist on a "square deal," thereby endangering the reformist vision of integration and highlighting a strident refusal to concede to racialized norms.[72] For many of the young women, the pachuca persona represented a positive affirmation, and an awareness that being American did not necessitate erasure of every semblance of their cultural heritage. Reformers, however, found it difficult to accept an identity that challenged authority and emphasized a nonwhite womanhood.

The visible discontent some so-called pachucas demonstrated about the dominant culture prompted attempts by reformers to halt underpinnings of ethnic nationalism by discouraging any retention of Mexican culture. As one juvenile official told a young Mexican American woman in residence at the infamous Ventura School for Girls, "Begin to plan and be ready when you leave Ventura to ... be a fine American girl and a good citizen. You will be doing your part in our great nation."[73] What, then, did it mean to be a "fine American girl"? The general consensus among juvenile officials was that as individuals, young Mexican American women seemed quite pleasant and pliable. Once befriended and influenced by fellow Mexicans, however, trouble ensued. Thus in an effort to combat cultural alliances, authorities frequently forbade Mexican American women from speaking Spanish within reformatory walls, conflating the use of a foreign language with a dangerous form of youthful rebellion. A young woman speaking Spanish represented a foreign outsider, not a citizen imbued with proper American values.[74]

In addition, court officials continually reprimanded Mexican American girls for interacting solely with young women of Mexican ancestry or for congregating in groups—behavior seen as a further hindrance to integration.[75] One probation officer disparaged the "unsatisfactory" behavior of her Mexican American client, remarking that the juvenile was "very clannish with Mexican girls and continue[d] to speak Spanish in spite of repeated requests not to do so."[76] The young women themselves often explained this "clannish" behavior as a natural choice, given their cultural background. Eva Flores, for instance, admitted to her case worker that she "finds it easier to identify with Mexican girls and felt that some of the American girls did not like her."[77] But for many law enforcement officials, manifestations of Mexican heritage among wayward youths represented a dangerous cultural pathology. Thus in addressing issues of juvenile delinquency, reformers tended to downplay the role of economic inequalities and racial discrimination, concentrating instead on instilling their wards with new cultural values.[78]

With such a stigma attached to the zooter identity, Mexican American women deemed pachucas often fell victim to discriminatory practices with very material consequences. At the Los Angeles Convent of the Good Shepherd, a religious boarding home and school for wayward girls of various backgrounds, the nuns in charge refused to accept any young women considered to be of the "pachuco type."[79] Eva Flores, the young Mexican American woman who stirred up trouble at El Retiro, found herself turned away from the convent. As Sister Germaine explained, "It is our policy not to accept Pachucos. When [Eva Flores] came to the Convent her hairdress [sic], her clothing and her speech indicated that she was a Pachuco and the girl, herself, declared that she was one. We therefore felt it advisable not to accept her even on trial."[80] Those Mexican American women who did not demonstrate "pachuco tendencies" until after their placement at the convent inevitably found themselves removed from the institution. In 1945, the convent admitted sixteen-year-old Sarah Villa, with some reservations, after the young woman was brought in for spending two nights away from home in the presence of African American and Mexican American young men. Sarah's later participation in a dormitory disturbance at the reformatory, combined with her previous "immoral" behavior, led the nuns to conclude that the young woman was "definitely the Pachuco type" and that her removal from the institution would be "beneficial to the Mexicans we now have."[81] The nuns at the convent were not alone in their hesitancy to assist pachucas; individual boarding homes accustomed to taking in wayward youths also expressed concerns regarding "girls of this type."[82] Left with few options, many young Mexican American women either failed to receive attention from juvenile authorities or found themselves transferred to the notorious Ventura School for Girls. Demonstrating a behavior understood as culturally pathological, these adolescent women were simply deemed irredeemable.

Mexican American women were not the only women of color whose behavior was considered a cultural pathology. As historian Regina Kunzel argues, during the World War II and postwar eras, social workers explained white out-of-wedlock pregnancy as a symptom of individual pathology—and thus a condition that might be changed—while they simultaneously reconceptualized black illegitimate pregnancy as a symptom of cultural acceptance and cultural pathology, intrinsic to black families. Reformers may have repudiated biological theories about African American life as racist, but in their place they invoked sociocultural explanations for deviant behavior.[83]

Thus Mexican parents faced similar blame. As biological understandings of race gave way to cultural and environmental explanations, court officials typically blamed zoot-suiting teens' behavior on the failure of the immigrant family to adopt and adjust properly to "American" ways. As a 1943 article in the *Los Angeles Times* explained, "Juvenile files repeatedly show that a language variance in the home—where the parents speak no English and cling to past culture—is a serious factor of delinquency. Parents in such a home lack control over their offspring."[84] Justice officials often assigned blame for the pachuca phenomenon on inadequate parenting skills, use of Spanish in the home, and low standards of living. According to Celia Harrison, a probation officer with the L.A. County Juvenile Court, "The pachucas (the girls) are taking to drink, often learning about liquor in homes with little or no furniture; if there is one bed it is a luxury."[85] Similarly, the social case worker assigned to Cecelia Preciado's case decried the fact that the girl's mother was "not at all Americanized and d[id] not speak any English nor really understand a good many of the American ways, and that she ha[d] no discipline over [Cecelia]." The case worker continued: "[Cecelia] is an extremely smart child able to outwit her mother at almost any point."[86] Disapproving of immigrant lifestyles and child-rearing practices, juvenile authorities often treated Mexican culture as an impediment to the second generation's "proper" integration into American life.[87]

Probation officers typically traced the roots of the pachuca phenomenon to the Mexican family's reliance on "Old World" moral standards in raising American-born daughters. According to juvenile authorities, the tendency of Mexican parents to restrict female behavior severely risked pushing daughters into a life of promiscuous behavior and gang activity. In one 1943 juvenile court case, the probation officer of thirteen-year-old Gloria Magaña placed the blame for the young girl's sexual experience and participation in gang fights squarely on her Mexican mother's shoulders. According to the court, Mrs. Magaña's refusal to grant any freedoms to her daughter had directly caused the girl's delinquent tendencies. "A cultural conflict seems to be the basis of [the] girl's difficulties," the probation officer explained. "[The] mother[,] apparently coming from low peon parents[,] has not become Americanized and wants [the] girl to grow up according to Old World standards. ... This American-born girl has rebelled against this paternalistic conception of the family and has sought an outlet in sexual freedom."[88]

Ironically, while the juvenile court system condemned Mexican families for their overly strict child-rearing practices, many immigrant parents—Mexican mothers in particular—also faced censure for parental behavior deemed morally lax. Just as Progressive Era reformers had frequently targeted Mexican mothers in their attempts to Americanize the Mexican population early in the twentieth century, World War II reformers similarly traced the roots of the pachuca identity to a lack of maternal role models with proper moral standards.[89] One official singled out blame for the phenomenon on Mexican mothers who were "leading immoral lives right in the home and that children were born to these mothers by different fathers."[90] Others found fault with the alleged propensity of Mexican women to engage in premarital sex since common-law marriages were socially acceptable in Mexico.[91] Many court officials simply considered Mexican parents—no matter what their child-rearing practices—incapable of supervising their daughters properly.[92]

Ultimately, the condemnation that Mexican parents faced at the hands of law enforcement officials and the wartime press and public brought the immigrant community to a complicated cultural crossroads. On the one hand, Mexican families had a very critical awareness of how being "American" threatened their values and their hold on their children. On the other hand, the immigrant generation remained apprehensive that they and their American-born offspring would be treated as enemy foreigners—a dangerous reality in a wartime environment of exacerbated xenophobia.

As rumors swirled about overtly sexual, troublingly nationalistic Mexican women, the Mexican-born generation grew increasingly alarmed that the pachucas' spectacular public presence would damage the image of respectable Mexican families trying to eke out an honest living in the United States. *La Opinión's* depiction of pachucas exemplifies such fears: The Spanish-language newspaper carefully chose the controversial term "malinches" to refer to pachucas in order to depict the young women not only as whores but as women who allowed pachucos—the hated enemy of respectable Mexican community members—to possess them sexually. Such terminology served to distance the more traditionally minded immigrant generation from the disreputable second-generation pachuca and to assert their own "civilized" position in contrast to that of the morally degraded young woman.[93] The defiant persona created by pachucas, women who seemingly rejected both traditional Mexican and mainstream American culture, significantly raised the level of anxiety among immigrant communities struggling to make sense of a new homeland and their place within it.

The immigrant generation's fears culminated as violence erupted between Euro-American servicemen and Mexican American youths during the Zoot Suit Riots in June 1943. After months of tense interactions and outright racial hostilities between the two groups, military men roamed Los Angeles in search of young men in zoot suits, dragging those they found into the streets, stripping them of their clothes, and beating them publically. Mexican American youths frequently fought back. Only after senior military officials declared Los Angeles off-limits to all servicemen did the ten straight days of violence come to an end. In the meantime, the local and national press publicized the clashes as yet another example of the second generation's disloyalty to the United States, as well as their supposed propensity toward violence.[94]

Not surprisingly, press coverage of the Zoot Suit Riots reflected heightened tensions about pachucas as well. The *Los Angeles Evening Herald and Express* featured a story of a girl zoot suiter who robbed a young man with a "blow to his chin," stealing five dollars from his pockets.[95] Just a few days later, the newspaper warned its readership that female "auxiliaries" to boy gangs were gearing up to join the battle in Los Angeles streets.[96] And according to an article that ran on n June 1943, merchants in Watts found "all their black shirts and green sweaters sold out as 'pachuco girls' outfitted themselves to join their menfolk in the mob disorders." The story ended with claims that "pachuquitas" staged a meeting to organize, shouting, "We won't quit. It's them or us."[97]

This "us vs. them" perception caused great alarm in the Mexican immigrant community. The *Los Angeles Times,* for instance, featured a photograph of Mrs. Vera Duarte Trujillo, an "irate mother" of a fifteen-year-old zoot-suiting youngster who was shot in the leg during a skirmish at a movie theater in Azusa, a small citrus community in the San Gabriel Valley. "We tried to keep him home but he kept slipping away and what has happened to him is his own fault," said the frustrated parent.[98] Many years later, a woman from the White Fence neighborhood of Los Angeles remembered her mother's humiliation over her choice of activities as a teenage pachuca. She reflected, "My mother used to feel embarrassed with me when I used to go out on the street with her—especially downtown—because, you know, white people would look at the way I was dressed and my mother thought I was a punk."[99] As witnesses to their children's expressions of discontent in the United States, particularly during a time of hyperpatriotism, Mexican parents struggled to maintain a respectable reputation and to demonstrate a certain amount of allegiance to their adopted homeland. But the immigrant community also hoped to see the best of their Mexican culture and traditions persist. In the end, the notoriety associated with the wartime pachuca threatened to undermine these first-generation visions of both racial uplift and cultural preservation.

Ultimately, the pachuca figure became both an element and an emblem of the changing cultural and gender landscape of World War II. For many Mexican American women, playing the part of the pachuca represented a liberating experience that provided them with a sense of personal freedom and control. But many so-called pachucas also learned all too quickly the limits of their individuality and autonomy. During the Second World War the United States looked for stability in social relations: women were expected to fulfill patriotic roles; minorities were expected to embrace Americanism. Pachucas seemed to do neither. Instead, their flaunting of a public sense of self and reveling in an unashamedly racialized identity appeared to threaten home front unity. In reality, many young Mexican American women worked in war jobs and wore coveralls by day, only to jitterbug dressed to the nines in pachuca attire by night. But as increasing numbers of women and people of color challenged traditional social relationships during the war, the wholesale stigmatization of pachucas served as a reminder to unconventional women of color that they should not stray too far from their "proper" place.

The flamboyant presence of the wartime pachuca would have long-lasting implications for a good number of women of Mexican descent coming of age in 1940s Los Angeles. She became at once the symbol and the reality of Mexican American women's new assertiveness and her unwillingness to stay in her traditionally assigned position in Mexican and Anglo society. And yet as the nation's war effort set in motion new federal policies and media opportunities to remedy the outsider status of the Mexican populace in the United States, more and more women of Mexican descent would feel compelled to consider the criteria by which they defined and presented themselves. This new generation would actively negotiate issues of femininity, nationality, and respectability on a daily basis, the legacy of women like Amelia Venegas never far from their minds.

Notes

1. "Brass Knuckles Found on Woman 'Zoot Suiter,'" *Los Angeles Times,* 10 June 1943, A.
2. Ibid.; *People v. Amelia Venegas,* Los Angeles County Superior Court, case number 93615, 1943, Los Angeles Superior Court Archives and Records Center. Venegas is deemed a "pachuco" in Watson, "Zoot Suit, Mexican Style," 10. Interestingly, in spite of how Venegas

is labeled, neither the court nor the press made mention of the young woman ever actually wearing a zoot suit. Likewise, as Catherine Ramirez observes, newspaper photographs do not show her wearing "identifying features of the pachuca look in wartime Los Angeles." Ramirez, *Woman in the Zoot Suit,* 83.

3. For an excellent study of the pachuca's fashion style and representation, see Ramírez, *Woman in the Zoot Suit.* Further descriptions of pachucas include Bogardus, "Gangs of Mexican-American Youth," 56; Adler, "1943 Zoot Suit Riots," 152; Griffith, *American Me,* 47; and McWilliams, *North from Mexico,* 219.

4. In utilizing juvenile court records to discuss the pachuca phenomenon, I do not mean to equate being "pachuca" with being delinquent. Rather, as I hope to demonstrate, the term "pachuca" held multiple and at times contradictory meanings during World War II, both inside and outside the juvenile justice system. As historical sources, juvenile court records remain valuable yet limited in their ability to shed light on the pachuca phenomenon. On the one hand, the files tell only those stories of women in conflict with the law and thus provide perspectives that are by and large mediated by unsympathetic outsiders. But given the paucity of primary sources on Mexican American women who adopted aspects of the pachuca identity—or were deemed "pachuca" by others—juvenile files can provide important insights into the ways in which so-called pachucas were conceived of and treated by parents and law enforcement, in addition to the ways in which the young women defined and thought of themselves, especially as they tried to articulate and defend their circumstances to court officials.

5. For in-depth discussion of Mexican American zoot-clad youth and zoot culture in wartime Los Angeles, see Alvarez, *Power of the Zoot;* Escobar, *Race, Police, and the Making of a Political Identity;* Pagán, *Murder at the Sleepy Lagoon;* Macias, *Mexican American Mojo.* Pagán and Alvarez document the zoot subculture among working- class African Americans, Asian Americans, and Euro-Americans as well.

6. Pagán, *Murder at the Sleepy Lagoon,* 11, 39, 108; Alvarez, *Power of the Zoot,* 83–84.

7. Pagán, *Murder at the Sleepy Lagoon,* 19–20; Alvarez, *Power of the Zoot,* 94.

8. Alvarez, *Power of the Zoot,* 18.

9. Ibid., 96.

10. Cosgrove, "Zoot-Suit and Style Warfare."

11. Alvarez, *Power of the Zoot,* 44.

12. Los Angeles passed a curfew ordinance in 1942 that prohibited anyone under seventeen from loitering in public places after 9:00 P.M. For a discussion of the conflict- ridden relationship between the LAPD and Mexican American youths during the war years, see Escobar, *Race, Police, and the Making of a Political Identity,* chaps. 8 and 9. According to Escobar, reported crime actually fell in Los Angeles during 1942–43—the years of the alleged crime wave—testifying to the fact that "large numbers of Mexican American youths found themselves arrested for no other reason than the fact that they were of Mexican descent" (Escobar, *Race, Police, and the Making of a Political Identity,* 174).

13. Pagán, *Murder at the Sleepy Lagoon,* 89. The phrase 'zoot suit' murder case" is from "Jury's Gang-Case Verdict Disproves 'Persecution,'" *Los Angeles Times,* January 14, 1943, A4. For

the history of the Sleepy Lagoon trial and its outcome, see Escobar, *Race, Police, and the Making of a Political Identity;* Pagán, *Murder at the Sleepy Lagoon;* Alvarez, *Power of the Zoot;* McWilliams, *North from Mexico;* and the PBS *American Experience* documentary "Zoot Suit Riots" (Boston: WGBH Educational Foundation, 2001).

14. For discussion of the SLDC and the diverse makeup of its membership, see Barajas, "Defense Committees of Sleepy Lagoon"; Bernstein, *Bridges of Reform,* 87–89; and Johnson, "Constellations of Struggle."

15. "Twenty-three Youths Indicted on Gang Murder Charges; 6 Additional John Does Also Accused; Case of 10 Girls Given to Juvenile Court," *Los Angeles Times,* 7 August 1942, A10; Ramirez, *Woman in the Zoot Suit,* 29; Ramirez, "Pachuca in Chicana/o Art, Literature and History," 20.

16. "Youthful Gang Evil, Vigorous Action Imperative in View of Seriousness of Situation," *Los Angeles Evening Herald and Express,* 4 August 1942, B2.

17. "Three Teen-Age Girls Held in Boy-Gang Slaying Inquiry; All Insist They Did Not Belong to Group Involved, in Investigation Undertaken by County Grand Jury," *Los Angeles Times,* 5 August 1942, A12.

18. See Pagán, "Sleepy Lagoon," 115–16 and 158–59; "Twenty-three Youths Indicted on Gang Murder Charges; 6 Additional John Does Also Accused; Cases of 10 Girls Given to Juvenile Court," *Los Angeles Times,* 7 August 1942, A10; Guy Endore, *The Sleepy Lagoon Mystery* (manuscript draft), 58, Box 2, Folder 4, SLDC Records; "150 Rounded Up in Killing Gang Terror," not dated, newspaper unknown, folder marked "News clippings, 1942–44," Ruiz Papers. See also the untitled 30 April 1943 summary of the injustices of the Sleepy Lagoon case by Rita Michaels, American Federation of Teachers, SLDC Records; and handwritten account of the trial, dated 29 October 1942, author unknown, SLDC Records.

19. See Guy Endore, *The Sleepy Lagoon Mystery* (manuscript draft), 58–63, Box 2, Folder 4, SLDC Records.

20. Dora Barrios, Betty Zeiss, and Juanita Gonzáles are listed as paroled from the Ventura School for Girls in 1943, although they officially remained wards of the state until their twenty-first birthdays. See "Paroled to Southern California Supervisor during 1943, Ventura School for Girls," Administrative Files, Corrections, Governors Prison Committee, Ventura School for Girls, 1937–1944, F3640:992, Warren Papers. Frances Silva is listed as being committed to the Ventura School for Girls in 1943 for "Mexican fights." See "Ventura School for Girls, Girls Over 18," Administrative Files, Corrections, Governor's Prison Committee, Ventura School for Girls, ¹93 7-¹944» F3640:992, Warren Papers. Discussion of Lorena Encinas's incarceration at the Ventura School can be viewed on the PBS *American Experience* documentary "Zoot Suit Riots." There is documentation of Bertha Aguilar's stay at the Ventura School in two court cases separate from that of the Sleepy Lagoon trial, referred to officially as *People v. Zammora. See The People, Respondent, v. Sam Marino Renteria, Apellant,* Crim. No. 3715, Court of Appeal of California, Second Appellate District, Division Three, 60 Cal. App. 2d 463; 141 P.2d 37; 1943 Cal App. LEXIS 541; and the

testimony of Bertha Aguilar, court case number CR025817, Ventura County Courthouse, 1943. Josephine Gonzáles testified at the Sleepy Lagoon trial that she had been sent to the Ventura reformatory for girls; see her testimony, Court Transcript, 764- 1168, SLDC Records. Lupe Ynostroza was eventually sent to Duarte Sanatorium; see Henry Ynostroza biography, SLDC Records.

21. My assessment of the type of inmate typically sentenced to the Ventura School comes from my readings of court case files brought before the Los Angeles County Superior Court, Juvenile Division, between the years 1939 and 1945. When the women of Sleepy Lagoon entered the school in late 1942, the institution's custodial and disciplinary procedures rivaled those of state prisons. A 1943 committee appointed by Governor Earl Warren to investigate California's penal institutions, for instance, described the punishments implemented in the Ventura School disciplinary cottage as a "disgrace to the state." See "Final Report of Governors Investigation Committee on Penal Affairs," 21 January 1944,110–1, Administrative Files, Corrections, Governor's Prison Committee, Reports, F304o:975, Warren Papers.

22. The cases cited in this chapter are examples of files where the labels "pachuco" and/or "pachuca" are included in the probation officer's description of the juvenile. Although the records used in this study are officially closed to the public, I petitioned the Juvenile Division of the Los Angeles County Superior Court for special permission to look at the files. Case files consist primarily of Los Angeles County Probation Department Intake Face Sheets and Los Angeles Police Department Juvenile Investigation and Disposition Reports; Probation Officer Reports and Recommendations based on interviews conducted with the juvenile family members, school and reformatory officials, and other related parties; and medical reports filed upon examination of the juvenile while in detention. To protect privacy and maintain confidentiality, I changed all names of the youths, friends, and family members mentioned in the juvenile case files. I have, however, tried to retain the ethnic characteristics of surnames.

23. Pagán, *Murder at the Sleepy Lagoon,* 37–39, 130–31.

24. Ramírez, *Woman in the Zoot Suit,* xii. Like Ramirez's, my descriptions of Mexican American women who adorned aspects of the zoot look during the World War II era come from contemporary photographs and interviews conducted with Mexican American women who either adopted the zoot style themselves or came of age when the zoot suit was popular with Mexican Americans.

25. Superior Court of California, County of Los Angeles Juvenile Court, case number 104932, Los Angeles Superior Court Archives and Records Center (hereafter cited as "case number").

26. Case number 103922.

27. Case numbers 107165, 116621.

28. Malagon, interview. Anna Morales Marquez similarly recalled wearing aspects of the zoot style during the 1940s but claimed in her interview that she did not self-identify as a "pachuca." Morales Marquez, interview.

29. Case number 106170.

30. Ruiz, *From Out of the Shadows,* 51–52; Odem, *Delinquent Daughters,* 44–45, 49.

31. Escobedo Atterbury, interview, 6 January 1998; Escobedo Atterbury, interview, 30 November 2010.

32. Case number 105230.

33. Velarde, interview; Hurtado Davis, interview.

34. Pallan Valadez, interview.

35. Hernández Jefferes, interview.

36. "Origenes de 'Pachucos' y 'Malinches,' *La Opinión,*" 26 August 1942, 2. The attitudes of *La Opinión* toward the pachuca/o population were not particularly surprising, given the political bent of the Spanish-language daily. Recognizing the vulnerability of the Mexican population in the United States, the newspaper urged the Mexican population to conduct themselves honorably while living in Los Angeles. See Garcia, *"La Frontera?"* 95–96. Discussions of La Malinche can be found in Romero and Harris, *Feminism, Nation, and Myth.* For further analysis of *La Opinión's* use of the term "malinches" to describe the pachuca, see Ramirez, *Woman in the Zoot Suit,* 38–39.

37. "Girl 'Zoot Suiters' Gird to Join Gangland Battle, Pachucas Stand by Beaten Pachucos," *Los Angeles Evening Herald and Express,* 10 June 1943, A3.

38. Case numbers 131627, 103259, 104932, 105230.

39. Pagán, *Murder at the Sleepy Lagoon,* 123. Several newspapers and magazines spoke of female gangs with names such as the "Black Widows" and the "Cherríes." See, for example, "Girl 'Zoot Suiters' Gird to Join Gangland Battle, Pachucas Stand by Beaten Pachucos," *Los Angeles Evening Herald and Express,* 10 June 1943, A3; "Youthful Gang Secrets Exposed," *Los Angeles Times,* 16 July 1944, A1; "Origenes de 'Pachucos' y 'Malinches,'" *La Opinión,* 26 August 1942, 2. See also Moore, *Going Down to the Barrio,* 27–29.

40. Mary Odem discusses similar issues regarding sexual delinquency charges and the social circumstances affecting turn-of-the-century working-class daughters in *Delinquent Daughters.*

41. Griffith, *American Me,* 52.

42. Case number 112504.

43. Ruiz, *From Out of the Shadows,* 83. Similarly, during a meeting of the Coordinating Council for Latin American Youth—a community group founded in 1941 to address the situation of Mexican American youths in urban barrios—it was stated that only 9/10 of 1 percent of Mexican girls were considered juvenile delinquents. See "CCLAY Minutes," 7 June 1943, Minutes, 1943, Folder 8, Box 3, Ruiz Papers.

44. Pagán, *Murder at the Sleepy Lagoon,* 132.

45. For a general discussion of fears surrounding women's changing roles during World War II, see May, "Rosie the Riveter Gets Married," 133–34.

46. For information about "victory girls" and increased efforts to police female sexuality during World War II, see Hegarty, *Victory Girls, Khaki-Wackies, and Patriotutes.* According to Hegarty, in an effort to cut down on prostitution and the spread of venereal disease

to servicemen, the 1941 May Act made prostitution in military areas a federal crime, giving federal agencies like the Social Protection Division of the Office of Community War Services "a powerful tool to control prostitutes and so-called promiscuous women" (Hegarty, *Victory Girls, Khaki-Wackies, and Patriotutes,* 19).

47. "Girl 'Zoot Suiters' Gird to Join Gangland Battle, Pachucas Stand by Beaten Pachucos," *Los Angeles Evening Herald and Express,* 10 June 1943, A3; "Youth Gangs Leading Cause of Delinquencies," *Los Angeles Times, 2* June 1943, A10; "Origenes de 'Pachucos' y 'Malinches,'" *La Opinión, 26* August 1942, 2.

48. For a discussion of twentieth-century miscegenation laws and understandings of Mexicans as legally "white," see Hollinger, "Amalgamation and Hypodescent," 1375-77; and Pascoe, *What Comes Naturally,* 120–23.

49. "Zoot Suits and Service Stripes: Race Tension Behind the Riots," *Newsweek, 21* June 1943, 35–36.

50. Case number 115630.

51. Case number 111288.

52. Ruiz, "'Star Struck,'" 133–37.

53. Tuck, *Not with the Fist,* 127.

54. Court officials eventually encouraged Mrs. Preciado to get her daughter away from her undesirable companions by placing her with relatives or her godmother. It is unclear from the court record if she ever took this course of action. As of January 1948, Cecelia remained in the home of her parents; her case was dismissed in July of that year. See Case number 122004. For an in-depth discussion of working-class, immigrant parents' use of the juvenile justice system to reform behavior of troublesome daughters during the late nineteenth and early twentieth centuries, see Odem, *Delinquent Daughters.*

55. Memo from Adele Calhoun to Frank J. DeAndreis, "Pachuco Situation in Los Angeles," 16 June 1943, Administrative, Department of Justice, Attorney General, Law Enforcement, 1943, F3640:2625, Warren Papers, 1–2.

56. For information on accusations of Sinarquista activities in the Mexican American community, see Barajas, "Defense Committees of Sleepy Lagoon"; and Escobar, *Race, Police, and the Making of a Political Identity,* 221–22, 227–28. For an example of the similarities in news coverage regarding the enemy Japanese and enemy Mexican gangs, see the front page of the *Los Angeles Times,* 10 August 1942, where the headlines "Allied Bombers Hit Japs in Rear" and "Police Seize 300 in Boys' Gang Drive" appear parallel to one another.

57. Case number 101591.

58. Case number 131627.

59. Case number 107502.

60. Myrdal, *American Dilemma, 1021.*

61. My thinking is informed here by scholar Nikhil Singh's discussion of Myrdal's *American Dilemma* and contemporary understandings of race and nation in World War II, in *Black Is a Country,* 38–42, 107–14.

62. Singh, *Black Is a Country,* 254 n. 30. See also Sollors, *Beyond Ethnicity.*

63. Singh, *Black Is a Country,* 113; Omi and Winant, *Racial Formation in the United States,* 14–18; Jacobson, *Whiteness of a Different Color,* 95–96; Gerstle, *American Crucible,* 187–96. Gerstle calls this belief in the erosion of ethnic differences "the growth of a common Americanness." See Gerstle, *American Crucible,* 196.

64. Several scholars, including George Lipsitz, Robin Kelley, and Luis Alvarez, have explored the important ways in which everyday cultural practices, including styles of clothing, can be viewed as examples of political expression and/or cultural politics. See, for instance, Lipsitz, *Rainbow at Midnight,* 83–86; Kelley, *Race Rebels,* and Alvarez, *Power of the Zoot.* In her book *Zoot Suit,* historian Kathy Peiss cautions against the "enduringly problematic practice of reading aesthetic forms as politics," calling upon scholars to "examine more closely the circumstances in which a cultural style may or may not be in fact political." Peiss does argue, however, that in Los Angeles—given campaigns by law enforcement and the press to denigrate zoot suits and to associate those who wore them with criminality—the look "took on a more politicized meaning," particularly for Mexican Americans. See Peiss, *Zoot Suit,* 1–14, 114–17 (quotations on 8, 4, 117).

65. Ruiz, *From Out of the Shadows,* 57.

66. Peiss, *Hope in a Jar,* 239–45; McEuen, *Making War, Making Women.*

67. Pagán, *Murder at the Sleepy Lagoon,* 102, 104. Mexican American women who came of age in wartime Los Angeles describe the "rat" as a beauty accessory consisting of a foam insert or patch of synthetic or human hair, placed on the head to add lift and fullness to the pompadour hairstyle. As described in Gonzáles Benavidez, interview, 6 November 2000; Rivera Cardenas, interview; Malagon, interview.

68. Case number 106170.

69. Alvarez, *Power of the Zoot,* 3.

70. Case numbers 103922, 114005. For further discussion of attempts by Mexican American youths to resist authority in California reform schools, see Chávez-García, "Youth, Evidence, and Agency."

71. "Reporters Transcript of Proceedings of Governor Earl Warrens Special Committee Investigating California Penal Institutions, Ventura School for Girls, vol. IX," 3 January 1944, F3640:956-1007, Warren Papers, 1666–68.

72. Ibid.; case number 101591 and Pagán, *Murder at the Sleepy Lagoon,* 7.

73. Case number 102135.

74. See case numbers 103193, 98670. George J. Sánchez discusses earlier reformers' Americanization efforts in "'Go after the Women,'" 256.

75. See case numbers 107165, 112504, and 101591.

76. Case number 98670.

77. Case number 101591.

78. For a discussion of similar failures within the juvenile justice system in Boston during the nineteenth and early twentieth centuries, see Schneider, *In the Web of Class.*

79. See, for example, case number 131627.

80. Case number 101591.

81. Case number 118703.

82. Case number 131627.

83. See Kunzel, *Fallen Women, Problem Girls,* 163–64.

84. "Youth Gangs Leading Cause of Delinquencies," *Los Angeles Times, 2* June 1943, A10.

85. Memo from Adele Calhoun to Frank J. DeAndreis, "Pachuco Situation in Los Angeles," 16 June 1943, Administrative, Department of Justice, Attorney General, Law Enforcement, 1943, F3640:2625, Warren Papers, 5.

86. Case number 122004.

87. See Sánchez, "'Go after the Women,'" 256; and Odem, *Delinquent Daughters,* 182.

88. Case number 107502.

89. According to historian George Sánchez, Mexican immigrant women became the target of Progressive Era Americanization programs by and large because they were seen as the individuals most responsible for the "transmission of values in the home." Reformers thus hoped to influence the second generation by way of their mothers while simultaneously teaching Mexican immigrant women the skills necessary to enter the labor market. See Sánchez, "'Go after the Women,'" 254–55.

90. Memo from Adele Calhoun to Frank J. DeAndreis, "Pachuco Situation in Los Angeles," 16 June 1943, Administrative, Department of Justice, Attorney General, Law Enforcement, 1943, F3640:2025, Warren Papers, 3.

91. Case number 109532.

92. Here, too, Mexican American mothers were not the only ones condemned. Ruth Feldstein discusses the perceived "maternal failure" of 1940s black and white women in her work *Motherhood in Black and White.*

93. "Orígenes de 'Pachucos' y 'Malinches,'" *La Opinión, 26* August 1942, 2. Eduardo Pagán makes a similar argument about pachucos and the middle class in his "'Who Are These Troublemakers?' "

94. For in-depth discussion of the Zoot Suit Riots, see Pagán, *Murder at the Sleepy Lagoon;* Mazón, *Zoot-Suit Riots;* McWilliams, *North from Mexico;* and PBS *American Experience,* "Zoot Suit Riots."

95. "Sailor 'Task Force' Hits L.A. Zooters, Send 5 to Hospital in Riots," *Los Angeles Evening Herald and Express,* 5 June 1943, A1, 4.

96. "Girl 'Zoot Suiters' Gird to Join Gangland Battle, Pachucas Stand by Beaten Pachucos," *Los Angeles Evening Herald and Express,* 10 June 1943, A3.

97. "Train-Attacking Zoot Gangs Broken Up," *Los Angeles Evening Herald and Express,* 11 June 1943, A.

98. Sánchez, *Becoming Mexican American,* 268; "Mother Tears Up Zoot Suit of Boy Wounded in Clash," *Los Angeles Times,* 11 June 1943, A.

99. Moore, *Going Down to the Barrio,* 71–72. Reading 5.2   Post-Reading Comprehension Questions

READING 5.3 POST-READING COMPREHENSION QUESTIONS

- Summarize the circumstances of the Sleepy Lagoon case.

- Describe how the pachuca identity complicated ideas about what it meant to be a Mexican American woman during WWII.

- Paraphrase the quote: "For many Mexican American women, playing the part of the pachuca represented a liberating experience that provided them with a sense of personal freedom and control."

End-of-Chapter Critical Thinking Questions

Directions: Respond to each of the questions about the image and the readings. Refer to these sources to support your answers.

- Explain the relationship between race and citizenship in the United States during World War II; how does soldiering affect that relationship?
- In what ways are Japanese internment and the Bracero Program connected?
- Identify and discuss some of the experiences of Mexican American Women during World War II.

Further Readings

Alvarez, Luis. *The Power of the Zoot: Youth Culture and Resistance During World War II.* Berkeley and Los Angeles, CA.: University of California Press, 2008.

Calavita, Kitty. *Inside the State: The Bracero Program, Immigration, and the I.N.S.* New York, NY.: Routledge, 1992.

Escobedo, Elizabeth Rachel. *From Coveralls to Zoot Suits: The Lives of Mexican American Women on the World War II Home Front.* Chapel Hill, NC.: University of North Carolina Press, 2013.

Galarza, Ernesto. *Merchants of labor: The Mexican Bracero Story: An Account of the Managed Migration of Mexican Farm Workers in California 1942–1960.* Santa Barbara, CA.: McNally and Loftin, 1964.

Gamboa, Erasmo. *Mexican Labor and World War II: Braceros in the Pacific Northwest, 1942–1947.* Austin, TX.: University of Texas Press, 1990.

Gluck, Sherna Berger. *Rosie the Riveter Revisited: Women, the War, and Social Change.* Boston, MA.: Twayne Publishers, 1987.

Griswold Del Castillo, Richard, ed. *World War II and Mexican American Civil Rights.* Austin, TX.: University of Texas press, 2008.

Kells, Michelle Hall. *Hector P. Garcia: Everyday Rhetoric and Mexican American Civil Rights.* Carbondale, IL.: Southern Illinois Press, 2006.

Lemke-Santangelo, Gretchen. *Abiding Courage: African American Migrant Women and the East Bay Community.* Chapel Hill, NC.: University of North Carolina, 1996.

Lichtenstein, Nelson. *Labor's War at Home: the CIO in World War II.* Philadelphia, PA.: Temple University Press, 2003.

Mazón, Mauricio. *The Zoot-Suit Riots: The Psychology of Symbolic Annihilation*. Austin, TX.: University of Texas Press, 1984.

Mercado, Juan Pablo, "Re-envisioning the Mexican American Experience in World War II: A Local History of Sacramento & the Mexican American WWII Generation" (2011). *Master's Projects*. 192.

Matsumoto, Valerie J. *Farming the Home Place: A Japanese Community in California, 1919–1982*. Ithica, NY: Cornell University Press, 1993.

Morin, Raul. *Among the Valiant: Mexican Americans in WWII and Korea*. Alhambra: Borden Publishing Company, 1966.

Nash, Gerald D. *World War II and the West: Reshaping the Economy* Lincoln, NE.: University of Nebraska Press, 1990.

Ramírez, Catherine Sue. *The Woman in the Zoot Suit: Gender, Nationalism, and the Cultural Politics of Memory*. Durham, NC: Duke University Press, 2009.

Ramos, Henry. *The American GI Forum: In Pursuit of the Dream, 1948–1983*. Houston, TX: Arte Publico Press, 1998.

Rivas-Rodriguez, Maggie. ed. *Mexican Americans and World War II*. Austin, TX: University of Texas Press, 2005.

Takaki, Ronald. *Double Victory: A Multicultural History of America in World War II*. Boston, New York, and London: Little, Brown and Company, 2000.

Zamora, Emilio. *Claiming Rights and Righting Wrongs in Texas: Mexican Workers and Job Politics During World War II*. College Station, TX.: Texas A&M University Press, 2009.

CHAPTER 6

The Postwar Period

....

Editor's Introduction

In the years after World War II the United States became the world superpower and was embroiled in a worldwide struggle with the Soviet Union for global dominance; the United States sought to win favor in the emerging nations of Africa and Asia. Yet as the self-imposed beacon of global liberty, it was becoming increasingly more difficult for the country to defend its Jim Crow domestic policies to the international community. The Soviet Union on the other hand sought to promote the concept that the United States was merely a racist and colonial empire looking to subjugate people abroad and at home. In part because of the pressure that civil rights groups put on the federal government to support their movement, and in part because of the need to challenge Soviet propaganda, the department of justice took a more active role in advocating for civil rights in the postwar period. Specifically, it filed an amicus brief in support of the NAACP in *Brown v. Board of Education*. It also marked many significant victories including the passage of the Civil Rights Act and the Voting Rights Act.

Although the United States was entangled with the Soviet Union in a "Cold War," the prosperity and opportunity for many Americans at home reached unprecedented levels. The GI bill, for instance, produced a generation of college-educated homeowners and set the stage for an important process of intergenerational transfer of wealth among many white American families. However, the opportunities and prospects for educational attainment and home ownership were far less certain for people of color. The experiences and contributions of people of color, and in particular Mexican Americans during the war years, provided an important foundation for the collective organizing of the so-called Mexican American generation in the postwar period. This was a generation of folks that sought to challenge explicit institutionalized discrimination and implicit destructive social practices using the legal and political system. They relied on legal and political advocacy, as well as a collective philosophy of working within the framework of the established systems, to transform and demand the rights of Mexican Americans living and working in the United States.

The lone source for this chapter highlights the struggle that Mexican Americans faced asserting their rights in postwar America, but also underscores the significant legacy of that resistance. In his article assessing the *Battle for Chavez Ravine*, Ronald W. López "... examines the vocal, organized resistance of the people of Chavez Ravine to the destruction of their community, and the displacement of the residents for the construction of a public housing project that was never built."[1]

Community Resistance and Conditional Patriotism in Cold War Los Angeles: The Battle for Chavez Ravine

In his article, López offers an important critique of the postwar period by highlighting the struggles of a Mexican American community to hold off displacement. López underscores the particular advocacy of Mexican American women as a key component to the resistance and offers the idea that the energy and activism of the Chicana and Chicano Movement of the 1960s and 1970s, in part, draws on the legacy and agency of the women from Chavez Ravine.

THINGS TO LOOK FOR AS YOU READ..

- The Cold War context
- Strategies of resistance
- Gendered discourse

---

1 Ronald W. López II, "Community Resistance and Conditional Patriotism in Cold War Los Angeles: The Battle for Chavez Ravine," *Latino Studies* 7 (2009): 458.

Community Resistance and Conditional Patriotism in Cold War Los Angeles

The Battle for Chavez Ravine

Ronald W. López II

Introduction

On 8 May 1959, the City of Los Angeles evicted the Aréchiga family from their Chavez Ravine home of 36 years. Once the family had been removed, a bulldozer reduced the home to a pile of rubble. Eminent domain proceedings had begun 8 years earlier, when the city planned to seize the land for a major public housing project. Long before the final evictions, however, the housing project had been canceled, and the Los Angeles City Council was in the process of transferring the land to the Los Angeles Dodgers, for the future site of Dodger Stadium. The 10-year debate over the use of the land leading up to the dramatic final evictions came to be known to the people of Los Angeles as the *Battle of Chavez Ravine* (Hines, 1982a).

This article examines the vocal, organized resistance of the people of Chavez Ravine to the destruction of their community, and the displacement of the residents for the construction of a public housing project that was never built. Largely women, they spoke out during public hearings, wrote letters, and made statements to the media in a gendered discourse of resistance to displacement. In a language of patriotic post-war motherhood, the women made direct references to husbands and sons in military service to underpin the moral legitimacy of their statements. And yet, they made it clear that their patriotism was conditional. They had worked hard, purchased property and sent their men to war despite

Ronald W. López II, "Community Resistance and Conditional Patriotism in Cold War Los Angeles: The Battle for Chavez Ravine," *Latino Studies*, vol. 7, no. 4, pp. 457-479. Copyright © 2009 by Springer Nature. Reprinted with permission.

the discrimination that they faced at home. If the Government could take their homes, the symbol of American belonging, it threatened the foundation upon which their patriotism was based, and suggested that the United States had failed to live up to its promise. The people of Chavez Ravine, moreover, challenged projects that were supported by the entire left, liberal, and labor community, projects that promised to help poor communities, including Mexican Americans, nationwide. In doing so, they opposed positions taken by Mexican American leaders, and allied themselves, if only briefly, with local conservatives.

Recently, significant new research on the history of Chavez Ravine has been published, but this work focuses on the role the residents played in the process, and the impact of these events on the residents of Chavez Ravine.[1] Early studies that explored the history of Chavez Ravine included Rodolfo F. Acuñas' (1984) history of East Los Angeles in the post-war era and Thomas Hines' (1982b) biography of modernist architect Richard Neutra. Most have focused on the protracted, citywide struggle to halt the public housing program and the sale of the Chavez Ravine land (for US$1!) to the Los Angeles Dodgers. Several excellent recent studies have covered aspects of the story, including Eric Avila's *Popular Culture in the Age of White Flight: Fear and Fantasy in Suburban Los Angeles* (2004); and Robert Sherrill's *First Amendment Felon: The Story of Frank Wilkinson, his 132,000-page FBI File, and his Epic Fight for Civil Rights and Liberties* (2005). Undoubtedly, the most prolific author in this area is Don Parson, who wrote *Making A Better World: Public Housing, The Red Scare, and the Direction of Modern Los Angeles* (2005), and several excellent articles (1991, 1993, 1999, 2005). Additionally, Raúl Homero Villa (1998) and David Díaz (2005) have recently examined the Latino urban experience, including Chavez Ravine. Most recently, Tara J. Yosso and David G. García's (2007) article "This is No Slum!" is exceptional. The story of Chavez Ravine has also inspired art, including a panel on the *Great Wall of Los Angeles* by artist Judy Baca, Don Normark's *Chavez Ravine 1949, A Los Angeles Story* (1999), and the play *Chavez Ravine* by the group Culture Clash (2003).[2] The struggle of the residents of Chavez Ravine to defend their community has become part of the living cultural memory of many Southern Californians, and has inspired both scholarly and artistic works. This piece, in particular, analyzes the methods and strategies adopted by diverse residents of Chavez Ravine, especially the women of the community.

---

1 This article is based on several chapters of my 1999 dissertation: *The Battle for Chavez Ravine, Public Policy and Chicano Community Resistance in Post War Los Angeles, 1945–1962*, Department of History, University of California, Berkeley.

2 Baca, J. (1983); Normark, 1999; Culture Clash, 2003; and Cooder, R. 2005.

Historical Context of Chavez Ravine

In late 1949, the residents of Palo Verde, Bishop Canyon, and La Loma—collectively known as Chavez Ravine—learned of a planned public housing project that required the entire community to be displaced and relocated. Located in the hills immediately northeast of downtown Los Angeles, Chavez Ravine was home to over 1100 families, many who had lived there for several generations. Developed as a Mexican suburb early in the century, Chavez Ravine had become a healthy, multigenerational Mexican barrio by the end of World War II. Since at least that time, the residents had been working to improve their community. They had petitioned the city council to put in streetlights, pave streets and provide bus service to the area. Through their own efforts, they had been successful in decreasing juvenile delinquency and crime, and in increasing attendance at the local schools. After all these efforts, they were shocked to learn that their community had been declared "a blighted area," and that they would have to move so that their homes and community could be destroyed, and public housing put up in its place (McWilliams, 1990, 203).[3]

The residents had good reason to defend their community. While Chavez Ravine had its share of social problems, it had the highest proportion of property owners and the highest social indicators of any Mexican American community in the Los Angeles area (Frank, 1949).[4] Furthermore, a shortage of affordable housing, residential segregation, and the exclusion of Mexican Americans from new housing developments made the prospect of being displaced and finding new homes especially onerous. A public housing project in Chavez Ravine would thus turn a sizeable group of homeowners into renters. Those who moved out did not receive adequate compensation for their homes and land, and found that segregation and high prices excluded them from many areas.

By opposing the public housing project, the people of Chavez Ravine were rejecting a program supported by the entire Mexican American and liberal establishment, including Councilman Edward Roybal, the first Mexican American elected to the City Council since the nineteenth century. Although he was one of the strongest and longstanding supporters of public housing, including the units planned for Chavez Ravine, Roybal steadfastly defended the residents' rights to fair treatment and a fair price for their homes. The City Center District Improvement Association (CCDIA), a Chavez Ravine community organization, publicly rejected assistance from the leftist Asociación Nacional

---

3 Chavez Ravine was only two thirds Mexican and Mexican American, but was widely considered a "Mexican" neighborhood. A designation of *blight* meant that 20 per cent or more of the homes in an area had one or more "substandard" elements and could be subject to *slum clearance* or *redevelopment*.

4 The term "Mexican American" is historically specific; see Tino Villanueva (1985) for an excellent analysis of the term.

México-Americana, or ANMA, refusing aid from any organization that did not adhere to "American Principles" (Urrutia, 1984; García, 1989, 199–227; and Gómez-Quiñones, 1990, 51).[5] Instead, the community allied itself with the conservative real estate lobby, which argued that public housing was "socialist," and that adequate low cost housing could be attained by the enforcement of existing laws and building codes. That the residents allied themselves with the real estate interests is not surprising, since their traditional allies were unanimous in supporting public housing. And yet, they were reluctant to denounce public housing altogether, refusing to adopt the real estate lobby's mantra that public housing was "socialist."

Most importantly, the majority of those who spoke out and wrote letters were women—Mexican, Mexican American, white and Asian American—who lived in Chavez Ravine. They spoke and wrote in the language of conservative post-war patriotism, but it was a tentative, conditional patriotism. Their sons, brothers and husbands fought in World War II, and in Korea. Speaking in the gendered discourse of mothers and wives of veterans, they emphasized their contributions to the "war effort" of World War II as citizens who had earned the right to enjoy their homes in peace. Settlers of Chavez Ravine, they were pioneers who built their homes with their own hands, and raised their children to be patriotic citizens, just like earlier generations of Americans. They had worked to improve their community, and they rejected a project that proposed to benefit others at their expense. In doing so, Chavez Ravine residents challenged, head on, the City Council and the dozens of high profile civic leaders and "experts" that supported the public housing projects, denouncing what they saw as an unjustified plan. They walked a fine line, both defining themselves as exemplars of American patriotism and suggesting that if the City forcibly displaced them, they might be radicalized in the process (Lopez, 1999).

Los Angeles, with a city administration dominated by liberal social planners, was one of the first cities to take advantage of the passage of the 1949 Housing Act, applying for $110,000,000 in Federal Funds to construct 10,000 units of low-rent public housing at 11 sites around the city. The housing plan was part of a coordinated citywide redevelopment program that would have linked freeway construction and urban redevelopment with slum clearance and public housing, while also addressing an ongoing housing shortage. In August 1949, the City Council unanimously approved the plan.

Two competing visions of Los Angeles' urban redevelopment had emerged in the post-war era: the conservative vision, favoring the free play of the market, and the

---

5 Juan Gómez Quinones mentions that ANMA was "involved in campaigns against police brutality, housing discrimination ... deportation raids, and the media stereotyping of Mexicans and other Spanish speaking people" (Gómez Quinones 1990, 51).

liberal vision that included desegregation and an aggressive public housing program. Supporters of the liberal program included organizations such as the Citizens Housing Council, organized labor, veterans, religious organizations, the National Association for the Advancement of Colored People (NAACP), the Community Service Organization (CSO), and Mexican American civic leaders such as Councilman Edward Roybal and, publisher Ignacio López. Advocates for public housing, called "public housers", argued that the infusion of federal money would provide jobs for workers, contracts for local businesses, housing for the needy, and would stimulate the local economy. They argued that slums and "blighted" conditions caused overcrowding and fostered delinquency and rat infestations that spread disease and endangered public health. A coordinated program of urban redevelopment, coupled with a racially integrated public housing program would address these ills.

The liberal program was backed by the Mayor, liberal Republican Fletcher Bowron, and the Director of the Los Angeles City Housing Authority (CHA) Howard Holtzendorff; but its most outspoken advocate was CHA Information Director Frank Wilkinson, who epitomized the social engineers who believed that razing the slums and building low-cost public housing would improve the living standards of the poor and reduce poverty, crime, delinquency, disease, and residential segregation citywide (Sherrill, 2005, 68).

Conservative interests, such as the real estate lobby that included the *Los Angeles Times*, and smaller groups like the Small Property Owners Association (SPOA) wanted slum clearance and urban redevelopment too, but argued that the need for housing was being met by private developers, and that public housing was socialism, or at least "creeping socialism." They pressured the City Council on public housing, and almost immediately after approving the program, council members shifted, one by one, from unanimous support for public housing, to a slight majority against it. Two weeks after the passage of Proposition 10, which made future housing programs subject to the approval of voters, the City Council approved the selection of 11 sites for public housing projects, this time by a majority. Chavez Ravine was one of the approved sites (Parson, 2005, 104).

The public housing project planned for Chavez Ravine would have included almost one-third of the units planned for the city. To be called "Elysian Park Heights," the project proposed a transformation of both architecture and geography. The mostly single family dwellings would be replaced with 163 two-story buildings and twenty four 13-story apartment towers. And, in an act of deliberate erasure, a name change would elevate the *Ravine* to the *Heights*. According to the citywide plan, Elysian Park Heights would be constructed first, providing relocation housing for people displaced by other slum clearance, redevelopment, and public housing projects. For their sacrifice, the displaced residents were promised, in writing, first choice of the new housing, without respect to race (Sherrill, 2005).[6]

The Residents' Fight to Stay

Despite these promises, the people of Chavez Ravine were shocked and angered; they had worked hard, built a thriving community, and many of them owned their own homes (Frank, 1949; Alexander and Bryant, 1951). Thus, building public housing there would destroy what was arguably the most successful barrio in the city, and would turn a sizable group of homeowners into renters. Along with the homeowners of a number of other areas, they refused to cooperate with the city's plans, and spoke out vigorously against the choice of their district at public hearings held before the Planning Commission and the City Council. Their resistance, although unsuccessful, was passionate and organized, and the rhetoric they employed and the alliances they forged ran counter to conventional expectations of Mexican American political behavior for that era (*Frontier*, 1957; Hines, 1982a).

Frank Wilkinson, accompanied by Ignacio "Nacho" López, walked door-to-door convincing Chavez Ravine residents to move (Urrutia, 1984; García, 1989). The CHA guaranteed them first priority on new housing, rent scaled to income, and no racial discrimination (Sherrill, 2005, 74). On the other hand, some residents reported being threatened with forcible eviction (Suazo, 1953), and were intimidated into selling their homes for a low price. Through guarantees of future rental housing, and through intimidation, a large number of residents reluctantly agreed to sell and left their homes (Roybal Papers *Torch Reporter*, 1959).

The CHA, the Planning Commission and the City Council held public hearings that were heavily attended by proponents and opponents of public housing. While it was later alleged that paid employees of the CHA were heavily represented among the supporters in attendance, the opponents included not only residents of "blighted" areas to be redeveloped, but also members of affluent communities adjoining proposed housing projects, as in the case of Rose Hills. Other opponents included members of the SPOA, a vocal opponent of public housing (Investigation of Public Housing Activities in Los Angeles, 1953).

The people of Chavez Ravine had been well organized as a community since at least the end of the war, long before the proposed project had been announced.

---

6 The promise of priority on housing is one of the most widely quoted aspects of the program, but non citizens were ineligible for public housing, so the Housing Authority may have made a promise it could not keep. Later events rendered this complication moot.

In particular, the CCDIA represented a number of Chavez Ravine residents, and was a leading force in opposing the housing project even before final agreement between the City and the Federal Housing Authority (Frank, 1949, 34–35, 48, 52–54; Alexander and Bryant, 1951, 60).[7] The CCDIA met with both City Councilman Ed Roybal, a supporter of public housing, and with the SPOA. Importantly, the people of Chavez Ravine made a very clear decision to organize their struggle according to the laws and principles of the United States, refusing assistance from the radical. Even the name of the organization—CCDIA—suggests that they wanted to distance themselves from any suggestion of foreignness or radicalism.

This decision illustrates the complexity of Mexican American civic life in the post-war era. In the case of CCDIA, their militancy reflects the fact that they viewed themselves not as foreigners but as citizens entitled to all the rights of citizens, including the right to own homes and preserve their community. According to historian Mario T. Garcia, this was characteristic of the emergent militancy of the Mexican American generation,

> Americans of Mexican decent ... like their middle class contemporaries, were now sufficiently acculturated to recognize and demand their rights as US citizens. Rather than leading to conformity, Americanization or acculturation gave rise to protests in pursuit of American principles of democracy. (García, 1989, 176)

At the same time, their protest was couched in the conservative language of post-war patriotism. Considering the political environment in Los Angeles at the time, this is no surprise: their traditional allies were all supporters of the public housing project. The people of Chavez Ravine were opposing a program that was supported by the entire Mexican American political establishment. Even City Councilman Ed Roybal, who steadfastly defended the residents' right to fair treatment and a fair price for their homes, supported the public housing project in Chavez Ravine. The community adopted the real estate lobby's position that affordable housing could be achieved by enforcement of existing building codes. Most white opponents of public housing argued that public housing was "creeping socialism," a position not enthusiastically embraced by the people of Chavez Ravine. They emphasized that their homes were not blighted. Many pointed out that their sons, brothers, and husbands had fought in World War II. Was this what they had fought and died for? Finally, many of the people who spoke out publicly were

---

7 Information on the City Center District Improvement Association is limited, but sources indicate sustained community activism to improve conditions both by petitioning the city, and by individual and group community improvement activities.

women—Mexican, Mexican American, white and Asian American—who lived in Chavez Ravine.

The Gendered Discourse of Resistance: The Public Hearings

The women of Chavez Ravine spoke out forcefully against the destruction of their community for the construction of Elysian Park Heights during two sets of public hearings held in April 1951, and June 1951. Those who spoke out included both men and women, with the CCDIA clearly occupying leadership. While men occupied the nominal leadership of the organization in the role of President and lead counsel, women clearly occupied the vanguard of the discursive attack on the housing project, and especially, on their own displacement for the project in Chavez Ravine. Specifically, the arguments presented by the men directly responded to statements made by proponents of the projects, while the women articulated their objections in terms of their role as patriotic mothers and wives of veterans, and spoke from a position of moral authority that the men on both sides of the issue could not.

The roles that Mexican American women play in Mexican American community politics have been explored by several authors, most notably Mary S. Pardo in *Mexican American Women Activists: Identity and Resistance in Two Los Angeles Communities* (1998). Traditionally, Mexican American women were expected not to engage in political or other public activities without the knowledge, assent, and even guidance of family members, ideally fathers or husbands. When women did become active, however, their "activism originated in family concerns and community networks, then generated broader political concerns and networks" (Pardo, 1998, 228). Thus, activities that are extensions of women's domestic roles, such as those involving the home, the Church, or the schools, were increasingly seen as acceptable or even appropriate areas for women's activism. In speaking about such issues, women had a moral authority that men did not, and occupied visible leadership positions, even when men occupied nominal leadership roles. Speaking about the Mothers of East LA, Pardo says they "based their theories about grassroots activism in everyday life and in their work as wives and mothers. Rather than allow themselves to be constricted by them, they used traditional and social identities in community action" (ibid, 230). The outspoken testimony by Chavez Ravine women at public hearings in defense of their community was thus consistent with their "family and community relationships," and obligations (ibid, 231).

The first set of hearings was held by the Planning Commission on the week of 26 April 1951. The hearings' official purpose was to determine if the project sites should be approved, but in truth, the contract between the City of Los Angeles and the Federal Housing Authority had been made, and there was no going back. The first day of hearings, held on 26 April 1951, was an emotional affair attended by at least 500 persons. Opponents packed the hearing chambers and harangued the council, making it clear that they had no faith in the intentions of the CHA, shouting "Don't believe them. They're trying to take your land. They've never cared about you before. Why should they now?" (Hines, 1982a; *Frontier*, 1957) Many carried placards with slogans like "MacArthur was kicked out ... Are We Next?" and "Priests should Stick to Religion—and Not Meddle in Politics," a reference to Monsignor Thomas J. O'Dwyer of the Citizens' Housing Council (*Frontier*, 1957). On the one hand was an impressive pantheon of civic leaders speaking on behalf of the proposed project: the CHA, representatives of the Catholic Church, and labor unions. On the other hand, speaking against the project were representatives from Chavez Ravine and their lawyer, Mr G.G. Bauman (La Opinión, 1951; Parson, 2005, 168).

CHA Executive Director Howard Holtzendorff opened the hearing, emphasizing that the Chavez Ravine project was "the keystone to the entire future of replanning downtown Los Angeles" (City Planning Commission, 1951, 1). Stanley Furman, Development Counsel for the CHA, noting that Chavez Ravine was a "large, partially vacant area" blighted by substandard housing, asserted that temporarily housed veterans would have first preference at the new housing, making no mention of the people of Chavez Ravine (ibid.). Others who spoke in favor of the project included Frank Wilkinson, CHA Director of Information, Architect Richard Neutra, Monsignor O'Dwyer of the Citizens' Housing Committee, and others. An impressive cross-section of experts and community interests favored public housing, including most Mexican American organizations, such as the CSO (ibid.).

After the pro-public housing testimony, the community, represented by the CCDIA, declared their desire to keep their homes and preserve their community. Women played a critical role as spokespersons, and reflected the multiethnic nature of the community. The CCDIA, said Baumen, had for several years been trying to improve conditions in the area, but to no avail.

> I represent a number of clients in this area who have for a number of years come to me and said "What can we do to get some improvement here? What about some street lights? Why can't we get the Health Department to give us help ... to improve the conditions that exist here?" If the Health Department is concerned, as they contend

they are now, about conditions in this area, it is within their power
to enforce the provisions of the City Code and the Health Laws
relating to these premises.

"In other words," Baumen continued, "we can keep the property in the hands of private owners, we can build up the community, [and] we can keep it on the tax roll without building high cost housing for low rent" (ibid, 12–13). That public housing would be a tax burden on the community became the most salient and compelling argument to the public, as the debate evolved from one specific site location to a national debate in which public housing was equated with socialism. Another issue, one that was dropped as time went on, was the immigrant and non-citizen status of many of the residents of Chavez Ravine. Baumen refuted earlier assertions that all current residents would be "given priority" for moving into Elysian Park Heights, noting that some of the people of Chavez Ravine were "of Mexican-Spanish descent, some Italians," and that "Federal Law does not permit them [to live in public housing] unless they are citizens" (ibid.). Homeowners were also ineligible for public housing (Land Purchase Policies, ND).

Responding to pictures of run down conditions, Manuel Cerda displayed photos of well-maintained properties, stating, "If you call this a slum, I don't know what would be a good house." Cerda emphasized the existing facilities in the Ravine, saying, "We have plenty of facilities in there. We have gas, water, lights." He also pointed to the city's failure to maintain the area, noting that, "The streets are very poor—but that is due to the City Engineer and Council. They have not done anything for us" (City Planning Commission, 1951, 13).

Mabel Hom, local Girl Scout troupe leader and an Asian American, did not mince words. Declaring, "I am an American Citizen," Ms Hom spoke at length, saying "I don't need all these fancy maps and charts to say what I have to say." She denounced veteran support of public housing, saying,

> I should think you know how it feels to go over to protect a piece
> of what you call your home. ... We did not know the Veterans were
> against our purpose of keeping our homes and ... I think it is very
> undemocratic of people to place the preference of Roger Young
> [Village Housing] Veterans over our 1100 families in Chavez Ravine.
> We have just as much right to a home as they have. (ibid.)

Furthermore, Ms Hom noted, the property owners of Chavez Ravine were "forced" to live there, because "discrimination forced us to buy into this area" when it was considered unsuitable for development. "But now these Capitolists (*sic*) find we have a lovely place, located close to every facility there is, and you want it." Additionally, rather than calling public housing "creeping socialism," Ms Hom suggested that the evicted residents might themselves become un-American, saying,

> If this plan goes through, I assure you there will be 1100 families that will not be as American, with attitudes that they should possess. I am sure if you label us 'Reds' from now on it will be the fault of the Housing Authority group which has no right to push people around, as they have been pushing 1100 families in Chavez Ravine. (ibid, 13–14)[8]

The pro-American tone of her statement, her defense of private property rights and her attack on both big government and big capital make her statement especially interesting. While she did not adopt the charge of "socialism," Ms Hom's perspective illustrates the intensity of the anti-public housing feeling that was felt by many, especially those who were threatened with losing their homes, that public housing as a conspiracy of powerful interests arrayed against them. Most importantly, Ms Hom suggested that displacing Chavez Ravine homeowners might radicalize them, make them less "American," even make them into "reds."

The final statement recorded in opposition was given by Agnes Cerda, the Secretary of the CCDIA, and the wife of Manuel Cerda. Speaking as a "taxpayer and American Citizen," and speaking on behalf of "the Mexican people," Mrs Cerda also spoke in language that was pro-American. She likened the early generations of Mexican American homeowners of Chavez Ravine to other generations of American pioneers who came to the United States in search of liberty, who built their homes with their own hands. She also denounced the CHA as un-American for taking their homes, saying,

> I represent all of ... the Mexican people ... they came out here to the land of liberty and justice for all. They started one by one to build to the best of their ability and, after all these years, the City Health Department never thought about coming in there to see that these homes were up-to-date and standard. Now, when they have them built, with the sweat of their brow ... The Housing Authority

---

8 Ironically, Mabel Hom lived just outside the boundaries of the redevelopment area, and her testimony was refuted on this basis in a written rebuttal submitted after the hearing.

comes in now and tries to take their homes away from them. It is
not justice and not American policy.

Mrs Cerda, emphasizing the Mexican people of the community, equated their experience with the American ideals of liberty and justice. Although she denounced the proposed public housing project in Chavez Ravine, Mrs Cerda, like Ms Hom, chose not to suggest that public housing was "socialistic," emphasizing "I don't say housing projects are not right. They might be all right for the people that want to live in them, but we, as property owners, we want to keep our homes." She also expressed skepticism about the motives of the Planning Commission and City Council, saying, "Let them live in those housing projects and give us their homes if they want to do so much for us." Finally, like Ms Hom, Mrs Cerda also warned the Commission about the disenchantment and anxiety that dispossession and dislocation would cause for the Mexicans and other people of the Ravine. Identifying herself as the mother of a combat veteran and an American citizen, she appealed to public sympathy for veterans and their families, saying,

> Take our homes away from us and you are taking away our incentive
> to be good American Citizens, [that] … we are trying to raise our
> children to be. I know, I had a boy in the Second World War. Thank
> God he was lucky to come back. I have another one that it won't
> be very long, if this keeps on, he will have to go too and when he
> comes back, is he going to fight over there and have to come and
> fight over here for a home he hasn't got? Would you put your mother
> out of your home to give it to the Housing Authority? You would
> not. (ibid, 15)

Mrs Cerda's words convey the nuance with which the people of Chavez Ravine sought to defend their homes. The women positioned themselves at the center of America's patriotic and pioneering spirit, building their own homes by "the sweat of their brow," and articulating their patriotism by raising their children to be good American citizens, even soldiers in wartime. But it was these idealized American values and trust in government that were now endangered by the very actions of the City Council and the CHA, representatives of both big business and big government. The expression of conditional patriotism was a warning—or was it a threat?—the idea that the people of Chavez Ravine would be radicalized by the process of dislocation and dispossession was clearly well-thought out, but it may also have been true.

Others also spoke: Louis J. Scott, John Lorenz, Bertha Withers, Samuel Fegestad, Alfonso Mirabal, Marie Stancil, Frank Sanchez, Richard Suazo, Mosher M. Meyer and Margaret C. Loya all spoke, but no written record remains. According to the Council recorder's note, "because their testimony was more or less reiteration of what previous speakers said it has been omitted." By omitting their statements from the formal record while including those of "experts" in favor of the project, the council recorder committed a deliberate act of erasure, similar to that planned for the residents of Chavez Ravine (ibid, 15–16).

Despite the thoughtful and strategic arguments of the residents, the policy-oriented arguments in favor of public housing prevailed. On 17 May, the City Planning Commission approved eight sites for public housing, including Elysian Park Heights. The *Los Angeles Times*, however, focused on the approval of the Rose Hills site, in the middle of a white middle-class suburb in a front-page blurb. Public housing would go forward, and it would be placed, among other places, in Chavez Ravine. The residents did not give up, but appealed the Planning Commission's approval of the Elysian Park Heights, Rose Hills and other sites. According to the *Los Angeles Times*, the appellants argued that the projects were not properly located and that the CHA did not have legal standing to seize their properties (*Los Angeles Times*, 1951a, b, c, d). The City Council agreed to hear the appeals of the Elysian Park Heights and two other sites as a Special Order of Business on 21 June (Los Angeles City Archives, 1951a). Meanwhile, the Council meeting was preceded by a series of articles in the *Los Angeles Times*, which argued that Los Angeles did not need public housing or rent control, that public housing was "creeping socialism," that apartment vacancies and home construction were on the rise, that private home builders needed to be free of restrictions to meet the demand, and that rent control was both unnecessary and detrimental to the economy (*Los Angeles Times*, 13–26 May 1951).

On 21 June, the City Council began what turned out to be a week of raucous public hearings. Hundreds of people packed the Council chambers, "vociferously opposing or favoring the proposals" (*Los Angeles Times*, 1951a,b,c,d,e). The Council agreed to hear groups from three proposed housing sites in one afternoon, granting each group 20 minutes to present their case. To further restrict the debate, the City Clerk asserted that the merits of public housing, having already been decided, were not an issue.

Speaking against the public housing project for the Chavez Ravine site were Manuel Cerda, Bertha Withers, John Lorenz, Marshall Stimson, Angie Villa and Lewis J. Scott. Speaking in favor of the Chavez Ravine site were 26 representatives of civic, veterans, minority, and labor organizations, including CHA Director Holtzendorff, Monsignor

Thomas J. O'Dwyer, and Trinidad Rodrígues of the Council of United Railroad Workers of America (Los Angeles City Archives, 1951a; *Los Angeles Times*, 1951a).[9]

Manuel Cerda, leader of the CCDIA, was the first speaker on behalf of Chavez Ravine property owners. Arguing that the will of the community was against the project, he asserted that, "The people of my district don't want to be renters. They want to be honest taxpayers. We don't want anybody else to have to pay our taxes." Finally, he said, "We don't want to be socialized" (*Los Angeles Times*, 1951a). Additionally, Cerda argued that the district was dirty because of the ongoing failure of the city to make necessary improvements. Marshall Stimson "representing certain citizens of the area" argued, as he had at the Planning Commission, that the project was economically wrong, that the area could be improved by other means, and that the City Council was acting illegally. Angie Villa stated that she had lived in Chavez Ravine for 39 years, that she and her father wanted to keep their home, and that public housing had poor living conditions (Los Angeles City Archives, 1951a). Bertha Withers testified that the $110,000,000 public housing "scheme" was the "biggest invitation to political graft that ever disgraced this community" (Los Angeles City Archives, 1951a).[10]

Speaking in defense of the projects, CHA chief Holtzendorff argued that if the $110,000,000 were not used in Los Angeles, it would be used elsewhere, despite the fact that Los Angeles paid taxes to create the funds. He also declared that the real estate lobby was behind opposition to the projects. Others argued that the housing projects would provide better living and a healthy environment for youth, that private development had failed to provide adequate and affordable housing, that it was a community responsibility to provide low-rent housing, that the human rights of the many must prevail over the property rights of the few, and that the benefit to the community as a whole offset the damage to a few individuals. Trinidad Rodrígues of the Railroad Workers union argued that the project would help the Mexican community, since the location was close to downtown where many Mexicans worked (*Los Angeles Times*, 1951a).

The following day was an all-day session at which opponents of the Rose Hills site spoke. Only a few homes were to be lost for the Rose Hills development, while the Chavez

---

9 Organizations advocating public housing included the American Legion, the Veterans Organizations Coordinating Council, the Veterans Advisory Committee, the Los Angeles Central Labor Council of the American Federation of Labor (AFL), the Citizens Housing Council, the Greater Los Angeles Congress of Industrial Organizations (CIO) Council, the League of Women Voters, the Los Angeles Urban League, the Los Angeles County District Council of Carpenters, the Council of United Railroad Workers of America, the Los Angeles Youth Project, the Watts Chamber of Commerce, the National Association for the Advancement of Colored People, the Regular Veterans Association, Americans for Democratic Action, the International Association of Machinists, the Los Angeles City Housing Council, the Catholic War Veterans and the American Council on Human Rights.
10 The testimony of Chavez Ravine appellants was paraphrased and truncated. Don Parson (2005) further discusses the role of Bertha Withers.

Ravine homeowners were to be forced out completely. The Rose Hills site representatives argued, in classic "not-in-my-backyard" fashion, that public housing would lower their property values, and that there were better ways to address the housing problem, in the words of one speaker, than "this proposed socialized concentration camp." One asked,

> Shall we light the match that spreads the conflagration which will destroy private homes and private enterprise in our city? Shall you gentlemen be the guards at the gate who tear it down to permit the entry of a Trojan horse which will destroy our American ideal of American privately owned homes? (*Los Angeles Times*, 1951b; Los Angeles City Archives, 1951b)

In response, Councilman Ed Davenport, previously one of public housing's most aggressive advocates, said "This is the most forceful and convincing presentation I have listened to in my six years of sitting of (*sic*) the City Council" (*Los Angeles Times*, 1951b). That the *Los Angeles Times*—and Davenport—should focus their sympathy so entirely on the white, middle-class Rose Hills residents, while stonewalling the mostly Mexican American residents of Chavez Ravine reveals the racism that permeated the era (Parson, 2005, 103–135).[11]

There were explicit examples of racial bias as well. Some letters to the City Council denounced the racial integration the public housing program proposed. For example, H. G. Tuthill, a Rose Hills property owner and author of several letters, said that he was one of those parents who,

> ... want their children to be free from the influence of a mass of negro, Mexican and a lot of others who have little regard for the better aspirations of American Citizenship ... we ... know it is hard enough to keep children out of trouble without moving them right into a nest of melting pot hudleums (*sic*) who care very little about what their children do or say. ... How would you like to have your own little girls (if you had any) be left to play with a bunch of rough negro, and others no better, would you like it? (Tuthill, 1951)

Tuthill's racial invective was wrapped in the language of citizenship, much like the statements of Ms Hom, Mrs Villa and Mrs Cerda, but to different effect. While they shared

---

11 See also Parson, 1999; I am deeply thankful to Mr Parson for sharing an advance copy of this article.

an opposition to public housing developments in their communities, Rose Hills residents vociferously embraced the argument that public housing was creeping socialism, and that integration threatened the racial integrity of their white daughters. The people of Chavez Ravine, on the other hand, were defending their already integrated community from complete destruction on the basis of their exemplary upholding of American ideals, such as their military service in World War II. The public hearings continued through the following Tuesday, 26 June 1951. During the packed, day-long session, Mr Bauman argued that since the people in the last election had passed Proposition 10, the City Council should place the issue on the ballot as a public referendum (Los Angeles City Archives, 1951b; *Los Angeles Times*, 1951c).

That same day, the Council approved resolutions denying the appeals of Manuel Cerda and the other residents of Chavez Ravine, and granted the final approval to the CHA to proceed with public housing in Chavez Ravine and the other sites (Los Angeles City Archives, 1951c). The *Los Angeles Times* editorialized that public housing had "expanded in significance beyond the expectations of proponents or opponents until it has reached the eminence of a city-wide issue," and echoed Bauman's demand that the Council place the issue on the ballot. Not surprisingly, the City Council took the *Los Angeles Times* more seriously than it took Mr Bauman, and a referendum on public housing was placed on the June 1952 ballot (*Los Angeles Times*, 1951d).

The Community Dwindles

After the approval of the Elysian Park Heights housing project, and with eminent domain looming, many Chavez Ravine residents gave up and sold their land to the CHA. Some held out, hoping for a reprieve, some stubbornly refused to leave, and some wrote, letters to the City Council, protesting their impending evictions. These women continued to express themselves in a discourse of conditionally patriotic mothers, such as Faustina Tele Ibarra, who wrote,

> I do not see the necessity of my paying rent or to be burdened with
> a debt in buying a home when I already own one, and ask, why it
> is that we mothers of veterans do not have a right to own property
> and live in peace without being molested? (Ibarra, 1951)

At 66 years old and in poor health, Maria Longoria Esparza, caring for her 11 orphaned grandchildren, was no longer able to work. She wrote that she would not be able to buy a new home for the price offered for her house, which was paid in full;

I plead to be able to keep my home, I have struggled so much to finish paying so that my poor children could have a roof over their heads ... my home is in good condition ... I do not know how the Housing Authority can condemn the home I went through so many hardships, sometimes without food, to get enough for the monthly payments, and now that I thought it was mine at last they tell me I must go from it. (Esparza, 1951)

Mrs Esparza's concerns were echoed by a neighbor, Margaret C. Ayala, who reiterated that many people would not be able to obtain new housing for what was offered. Reminiscent of the real estate lobby's slogan; "Don't Pay Someone Else's Rent!" she suggests that people like Mrs Esparza might become wards of the state, saying,

Some homes are owned by older people who have very little income yet they have been too proud to ask for any assistance while they had a roof over their heads. With their homes about to be taken from them and at the prices the Housing Authorities are quoting the acquisition of another house will be out of the question, then instead of taxpayers they would become burdens of the government. (Ayala, 1951)

Ms Ayala alludes to the same feeling expressed by Mabel Hom and Agnes Cerda, that the taking of their homes threatened their faith in the government, and undermined their incentive to be good citizens;

Our homes we thought were ours to have and to hold seem to be ours only as long as bureaucrats wish us to have them. What assurance can we have that we won't have to go through the same thing again[?]. The sense of security, the incentive, the pride that goes in owning your home is now for us a matter of "what's the use, where can we go?" (ibid.)

Finally, Ms Ayala tells the member of the City Council that she, and others, despite their fear of the courts, would resist, defend their homes, and that they had no faith in the CHA to give them a fair hearing. She hastens to add that she has "no alternative,"

As one of the more stubborn ones in this area I know that eventually I will be served with a Condemnation suit, I do not welcome such action ..., however, I have no alternative, threatened with the injustice and lack of consideration to the extent of losing our home we must make an effort to defend ourselves. Like me, there are people who ... have very little doubt but that these suits will in all probability be only mere formalities. (ibid.)

Ms Ayala's letter to the council was well written and very polite. Yet even here, Ms Ayala alerts the Council to layers of injustice involved in displacing poor and elderly residents from their homes. People like Mrs Esparza, sick and elderly, might not be able to resist, but Ms Ayala's letter said that she would put up a fight.

By August of 1951, two-thirds of the Chavez Ravine residents had packed up, sold their homes and land, and moved on. Those that remained refused to sell. Women such as Agnes Cerda, Angie Villa and Arana Aréchiga, who were leaders in the struggle to preserve Chavez Ravine from redevelopment, expressed resentment at their treatment by the City, and their determination to continue the fight to retain their homes (*Los Angeles Times*, 1951e; Roybal interview, 1990).

The concerns of the women mirrored those expressed months before at the public hearings. "If these are slums," queried Agnes Cerda, one of the guiding forces of the holdouts, "why did they not come to us 10 years ago and tell us they were slums. Then we might have been able to do something about them," adding that "We built our homes here, not the government. ... Taking away our homes takes our incentive to be good American citizens." Avrana Aréchiga concurred, adding that "I know nothing of slums. I only know this has been my home and it was my father's home and I do not want to sell and move. I am too old to find a new home. Here is where I live. Here, in Chavez Ravine" (*Los Angeles Times*, 1951e).

Their desire to stay was reinforced by the negative experiences of those who had moved out before, only to suffer discrimination and hostility in their new neighborhoods. Mrs de León reported that "There are families that have moved into the City and they have come back to us and they have had tears in their eyes. And they say they are not accepted outside." Angie Villa expressed her hope that the Court of Appeals would rule in their favor, but they all seemed sadly conscious that the departure of so many of their neighbors meant that the community that they had fought to defend no longer existed. "I swear I will never sell and others swear the same," Villa said sadly, "But they see so many move away that they are afraid and they sell and go too." By this time, less than a third of the original property owners remained (ibid.; Roybal interview).

Earlier in the year, the property owners had met with Los Angeles City Councilman Edward Roybal. A progressive Mexican American leader and a consistent supporter of public housing, he understood, from experience, the challenges faced by the residents of Chavez Ravine. During their meetings, he advised the property owners that they would only be fairly paid for their property if they remained united, collectively refused to sell their properties to the CHA, and demanded a higher price from the CHA. According to Roybal,

> Those that sold [their property to the CHA] made a mistake in my opinion. I had meetings with them and I told them "Don't sell; stick together and you're going to win this." They didn't stick together. Because one of them sold one [property] here, the other one over there. They gave them a hundred dollars more in one place, another two hundred in the other. And pretty soon they divided the whole thing, and three-fourths of them sold [their property to the CHA]. (Roybal interview)

Roybal maintained that all of the homeowners of Chavez Ravine, but especially those who sold their homes first, "got gypped" (ibid.). While Roybal had encouraged the homeowners of Chavez Ravine to act together to secure higher prices, the SPOA had encouraged them to reject public housing altogether. The liberal magazine *Frontier* denounced the SPOA's gall in spreading "the gospel of free enterprise to people who hadn't known before how heavily their problems weighed on the business community" (*Frontier*, June 1957).

The residents of Chavez Ravine were supposedly offered "market prices" for their land. Some officials even argued that they were being offered more than their land was worth. Although the CHA was to provide relocation assistance in finding new living quarters, *Frontier* noted that "those residents of the area who had owned their own homes faced the typical difficulty of matching the sale price of their old property with the purchase price of the new" (ibid.). Roybal also said that the people were not paid fairly, saying "Under the right of eminent domain they went in there and took their property." The CHA "told them your house is worth 'so much,' and that's all there was to it" (Roybal interview).

Many resisters, such as the Aréchigas, De Leons, Cerdas and Angie Villa, stayed on, fighting the evictions in the courts. During the Condemnation proceedings the Aréchigas were offered $10,500 for three lots and two houses. Unsatisfied, the Aréchiga family hired a private appraiser, who appraised their properties at $17,000. Challenging the condemnations in court, the Aréchigas lost and the courts set the price at $10,050. When the Aréchigas refused to accept the money, the payment was placed in an account in their name and the sale declared consummated by the judge. Eviction proceedings began, but no actual eviction took place until 1959 (Roybal Papers; Aréchiga *et al*, 1953; *Lincoln Heights Bulletin News*, 7 June 1959). In all, the Aréchiga family resisted the City Council, police officers and the courts for 10 years.[12]

Red Scare

On 3 June 1952, Los Angeles voters rejected the public housing program in a citywide referendum, but the vote was merely symbolic; the courts had ruled that the measure would have no effect, and that public housing in Los Angeles would continue. The property owners of Chavez Ravine had been unable to prevent the mass condemnation of their properties, and they had been unable to obtain satisfactory prices for their homes. Those who refused to accept the prices offered, like the Aréchigas, found that the CHA brought the matter to superior court, where their lands were condemned, prices set low and "sales" forced on unwilling landowners.

In late August 1952, Frank Wilkinson was testifying at a condemnation hearing for a Chavez Ravine property. Felix H. McGinnis, a lawyer for a Chavez Ravine landowner, had been given an FBI brief detailing Wilkinson's communist party associations. After cross examining Wilkinson on blighted conditions, McGinnis abruptly changed the subject and asked Wilkinson "what organizations, 'political or otherwise,'" he had been a member of since 1929? (Hines, 1982a, 139–140). Wilkinson described his professional associations, and his work experience, but when McGinnis pressed him to name his political associations, Wilkinson refused, saying that he was "compelled by matters of personal conscience" and that "to answer such a question might in some way incriminate me" (Hines, 1982a, 80; Parson, 2005, 118; Sherrill, 2005, 75). Wilkinson was immediately suspended.

Los Angeles exploded in a frenzy against "communist infiltration" in the CHA. While the enemies of public housing had always argued that public housing was socialistic, Wilkinson's invoking of his Fifth Amendment right against self-incrimination gave them all the ammunition they needed. Two months later, Wilkinson again refused to answer the question, this time before the California Senate Fact-Finding Committee on Un-American Activities. This time, for refusing to answer, Wilkinson and five other public housing officials were fired and blacklisted (Seventh Report of the Senate Fact-Finding Committee on Un-American Activities, 1953; Sherrill, 2005, 135–141; Parson, 2005, Appendix A, 204).

---

12 A dozen other households also refused to leave, and were similarly evicted. The Aréchigas, however, were the most public about their opposition, and the most willing to use the media to their advantage, including alerting the media to the day they expected the eviction.

With Wilkinson fired and the public housing program discredited, the *Los Angeles Times* drafted Congressman Norris Poulson, an undistinguished Republican, to challenge Mayor Fletcher Bowron in the 1953 mayoral election. The House Subcommittee on Government Operations, chaired by Poulson's friend Clare Hoffman, held a Special Subcommittee on Public Housing in Los Angeles shortly before the June 1953 election, keeping the recent scandal alive in the minds of voters. Predictably, Bowron lost the election (Poulson, 1966, 155).

Within a week of taking office, the new Mayor suggested a compromise to end the controversy. CHA Director Holtzendorff would agree to renegotiate the contract between the Federal Housing Authority and the City of Los Angeles that would cancel the controversial Chavez Ravine and Rose Hills projects, and Poulson would leave the remaining public housing intact, and ask his allies in Congress and Los Angeles to end their attacks. Mayor Poulson, City Attorney Roger Arnebergh, Holtzendorff and others met with the Federal Housing Administrator in Washington DC. Not only were the Chavez Ravine and Rose Hills projects canceled, but the City of Los Angeles was given an option to buy the Chavez Ravine land owned by the CHA for its acquisition costs (ibid, 224; Assembly Interim Committee, 1958).

Behind the scenes, however, the City Attorney's office continued to condemn Chavez Ravine properties until the very minute they received word that public housing there was officially canceled. The Rose Hills properties were left untouched. The people of Chavez Ravine had their land seized under eminent domain for a purpose that no longer existed. Dispossessed of their land and forced to move, they were largely forgotten. Even the Spanish language daily *La Opinión* turned its attention to the hysteria over the discovery that "reds" had infiltrated the CHA.[13] Los Angeles was able to buy the land in Chavez Ravine for a minimal sum, and a few years later succeeded in attracting the Brooklyn Dodgers to the city by offering them 315 acres of Chavez Ravine (*The Californian*, 13 September 1960; López II, 1999; Arnebergh, ND).[14]

There were still some of the old residents living there, however, who had to be forcibly evicted, including the Aréchigas, who were evicted in May 1959. The home was bulldozed moments after the eviction, and the family conducted a "sit-down strike," camping out for a week on the site. Aurora Vargas, a daughter of the Aréchigas and a war widow, hung her husband's dress uniform up in front of the wreckage of the house with a handwritten sign that declared; "My husband died in World War II to Protect Our

---

13 *La Opinión*, the Spanish language daily newspaper of Los Angeles, was sometimes more extensive in its coverage, but it rarely diverged significantly from the politically powerful *Los Angeles Times*.

14 Efforts to interview Dodger officials were unsuccessful. I was told that Neil J. Sullivan, *The Dodgers Move West*, (1987) was their preferred version of events.

Home" (Parson, 1993). The dramatic eviction and its aftermath quickly overshadowed the earlier struggle of the people to preserve their homes 8 years earlier. Although there were other evictions, it was the Aréchiga eviction, filmed by television reporters and covered in detail by the newspapers, that seared the fate of Chavez Ravine into the minds of Los Angeles residents.

Conclusion

The residents of Chavez Ravine fought to preserve their community against destruction by the intrusion of a public housing project during the years 1950–1952. They had good reason to do so, as Chavez Ravine was probably the nicest "blighted" area one could hope to live in at the time, especially if one were Mexican or Mexican American. With its spacious semi-rural environment, and a core of residents whose parents had moved there early in the century, Chavez Ravine had a strong sense of community pride. Decent, affordable housing was in short supply, and most new housing was too costly and restricted to "whites only." There was more at stake than a few homes; what the CHA proposed was the displacement of the entire community. The people who spoke on behalf of Chavez Ravine used a variety of arguments, but were consistent in their expressed belief in American political principles and ideals, and their commitment to the democratic process. Largely women, they spoke in a highly gendered language, making unambiguous references to husbands and sons in military service to underpin their moral legitimacy. The women made it clear, however, that their patriotism was tentative and conditional; they had worked hard, purchased property and sent their men to war despite the discrimination they faced at home. If the Government could take their homes, the symbol of belonging in the American system, they argued, it threatened the very foundation upon which their patriotism was based. This subtle threat suggests a lingering distrust of government, a sense that the United States had yet to live up to its promise. The people of Chavez Ravine, moreover, were challenging projects that were supported by the entire left-liberal and labor community, projects that promised to help poor communities, especially Mexican Americans, and other minorities nationwide. They opposed the positions taken by the acknowledged Mexican American leaders of the day, and allied themselves, if only briefly, with local conservatives. While the story of Chavez Ravine continues to be explored by academics, journalists, and artists, few have acknowledged the centrality of the community's militancy in delegitimizing public housing in Los Angeles.[15] The residents rejected a sacred cow of liberal ideology of the

---

15 The exceptions are cited above; Baca, 1983, Normark, 1999, Culture Clash, 2003, Cooder, 2005; and Yosso and García, 2005.

era—that public housing was a greater good destined to help Mexican Americans, and other poor communities. Their protest challenged contemporary expectations of Chicano political behavior of the era: they were not simply poor, hapless slum-dwelling Mexicans, but politically astute Mexican Americans determined to defend their community. In the end, although their opposition to the redevelopment of Chavez Ravine was unsuccessful, the refusal of the landowners to willingly move away proved to be the opening salvos of a political conflict that would dominate Los Angeles politics for 10 years, and that would be resolved only by the physical evictions of the Aréchigas, and other families. Furthermore, the struggle to preserve Chavez Ravine became part of the popular memory of Los Angeles' Mexican American community. The residents of Chavez Ravine spoke out in defense of their homes, and their politically complex position impacted Los Angeles city politics. They rejected the liberal establishment's social engineering because, despite their desire to be fully included in the American body politic, it would be they, and not the liberal social planners, who would pay the price.

Acknowledgement

I acknowledge the support of my wife Christina Zapata, my family, mentors, and the editors of Latino Studies. This article is dedicated to the people of Chavez Ravine, their descendants, and displaced people everywhere.

About the Author

Ron López II is an assistant professor in the Department of Chicano and Latino Studies at Sonoma State University. Born and raised in Ventura and Los Angeles, California, he received his BA from UCLA in History in 1988, and his PhD in History from U.C. Berkeley in 1999. He taught Mexican and Latin American Studies and United States History at Laney College, and United States History at Chaffey College. He is currently conducting research on the Chicano community in Santa Rosa, California.

References

Acuña, R.F. 1984. *A Community Under Siege: A Chronicle of Chicanos East of the Los Angeles River, 1945–1975*. Los Angeles, CA: Chicano Studies Research Center Press, University of California.

Alexander, R.E. and D. Bryant. 1951. *Rebuilding the City: A Study of Redevelopment Problems in Los Angeles*. Los Angeles, CA: The Haynes Foundation.

Aréchiga, M. and A. Aréchiga. 1953. *Appellants, vs Housing Authority of the City of Los Angeles, et al., respondents.*

Arnebergh, R. ND. Letter to Editor by Los Angeles City Attorney R. Arnebergh on unmarked undated newspaper clipping, probably from May or June, 1959.

Avila, E. 2004. *Popular Culture in the Age of White Flight: Fear and Fantasy in Suburban Los Angeles.* Berkeley, CA: University of California Press.

Ayala, M.C. 1951. Letter to the City Council, 25 May; Archives of the City of Los Angeles.

Baca, J. 1983. *Division of the Barrios and Chavez Ravine, Segment of the Great Wall of Los Angeles.* Los Angeles, CA: Social and Public Art Resource Center.

The Californian. 1960. Roybal Papers, 13 September.

California Legislature Assembly. 1940. Assembly Interim Committee on Governmental Efficiency and Economy, Chavez Ravine Hearings, Sacramento, CA.

City Planning Commission. 1951. Minutes of public hearing on Elysian Park Heights Housing Project. 26 April. Archives of the City of Los Angeles.

Culture Clash. 2003. *Chavez Ravine,* (Theater Production). Los Angeles.

Cooder, R. 2005. *Chávez Ravine A Record by Ry Cooder,* Nonesuch Records, Los Angeles.

Díaz, D.R. 2005. *Barrio Urbanism: Chicanos, Planning, and American Cities.* New York: Routledge.

Esparza, M.L. 1951. Letter to the City Council, 28 May; Archives of the City of Los Angeles.

Frank, E.R. 1949. Background for planning. *Welfare Council of Metropolitan Los Angeles*, Welfare Council of Metropolitan Los Angeles, pp. 48, 52 53.

Frontier. 1957. *The voice of the New West.* Los Angeles, CA, June.

García, M.T. 1989. *Mexican Americans: Leadership, Ideology, & Identity, 1930–1960.* New Haven, CT, London: Yale University Press, 84 112.

Gómez Quiñones, J. 1990. *Chicano Politics: Reality and Promise 1940–1990.* Albuquerque, NM: University of New Mexico Press, 51.

Hines, T.S. 1982a. Housing, Baseball, and Creeping Socialism, The Battle of Chavez Ravine, Los Angeles, 1949 1959. *Journal of Urban History* 8(2): 123, 136 137.

Hines, T.S. 1982b. *Richard Neutra and the Search for Modern Architecture: A Biography and History.* New York, NY: Oxford University Press.

Ibarra, F.T. 1951. Letter to the City Council, 29 April, typed translation of Spanish handwritten letter to the City Council; Archives of the City of Los Angeles.

Investigation of Public Housing Activities in Los Angeles. 1953. House of Representatives Hearings before a Special Subcommittee on Government Operations, US Congress, 83rd Congress, First Session, 13, 18–21 and 27 May.

La Opinión. 1951. Acalorada Audienciaen el Caso de Palo Verde. Making a better world. 27 April: 168.

Housing Authority of the City of Los Angeles. ND. Land Purchase Policies: Policies on Relocation Assistance to Site Residents. City Planning Commission, attachment to minutes of public hearing on Elysian Park Heights Housing Project, 26 April 1951. Los Angeles City Archives.

Lincoln Heights Bulletin News. 1959. Edward Ross Roybal Papers (Newspaper clippings) June.

López II, R.W. 1999. The Battle for Chavez Ravine: Public Policy and Chicano Community Resistance in Post War Los Angeles, 1945–1962. PhD Dissertation, University of California Berkeley.

Los Angeles City Archives. 1951a. Transcript of Hearings City Council Meeting, 21 June.

Los Angeles City Archives. 1951b. Transcript of Hearings Before the City Council, 25 June.

Los Angeles City Archives. 1951c. Transcript of Hearings Before the City Council, 26 June.

Los Angeles Times. 1951a. Housing Hearing Start Brings Storm, 22 June.

Los Angeles Times. 1951b. Housing Projects Socialistic, Opponents Tell Councilmen, 23 June.

Los Angeles Times. 1951c. Council Acts Today in Housing Dispute, 26 June.

Los Angeles Times. 1951d. Council Votes for Low Rent Housing Plan, 27 June.

Los Angeles Times. 1951e. Settlement Losing Battle for its Life, 20 August.

McWilliams, C. 1990. *North From Mexico, The Spanish Speaking People of the United States*, updated edn. New York: Praeger Publishers.

Normark, D. 1999. *Chavez Ravine 1949: A Los Angeles Story*. San Francisco, CA: Chronicle Books.

Pardo, M.S. 1998. *Mexican American Women Activists: Identity and Resistance in Two Los Angeles Communities*. Philadelphia, PA: Temple University Press.

Parson, D. 1993. "This Modern Marvel:" Bunker Hill, Chavez Ravine, and the Politics of Modernism in Los Angeles. *Southern California Quarterly* 75(Fall/Winter): 343.

Parson, D. 1999. "The Darling of the Town's Neo Fascists:" The Bombastic Political Career of Councilman Ed. J. Davenport. *Southern California Quarterly* 81(Winter): 467 505.

Parson, D. 2005. *Making a Better World: Public Housing, The Red Scare, and the Direction of Modern Los Angeles*. Minneapolis, MN: University of Minnesota Press.

Poulson, N. 1966. *Who Would Have Ever Dreamed?* Oral History. Los Angeles: Oral History Program, University of California, Los Angeles, p. 155.

Roybal, E.R. 1983. (papers), Los Angeles: University Research Library's Special Collections Room, University of California.

Roybal, E.R. 1990. Interview with Congressman Edward R. Roybal, formerly a Los Angeles City Councilman, in Los Angeles, 27 November 1990.

Seventh Report of the Senate Fact Finding Committee on Un American Activities 1953. Hearings on the Los Angeles City Housing Authority, California Legislature, Sacramento.

Sherrill, R. 2005. *First Amendment Felon: The Story of Frank Wilkinson, His 132,000 page FBI File, and His Epic Fight for Civil Rights and Liberties*. New York: Nation Books.

Suazo, S. 1953. Investigation of Public Housing Activities in Los Angeles, House of Representatives Hearings before a Special Subcommittee on Government Operations, US Congress, 83rd Congress, First Session, 13, 18–21 and 27 May. Testimony of a resident of Chavez Ravine. 20 May, p. 329.

Sullivan, N.J. 1987. *The Dodgers Move West.* New York: Oxford University Press.

The Torch Reporter. 1959. Roybal papers (magazine clippings) (May) 2.

Tuthill, H.G. 1951. To Councilman Ernest Debs, Los Angeles City Archives, letter from H.G. Tuthill to Councilman Debs, 14 June.

Urrutia, L. 1984. An Offspring of Discontent: the Asociación Nacional México Americana, 1949 1954. *Aztlán, International Journal of Chicano Studies Research* 15(1): 177–184.

Villa, R.H. 2000. *Barrio Logos: Space and Place in Urban Chicano Literature and Culture.* Austin: University of Texas Press.

Villanueva, T. 1985. *Chicanos: (Selección).* México: Fondo de Cultura Económica.

Yosso, T.J. and D.G. García. 2007. This is No Slum!" A Critical Race Theory Analysis of Community Cultural Wealth in Culture Clash's Chavez Ravine. *Aztlán: A Journal of Chicano Studies* 32(Spring): 145–179.

READING 6.1   POST-READING COMPREHENSION QUESTIONS

- Summarize why residents of Chavez Ravine were skeptical of the planned public housing project.

- Define conditional patriotism.

- Paraphrase the passage: "Their protest challenged contemporary expectations of Chicano political behavior of the era: they were not simply poor, hapless slum-dwelling Mexicans, but politically astute Mexican Americans determined to defend their community."

End-of-Chapter Critical Thinking Questions

Directions: Respond to each of the questions about the reading. Refer to the source to support your answers.

- Describe the significance of the political activism of Mexican Americans during the postwar period.
- Explain some of the strategies that the Chavez Ravine community used to advocate for their rights.
- How does the cold war context influence our understanding of this period?

Further Readings

Acuña, Rodolfo. *A Community Under Siege: A Chronicle of Chicanos East of the Los Angeles River, 1945–1975.* Los Angeles, CA.: Chicano Studies Research Center, Publications, University of California at Los Angeles, 1984.

Avila, Eric. *Popular Culture in the Age of White Flight: Fear and Fantasy in Suburban Los Angeles.* Berkeley, CA.: University of California Press, 2004.

Carroll, Patrick James. *Felix Longoria's Wake: Bereavement, Racism, and the Rise of Mexican American Activism.* Austin, TX.: University of Texas Press, 2003.

Cohen, Lizabeth. *A Consumers' Republic: The Politics of Mass Consumption in Postwar America.* New York, NY.: Knopf Random House, 2003.

Daniel, Cletus E. *Chicano Workers and the Politics of Fairness: The FEPC in the Southwest,1941–1945.* Austin, TX.: University of Texas Press, 1991.

Dudziak, Mary L. *Cold War Civil Rights: Race and the Image of American Democracy.* Princeton, NJ.: Princeton University Press, 2002.

Galarza, Ernesto. *Farm Workers and Agri-business in California, 1947–1960.* Notre Dame, IN.: University of Notre Dame Press, 1977.

García, Ignacio M. *Hector P. García: In Relentless Pursuit of Justice.* Houston, TX.: Arte Público Press, 2002.

García, Mario T. *Memories of Chicano History: The Life and Narrative of Bert Corona.* Berkeley, CA.: University of California Press, 1994.

Hernández, Kelly Lytle. *Migra!: A History of the U.S. Border Patrol.* Berkeley, CA.: University of California Press, 2010.

Laslett, John H.M. *Sunshine Was Never Enough: Los Angeles Workers, 1880–2010*. Berkeley and Los Angeles, CA.: The University of California Press, 2012.

Orozco, Cynthia. *No Mexicans, Women, or Dogs Allowed: The Rise of the Mexican American Civil Rights Movement*. Austin, TX.: University of Texas Press, 2009.

San Miguel, Guadalupe. *"Let All of Them Take Heed": Mexican Americans and the Campaign for Educational Equality in Texas, 1910–1981*. Austin, TX.: University of Texas Press, 1987.

Self, Robert O. *American Babylon: Race and the Struggle for Postwar Oakland*. Princeton, NJ.: Princeton University Press, 2003.

CHAPTER 7

El Movimiento

Editor's Introduction

There is no doubt that there were very significant gains made by the Mexican American generation of the 1940s and 1950s, yet by the 1960s and early 1970s there were more Mexican American students attending segregated schools than there were in the 1940s. Additionally, by the 1960s more and more Mexican American families were falling deeper into poverty as a result of being tracked into low-wage labor and explicit public policy directed at extending a second-class citizenship to this group of people. Like their predecessors before them, many of the younger generation were fed up with these circumstances but now were increasingly unwilling to accept what they perceived as accommodationist strategies to reverse their conditions. What came to fruition during this period was the development of a political consciousness that shifted the way that Mexican Americans understood themselves, their politics, and their place within American Society; what resulted was a new Chicano consciousness.

Historian Ignacio Garcia writes that "A political consciousness of being 'Mexicano' in the United States gave rise to a militant ethos that became the impetus for this social upheaval. This ethos sought to synthesize the problems of the Mexican American community in terms that most Mexican Americans could understand and to which they could relate." Garcia goes on to note that the Chicano militant ethos should be understood as the collective mechanisms that the Mexican American community used to combat racism, discrimination, poverty, and segregation, and to define itself politically and historically.[1] Thus it is appropriate to understand the Chicana and Chicano Movement (CCM) as a creative and revivalist surge that absolutely championed civil rights amidst a larger set of social movements that fought for political recognition, an end to racial violence, and legal respect.

---

1 Ignacio M. García, *Chicanismo: The Forging of a Militant Ethos Among Mexican Americans* (Tucson, AZ.: University of Arizona Press, 1997), 3–4.

More to the point, however, the CCM was a confluence of many significant struggles all aimed at social justice.[2] The readings in Chapter Seven are a mix of primary and secondary sources that all speak to the political and social militant resurgence that took place during the 1960s and 1970s, and specifically assess the three main strands that made up *El Movimiento*; the student movement, the farmworkers' movement, and the anti-war movement.

Manifesto, Excerpt from El Plan de Santa Barbara

El Plan de Santa Barbara was the applied manifestation of much of the activism and energy of the Chicana/o student movement. Its main focus was trying to develop the institutional mechanism that could fuse higher education with the needs of the community. "The statement of a Chicano philosophy of education was inclusive and progressive, a unique concept beyond the usual limiting university concerns to a selected few. Thus, the plan's primary importance was its concern, and focus on, the Chicano community."[3] The entire plan, written in 1969, is actually more than 150 pages long and includes a detailed outline for an associate degree, bachelor's degree, and a full academic program—all in Chicano studies. This is a short excerpt from the opening manifesto. It begins with a historical recentering of the circumstances and calls for a strategic use of education to challenge the structural racism and violence experienced by Chicanos and Chicanas in American society.

THINGS TO LOOK FOR AS YOU READ..

- The cost of assimilation
- Historical context
- Definition of Chicano

---

2 Juan Pablo Mercado, "From Siqueiros to SPARC: The Ideological and Historical Roots of a Chicana Mural Movement," in *Rewriting the Chicano Movement: New Histories of Mexican American Activism in the Civil Rights Era, eds.* Mario Garcia and Ellen McCracken (Tucson, AZ.: University of Arizona Press, 2021).

3 Juan Gómez-Quiñones and Irene Vásquez, *Making Aztlán: Ideology and Culture of the Chicana and Chicano Movement, 1966–1977* (Albuquerque, NM.: University of New Mexico Press, 2014), 169.

Manifesto, Excerpt from *El Plan de Santa Barbara*

Chicano Coordinating Council on Higher Education

For all people, as with individuals, the time comes when they must reckon with their history. For the Chicano the present is a time of renaissance, of renacimiento. Our people and our community, el barrio and la colonia, are expressing a new consciousness and a new resolve. Recognizing the historical tasks confronting our people and fully aware of the cost of human progress, we pledge our will to move. We will move forward toward our destiny as a people. We will move against those forces which have denied us freedom of expression and human dignity. Throughout history the quest for cultural expression and freedom has taken the form of a struggle. Our struggle, tempered by the lessons of the American past, is an historical reality.

For decades Mexican people in the United States struggled to realize the "American Dream." And some—a few—have. But the cost, the ultimate cost of assimilation, required turning away from el barrio and la colonia. In the meantime, due to the racist structure of this society, to our essentially different life style, and to the socio-economic functions assigned to our community by anglo-american society—as suppliers of cheap labor and a dumping ground for the small-time capitalist entrepreneur--the barrio and colonia remained exploited, impoverished, and marginal.

As a result, the self-determination of our community is now the only acceptable mandate for social and political action; it is the essence of Chicano commitment.

Culturally, the word Chicano, in the past a pejorative and class-bound adjective, has now become the root idea of a new cultural identity for our people. It also reveals a growing solidarity and the development of a common social praxis. The widespread use of the term Chicano today signals a rebirth of pride and confidence. Chicanismo simply embodies an ancient truth: that man is never closer to his true self as when he is close to his community

... We recognize that without a strategic use of education, an education that places value on what we value, we will not realize our destiny.

READING 7.1 POST-READING COMPREHENSION QUESTIONS

- Summarize the social and political reawakening taking place in the Mexican American community.

- Describe how Chicanismo is defined in this excerpt.

- Paraphrase the line: "We recognize that without a strategic use of education, an education that places value on what we value, we will not realize our destiny."

"Sí Se Puede": The United Farm Workers

"Sí Se Puede": The United Farm Workers by Fred B. Glass provides an important look at California labor history and specifically focuses on the strategies and contributions of the United Farm Workers (UFW) in order to secure unionization rights in California. This source charts the seminal event of that effort—the consumer grape boycott of 1965—but also goes deeper to examine some of the important gains and internal challenges that faced farmworkers in their struggle for fair and decent working conditions in the agricultural industry.

THINGS TO LOOK FOR AS YOU READ...

- Union accomplishments
- Strategies of resistance
- Contributions of *manong* farmworkers

"Sí Se Puede"

The United Farm Workers

Fred B. Glass

....

For more than a century farmworkers had been denied a decent life at work in the fields and in the communities of California's rich agricultural valleys. Essential to the state's biggest industry—but only so long as they remained exploited and submissive—farmworkers and their supporters in the labor movement had tried but failed so many times to organize the giant agribusiness farms that most observers considered it a hopeless task.

But by the early 1960s things were evolving. Within fifteen years close to 100,000 farmworkers were protected by union contracts. The union, the United Farm Workers of America (UFW), was a cross between a labor organization and a social movement. Its leader, Cesar Chavez, had become a nationally revered civil rights crusader. The farmworkers' newfound power was reflected in passage of a state law, the Agricultural Labor Relations Act—first of its type in the nation—that forced the growers to play by the rules of common decency. Wages rose; toxic pesticides were no longer sprayed by growers with impunity on crops and workers alike; workers and their families began to participate in the American Dream and achieve the dignity so long denied them. What had happened?

End of the Bracero Program

The Bracero Program, an informal arrangement between the United States and Mexican governments, became Public Law 78 in 1951. Started during World War II as a way to provide Mexican agricultural workers to take up the slack for farmworkers who had left for military service and better-paid war industry jobs on the coast, the Bracero Program nonetheless continued after the war ended. It undercut unionization efforts by providing cheap labor and replacements for striking workers.

Recalled Jessie De La Cruz, who later organized farmworkers for the UFW, "When my husband used to go up to Stockton to pick tomatoes, he was getting 25 cents a box for picking tomatoes, those forty-pound boxes, and when the *braceros* came they were paid 12 cents, half of what we were getting." Because of the ever-present threat of deportation, *braceros* were usually afraid to protest employer abuses, of which there were many.

One of the worst consequences of the Bracero Program was that stable, family-based communities of mostly Chicano farmworkers around the edges of major growing areas—fertile ground for union organizing, because they lived in the same place all year round—were broken up. These workers were instead forced to follow crops around the state and even into other states. The Bracero Program brought hundreds of thousands of temporary, disposable Mexican workers to the California fields each year.

Over time, however, farmworkers were able to call upon allies in other unions, and in churches and community groups affiliated with the growing civil rights movement, to put enough pressure on politicians that the Bracero Program was finally phased out of existence by 1964. This occurred despite the loud protests of the growers that their business would fall apart without the *braceros*. Of course no such thing happened. An important obstacle to farmworker unionization had been removed.

Conditions of Farmworkers and Their Work

But in some respects things hadn't changed much since the Wheatland Hop Affair in 1913. Grape pickers in 1965 were making an average of $1.20 per hour, plus ten cents per "lug" (a 28-pound wooden basket) picked. State laws regarding working standards were loosely enforced, if at all. At one farm the boss made the workers all drink from the same "cup"—a beer can—in the field; at another ranch workers were forced to pay a quarter per cup. Many ranches had no portable field toilets. Jessie De La Cruz described a typical arrangement.

> What they do instead of supplying restrooms and clean water where we can wash our hands, is put posts on the ground with a piece of gunny sack wound around them. That's where we went. And that thing was moved along with us. It was just four stakes stuck in the ground, and then there was canvas or a piece of gunny sack around it. You would be working, and this restroom would be right there. The canvas didn't come up high enough in front for privacy.

Workers' temporary housing was segregated by race, and they paid two dollars or more per day for unheated metal shacks with no indoor plumbing or cooking facilities. Often the accommodations were infested with mosquitoes. Room and board were deducted from workers' pay. Farm labor contractors played favorites with workers, selecting friends first, sometimes accepting bribes. Child labor was rampant, and many workers were injured or died in easily preventable accidents. The average life expectancy of a farmworker was forty-nine years.

New Organizations, New Possibilities

Two organizations were attempting in different ways to represent and organize the farmworkers. One had been formed in 1959 by the AFL-CIO. The Agricultural Workers Organizing Committee (AWOC) was dominated in the beginning by white AFL-CIO staffers, who held the purse strings. But most active AWOC members were older Filipinos, with some Chicano, Anglo, and black workers as well. The Filipino workers in particular had had experience organizing unions and with strikes in the fields.

This core of veteran *manong* (first-generation Filipino immigrants) kept the organization going, even while much attention and funding were directed to various high-profile organizing projects that never got off the ground. Some workers, like Larry Itliong, had participated in leadership roles in other unions, such as the short-lived Filipino Agricultural Laborers Association, which led an impressive one-day strike of several thousand asparagus workers around Stockton in April 1939 to restore wage rates. Itliong and another Filipino, Philip Vera Cruz, had also taken part in a large scale but less successful 1948 asparagus strike.

At fifteen, in 1929, Itliong came to the United States from the Philippines. Like many of the *manong,* he worked as a migrant laborer in West Coast agriculture but also took jobs on the railroad and in canneries. He helped found a salmon cannery workers union, originally chartered as a federal AFL local in 1933 in Seattle and Stockton, which became UCAPAWA, and then Food, Tobacco, Agricultural and Allied Workers (FTA) Local 7. When the FTA folded in 1950, Local 7's members affiliated with the International Longshoremen and Warehousemen's Union as Local 37. Itliong served as a shop steward and was then elected vice president in Local 37 in Stockton. Due to this resume, he was hired by the Agricultural Workers Organizing Committee (AWOC) as an organizer.

Vera Cruz arrived in the United States three years before Itliong, but he spent seventeen years in Vancouver, Chicago, and other cities outside California before landing in the San Joaquin Valley in 1943 to pick grapes. He was thirty-nine, discharged from the army, and had a cousin in Delano, a farm town north of Bakersfield. He lived for years in labor camps in order to save money and to send some home to his family, who had sacrificed to send their son overseas. Eventually he was able to buy a small house in Richgrove, ten miles east of Delano. Although Vera Cruz served as president of the National Farm Labor Union local in Delano in the 1950s, he had become inactive by 1965, when he joined AWOC.

The other organization was the National Farm Workers Association (NFWA), started by thirty-five-year-old Cesar Chavez in 1962. Chavez was frustrated with the Community Services Organization (CSO) despite having become national director. He believed in the CSO methods of working with communities to solve problems through organizing and direct action, based on the principles of community organizers Saul Alinsky and Fred Ross. But when CSO leaders refused to allow a pilot program to organize farmworkers to move forward, Chavez left to found the NFWA. From his home in Delano, over a period of three years he traveled from town to town in southern San Joaquin Valley, meeting with groups of farmworkers in their living rooms, tirelessly building an organization that he hoped would one day become an effective union. Dolores Huerta, meanwhile, did the same work in the northern valley counties.

They deliberately set dues rates relatively high for the association (Chavez preferred to avoid the term "union" until the organization was on a stable footing). Chavez believed that at $3.50 per month it would be a stretch for most workers, but in the process help the members form a commitment to the NFWA. He was right. Within two years the organization claimed close to a thousand members and was able to pay modest salaries to Chavez and NFWA cofounder Dolores Huerta.

Like Chavez, Huerta had gained organizing skills in CSO after recruitment by Fred Ross. As a small child she had lived in New Mexico while her father worked in the mines, until the mine owners blacklisted him for union activities. After her parents divorced, Huerta and her brothers moved with their mother, who supported the family by running a restaurant and hotel, to Stockton. Self-confident and assertive, Huerta went to college and became an elementary school teacher but also began volunteering for CSO in 1955. She set up the Stockton-based Agricultural Workers Association together with a Catholic labor priest, Thomas McCullough, while raising a growing number of children (eventually eleven). She went to work for AWOC and became its secretary-treasurer. But eventually she left the organization because she disagreed with its approach to organizing.

Huerta thought that organizing meant talking with workers. The AFLCIO staffers running AWOC took a shortcut; they organized the labor contractors, the middlemen who put together workers and employers for a fee. Their tactics included short strikes when necessary, and gained raises in pay, but resulted in little collective spirit or worker loyalty to an ongoing organization.

This was not AWOC's only mistake. Despite the agreement of May 1950 that ended the three-year DiGiorgio strike, some copies of the ill-fated documentary film *Poverty in the Valley of Plenty* survived. One turned up in the possession of AWOC in 1959. Blissfully unaware of its legal history, or aware but uncaring (former AWOC staffers disagree on this point), the new AFL-CIO union made prints and began screening them in meetings around the San Joaquin valley. DiGiorgio's lawyers hauled the union into a Stockton court on charges of libel. A young labor attorney named Victor Van Bourg, whose experiences on the DiGiorgio picket lines in 1948 as a teenaged painters' union apprentice had steered him in the direction of his future career, attempted to defend AWOC against DiGiorgio's legal department.

Van Bourg, who later became the head of the largest labor law firm on the West Coast, said that he never argued a case better in court. He remained convinced that had the case been tried outside of the San Joaquin Valley the film would not have been found libelous: "In the atmosphere of the times, you couldn't expect a decision in Stockton to go against the growers for something like this." On appeal the $150,000 settlement against the union was reduced to $60,000 in 1961. But the libel decision remained, and the AFLCIO leadership lost considerable enthusiasm for farmworker organizing. AWOC continued, although with diminished support from the national federation.

Before the Beginning

Two short strikes occurred in the spring of 1965. Eighty-five farmworkers in a McFarland rose farm asked the NFWA to help them form a union and gain a wage increase. Assisted by Chavez and Huerta, the workers struck. After a few days the growers agreed to the wage increase but not the union. The workers contented themselves with the wage increase and returned to work.

Around the same time AWOC members led a much larger walkout of hundreds of Filipino and Mexican grape pickers in Coachella Valley. Although the Bracero Program had officially ended the year before, a new agreement between the United States and Mexico allowed growers to import Mexican workers if they were paid $1.40 an hour, and never paid more than domestic workers. When Coachella grape growers indeed attempted to pay the domestic workers less than the imported workers, the Filipinos, many of whom were AWOC members, refused to work. Philip Vera Cruz explained why.

> We had a strong labor consciousness. We had been working in
> this country for over 40 years, and we were aware of prices and
> profits because we listened to market reports on the radio and

then discussed these reports in Ilocano, our dialect. This "workers' consciousness" helped us to be the most organized and united of all the different ethnic groups of farm workers at that time.

Coachella grapes, grown in southern California, ripen first in the state. Getting the grapes picked and to market quickly is crucial to Coachella growers' profits. Ten days later the growers decided to pay everyone, including Chicanos who had joined the Filipinos, $1.40 per hour. Once more, however, no union contract was signed.

It Started in Delano

At the end of summer the grapes were ripening in the fields around Delano. Farmworkers from the successful Coachella action had come up to Delano, trailing the grape harvest. Many lived in Delano year round but had traveled south to follow the seasonal work. Expecting to be paid $1.40 per hour, the farmworkers were furious at being offered less once more. On September 8 they struck nine farms. The strike organizer was AWOC's Larry Itliong.

After five days the growers began to bring in Chicano scabs. Itliong approached Chavez and asked the NFWA to join the mostly Filipino strike. At a meeting on September 16, in an old hall in Delano packed with hundreds of workers, the NFWA voted unanimously, to shouts of "Viva la Huelga!" to strike too. Chavez was apprehensive. Asked later when he felt his organization—which had $100 in its bank account—would have been ready to go out on a big strike, he replied, "About 1968."

But the NFWA didn't have until 1968. Events moved quickly, and the NFWA had to march alongside or get left behind. In joining the strike, the NFWA took the lead, for it had many more members than AWOC. It also changed the ethnic makeup of the strike; now the majority of workers involved were Chicano. By September 20 more than thirty farms were struck, with several thousand workers leaving the fields. Despite the large numbers of striking farmworkers, the workers could not muster picket lines at all the ranches simultaneously. For one thing most of the workers couldn't stick around Delano—they had to work and left the area to find crops elsewhere. And as one strike supporter described the situation,

> It's like striking an industrial plant that has a thousand entrance gates and is four hundred square miles large. And if that's not bad enough, you don't know each morning where the plant will be, or where the gates are, or whether it will be open or closed or what wages will be offered that day.

NFWA and AWOC set up a system of roving pickets, with different fields picketed each day. Fifteen or twenty cars full of pickets would go to a field where a grower was attempting to use strikebreakers. Striking workers, often harassed by the growers and police, sometimes violently, would try to get the scabs to leave the fields. Remarkably, their appeals were successful much of the time in emptying the ranches of workers, who were persuaded it was in their interest to strike.

The growers, overconfident, made a mistake almost immediately. They had always been able to end strikes with small wage concessions. Soon after the strike began they raised wages to $1.40 per hour. But this time they were shocked to discover it wasn't enough. The raise merely encouraged the strikers to believe they were being effective. Now there had to be a union contract, too.

Squeezing the Companies with a Boycott

A couple months after the strike erupted, Chavez and Huerta, on a suggestion from attorney Stewart Weinberg, initiated a crucial tactic, one that the farmworkers used to remarkable effect: a consumer grape boycott. The union called upon the public to refrain from buying grapes without a union label. Union volunteers were sent out to big cities, where they established boycott centers that organized friendly groups—unions, churches, community organizations—to not buy grapes and to publicize the boycott and pressure stores to remove grapes from their shelves.

This was not a first. The National Farm Labor Union had used the tactic with some success during the DiGiorgio strike. But the grape strike took things to a new level. Combined with the union's public disavowal of violence, this boycott was better funded, more extensive, more organized, and more effective. For one thing, it included a secondary boycott of stores selling grapes, not simply the primary boycott of the product itself. Although part of the difficulty farmworkers faced in organizing stemmed from their exclusion from the National Labor Relations Act, an advantage of being outside the law was their ability to use secondary boycotts, which had been removed from the NLRA by Taft-Hartley in 1947.

The strikers' cause was boosted by other events in the nation at the same time. The civil rights movement had created strong public awareness of the effects of racism, including lowered standards of living for the victims of prejudice in housing, employment, schools, and other areas of daily life. The civil rights movement focused attention on the treatment of African Americans in the south. But once revealed, the situation in the California fields looked similar. The largely Chicano and Filipino farmworkers benefited by the new public understanding of racism.

Sympathetic young people, some of whom participated the year before in the Freedom Summer voter registration drive in Mississippi, or in the University of California at Berkeley's Free Speech Movement, flocked to *la causa*. Many joined in the boycott effort. Others came to Delano to help with strike support. This was the "New Left," idealistic college-educated young people who devoted time and energy to bring about their vision of social justice.

Youthful movement energy fused with solidarity offered by the progressive wing of American labor—at its peak moment of numerical strength and political influence—to give the UFW critical backing. Key leaders like Walter Reuther of the United Auto Workers sent organizers and funding. Politicians like U.S. senator Robert Kennedy enrolled in the cause. Rank and file union members respected picket lines and joined the boycott. ILWU members refused to handle shipments of grapes, leaving them to rot on the San Francisco docks, and ILWU Local 10 formed a "five dollar a month" club so that members could contribute regularly to the farmworkers.

The farmworkers did not forget these acts of solidarity. When the ILWU longshore division went on strike in 1971, Don Watson, a "five dollar a month" club leader, asked the UFW if the farmworkers could help. Recalled Watson, "The next thing I knew they put together this huge food caravan for us. This long grape truck came to the San Francisco waterfront from the Central Valley. There were several trucks from Salinas. They had all this produce. Maybe 150 farmworkers arrived too."

Thousands of volunteers handed out boycott literature in front of stores selling grapes. Enormous publicity was generated for the strikers' cause, and millions of consumers learned about how their table grapes were grown through the exploitation of farmworkers. The boycott stimulated hostile reactions as well. Ronald Reagan, elected governor of California in November 1966, staged high-profile events with growers at which he made a point of eating grapes in front of cameras.

The Catholic Church split badly over the issue, but many priests played important roles building support in their communities and in the church hierarchy for the strike and boycott. Although debates raged as to the precise impact of the boycott on grape sales—and it varied widely from place to place—there can be no doubt it served a crucial function in the strike.

The Bigger They Are ...

The two biggest growers in the Delano area, Schenley and DiGiorgio, were the most vulnerable to the boycott. Both companies were owned by corporate entities with headquarters far from Delano. For each company grape growing was a relatively minor part of a larger economic empire. And crucially, Schenley and DiGiorgio had union contracts with workers in other parts of their businesses. The boycott had the potential to hurt sales in other product areas and to harm labor relations with their other workers. It didn't help the company's image with the public when soon after the strike began Schenley sprayed striking workers with fertilizer and insecticide.

Schenley was the first to crack. But it took another innovative action to bring the grower to the negotiating table: the NFWA and AWOC organized a march to Sacramento. Seventy strikers left Delano on foot on March 17, 1966, led by Chavez. They walked nearly three hundred miles in twenty-five days. Along the route of *la peregrinacion*, as they called it, they picked up hundreds of friends. They met and talked and rallied with thousands. A Chicano theater group, El Teatro Campesino, staged skits about the struggle from the back of a flatbed truck every night. One of its members, Luis Valdez, wrote a proclamation, "Plan of Delano," updating Emiliano Zapata's manifesto from the Mexican Revolution, which he read at each stop along the way. In the preamble it stated, "Our sweat and our blood have fallen on this land to make other men rich. The pilgrimage is a witness to the suffering we have seen for generations."

The march attracted media attention, public support, and helped generate the strikers' first substantial victory. Arriving in Sacramento on Easter morning, Chavez announced to a cheering demonstration of 10,000 supporters in front of the capital building that Schenley had bowed before the pressure and signed an agreement—negotiated by Dolores Huerta—with the union.

Within weeks, DiGiorgio agreed to hold a representation election. But before the election could be held a complication arose. The International Brotherhood of Teamsters (IBT), an independent union since its expulsion from the AFL-CIO in 1957 and the largest union in the country, offered to be on the ballot too. The IBT represented workers in many agriculture-related industries in California. If field workers were represented by another union and that union decided to strike, Teamster workers might be thrown out of work for the strike's duration. Ignoring the questions of social justice at the core of the farmworkers' campaign for union recognition, the IBT offered itself to DiGiorgio as a conservative alternative to the NFWA/ AWOC. The grower eagerly assented. Chavez and the NFWA called for the workers to boycott the election. Heeding the union, more than half the eight hundred workers at DiGiorgio's Sierra Vista ranch refused to vote.

Behind in the polls in a gubernatorial election year and needing union and Chicano votes, Pat Brown yielded to pressure and appointed an arbitrator to decide whether to hold another representation election at Sierra Vista. The arbitrator ordered another election for the end of August. This time the NFWA beat the Teamsters decisively, and the two largest growers in Delano were employers of union labor. Although it took seven months to negotiate a contract with DiGiorgio, the workers ended up with a union shop, a new base rate of $1.65 per hour, a week's paid vacation for workers employed at least forty weeks per year, and reporting and standby pay if no work was available.

La Huelga Continues

There were many more growers than Schenley and DiGiorgio, however. The strike dragged on at dozens of grape farms throughout the Delano area. In the past a farmworkers' union would have been unable to survive such a long conflict. But things were different now. More farmworkers joined after the first victories.

Consolidating strength, NFWA and AWOC formally merged during the summer, just before the DiGiorgio election. On August 22, the two organizations became the United Farm Workers Organizing Committee, AFL-CIO (UFWOC). The new union received a steady stream of organizing funds from the AFL-CIO, as well as ever-growing strike support from other unions, consisting of food, cash donations, and equipment for use in the union offices and field operations. UFWOC was able to extend its influence in the fields far beyond the Delano area.

By 1967 the union had over 17,000 members. On the same day in July that year that the UFWOC and IBT announced a jurisdictional agreement giving UFWOC uncontested right to organize fieldworkers, Gallo and Paul Masson, two large growers, announced they were ready to hold elections, realizing they could no longer play off one union against another. Unfortunately, the IBT/UFWOC accord proved to be short-lived. Over the next few years the Teamsters signed dozens of "sweetheart contracts" with growers without any evidence of support from workers.

But over the same period of time UFWOC continued to pick up momentum. Organizing steadily in the fields, the union had contracts covering one-third of all table grape companies, representing 50,000 workers, by mid-1970—by far more than had ever been represented by a union in the history of California agriculture. The most important symbolic moment of victory came in July, when two dozen Delano-area growers signed agreements committing to $1.80 an hour in wages plus a 25 percent increase in the piece rate per lug. Gains included union-run hiring halls to dispatch the workers and a growing set of services: a health clinic and health plan to be paid by an hourly grower contribution. The UFWOC also offered a credit union, community center, and cooperative gas station to members.

The hiring hall meant a serious barrier to discrimination and favoritism by labor contractors, much as the ILWU hiring hall had brought fairness in hiring for longshoremen in San Francisco thirty-five years before. For instance, in March, seventeen black farmworkers were dispatched to the Perelli-Minetti grape ranch from the union hall. It was the first time African American farmworkers had ever been employed there.

The United Farm Workers Organizing Committee (renamed in 1970 the United Farm Workers of America), as Chavez had envisioned, had become both a union and a civil rights movement, and this was the key to its success. The dual character of the farmworkers organization gave it a depth of moral pressure and sense of mission felt by members and supporters alike. It brought the union its victories but also the determined, long-term enmity of the growers, which mobilized all the considerable forces under its influence in the central valleys.

In the late summer and fall of 1970, lettuce and strawberry workers around the Salinas area, who had waited impatiently for the grape strike to be settled, were no longer willing to wait. Emboldened by the victory in grapes, they pushed the UFW to help them gain contracts, as did farmworkers throughout the state.

The UFW leadership told Salinas workers they would help organize after grape contracts were put in place. But before details could be hammered out, the floodgates opened. Besides the workers' impatience, magnifying the urgency of the situation was an unfortunate development: Chavez and the Salinas workers learned that the area's growers had signed secret contracts with the Teamsters covering more than ten thousand workers. Not one worker had been involved in negotiations or even knew about them. The UFW leaders were furious but not as angry as the workers.

Their wrath propelled mobilizations and actions including a mass march, rolling strikes, the threat of a boycott leveled against one of the major growers' corporate parent (United Fruit Corporation), a six-day fast by Chavez, and very effective field organizing by what was now a large, experienced cadre of UFW activists, ultimately ending up with a number of new contracts.

Over the next several years the union sought to consolidate and extend its collective bargaining realm but had to defend every inch of the terrain it had won against counter-attacks launched by the growers in the fields, the legislature, the courts, and in the media.

Farmworkers and their supporters were injured and killed in acts of violence by growers, their hired goons, law enforcement, and Teamsters, who pitted themselves against the UFW in hundreds of representation elections. When the courts ruled that the union could only use bullhorns to call out the workers in the fields for an hour a day, and limited picketing to one picket every hundred feet, the UFW responded with campaigns of mass civil disobedience. In four months of spring and summer in 1973, more than 3,500 farmworkers and supporters were arrested, clogging the jails of Kern County in a situation reminiscent of the Wobblies' free speech fights in Fresno over a half century before.

Figure 7.2.1 Born in the context of mass social movements and organized labor at its peak, Cesar Chavez's United Farm Workers declined as the political climate shifted right. Dennis Kelly, photo.

Although Chavez and the union leadership consistently preached the gospel of nonviolence to UFW members, the message did not always maintain discipline in the ranks, especially in the face of continuous provocations on picket lines, in labor camps, and on the streets of the small towns dotting the agricultural map.

The violence crested with two farmworker deaths in August. A Yemeni farm laborer, Nagi Daifullah, had served as a UFW picket captain. He was standing in front of a bar in Lamont with friends celebrating UFW members' release from jail. After an argument with a deputy sheriff, the twenty-four-year-old Daifullah was dead—an accident, said the police, but murder, according to UFW witnesses. A few days later, Juan de la Cruz, picketing the Giumarra ranch southeast of Bakersfield, was shot dead by two men passing in a pickup truck.

The deaths triggered wide-ranging discussions within the union and a refocusing of tactics, for a time, from picket lines to the boycott, and ultimately to political action. The UFW helped Jerry Brown win election to the governor's office in 1974, with the expectation that Brown—the son of former governor Pat Brown—would sign a law, the Agricultural Labor Relations Act (ALRA), legalizing collective bargaining for farmworkers. Like many private sector workers before passage of the National Labor Relations Act in 1935, farmworkers were already negotiating contracts with employers. But such bargaining occurred in a tumultuous, unpredictable environment, dependent on power matched against power, with inconsistent rules from one situation to the next, and the constant threat of violence lurking beneath the surface.

Crucial to the act, from the UFW's perspective, was creation of an Agricultural Labor Relations Board to enforce the law. The ideal ALRA should ensure the safety of union activists, protect access by organizers to workers, and see that implementation of farm labor elections was not ignored or delayed, often for years, by growers through the courts.

The growers, for their part, pushed for provisions outlawing strikes during harvest and removing secondary boycotts from the workers' tool kit. Such a law had been signed in Arizona in 1971. It was during the campaign against this legislation that, in refusing admonitions to give up, Dolores Huerta responded, "*Sí se puede*" (Yes, we can). When Governor Brown signed the ALRA in June 1975, it allowed harvest strikes but excluded secondary boycotts.

The governor appointed a proworker majority to the board and provided it with enough funding to open field offices across the state, hire attorneys and staff, and carry out its mission to encourage and oversee collective bargaining. There were scores of elections within the first year. The union's membership, which had sunk below ten thousand, climbed back over twenty thousand. But the growers came up with a new strategy. They filed hundreds of charges against the union and simultaneously persuaded friendly state legislators to withhold funding for the board, which quickly became overwhelmed by its huge case backlog.

The UFW mobilized its volunteer army in the cities to collect signatures and place Proposition 14 on the ballot, which stipulated adequate funding for the board and reiterated the right of the UFW to talk with farmworkers. Proposition 14 lost in November 1976, falling before a heavily bankrolled opposition campaign. But the rights to field access were upheld by a Supreme Court decision. And after the Teamsters signed a pact in 1977 pledging to stay out of the fields, the union won election after election. By 1980 the UFW claimed a hundred thousand members, enrolled under hundreds of contracts.

The forward momentum did not last. The next decade saw a steady reassertion of grower power as the crucial external support for the UFW in labor and public opinion eroded. Born in a context of mass social movements and with the support of organized labor at its peak, the UFW declined as the movements receded and industrial unions were hammered by political attacks and the globalization of the economy. The union struggled to administer contracts and organize in an increasingly hostile political climate. The Agricultural Labor Relations Board turned out to be a two-edged sword after Republican George Deukmejian, elected governor in 1982, appointed a pro-grower majority to the board.

Matters were not helped by problems inside the UFW. Larry Itliong had left the union in 1971, frustrated over his relegation to the fringes of leadership. In 1977 Philip Vera Cruz resigned in protest when Chavez accepted an award from Philippines dictator Ferdinand Marcos. Chavez's insistence on calling undocumented workers "illegals" and pushing for their deportation split the Chicano community. Internal battles over union democracy and purges of longtime UFW staff and other leaders left the union ill-prepared to cope with the new political environment.

A Balance Sheet

If the UFW ultimately could not live up to the expectations created by its early successes, that doesn't mean it was a failure. In a country where labor history is mostly a history of defeats, and in an industry with such an imbalance of power between workers and owners, the UFW meant something much more.

Prior to the UFW, any advances won by farmworker unions were always brief, eroded by the determination of the solid ranks of growers and by the marginal status of mostly immigrant farmworkers in the economic and political life of the state. Despite herculean efforts, sometimes entailing the sacrifice of lives, workers never managed to build a union in the fields that lasted even a decade.

The United Farm Workers' singular achievement was that it was the first farmworker union that lasted. As a result it had a profound impact on the labor movement and on the public's understanding of where its food came from and how it was produced. A generation of labor activists, leaders, and staff emerged from the crucible of the boycott and farmworker organizing.

The UFW and its struggle provided a central point of reference for the emergence of Chicano identity and culture, not only in California but the United States. The red and black Aztec Thunderbird logo cast a long shadow over Chicano graphic design and visual arts, as did marching farmworkers, grapes, and the iconic faces of Cesar Chavez and Dolores Huerta. The union's successes and stubborn survival provided a foundation for rethinking and rewriting the historic role of people who came from Mexico to California.

The union also made a classroom for consumers out of its struggle. It educated millions of people who, living in urban centers, had lost the ancient, basic human connection with growing the food they ate. Through the strikes, boycotts, and astute publicity efforts, the UFW taught the public about the exploitation of the people who produced what appeared, somewhat mysteriously, in supermarkets and on their tables. They learned about the health problems, for workers and consumers alike, that might be associated with a heavy reliance on pesticides in agriculture. And with the union's struggles, people found that, even against great odds, sometimes these wrongs could be righted. *Sí se puede.*

Sources

Chavez, Cesar. *An Organizer's Tale: Speeches.* New York: Penguin Books, 2008. Print.

Glass, Fred, ed. "California Labor History, Part IX: *Poverty in the Valley of Plenty*," *California Classified Exposition* 10.3 (1994). Print.

Huerta, Dolores. Personal conversations. 1994–1995, 2015.

Scharlin, Craig, and Lilia Villanueva. *Philip Vera Cruz: A Personal History of Filipino Immigrants and the Farmworkers Movement.* Los Angeles: UCLA Labor Center, Institute of Industrial Relations, and UCLA Asian American Studies Center, 1992. Print.

Soto, Gary. *Jessie de la Cruz: A Profile of a United Farm Worker.* New York: Persea Books, 2000. Print.

READING 7.2   POST-READING COMPREHENSION QUESTIONS

- Summarize the working conditions of farmworkers.
- Describe the strategy and effectiveness of the grape boycott.
- Paraphrase the line: "In a country where labor history is mostly a history of defeats, and in an industry with such an imbalance of power between workers and owners, the UFW meant something much more."

Ester Hernandez: Sun Mad

Ester Hernandez is a prolific artist and activist who made some significant contributions to the Chicana and Chicano Movement. When we think about the activism and struggles that took place in the 1960s and 1970s, we tend to acknowledge the work of political and labor leaders and those within academic institutions—and rightfully so. However, we must also acknowledge the work of the cultural producers. Hernandez produced one of the most iconic images of Chicana/o art with her screenprint Sun Mad in 1982. It was a fusion of Chicana activism, environmental justice, human rights, and labor rights in the form of a political poster. The beauty and genius of this work has not gone unnoticed and, as mentioned in this article, should be understood as a powerful contribution to the broader struggles against traumas of economic globalization.

THINGS TO LOOK FOR AS YOU READ

- The significance of political posters
- The association of labor and environmental practices
- The connection between the Chicana/o Movement and art

Ester Hernandez

Sun Mad

Rowan Bain

....

A first-generation Chicana, Ester Hernandez is a key figure in the Chicano civil rights art movement that emerged in America in the late 1960s. Her most famous image, the screen-printed poster *Sun Mad*, was first created in 1981 and expresses her anger at the human and environmental cost of pesticide use in commercial grape growing in California. A second edition of the screenprint, printed in 1982, has recently been acquired by the Victoria and Albert Museum and will feature in the forthcoming exhibition "A World to Win: Posters of Revolution and Protest."[1]

Making or displaying a poster is often a political, sometimes even a dangerous act, and for many social and political movements poster production has been an important form of cultural output. As the repository of the UK's national poster collection, the V&A holds an impressive range of political posters, about 70 of which will be represented in the exhibition. Produced over the course of a century, from the Votes for Women campaign to the recent Occupy movements, these images were created to mobilize, educate and organize people to produce change. Hernandez's print is important as a vibrant example of Chicano political art (not broadly represented in the UK), an early dramatization of environmental awareness and a potent subversion of corporate branding.

Born in 1944, Hernandez grew up in Dinuba, a rural town in California's San Joaquin Valley, sometimes described as "the salad bowl of America."[2] While much of the country's produce is grown in this area, the metaphor has another connotation, pertinent to understanding how Hernandez and many other Chicano artists identify themselves. Unlike its semantic forebear, the "melting pot," which was coined in the late 19th century to describe the fusion of European immigrants into a common

Rowan Bain, "Ester Hernandez: Sun Mad," *Art in Print*, vol. 3, no. 6, pp. 28-29. Copyright © 2014 by Art in Print Review. Reprinted with permission.

American culture, "salad bowl" describes a melange of ethnic groups tossed together while retaining their separate identities. In the 1960s, the term "Chicano" was adopted by people of Mexican descent living in the United States who had become politicized by their experience. Chicano art was, from its very beginning, an art of protest, connected to social politics and the labor movement and concerned with creating distinctive work that reflected the Mexican experience in the United States.

During the Great Depression, Hernandez's grandparents immigrated to California from Mexico to work on commercial grape farms. Having been forced to cut short their own educations, her parents were determined that their daughter finish high school. After graduating, she moved to the San Francisco Bay Area, got married and had a son. In her late twenties she went back to school, eventually enrolling at the University of California, Berkeley, to study anthropology. During her studies she shifted her focus to the visual arts, working with emergent Chicano artists, and later joined the Mujeras Muralistas, a group of female artists creating large-scale murals depicting the social concerns and everyday life of the Mexican community in San Francisco's Mission District. In the post-1968 era of grassroots activism, posters became tools of empowerment. They were used, for example, to publish images of black power and beauty, or of women daring to revolt. Like many Chicano artists, Hernandez was drawn to screenprints, which are inexpensive, can be reproduced and circulated easily, and suit her bold use of graphics and color.

In response to the African-American Civil Rights Movement of the late 1950s and early '60s, Mexican-American groups also organized to fight for social and political change. Unfair labor practices, voting restrictions and housing discrimination were common experiences for Chicanos and Mexican immigrants in America. For the many Mexican-American migrant workers, the formation of the United Farmworkers of America (UFWA) was a critical development. From 1965 the UFWA, led by César Chávez and Dolores Huerta, organized a series of successful strikes and boycotts against major American grape growers, demanding better wages and employment rights. The boycotts thrust the issue of conditions for farmworkers onto the dinner tables of America. Hernandez became involved with the UFWA, which, along with her engagement in the politically charged Berkeley community in the 1970s, confirmed her sociopolitical artistic identity and commitment to activism.

Against this backdrop Hernandez learned that pesticides used on the grape farms surrounding Dinuba had leeched into the ground and contaminated the town's water sources. Concerned for her family and friends and feeling a responsibility to speak up for those who could not speak up for themselves, Hernandez created *Sun Mad* in 1981. She chose Sun-Maid Growers of California, a privately held cooperative, as her target because the raisin grapes harvested in her hometown went to the cooperative for processing.

One of the most memorable company emblems ever created, the Sun Maid embodies a vision of California sunshine and prosperity. As the official company history tells us, the original Sun Maid was Lorraine Collett, a California fruit packer who was discovered by company representatives in 1915. Her image is so established in American popular culture, in 1988 Collett's original red bonnet was acquired by the Smithsonian Institution in Washington and now forms part of its permanent collection, alongside Dorothy's red shoes from *The Wizard of Oz* and the tattered flag that prompted Francis Scott Key to pen "The Star-Spangled Banner."

Packaged in small, child-sized boxes, Sun-Maid Raisins have been a staple in school lunch boxes for generations; as a result, many people associate them with the innocent pleasure of childhood. Hernandez reproduced the familiar raisin box composition, with its tomato-red background, yellow disk of sun and bonneted figure bearing grapes. But in place of a friendly young face looking out from beneath the oversized red bonnet we find the leering face of death. The poster's small print explains the Sun Maid has been poisoned by "insecticides, miticides, herbicides, fungicides."

Hernandez's skeleton dramatizes the lethal consequences of pesticides and at the same time firmly locates the print in the tradition of Mexican printmaking dating back to José Posada, whose *calavaras* (skull) illustrations satirized Mexican society at the end of the 19th century. Posada's work has influenced many Mexican artists and has come to define the visual imagery associated with Day of the Dead festivities, which are celebrated around the world.

Although Hernandez and other Chicano artists identify as part of an artistic movement rooted in cultural difference, many have extended their concerns and political outrage by creating protest posters for a wide range of causes including the Vietnam War, apartheid and Palestinian rights. *Sun Mad* points to the plight of farm-workers but also calls attention to the risks to consumers. Hernandez has been credited with creating one of the first images to link the plight of farmworkers to effects on consumers and the environment.[3]

In 1982, when Hernandez first printed *Sun Mad*, no one took much notice of it.[4] Due to her growing reputation as an artist, however, and following its inclusion in a number of seminal exhibitions and publications on Chicano art, *Sun Mad* has gained her more attention.[5] With the growth of the environmental movement, its cautionary message about over-reliance on pesticides continues to resonate as consumers have increasingly demanded to know what goes into their food. Sun-Maid has never publicly commented on the work.

Figure 7.3.1 Ester Hernandez, *Sun Mad* (1982), screenprint, 26 x 20 inches. Edition of 53 (second edition). Printed by Ester Hernandez, San Francisco. ©Ester Hernandez.

In recent decades, as artists have responded to the traumas of economic globalization, the poster has become a way to undermine corporate media dominance: artists hijack big brands, alter logos and manipulate company slogans or straplines. *Sun Mad* is an early example of such "subvertised" posters, and a particularly powerful one.

Notes

1. The exhibition opens at the V&A on 1 May 2014. The exhibition looks at the defining features of protest graphics produced by individual artists, graphic designers and print collectives.

2. http://ceres.ca.gov/geo_area/bioregions/San_Joaquin_Valley/about.html. See also Alex Van Tol, *Dolores Huerta: Voice for the Working Poor* (Hove, UK: Crabtree Publishing Company, 2011), 14.

3. Maria X. Martinez, "The Art of Social Justice," *Social Justice* 34, no. 1 (2007), 9.

4. Email correspondence from Ester Hernandez with the author, 20 January 2014.

5. For a list of exhibitions and publications see http://www.esterhernandez.com/.

READING 7.3   POST-READING COMPREHENSION QUESTIONS

- Summarize some of the conditions that the Sun Mad poster is addressing.

- Describe how activism can inform artistic practice.

- Paraphrase the passage: "Hernandez's print is important as a vibrant example of Chicano political art, an early dramatization of environmental awareness and a potent subversion of corporate branding."

Ten Point Program, Brown Berets (1968)

The Brown Berets were a group of young activists who were dedicated to the strategic use of Chicano Militancy in its many forms. While it is true that the Brown Berets were influenced by many groups involved in the modern civil rights movement, they also had very particular demands in relation to the effect on their communities. The "Ten Point Program" offers an explicit view of the demands that the group sought but also suggests a broader reimagination of what liberty and democracy ought to look like for Mexican Americans in the United States.

THINGS TO LOOK FOR AS YOU READ

- Similarities and distinctions between the demands
- The language of the demands
- The goals of the demands

Ten Point Program

Brown Berets

1. Unity of all of our people, regardless of age, income, or political philosophy.
2. The right to bilingual education as guaranteed under the treaty of Guadalupe-Hidalgo.
3. We demand a Civilian Police Review Board, made up of people who live in our community, to screen all police officers, before they are assigned to our communities.
4. We demand that the true history of the Mexican American be taught in all schools in the five Southwestern States.
5. We demand that all officers in Mexican-American communities must live in the community and speak Spanish.
6. We want an end to "Urban Renewal Programs" that replace our barrios with high rent homes for middle-class people.
7. We demand a guaranteed annual income of $8,000 for all Mexican-American families.
8. We demand that the right to vote be extended to all of our people regardless of the ability to speak the English language.
9. We demand that all Mexican Americans be tried by juries consisting of only Mexican Americans.
10. We demand the right to keep and bear arms to defend our communities against racist police, as guaranteed under the Second Amendment of the United States Constitution.[37]

READING 7.4 POST-READING COMPREHENSION QUESTIONS

- Summarize in your own words a few of the main demands of the "Ten Point Program."
- Describe how the demands of the "Ten Point Program" are rooted in the United States Constitution.
- Paraphrase the fourth demand: "We demand that the true history of the Mexican American be taught in all schools in the five Southwestern States."

Brown Berets, "Ten-Point Program," 1968.

Birth of A New Symbol: The Brown Berets

In his chapter "Birth of a New Symbol: The Brown Berets," Ernesto Chávez uncovers the depth and nuance that went into organizing one of the most recognized groups of the Chicana and Chicano Movement. Chávez introduces the key players and pivotal moments within the group's history, while also examining the many external and internal challenges that they faced. Moreover, he makes clear the important connections between the Berets and other groups involved in the broader struggles of the modern civil rights movements.

THINGS TO LOOK FOR AS YOU READ...

- The origins of the Brown Berets
- The goals of the Brown Berets
- Organizational challenges within the group

"Birth of a New Symbol"

The Brown Berets

Ernesto Chávez

I n January 1967 *Time* magazine declared: "The Man of the Year 1966 is a generation: the man—and woman—of 25 and under."[1] The youth of the sixties, observed *Time,* are "well-educated, affluent, rebellious, responsible, pragmatic, idealistic, brave, 'alienated,' and hopeful."[2] People of color were not well educated and affluent, but their desire to be so and also to eliminate racial and ethnic discrimination in American society caused them to strike out at that society in ways that were both similar to and strikingly different from the efforts of earlier generations. For Mexican Americans, no group better illustrated the rebellious 1960s and 1970s than the Brown Berets.

As shown in the previous chapter, by 1966 the Mexican American Political Association's approach to empowering Mexican Americans had proved inadequate. This ineffectiveness combined with the general protest environment of the later 1960s to ensure a new style of politics known as the Chicano movement. The Mexican protonationalism that an older generation used as an oppositional tool was transformed into a Chicano nationalism when suffused with the anti-Americanism of the Vietnam era. Though the issues faced by the ethnic Mexican community were similar to those confronted earlier, the approach to them now differed. Instead of relying on the ballot box, Chicano activists took to the streets and demanded change through protest. This is not to say that protest was nonexistent in prior years, but, rather, that it now attracted mainstream attention, especially from the media and young people, the "baby boomers" who had come of age in the 1960s.

Like other ethnic groups in post–World War II America, the ethnic Mexican community experienced a population boom, its numbers almost doubling from 156,356 in 1950 to 291,959 in 1960.[3] The increase reflected a birth rate 50 percent higher than that of the general population, and resulted in a disproportionately large number of youths in the impoverished community, a fact not lost on the McCone Commission which investigated the causes of the 1965 Watts rebellion in south-central Los Angeles. "Recommendations regarding the Negro problem in Los Angeles," observed the commission, "apply with equal force to the Mexican-Americans ... whose circumstances are similarly disadvantageous and demand equally urgent treatment."[4] The post-Watts atmosphere created a sense of urgency in the city and prompted the Los Angeles County Human Relations Commission, formed following the 1943 zoot-suit riots, to join with the Wilshire Boulevard Temple's Camp Hess Kramer in sponsoring a conference for Mexican-American young people in April 1966.[5]

This event, with the prosaic name of the Mexican-American Youth Leadership Conference, became the vehicle for igniting a new generation of Mexican-American reformers.[6] The conference's purpose was to "examine emotions, feelings, values, identity and the label 'Mexican American.'" Attendees were high-school leaders who were urged to discuss what they shared in common, in the hope that they would forge alliances to bring about positive changes in their neighborhoods.[7] The conference lasted only three days, but some of those present continued to talk about issues that troubled them. In May 1966 six of them—Vickie Castro, David Sánchez, Moctesuma Esparza, Ralph Ramírez, Rachel Ochoa, George Licón, and John Ortiz—created Young Citizens for Community Action (YCCA).[8] Far from being radicals, they believed in the principles of President Lyndon Johnson's "war on poverty" and had faith in the electoral process. With headstrong, eighteen-year-old Roosevelt High School senior Vickie Castro as president, they surveyed student needs, discussed school problems with education officials, and gathered information about candidates running for election to the Los Angeles Board of Education. They were convinced that the flaws in the school system could be remedied only through political action, and their first move was to support Julian Nava, a state-college professor in the San Fernando Valley, in what became his successful bid for a seat on the school board. They followed their "Youth for Nava" campaign with membership in Los Angeles Mayor Samuel Yorty's Youth Advisory Council. Later, some of them served on the California Governor's Youth Advisory Council during the administrations of Governors Gerald "Pat" Brown and Ronald Reagan.[9]

These youths gradually began focusing on issues other than schools, especially police brutality and the need to improve the quality of life in their communities. Particularly strong encouragement came from Father John B. Luce, rector of the Episcopal Church of the Epiphany in Lincoln Heights and before that a pastor in the poor neighborhoods of East Harlem in New York City and Jersey City, New Jersey. In October 1965 he relocated to Los Angeles at the request of the local Episcopal bishop who encouraged him, as well as others, "to try to reach out and work with all sorts of different groups and kids, drug addicts, people that had been troubled with the law."[10] The challenge excited Luce, who shared the bishop's conviction that "the support of indigenous organizations of the people themselves will build real democracy in this country."[11]

The church formed part of an ever-growing network of urban groups that encouraged the YCCA in its efforts. Across the street from the church was the California Center for Community Development's Social Action Training Program, an organization funded by the Southern California Council of Churches through the federal Office of Economic Opportunity. The Social Action Training Center, in turn, introduced the YCCA youths to a Community Service Organization young people's group—the Young Adult Leadership and Community Development Project—dedicated "to train[ing] young adults in East Los Angeles in community action by involving them in neighborhood improvement and community participation projects."[12] No longer actively involved in electoral politics, CSO now concentrated on providing much-needed community services, such as a credit union and a "buyers club" that provided opportunities to buy food, clothing, and other items in bulk and at reduced rates.[13] Through CSO the YCCA members met Richard Alatorre, who schooled them in the ways of practical politics and community organizing and who also introduced them to the now famed César Chávez.[14] These numerous contacts left them not only better informed but also with greater pride in their own ethnicity that was reflected in the new name they gave their organization: Young Chicanos for Community Action (YCCA).[15]

These energetic youth, in addition, became more visible in the community. With the financial help of Father Luce, in 1967 they opened "La Piranya," a coffeehouse located on East Olympic Boulevard in an industrial section of unincorporated East Los Angeles. La Piranya served as an office and meeting place, where prominent civil rights leaders expressed their views to an ever-increasing number of Chicano youth. Among those making appearances were César Chávez, Reies López Tijerina of New Mexico's Alianza Federal de Mercedes, and African-American leaders Hubert "Rap" Brown and Stokely Carmichael of the Student Non-Violent Coordinating Committee and Ron Karenga of United Slaves (US).[16] The coffeehouse also sponsored "Educational Happenings," designed to encourage youth to get a college education.[17] Usually present on these occasions were representatives from nearby colleges and universities as well as speakers from other community groups—for example, the United Council Community Organizations and the United Parents Council—and sometimes a political leader or representative from a congressional field office. The coffeehouse remained, however, a gathering place for young people run by young people, with little and only nominal adult supervision.

As *La Raza,* a local Chicano newspaper, observed, "Many nights you will hear live music ... but mostly you will find young Chicanos like yourself."[18]

The gatherings also attracted Los Angeles County sheriff's deputies, who harassed La Piranya patrons on the grounds that the coffeehouse was a hangout for Chicano "hoodlums." The deputies would frequently drive by and shine their lights into the windows, as well as question and illegally search customers as they left the building. Angered by such affronts, the YCCA organized protest demonstrations at the nearby East Los Angeles sheriff's station.[19]

These protests marked a change in the leadership of YCCA, for they occurred at a time when some members began their college studies and gradually drifted away because of the pressure of classes. Licón, Esparza, Ochoa, and the group's president, Vickie Castro, were among them. Now assuming leadership positions were people like David Sánchez, the new president, who had little patience with police harassment and urged a more militant stance. In January 1968 this attitude took the symbolic form of khaki military clothing and a name change to the Brown Berets. Law-enforcement abuses had transformed them from moderate reformers into visually distinctive and combative crusaders on behalf of justice for Chicanos. Residual Mexican cultural nationalism was becoming Chicano nationalism, the core value of the now-emerging Chicano movement.

Besides the khaki attire, the most revealing feature of their apparel was the beret and the emblem attached to it, depicting a yellow pentagon with two bayoneted rifles behind a cross and the words *La Causa* ("The Cause") above them. The design originated with a new member, Johnny Parsons, but others instinctively shared the message he sought to convey.

> We asked him why [are you designing an emblem]? He said, "Look, it's like an emblem for guerrillas, ... a symbol of guerrillas, and in this case like urban guerrillas." He started telling us how there were green berets, how the French guerrillas and the Spanish guerrillas had worn it during the Spanish Civil War and that we should wear a brown beret. So, we thought it was a good idea. So we started wearing the brown beret and the khaki jacket—the bush jacket. But we didn't call ourselves the Brown Berets. [Those] who started calling us the Brown Berets were the East L.A. Sheriffs ... and we got pissed off. We would hear it because every time they had us up against the wall we'd hear all the radio messages from the patrol cars, "Brown Berets here" and "Brown Berets over here," and so then it stuck. So, then we just stayed with it.[20]

A new member had proposed the group's outward symbols, but someone who had been with the organization from the outset, eighteen-year-old David Sánchez, expressed in writing the anger and goals shared by all the Berets. Following his arrest in February 1968 and a sixty-day jail term for participating in an unlawful assembly, Sánchez wrote "The Birth of a New Symbol" in a setting reminiscent of Martin Luther King Jr.'s imprisonment in 1963, when he wrote his "Letter from a Birmingham Jail." Instead of the nonviolent philosophy advocated by King, however, Sánchez, using words suggestive of Malcolm X, called on Brown Berets to use "any and all means necessary … to resolve the frustrations of our people."

"As a Brown Beret," he admonished his followers, "you are to be considered prophets of [a] disillusioned past" and a "symbol of hope" who should "preach hope. … By merely standing on a street corner, [and] wearing a Brown Beret … people [can] observe you and gather information and form an opinion about the Brown Berets." The Berets' mission was conversion: "Talk to every potential Chicano who crosses your path. Because every Chicano that you miss is a potential enemy." But avoid "Anglos," he cautioned. "do not talk to the enemy, for he is either a dog or a devil. … For over 120 years, the Chicano has suffered at the hands of the Anglo Establishment" and the only way to "stop discrimination and the many injustices against our people" demands "pressure." Sánchez outlined three escalating stages of pressure. The first was "communication," sending telegrams and letters and making telephone calls to elected officials and other authorities. The second was to "embarrass and expose those who are in the wrong." The final stage consisted of "alternatives," which he ambiguously described as "any and all means necessary." Similar statements coming from Malcolm X and the Black Panthers had probably inspired this last option.[21]

Success required self-discipline. "Because your people, the land, and the enemy are watching you, you must look good, act right and move with the precision of a clock," lectured Sánchez.[22] This required unquestioning obedience to superiors in the group, the more so because they are the "best qualified to handle any situation" and fully aware of Anglo "trickery."[23] Success also demanded high standards of personal conduct. Avoid scandal because it will only "reflect upon the organization in a bad way" and alienate it from the community. Avoid as well "theory and ideology" because "intellectuals aren't able to communicate with the dude on the street." In addition, when out of uniform Berets should wear "simple dress" since "if you dress like the greater part of the community, you will usually be accepted. If you dress different," Sánchez cautioned, "and are sloppy or dirty, you usually aren't accepted and your channel of communication is broken."[24]

Also suffusing Sánchez's "Birth of a New Symbol" and the organizational structure were gendered notions of nation. All Beret officers were male. Sánchez served as "prime minister," Carlos Montes was "minister of information," Cruz Olmeda held the post of "chairman," and Ralph Ramírez that of "minister of discipline." These titles, similar to those adopted earlier by the Black Panthers, reflected the militaristic, masculine, and hierarchical nature of the group.[25] Permeating all subsequent Beret statements and documents were these emphases on strict discipline, clean and unostentatious living, Anglos as the enemy, the leadership role of Berets, and Chicano identity and solidarity.[26]

The Brown Berets first gained wide notoriety in March 1968 when they became involved in student boycotts, known as "blowouts," of five East Los Angeles high schools. Prompting the protest was the high percentage (over 50 percent) of Chicano high-school students forced to drop out of school either through expulsion and transfers to other schools or because they had not been taught to read and thus failed their classes. Overcrowding and dilapidated buildings were endemic at Chicano schools, where teachers, a majority of whom were Anglo, often discriminated against their Mexican-Americans students, calling them "dirty Mexicans" and encouraging them to join the workforce rather than attend college.[27] Angered by the treatment, students demanded more Chicano teachers and administrators and better schools.[28]

The Berets did not directly participate in the planning of the demonstrations, but they did "back up, advise, and assist" those who did. This initially took the form of allowing students to meet at La Piranya and then involved defending them when the police used violence to crush the boycott.[29] "The Chicano students were the main action group," stated Sánchez later. "The Brown Berets were at the walkouts to protect our younger people [the students ranged in ages from 14 to 18, while the Berets were 18 to 24 years old]."[30] Such action won wide approval among the students. "Who Are the Brown Berets?" asked the *Chicano Student News*. They are people, who "served, observed and protected the Chicano community."

> When the cops moved in, it was the Berets that were dragged behind bars. THE BROWN BERETS became a target for the PLACA [the police], and anyone wearing one [a brown beret] was suspect to be picked up. It is the brown berets who are presently behind bars or have warrants out for their arrests. You know, *ese,* when you lay it on the line, there are people who mouth about taking care of business, and there are people who take care of business. The BROWN BERETS take care of business and leave the "politicking" and mouthing to others. The brown berets are strictly a defense organization but reserve the right and duty to defend themselves, Chicanos and La Raza wherever and by whatever means necessary. Already many

community organizations have found this out and are in full support behind these young Chicanos who stand ready. Their numbers are growing, growing, GROWING. BUENO YA. … NO SE DEJAN.[31]

Support for the Berets increased when five of them (along with several other participants in the Blow Outs) were indicted by the Los Angeles County Grand Jury for engaging in conspiracies to disrupt the public schools, a felony punishable by up to forty-five years in the state penitentiary.[32] Following the arrests, *Inside Eastside* (a student newspaper) protested that "We will not tolerate the felony charges which … will prevent the Brown Berets from being effective because its leaders … will most likely be jailed."[33] The Berets quickly secured release on bail, but it took two years of litigation before the charges against the "conspirators" were dropped.[34] *La Raza* (a paper published by young Chicanos affiliated with the Church of the Epiphany) rallied to the defense of the Berets, arguing that Anglo injustices were the reason for their creation.

> Because these injustices have existed and the Anglo Establishment shows no sign of changing them, because the cries of individuals have gone unheard and fallen upon deaf ears, a group of young Chicanos have come together under the name of the Brown Berets to demand an immediate end to the injustices committed against the Mexican-American. … The Brown Berets are not a gang, car club, or private social group; it is an organization of young Chicanos dedicated to serving the Mexican American community.[35]

The growing publicity about the Berets prompted the group to reexamine its mission and in June 1968, in emulation of the Black Panthers,[36] whom they admired, to circulate a "Ten Point Program":

1. Unity of all of our people, regardless of age, income, or political philosophy.
2. The right to bilingual education as guaranteed under the treaty of Guadalupe-Hidalgo.
3. We demand a Civilian Police Review Board, made up of people who live in our community, to screen all police officers, before they are assigned to our communities.
4. We demand that the true history of the Mexican American be taught in all schools in the five Southwestern States.
5. We demand that all officers in Mexican-American communities must live in the community and speak Spanish.

6. We want an end to "Urban Renewal Programs" that replace our barrios with high rent homes for middle-class people.

7. We demand a guaranteed annual income of $8,000 for all Mexican-American families.

8. We demand that the right to vote be extended to all of our people regardless of the ability to speak the English language.

9. We demand that all Mexican Americans be tried by juries consisting of only Mexican Americans.

10. We demand the right to keep and bear arms to defend our communities against racist police, as guaranteed under the Second Amendment of the United States Constitution.[37]

The ten points were reformist, not revolutionary. The Berets did not call for the overthrow of the U.S. government, but, rather, grounded many of their demands on the U.S. Constitution, the Bill of Rights, and the Treaty of Guadalupe Hidalgo. They also saw themselves as safekeepers of the Chicano community, a responsibility that found expression in their new three-part motto: "to serve, to observe, and to protect." "To serve" meant giving "vocal as well as physical support to those people and causes which will help the people of the Mexican-American communities," while "to observe" required keeping "a watchful eye on all federal, state, city and private agencies which deal with the Mexican American, especially law enforcement agencies." As for the words "to protect," they meant working to "guarantee … and secure the rights of the Mexican American by all means necessary." The "means necessary" (reminiscent of Sánchez's "any and all means necessary"), explained the Berets, depended upon the actions of those in power. If the Anglo establishment accommodated their demands "in a peaceful and orderly process, then we will be only too happy to accept this way. Otherwise, we will be forced to other alternatives."[38]

Like the Black Panthers, the Berets expressed a fondness for Marxism, with some of them also seeking guidance in the writings of Mao Zedong and arguing for the need to be "one with the masses of the people."[39] This caused tension within the organization, especially when Cruz Olmeda and several others took Mao's words to heart and insisted that the Berets be transformed into a militia in the service of the community. Sánchez, on the other hand, believed that the Berets should only *appear* to be a military group, projecting the image rather than the reality of a revolutionary cadre. His Cold War upbringing had produced in him a deep fear of Communism that became so intense that he burned Marxist literature. He also knew firsthand about violent police repression and believed the police would destroy the Berets if they moved in a Marxist direction.[40]

At first, Beret leaders also disagreed among themselves about the group's recruitment policies. The approximately thirty members who had joined the Berets by mid-1968 were mostly recruited from local high schools and now ranged in ages from 14 to 18.[41] Sánchez wanted to continue the emphasis on enlisting high-school students but Olmeda disagreed, arguing that such a policy would prevent the group from reaching a revolutionary takeoff point and relegate it to being just another pacifist organization. These differences were exacerbated by each man's personal desire to control the organization. The conflicts ended only when Olmeda and seven of his followers left the Brown Berets in July 1968 and founded a group called "La Junta," which recruited former gang members and aligned itself with adult leftists, reputed members of the Communist Party.[42]

The bickering among the Berets was accompanied by some criticism of the group from Mexican Americans. Not everyone shared the Berets' alienation from American society. In a letter in *La Raza,* a Lincoln High School student proclaimed his opposition to the group. "This is our country—the greatest country in the world and this is our school—the best there is!!! We love our country and our school so let's tell it like it is." The Berets, declared the student, were "outsiders" who had done nothing for "our country" or for "our community. ... WE, THE REAL STUDENTS OF LINCOLN HIGH, demand that all you BROWN BERETS and outsiders leave our school alone. we don't need you or want you. GET OUT!!!"[43]

Most residents, however, were either silent or vigorously defended the Berets. The student letter, for example, sparked a hostile response accusing the writer of doing the work of "The Man" and going "along with the white man's disinterest." The Berets, declared the rejoinder, were helping the community and fighting discrimination, as evidenced by their participation in "the Poor People's Campaign" organized in Washington, D.C., by the Southern Christian Leadership Conference. Moreover, they supported the United Farm Workers' struggle and, locally, were promoting educational reform and the introduction of classes in Mexican history, "not Anglo history that excludes the contributions of your forefathers."[44]

Although other periodicals reported on the Berets' activities, the organization initiated its own newspaper, *La Causa,* on May 23, 1969. Describing the monthly as "a Chicano newspaper dedicated to serve the Chicano barrio with local and national news," the Berets promised to reveal "the many injustices against the Chicano by the Anglo establishment," to inform "the Raza of current and coming events," and to seek "to better relations and communications between barrios throughout the country."[45] Sánchez, the editor, exhorted the Berets to redouble their efforts on behalf of the community and kept coming back to what he called the "8 Points of Attention": "(1) Speak politely to the people; (2) Pay fairly for what you buy from the people; (3) Return everything you borrow; (4) Pay for anything you damage; (5) Do not hit or swear at the people; (6) Do not damage property or possessions of people; (7) Do not take liberties with women; and (8) When working with the people do not get loaded."[46]

Though Sánchez exercised a powerful influence over the organization, he was not present at an incident that first dramatically brought the Brown Berets to the attention of those outside the Chicano community. This took place at Los Angeles's Biltmore Hotel during the third annual "Nuevas Vistas" Conference in April 1969. Arranged by State Superintendent of Public Instruction Max Rafferty, the convocation was a gathering of Mexican-American educators charged with exploring ways to improve relations between the schools and the Mexican-American community. Also participating were students from chapters of the United Mexican American Students (UMAS) at UCLA and the California State College campuses at Los Angeles, Long Beach, Fullerton, and North-ridge. The keynote speaker for the Friday night banquet was Governor Ronald Reagan, whose election in 1966 had weakened the power base of Mexican Americans in Sacramento. As a preeminent symbol of the "Anglo establishment," his presence almost guaranteed a disruption.[47]

Reagan had hardly begun his speech before shouts from some in the audience tried to drown him out. The protesters loudly denounced the condescending attitudes of educators and cuts in affirmative action programs. Firecrackers dropped from the mezzanine to the Biltmore Bowl floor, as fourteen demonstrators began doing the "famous Chicano clap." The governor shouted over the din that "these are the few that are wrecking what we are attempting to build," but the protesters succeeded in breaking up the proceedings and taking over the dance floor, until approximately fifty police and Biltmore security officers arrested them for disrupting a public assembly.[48]

In the meantime, authorities outside the banquet hall had barred other ticket-holding Mexican Americans from entering. When they heard the claps coming from inside, those waiting at the door joined in and began shouting "Viva la Raza!" The chants and claps subsided when the Chicanos realized that those emerging from the room were mostly non-Mexicans.[49] By that time, fires had broken out on the mezzanine and the second, fourth, ninth, and tenth floors. The blazes remained small and confined to linen closets, where they had been started with highway-type flares. Some guests had to be removed from their rooms, but no one was evacuated from the hotel. The damage was later estimated at $15,000.[50]

On June 9 the Los Angeles County Grand Jury indicted ten Chicanos for starting the fires.[51] The indictments were based on testimony provided by Fernando Sumaya, an undercover Los Angeles police officer who had infiltrated the Berets. The charges carried a possible maximum sentence of life in prison for each of those involved.[52] The first trial of two of those who were indicted (Ramírez and Cebada) ended in a mistrial in August 1971. Their second trial ended in May 1972 with acquittal verdicts on the grounds of insufficient evidence. Seven of the eight others indicted were never tried. Montes, who out of fear for his life went into hiding in 1970, was not brought to trial until 1979, when he was acquitted for lack of evidence.

The Berets believed that law enforcement agencies were the principal threat to Mexican Americans in the United States. They became even more convinced with the disappearance of Montes following his indictment for the Biltmore fire. *La Causa* attributed his disappearance to his being kidnapped by the CIA: "Sergeant Abel Armas (LAPD) of the Special Operation Conspiracy (SOC) has conspired to destroy Carlos Montes and Brown Beret leaders by taking the law into their own hands which is typical of CIA policy." Montes was "truely [sic] a Chicano Revolutionist that has put his life on the line more than once for his Raza."[53] *La Causa* featured a likeness of him on its masthead for six months, effectively raising Montes's heroic status to mythical proportions.[54]

In the meantime, Montes had fled with his wife to El Paso, Texas, where he changed his name to Manuel Gómez and worked for seven years as a carpenter and a maintenance mechanic in the garment industry. In 1979 he returned to Los Angeles, where he voluntarily surrendered to authorities, was tried for conspiracy to commit a felony (arson), and acquitted.[55]

Sumaya's testimony during Montes's trial revealed that the Los Angeles Police Department had been systematically monitoring the Berets for four months. Going by the LAPD code name of S-257, Sumaya had joined the Berets in December 1968, grown a beard, and posed as a dedicated rebel. He alleged that on the day of the Biltmore Hotel incident he had met with Ralph Ramírez and Carlos Montes at the Brown Beret headquarters at 11 a.m. that morning. The three then went to the Biltmore and picked up Esmeralda Bernal, who was a San Jose State College student attending the conference. They drove to East Los Angeles College for a meeting of "La Vida Nueva," the campus's Mexican-American group. There, Willie Mendoza, an East Los Angeles College student, conducted a workshop on guerilla warfare tactics and civil disobedience. At the workshop Montes interrupted Mendoza, telling him that those present should not just talk about such acts but should actually perform them. The time to begin, he announced, was that night at the Biltmore Hotel, where they should disrupt Reagan's speech by breaking windows, turning off electrical power, and setting off fire alarms. Those present agreed. Montes added that he would purchase flares to ignite in the hotel. He also suggested that everyone choose a partner. That night about twenty people (including Ramírez, Montes, James Vigil, Ernesto Eichwald Cebeda, Moctesuma Esparza, and Rene Nuñez) gathered in Bernal's room (number 7341 of the Biltmore) to plan the evening's activity.[56]

Most of those present advocated walking out as soon as Reagan commenced his speech, while others proposed cutting the wires to the microphone. With a course of action unresolved, Ramírez, Montes, Cebeda, and Sumaya decided to take matters into their own hands. They left the room and went downstairs to look for an electrical power switch. When they failed to locate one, they went to the hotel's roof, where Montes spotted a metal cabinet labeled "Danger High Voltage." He stated that he would return to the roof after dark. The four then went back to room 7341 where they learned that in their absence the others had decided on a course of action. Two people would stand up in the middle of Reagan's speech. That would be a signal to the others to rise and begin shouting in order to silence the governor. Someone would then cut the wires to the microphone. In the meantime, two people stationed at the doors would let in those waiting outside so they could participate in disrupting the meeting.[57]

At Montes's trial, Sumaya testified that Montes had set the fires. According to his account, at approximately 7 p.m. he and Ramírez picked up Juan Ortiz, a "La Vida Nueva" member, in East Los Angeles and then returned to the Biltmore a half hour later. As they entered the lobby, they encountered Montes who announced, "Well that's one fire." Then, at approximately 8:15 p.m. Montes and Sumaya went to a mezzanine-level men's room near the Grand Avenue entrance of the hotel, where Montes told Sumaya, "Wait outside and call me if someone comes." Sumaya waited for about thirty minutes and then left. As he did so, he saw Montes igniting papers piled against the men's room door.[58]

At his trial, Montes accused Sumaya of starting the fire in the men's room. Sumaya had a history of violence, he claimed, citing in particular Sumaya's later involvement in the firebombing of a Safeway supermarket on May 10, 1969. According to Montes, on that occasion, Sumaya drove the car, provided the Molotov cocktails, and threw one of them into the store. He was accompanied by two youths to whom he promised membership in the Berets for helping him; the two were later arrested for the Safeway fire. Montes also accused Sumaya of openly using and advocating the use of such drugs as marijuana, "reds," and Seconal. In addition, he claimed that the undercover agent had advocated violence against the police and more militant actions on the part of the Brown Berets. Sumaya, stated Montes, was "a typical agent provocateur, advocating and committing illegal acts with the whole idea to get other members of the organization or their leaders busted, with the whole idea of trying to disrupt or destroy the movement of the Brown Berets."[59]

La Causa leveled similar charges against Sumaya. In an article entitled, "Is There a Frito Bandito in Your House?" the newspaper also criticized his personal life.

Brown Beret Intelligence reveals that the SUPER-HERO of the Dudley do-rights of the Protect and Serve Nazi Troops ... was not so much in "the line of duty," but a married man who committed adultery, and a seducer of innocent young girls, and known by many males in this organization to be continuously looking for a girl. Casanova Sumaya had a tendency to have no self-control in the hand department, among other things. He was always trying to pick up young Chicanas from our barrios, and was a common sight on Whittier Blvd., trying to do his thing. There is no telling how many unwed mothers he left behind.[60]

Despite police infiltration and setbacks caused by trials, the Brown Berets persisted in their work on behalf of the Chicano community. A notable achievement was the creation of a free medical clinic in East Los Angeles, which opened in 1969.[61] The Berets established the clinic because they saw the need for free medical services for the East Los Angeles ethnic Mexican community. Modeled after the Fairfax Free Clinic in Hollywood, the facility opened on May 31, 1969, at 5016 East Whittier Boulevard and offered free social, psychological, and medical services as well as draft counseling. The only requirement for gaining entry was the "need to see a doctor." Open four days a week, the facility operated from 10 a.m. to 10 p.m. and maintained itself through donations from merchants, doctors, and other private benefactors, including the Ford Foundation, which provided funds for an endowment. Managing the facility was a board of directors composed of representatives from the community as well as medical professionals.[62]

Another project that attracted Beret participation was the Chicano antiwar effort. Despite their disparaging attitude toward college students, the Brown Berets joined with them to mount a major campaign against the Vietnam War. Among students, the initiative came from a group of Chicanos at UCLA who were particularly upset about the disproportionate number of Chicanos dying in the war, at a 3-to-1 ratio to whites.[63] In December 1969 the Berets and a group of college students formalized their alliance against the war by creating the Chicano Moratorium Committee, with David Sánchez of the Brown Berets and Rosalio Muñoz, a UCLA student, serving as co-chairs. Almost immediately, on December 20, they staged a demonstration against the war that attracted three thousand protesters. They had obviously touched an issue of widespread concern, one that also aroused hundreds of thousands of people of every ethnicity across the nation. But for Chicanos, as *La Causa* declared, the war was seen as "a matter of survival" and "freedom." The newspaper believed that the "the Vietnam War is the ultimate weapon of genocide of non-white peoples by a sick decadent *puto* western culture." It viewed the war as "a turning point in the history of mankind" because the "Vietnamese have shown that man's spirit and will to survive can overcome the most brutal punishment ever netted [*sic*] out to any nation." The newspaper went on to suggest parallels between the Vietnamese peoples' struggle for liberation and that of Chicanos. It called for Chicanos to learn from the Vietnamese "that to resist is to survive a free man and to submit is to be a *puto* and thus a slave. Dare to Struggle, Dare to Win—Hasta La Victoria Siempre!"[64]

During the next three years the Brown Berets proclaimed their message in other demonstrations and through symbolic acts. In an effort to "reconquer [Chicanos'] rights to be treated like people, and not like second-class citizens," the Berets initiated "La Caravana de la Reconquista" and drove through five southwestern states (California, Arizona, Colorado, New Mexico, and Texas) between October 1971 and August 1972.[65] Led by David Sánchez, the Berets participating in the "Caravan" issued their goals for the "National Policies of 1972," proclaiming "absolute militarism ... [as] the fastest and strongest way to Chicano power."[66] They also underscored their intense sense of cultural nationalism and their view of themselves as a conquered people in their own land.

> We the Chicano people of the Southwest hereby declare ourselves a nation, and as a nation that has been the subject of a profit-making invasion. We are a nation with a land that has been temporarily occupied. And we are a nation with the ability to survive. We are a nation with great natural culturability. We are a nation, we who come from different ways, combining ourselves in one nation.[67]

The Berets called for reclaiming the Southwest and dramatically, though only symbolically, demonstrated their resolve on August 30, 1972, by "invading" Santa Catalina Island off the southern California coast and remaining there for nearly a month until September 22. The pretext for the invasion was their contention that the isle, along with the other Channel Islands off the California shore, had not been included in the lands ceded to the United States by the Treaty of Guadalupe Hidalgo following the U.S.–Mexico War.[68] The invasion was undoubtedly inspired by a similar action, the American Indian Movement's (AIM) takeover of Alcatraz Island in San Francisco Bay, from November 1969 to June 1971.[69] When, on August 30, 1972, in "Project Tecolote" (Project Owl) twenty-six Berets marched off the Catalina ferry and set up camp on land owned by the Santa Catalina Island Company, they attracted considerable public attention.[70] They left when asked to go by Judge William B. Osborne who, accompanied by Los Angeles County sheriffs, told them that they were in violation of an Avalon ordinance prohibiting camping in an area zoned for single-family dwellings. Following the warning, they unceremoniously abandoned "Campo Tecolote."[71]

The Catalina Island incident marked the last of the Berets' attention-grabbing exploits. Shortly thereafter, quarreling among the leaders robbed the organization of its effectiveness and it gradually disappeared. The bickering seems to have begun because of the ever-larger role being played by David Sánchez. He had always been prominent, first because of his inspiring jailhouse writings that galvanized the Berets during their earliest months, and later because of his role as editor of *La Causa*. Now, however, he was seen as exceeding his authority, writing about Beret policy without first getting permission of the Brown Beret National Headquarters Central Committee. He was also accused of having violated basic Beret tenets by killing a fellow member and committing rape. The final insult came when the Central Committee charged him with stealing money from the Berets. The committee fired him on October 21, 1972.[72]

Sánchez responded by calling a press conference and announcing that he was resigning and disbanding the organization. The Berets, he claimed, had a membership of five thousand in ninety chapters, but he was dissolving the group because others were using it "as a vehicle for their own purposes" and he feared there would be bloodshed. He also attributed his action to "police harassment and infiltration, internal squabbles and 'hippie-ism' among members, which ruined discipline."[73] Perhaps one reason for the Brown Berets' demise was Sánchez's narrow vision of a male-dominated Chicano community.[74] The Brown Berets disseminated a highly masculine view of what it meant to be a Chicano and they practiced this concept in symbolic ways: the organization's paramilitary structure, the exclusion of women from leadership positions, and the emphasis on recruiting young men as members.[75] Almost every issue of *La Causa* featured a recruitment appeal that urged readers to "Join Today" (listing meeting dates and times) and primarily targeted lower-income males who had little formal education and were gang members, the so-called "*vatos locos.*" Illustrations depicted potential recruits as wearing *cholo* garb and carrying a bottle of beer underneath a banner proclaiming "Bato Loco Yesterday." That picture was followed by another showing the same man in a Beret uniform, with his right arm outstretched and his fist clenched in the power symbol. A banner above proclaimed "Revolutionist Today, Be Brown, Be Proud, Join the Brown Berets" (see figures 7.5.1 and 7.5.2).[76] Like the Boy Scouts of nineteenth-century England, the Berets sought to create a healthy nation of clean-living young men.

The Berets disparaged college students, however, even those belonging to UCLA's Movimiento Estudiantil Chicano de Aztlán (MEChA), as "bureaucrats" and out of touch with the community.

Figures 7.5.1 and 7.5.2 "Bato Loco Yesterday" and "Brown Beret Today" illustrations in the Brown Beret Newspaper *La Causa* depicted the organization's targeted audience (or represtative subject).

They have never related to the off-campus Chicano community in Venice or the Eastside and have alienated a substantial number of the current Hi-Potential students [a special admissions program at UCLA]. This group used to be on an ultra cultural nationalist kick, affecting the speaking of the Cholo dialect which sounded ridiculous because its pronunciation had a heavy English accent. Most of these people never toked a joint until they came to college—a white hippy undoubtedly taught them how, however they were and are extolling the virtues of the Cholo.[77]

As for women, the Berets patronized them and saw their contributions as of a lesser order of importance. Women were welcomed into the organization, but their roles were subordinate to those of men. They met at different times and in different buildings, where they focused on serving the male leadership's needs: bailing them out of jail, organizing a fundraiser for their activities, or typing the newspaper that carried information about men's actions. The men, on the other hand, busied themselves with the more weighty questions: planning demonstrations and discussing Beret policies and strategies. Women played a significant role, stressed *La Causa,* yet the newspaper's description of their activities indicated otherwise.[78] In an article entitled "Beautiful Bronze Women All Over Aztlán," Gloria Arellanes wrote that women "are beginning to realize how valuable they are in beauty and the movement."

> Your role will be whatever you have to offer your people, whether it be leadership, a good rap, cooking or just to become involved, aware and educated, but find out. Every person has something to offer, every person is valuable. Get your head together, be aware—teach your awareness to those that are lost—teach your awareness to all those around you.[79]

That "awareness" took the form of an anonymously written love poem, "Mi Amor," in a subsequent issue. "To my eyes/A Chicana is an exotic queen,/She radiates a glow of exquisite sheen." Certainly, these saccharine lines only heightened the objectification of women. They were, as George Mosse has said of women within other national discourses, "sedate rather than dynamic," providing the "backdrop against which men determined the fate of nations."[80] In another *La Causa* article, "Chicanas de Aztlán," the author claimed that "women in the Brown Beret organization have left behind the traditional role that the Chicana has held for the past hundreds of years," but his description of their new "duties and assignments" were supportive roles: "anything from getting a brother out of jail to planning a fund raiser." Frequently, women acknowledged their traditional status. "We're not talking about women's liberation," announced one woman, "because, like that's not ours—we're talking about our Raza's liberation and in order to get our Raza liberated we all have to work together within our Raza."[81] By denying women full and meaningful participation in the struggle for liberation, the Brown Berets not only had a restricted concept of community but also lessened the attractiveness of their organization to women's participation.[82]

Yet gender bias and internal bickering were not the only reasons for the Berets decline. From the beginning they were plagued by harassment from law-enforcement authorities and weakened by infiltrators. Besides Sumaya, there were at least two other local infiltrators. Police officer Abel Armas began working within the Berets in 1967 while a member of the LAPD's Criminal Conspiracy Section. A year later, he was joined by Los Angeles County Deputy Sheriff Robert Acosta, who remained undercover from May 1968 through April 1969. Their assignments resulted from a law enforcement belief that the Berets were a subversive organization involved in bombings, fires, and the killing of deputy sheriffs and policemen. Acosta later testified that he attended many Beret functions, but never saw anyone commit a criminal act.[83] Documents obtained through the Freedom of Information Act reveal that beginning in March 1968 the Federal Bureau of Investigation also began investigated the organization.[84] The reason for doing so was the FBI's belief (shared by other law enforcement agencies) that the Berets were controlled by "rabble rousing" Mexican Americans who were apt to incite "racial violence" and therefore posed a threat to national security. The FBI continued their surveillance for more than five years, until the group's dissolution in November 1973, focusing not only on activities in Los Angeles but also on ethnic Mexican communities outside of California.[85] Eventually, the FBI came to the conclusion that the Berets were not acting in a subversive manner.[86]

The Brown Berets' short-lived, yet celebrated, existence, as "a new symbol" for challenging the "Anglo Establishment" mirrored the Black Panthers' experience. Like the Panthers, they pushed a paramilitaristic form of cultural nationalism that captured the imagination of the young, particularly young men, beginning with the "Blow Outs." Later, they caught the attention of a larger audience in their support of health projects and especially in their protests against the Vietnam War. Though the Brown Berets did little to change the status quo, they were not without significance, for their example inspired others equally dedicated to reform and the creation of Aztlán.

Notes

1. "Man of the Year: The Inheritor," *Time,* January 6, 1967, p. 18.

2. Bernhard M. Auer, "A Letter from the Publisher," *Time,* January 6, 1967, p. 11.

3. Helen Rowan, "A Minority Nobody Knows," *Atlantic,* June 1967, p. 47.

4. Governor's Commission on the Los Angeles Riots. "Violence in the City—An End or a Beginning?" In *The Los Angeles Riots,* ed. Robert M. Fogelson, (New York: Arno Press; New York: New York Times, 1969), 5.

5. Transcript of Los Angeles Commission on Human Relations meeting, March 21, 1966, p. 28, Oscar Zeta Acosta Papers, University of California at Santa Barbara, Department of Special Collections.

6. Organizing among Mexican American youth was not new; it had happened throughout the twentieth century. The best example of this phenomenon was the Mexican American Movement (MAM) of the 1940s and 1950s. This Los Angeles–based group focused on educational reform but never included a large following. Like the Brown Berets, it too emerged from a youth conference (sponsored by the YMCA). For more on MAM,

see George J. Sánchez, *Becoming Mexican American: Ethnicity, Culture, and Identity in Chicano Los Angeles, 1900–1945* (New York: Oxford University Press, 1993).

7. Program for Fourth Annual Camp Hess Kramer Leadership Conference for Mexican-American Youth, April 3–5, 1966, p. 1 (in author's possession).

8. Victoria Castro, interview by author, tape recording, Los Angeles, May 24, 1993.

9. Castro, interview; Gerald Paul Rosen, *Political Ideology and the Chicano Movement: A Study of the Political Ideology of Activists in the Chicano Movement* (San Francisco: R & E Research Associates, 1975), 73.

10. "Transcript of the John B. Luce testimony before the Los Angeles County Grand Jury," p. 397, Oscar Zeta Acosta Papers, Department of Special Collections, University of California at Santa Barbara.

11. Ibid., p. 440.

12. CSO, "Community Service Organization: 25th Anniversary Program" (Los Angeles: Community Service Organization, 1972), 8.

13. Ibid., 8–9.

14. "Transcript of the John B. Luce testimony before the Los Angeles County Grand Jury," pp. 396–405, Oscar Zeta Acosta Papers, Department of Special Collections, University of California at Santa Barbara.

15. Castro, interview.

16. Ruben Salazar, "Brown Berets Hail 'La Raza' and Scorn the Establishment," *Los Angeles Times,* June 16, 1969, sec. 1, p. 24.

17. "It's Happening," *La Raza* (newspaper), January 15, 1968, p. 2.

18. *La Raza* (newspaper), November 15, 1967, p. 6.

19. "Sheriff's Harass," *La Raza* (newspaper), January 15, 1968, p. 1.

20. Cruz (Olmeda) Becerra, interview by author, tape recording, Alhambra, California, 15 May 1993.

21. David Sánchez, "The Birth of a New Symbol," pp. 1–2, Richard and Gloria Santillán Collection, University of California at Berkeley, Chicano Studies Library. For more on the Black Panthers' rhetoric, see Phillip S. Foner, ed., *The Black Panthers Speak* (New York: J. B. Lippincott, 1970); for Malcolm X, see Malcolm X with Alex Haley, *Autobiography of Malcolm X* (New York: Ballantine Books, 1965), and David Gallen, ed., *Malcolm X: The FBI File* (New York: Carroll and Graf Publishers, 1991). Here, too, the first glimpses of the Berets' masculinist and nationalist ideology first emerged. The document concretely shows Anne McClintock's notion that all nationalisms are gendered and invented (for more on this, see Anne McClintock, *Imperial Leather: Race, Gender, and Sexuality in the Colonial Contest* [New York: Routledge, 1995]). Sánchez's ideas also reflect historian George Mosse's ruminations that "the ideal of manliness" is "basic to the national ideology" (see George Mosse, *Nationalism and Sexuality: Middle-Class Morality and Sexual Norms in Modern Europe* [Madison: University of Wisconsin Press, 1985], 23). We can read Sánchez's words as his attempt to construct a new society in which the young Chicano man would be the

representative subject. Thus, in his "imagined community," men are privileged and indeed are metonymic to the idea of nation.

22. Sánchez, "The Birth of a New Symbol," 2.

23. Ibid.

24. Sánchez, "The Birth of a New Symbol," 3.

25. "Brown Berets: Serve, Observe, and Protect," *La Raza* (newspaper), June 7, 1968, p. 13. According to Cruz (Olmeda) Becerra, the structure implied by the titles never took hold and existed only on paper (Becerra, interview).

26. In Sánchez's conception of the organization, as expressed in "The Birth of a New Symbol," the Berets ideally were young men that would change the course of, and indeed, create a new history. The colonial manifestation of community would be reconstituted and a new imaginary would emerge. The role of men within the document is reminiscent of Mosse's notion of masculinity in the early modern era in Europe. He states, "The ideal of manliness was basic both to the self-definition of bourgeois society and to the national ideology. Manliness was invoked to safeguard the existing order against the perils of modernity, which threatened the clear distinction between what was considered normal and abnormality" (see Mosse, *Nationalism and Sexuality,* 23). So, too, was manliness invoked as a safeguard against the normal and the abnormal in Sánchez's rendering of society. The Brown Beret would act as prophet and bring about the "true" nature of Chicano nationalism and identity—the normal—and safeguard it against the infringement of Anglo society—the abnormal.

27. Dolores Delgado Bernal, "Grassroots Leadership Reconceptualized: Chicana Oral Histories and the 1968 East Los Angeles School Blowouts," *Frontiers* 19, no. 2 (1998): 120.

28. Rodolfo Acuña, *Occupied America: A History of Chicanos,* 3d ed. (New York: Harper and Row, 1988), 336.

29. David Sánchez, *Expedition Through Aztlán* (La Puente, Calif.: Perspectiva Press, 1978), 2.

30. Ruben Salazar, "Brown Berets Hail 'La Raza' and Scorn the Establishment," *Los Angeles Times,* June 16, 1969, sec. 1, p. 24.

31. "Who Are the Brown Berets?" *Chicano Student News,* March 15, 1968, p. 5.

32. Oscar Zeta Acosta, "The East L.A. 13 vs. the L.A. Superior Court," *El Grito* 3, no. 2 (winter 1970): 12.

33. Victor Franco, "E.L.A. Raided," *Inside Eastside,* June 10–13, 1968, p. 3.

34. Becerra, interview.

35. "For the Black Panthers' "Ten Points", see "October 1966 Black Panther Party Platform and Program: What We Want and What We Believe," in Foner, *The Black Panthers Speak,* 2–4.

36. "Brown Berets: Serve, Observe, and Protect," *La Raza* (newspaper), June 7, 1968, p. 13.

37. Ibid.

38. Ibid.

39. Becerra, interview.

40. Ibid.

41. In May 1969 the Beret newspaper *La Causa* reported that the organization had twenty-eight chapters in cities including San Antonio, Texas; Eugene, Oregon; Denver, Colorado; Detroit, Michigan; Seattle, Washington; Albuquerque, New Mexico; and most major California cities (see *La Causa*, May 23, 1969, p. 2).

42. Becerra, interview.

43. "The East Los Angeles 13 Are Ready," *La Raza* (newspaper), October 15, 1968, p. 13.

44. Ibid.; Della Rossa, "Poor People's Coalition," *La Raza* (newspaper), July 10, 1968, p. 7.

45. "News for a More Aware Community," *La Causa*, May 23, 1969, p. 8.

46. "Brown Berets: 8 Points of Attention," *La Causa*, December 1970, p. 19. The Brown Berets appear to be modeled after Mao Zedong's 1928 "Eight Rules" for the Red Guard; for more on this, see Zhong Wenxian, ed., *Mao Zedong: Biography, Assessment, Reminiscences* (Beijing: Foreign Language Press, 1986), 60–61. The Black Panthers also had a similar "Eight Points"; for these, see Foner, *The Black Panthers Speak*, 6. One such recruitment message was entitled "Becoming A Brown Beret: A Reason For Existing" (see *La Causa*, December 1970, p. 12).

47. "Third Annual Nuevas Vistas Conference" program, April 1969, Richard and Gloria Santillán Collection, University of California at Berkeley, Chicano Studies Library.

48. Those arrested were Chris Augustine, Luis Arroyo, Chris Cebada, Jaime Cervantes, Adelaida R. Del Castillo, Ernest Eichwald, Moctesuma Esparza, Reynaldo Macías, Francisco Martínez, Rene Núñez, Frank Sandoval, Victor Resendez, James Vigil, Thomas Varela, and Petra Valdez ("Ronnie's Show Flops as Biltmore Burns," *La Raza* [newspaper], April 30, 1969, p. 3).

49. "Ronnie's Show Flops as Biltmore Burns," *La Raza* (newspaper), April 30, 1969, p. 3; and Tom Newton, "Demonstration Disrupts Talk by Governor," *Los Angeles Times*, April 25, 1969, sec. 1, p. 1.

50. "14 Jailed in Biltmore Hotel Outburst," *Los Angeles Herald-Examiner*, April 25, 1969, sec. 1-A, p. 1.

51. The ten were Anthony Salamanca, Esmeralda Bernal, Carlos Montes, Ralph Ramírez, Thomas Varela, Rene Núñez, Ernest Eichwald Cebeda, Juan Robles, Moctesuma Esparza, and Willie Mendoza ("Nuevas Vistas 10," *La Raza* [newspaper], July 1969, p. 13).

52. "Nueva Vistas 10," *La Raza* (newspaper), July 1969, p. 10.

53. "Carlos Montes Disappears," *La Causa*, February 28, 1970, p. 9.

54. These issues were vol. 1, nos. 6–10, and vol. 2, nos. 1–2.

55. "Opening Statement Recorded on the Carlos Montes Trial," October 2, 1979; and "Superior Court of the State of California for the County of Los Angeles—The People vs. Carlos Michael Montes" (trial transcript), February–April 1979, p. 579; both in Oscar Zeta Acosta Papers, Department of Special Collections, University of California at Santa Barbara.

56. Ron Einstoss, "Undercover Officer Describes Role at Biltmore Fire Trial," *Los Angeles Times*, June 7, 1969, p. 2.

57. Los Angeles Police Department, Intelligence Report, file S-257.

58. Ibid.

59. "Opening Statement Recorded on the Carlos Montes Trial," October 2, 1979, pp. 3–4, Oscar Zeta Acosta Papers, Department of Special Collections, University of California at Santa Barbara.

60. "Is There a Frito Bandito in Your House?" *La Causa,* July 10, 1969, p. 3.

61. "Serving the People: The E.L.A. Free Clinic," *La Causa,* December 16, 1969, p. 2.; Ruben Salazar, "Brown Berets Hail 'La Raza' and Scorn the Establishment," *Los Angeles Times,* June 16, 1969, sec. 1, p. 24.

62. "Serving the People: The E.L.A. Free Clinic," *La Causa,* December 16, 1969, p. 2.; Ruben Salazar, "Brown Berets Hail 'La Raza' and Scorn the Establishment," *Los Angeles Times,* June 16, 1969, sec. 1, p. 24.

63. Though Sánchez claims, in *Expedition Through Aztlán* (p. 4), that he came up with the idea for the group, my research shows that Rosalio Muñoz, a UCLA student, was thinking along the same lines, and along with fellow Bruin, Ramsés Noriega, formed an organization, "Chale Con La Draft," to bring awareness on the draft to the Chicano community (see chapter 3).

64. "Chicano Moratorium: A Matter of Survival," *La Causa,* February 28, 1970, p. 1.

65. "La Caravan De La Reconquista is Coming," *La Causa,* ca. 1972, p. 1.

66. "Brown Berets National Policies" *La Causa,* ca. 1972.

67. Ibid.

68. Sánchez, *Expedition Through Aztlán,* 174–81.

69. For more on AIM's invasion of Alcatraz, see Paul Chaat Smith and Robert Allen Warrior, *Like A Hurricane: The Indian Movement from Alcatraz to Wounded Knee* (New York: The New Press, 1996).

70. Sánchez, *Expedition Through Aztlán,* 174–81.

71. Ibid.; and Al Martinez, "Judge Asks Berets to Leave—They Do: Chicano Group Quits Catalina Without Incident," *Los Angeles Times,* September 23, 1972, sec. 2, p. 1.

72. "National Brown Beret Organization Termination Notice," ca. October 22, 1972, Centro de Acción Social Autónomo [hereafter CASA] Papers, M325, box 25, folder 9, Stanford University Library, Department of Special Collections.

73. Dale Torgenson, "Brown Beret Leader Quits, Dissolves Units," *Los Angeles Times,* November 2, 1972, p. 9; and Memorandum to the Acting Director, March 29, 1973, Brown Beret file, no. 105-178715-273, U.S. Department of Justice, Federal Bureau of Investigation.

74. Two previous works point to the gendered nature of Chicano nationalism by surveying literary works, but they do not provide case studies of specific political groups: see Angie Chabram-Dernersesian, "I Throw Punches for My Race, but I Don't Want to Be a Man: Writing US—Chica-nos (Girl Us)/Chicanas—into the Movement Script," in *Cultural Studies,* ed. Lawrence Grossberg, Cary Nelson, and Paula A. Treichler (New York: Routledge, 1992), 81–95; and Ramón A. Gutiérrez, "Community, Patriarchy, and Individualism:

The Politics of Chicano History and the Dream of Equality," *American Quarterly* 45, no. 1 (March 1993): 44–72.

75. The case of the Brown Berets upholds Elleke Boehmer's notion that the male role in the nationalist scenario is typically "metonymic," i.e., men are contiguous with each other and with the nationalist whole. She goes on to argue that "the idea of nationhood bears a masculine identity" (see Boehmer, "Stories of Women and Mothers: Gender and Nationalism in Early Fiction of Flora Nwapa," in *Motherlands: Black Women's Writings from Africa, the Caribbean and South Asia,* ed. Suheila Nasta [New Brunswick, N.J.: Rutgers University Press, 1992], 6).

76. *La Causa,* April 1971, pp. 10–11.

77. "Chicanos at UCLA Blow-it," *La Causa,* August 29, 1970, p. 4.

78. "Brown Berets: To Serve ... Observe ... Protect," *La Causa,* December 16, 1969, 7.

79. Gloria Arellanes, "Palabras Para La Chicana," *La Causa,* July 10, 1969, p. 6.

80. Mosse, *Nationalism and Sexuality,* 23.

81. "The Adelitas Role En El Movement," *La Causa,* February 1971, p. 10.

82. For more on women in the Brown Berets, see Dionne Espinoza, "Pedagogies of Gender and Nationalism: Cultural Resistance in Selected Practices of Chicana/o Movement Activists, 1967–1972" (Ph.D. diss., Cornell University, 1996).

83. "Declaration of Robert Acosta," Los Angeles, December 1978, Oscar Zeta Acosta Papers, Department of Special Collections, University of California at Santa Barbara.

84. The FBI file contains 1,934 pages on the organization, of which 1,260 were made available to me through the Freedom of Information Act.

85. Memorandum, W. R. Wannall to W. C. Sullivan, March 26, 1968, Brown Beret file, no. 105-178715, U.S. Department of Justice, Federal Bureau of Investigation.

86. Memorandum, FBI Director to SAC [special agent in charge], Denver, March 2, 1976, Brown Beret file, no. 105-178715-299, U.S. Department of Justice, Federal Bureau of Investigation.

Bibliography

University of California at Berkeley, Chicano Studies Library

Richard and Gloria Santillán Collection

Oscar Zeta Acosta Papers, Department of Special Collections

California. Governor's Commission on the Los Angeles Riots. *Violence in the City: An End or A Beginning?* Los Angeles, 1965.

U.S. Bureau of the Census. *United States Census of Population, 1950. Special Reports. Persons of Spanish Surname.* Washington, D.C.: Government Printing Office, 1953.

———. *U.S. Census of Population and Housing: 1960. Census Tracts, Final Report. PHC (1)-82.* Washington D.C.: Government Printing Office, 1962.

_____. *U.S. Census of Population: 1960; Subject Reports. Persons of Spanish Surname. Final Report PC (2)-1B.* Washington D.C.: Government Printing Office, 1963.

_____. *U.S. Census of Population and Housing: 1970. Census Tracts, Final Report. PHC (1)-82.* Washington D.C.: Government Printing Office, 1972.

U.S. Department of Justice. Federal Bureau of Investigation.

Brown Beret file, no. 105–178715

Atlantic, 1967

La Causa, 1969–72

Chicano Student News, 1968

Inside Eastside, 1968–69

Los Angeles Herald-Examiner, 1949–70

Los Angeles Times, 1949–2001

La Raza (newspaper), 1967–70

Time, 1967

Becerra, Cruz (Olmeda). Interview by author. Tape recording. Alhambra, California, May 15, 1993.

Castro, Victoria. Interview by author. Tape recording. Los Angeles, May 24, 1993.

Acosta, Oscar Zeta. "The East L.A. 13 vs. the L.A. Superior Court." *El Grito* 3, no. 2 (winter 1970): 12–18.

Acuña, Rodolfo. *Occupied America: A History of Chicanos.* 3d ed. New York: Harper and Row, 1988.

Bernal, Dolores Delgado. "Grassroots Leadership Reconceptualized: Chicana Oral Histories and the 1968 East Los Angeles Blowouts." *Frontiers* 19, no. 2 (1998): 113–42.

Boehmer, Elleke. "Stories of Women and Mothers: Gender and Nationalism in Early Fiction of Flora Nwapa." In *Motherlands: Black Women's Writing from Africa, the Caribbean and South Asia,* ed. Suheila Nasta. New Brunswick, N.J.: Rutgers University Press, 1992.

Chabram-Dernersesian, Angie. "I Throw Punches For My Race, but I Don't Want to Be a Man: Writing US—Chica-nos (Girl Us)/Chicanas—into the Movement Script." In *Cultural Studies,* ed. Lawrence Grossberg, Cary Nelson, and Paula A. Treichler, 81–95. New York: Routledge, 1992.

Espinoza, Dionne. "Pedagogies of Gender and Nationalism: Cultural Resistance in Selected Practices of Chicana/o Movement Activists, 1967–1972." Ph.D. diss., Cornell University, 1996.

Foner, Phillip S., ed. *The Black Panthers Speak.* New York: J. B. Lippincott, 1970.

Gutiérrez, Ramón A. "Community, Patriarchy, and Individualism: The Politics of Chicano History and the Dream of Equality." *American Quarterly* 45, no. 1 (March 1993): 44–72.

Malcolm X, with Alex Haley. *The Autobiography of Malcolm X.* New York: Ballantine Books, 1965.

McClintock, Anne. *Imperial Leather: Race, Gender, and Sexuality in the Colonial Contest.* New York: Routledge, 1995.

Mosse, George L. *Nationalism and Sexuality: Middle-Class Morality and Sexual Norms in Modern Europe.* Madison: University of Wisconsin Press, 1985.

Rosen, Gerald Paul. *Political Ideology and the Chicano Movement: A Study of the Political Ideology of Activists in the Chicano Movement.* San Francisco: R & E Research Associates, 1975.

Salazar, Ruben. *Border Correspondent: Selected Writings, 1955–1970,* edited with an Introduction by Mario T. Garcia. Berkeley: University of California Press, 1995.

Sánchez, David. *Expedition Through Aztlán.* La Puente, Calif.: Perspectiva Press, 1978.

Sánchez, George J. *Becoming Mexican American: Ethnicity, Culture, and Identity in Chicano Los Angeles, 1900–1945.* New York: Oxford University Press, 1993.

Smith, Paul Chaat, and Robert Allen Warrior. *Like A Hurricane: The Indian Movement from Alcatraz to Wounded Knee.* New York: The New Press, 1996.

READING 7.5   POST-READING COMPREHENSION QUESTIONS

- Summarize the main problems the Brown Berets sought to challenge in their communities.

- Describe what the Brown Berets' three-part motto signifies: "To serve, to observe, and to protect."

- Paraphrase the quote: "Instead of relying on the ballot box, Chicano activists took to the streets and demanded change through protest."

End-of-Chapter Critical Thinking Questions

Directions: Respond to each of the questions about the readings. Refer to these sources to support your answers.

- Explain the role that education plays in the movement for freedom and human dignity.
- Describe how the farmworker struggle and more specifically the UFW profoundly shaped Chicana/o identity and culture.
- What can we learn about the Chicana and Chicano Movement by better understanding the Brown Berets?

Further Readings

Blackwell, Maylei. *Chicana Power!: Contested Histories of Feminism in the Chicano Movement.* Austin, TX.: University of Texas Press, 2011.

Chávez, Ernesto. *"¡Mi Raza Primero!": Nationalism, Identity, and Insurgency in the Chicano Movement in Los Angeles, 1966–1978.* Berkeley, CA.: University of California Press, 2002.

Gómez-Quiñones, Juan. *Chicano Politics: Reality and Promise, 1940–1990.* Albuquerque, NM.: University of New Mexico Press, 1990.

Gómez-Quiñones, Juan, and Irene Vásquez. *Making Aztlán: Ideology and Culture of the Chicana and Chicano Movement, 1966–1977.* Albuquerque, NM.: University of New Mexico Press, 2014.

García, Ignacio M. *Chicanismo: The Forging of a Militant Ethos Among Mexican Americans.* Tucson, AZ.: University of Arizona Press, 1997.

Garcia, Mario, and Ellen McCracken. *Rewriting the Chicano Movement: New Histories of Mexican American Activism in the Civil Rights Era.* Tucson, AZ.: University of Arizona Press, 2021.

García, Matt. *From the Jaws of Victory: The Triumph and Tragedy of Cesar Chavez and the Farm Worker Movement.* Berkeley, CA.: University of California Press, 2012.

Haney-López, Ian. *Racism on Trial: The Chicano Fight for Justice.* Cambridge, MA.: Belknap Press of Harvard University Press, 2003.

Mariscal, George. *Brown-Eyed Children of the Sun: Lessons from the Chicano Movement, 1965–1975.* Albuquerque, NM.: University of New Mexico Press, 2005.

Marquez, Lorena. *La Gente Struggles for Empowerment and Community Self-Determination in Sacramento.* Tucson, AZ.: University of Arizona Press, 2020.

Montejano, David. *Quixote's Soldiers: A Local History of the Chicano Movement, 1966–1981.* Austin, TX.: University of Texas Press, 2010.

Muñoz, Carlos. *Youth, Identity, Power: The Chicano Movement.* London, UK. and New York, NY.: Verso, 1989.

Oropeza, Lorena. *¡Raza Si! ¡Guerra No!: Chicano Protest and Patriotism during the Viet Nam War Era.* Berkeley, CA.: University of California Press, 2005.

Patiño, Jimmy. *Raza Sí, Migra No: Chicano Movement Struggles for Immigrant Rights in San Diego.* Chapel Hill, NC.: University of North Carolina Press, 2017.

CHAPTER 8

Cultural Resistance

··

Editor's Introduction

Culture and identity have always played a central role in how people understand their lives and their place within society. Noted historian Juan Gómez-Quiñones wrote that "[q]uestions and answers on culture are basic to historical analysis and political discourse." He went on to note that, in fact "[c]ulture is the context in which struggle takes place ..."[1] Understanding culture as a critical complement of how folks define themselves, resist conditions of subjugation, and create opportunities for survival is the subject of this last chapter.

Denise M. Sandoval documents an understudied yet critical period of Black and Brown cultural history in Los Angeles by focusing on Lowriding. Her research is an attempt to "... offer possible insight into how cultural expressions such as lowriding offer avenues for understanding the ways these two communities have historically lived, worked, played, and created a 'brotherhood' by cruising together."[2] By highlighting film, music, and Lowriders, Sandoval weaves together a riveting combination of cultural expression to build an important historical narrative that demonstrates the power of cultural resistance. Cherríe Moraga, on the other hand, uses an inventive combination of poetry and prose to unpack a long and complicated history of cultural nationalism, political and social resistance, and many of the contradictions that arose within those spaces of struggle during the modern civil rights movements. Part of the issue that Moraga works through in the piece is the fact that she wants to stay connected to her family and her culture, and realizes the significance of familial and cultural history, while at the same time recognizing

1 Juan Gómez-Quiñones, "On Culture," *Revista Chicano-Riqueña* 5, no. 2 (1977): 29.
2 Denise M. Sandoval, "The Politics of Low and Slow/Bajito y Suavecito: Black and Chicano Lowriders in Los Angeles, from the 1960s through the 1970s," in *Black and Brown in Los Angeles: Beyond Conflict and Coalition*, eds. Josh Kun and Laura Pulido, 176–200. (Oakland, CA.: University of California Press, 2014), 178.

that she is not always welcome, accepted, or safe within those cultural constructs. It is an amazing use of *historia* to not only challenge some of the extremely destructive attitudes within the community, but also to provide a very important intervention to those problems.

The Politics of Low and Slow/Bajito y Suavecito: Black and Chicano Lowriders in Los Angeles, from the 1960s through the 1970s

In this vibrant and forceful reading, Sandoval illustrates the dynamic and multiple ways in which Lowriding can "... express vividly the intersections of race, class, and gender, along with respect and pride."[3] The author covers the unique history of Lowriding car culture in Los Angeles while also highlighting the very critical connections this art form has for the potential of cross-racial solidarity.

THINGS TO LOOK FOR AS YOU READ..

- Politics of Bajito y Suavecito
- Black and Brown interconnectedness
- *Carnalismo*

---

3 Sandoval, "The Politics of Low and Slow/Bajito y Suavecito," 179.

The Politics of Low and Slow/ *Bajito y Suavecito*

Black and Chicano Lowriders in Los Angeles, from the 1960s through the 1970s

Denise M. Sandoval

As far as I am concerned, it all started here [Los Angeles].
Period. This is the lowrider capital of the world. Everybody
tries to imitate what's done here. That's always how it's going
to be. ... LA is it.
—Ted Wells, Professionals Car Club

We had three cultures. We had our Mexican culture at home.
Our mother spoke to us all in Spanish. Then we had our
pachuco culture—we were pachucos. And we had our Black
brothers out there. We had a variety and that was good.
—Fernando Ruelas, Dukes Car Club

Introduction

Hollywood movies have often presented sensationalized and racialized images of
lowrider culture in Los Angeles that have commonly led to the misconception that
lowriders are "gangs on wheels." *Boulevard Nights* (1979) was one the first movies
that visualized lowrider culture in East Los Angeles by connecting it not only to
the culture of "gangs," or *la vida loca,* but also to Chicano culture by capturing the
lingo, music, art, and cruising of Chicano lowriders in the late 1970s. In one scene,
the protagonist, Raymond, takes his *ruca*/girlfriend and younger brother, Chuco,

Denise M. Sandoval, "The Politics of Low and Slow/Bajito y Suavecito: Black and Chicano Lowriders in
Los Angeles, from the 1960s through the 1970s," *Black and Brown in Los Angeles: Beyond Conflict and
Coalition,* ed. Josh Kun and Laura Pulido, pp. 176-200. Copyright © 2013 by University of California
Press. Reprinted with permission.

to cruise on Whittier Boulevard on a Friday night in his royal blue 1976 Monte Carlo (with its small chain-link steering wheel and hydraulics setup) as disco music blares in the background. When Chuco sees his *cholo* friends, he gets out of his brother's car and into a 1940s lowrider that is blasting oldies. The movie shows the links between the lowrider pachuco past and the Chicano urban reality of the late 1970s, and it has been a very popular movie within many Chicano communities.

Yet, what I find significant is that it also portrays lowriding as a primarily Chicano cultural scene. Twelve years later, not only would *Boyz n the Hood* (1991) put lowriding in South Central (and Crenshaw Boulevard) on the map, but also it celebrated the popularity of gangsta rap on the West Coast. The night scene on Crenshaw has gang member Doughboy (played by Ice Cube) sitting in his champagne gold 1963 Chevy Impala convertible, discussing religion and street politics with his homies as other lowrider cars line up on the boulevard, socializing. When schoolboy Tre and his childhood friend Rick, a star athlete and Doughboy's brother, join them, there is a gang confrontation, Crips and Blood signs are flashed, and then the social scene on the Shaw is disrupted by the gunfire of an AK-47. Lowriding on Crenshaw in the early 1990s is portrayed in the film as a primarily African American activity, when in fact that era saw the community undergoing a demographic shift toward Latinos, and both Black and Chicano lowriders frequented "the Shaw."

Boyz n the Hood and *Boulevard Nights* share themes of gang violence, family connections, hypermasculinity, and brotherhood, as well as the struggle to move out of one's neighborhood for a better way of life. Yet, each movie portrays lowriding as racially/ethnically specific to the urban spaces of East Los Angeles and South Central. What is overlooked, however, is that each of these communities, Black and Chicano, has shared a similar history of struggle in Los Angeles and that at moments cultural expressions, such as lowriding, have led to interconnections and the creation of multicultural spaces. It is the passionate love affair for lowrider cars that has often bridged the gaps between East Los Angeles and South Central or South Los Angeles.

Los Angeles Lowriders

Lowriders in Los Angeles not only reveal their owners' passion for classic cars but also speak to the importance of visualizing and communicating cultural identity and community.[1] Using their vehicles as canvases for creative expression within the urban landscape, lowrider owners document the rich and vibrant social and cultural history of *nuestra ciudad* (our city). Lowriding is an everyday cultural practice for some Chicanos, and they are often cited as one of the creators of their culture (Trillin 1978; Plascencia 1983;

Lipsitz 1990; Stone 1990; Bright 1995; Mendoza 2000; Penland 2003; Sandoval 2003). More important, the history of lowriding speaks to the long history of interconnection between Chicano and Black communities in Los Angeles, reaching back to the swing and jazz scene of the 1940s and to the R&B and rock 'n' roll scene of the 1950s, 1960s, and 1970s. The West Coast sound created by single artists and groups such as Lalo Guerrero, Chuck Higgins, Etta James, Richard Berry, Brenton Wood, Thee Midniters, Tierra, and War, who explored the rhythms and beats of jazz, swing, blues, R&B, mambo, and rock music (Lipsitz 1990; Macías 2008), became the soundtrack for lowriding in Los Angeles, especially the music of Thee Midniters, Tierra, and War, who wrote songs that specifically catered to the lowrider community (Reyes and Waldman 1998; Molina 2002). The explosion of hip-hop culture in the 1980s and 1990s in Los Angeles also displayed this interconnectedness and transformed lowrider culture. Groups and artists such as N.W.A., Ice-T, Cypress Hill, and Kid Frost consistently employed lowriders in their videos as part of the West Coast hip-hop culture, and this had an impact both nationally and internationally. Los Angeles history reveals moments in which Mexican Americans and African Americans have used the dominant urban landscape in order to re-create their community and their cultural identities.

In the years since the 1965 Watts Riots, Los Angeles has often been portrayed as a city full of racial tensions, and the mainstream media have focused in particular on "Black and Brown" tensions in South Central, resulting from gang violence, issues over immigration, and even interactions between Blacks and Latinos in schools. Often overlooked, though, are the many historical moments in which these communities have come together through their love of similar cultural expressions, such as fashion, music, and cars. Documenting and understanding the earlier Black and Brown cultural histories of Los Angeles through lowrider history will, I hope, help illuminate the present and offer possible insight into how cultural expressions such as lowriding offer avenues for understanding the ways these two communities have historically lived, worked, played, and created a "brotherhood" by cruising together. A core theme found within the many stories of lowriding is the pride and respect lowriders feel for their cars, their car clubs, and for other lowrider participants. Other themes include the importance of family and brotherhood. "Brotherhood" is a particularly fascinating and important aspect of these communities that embrace and practice multiculturalism. In my many years of research, I often heard that the love of lowrider cars is what brings these men together, and this precedes any "race" solidarity. But, as these stories reveal, "race" is, in fact, an aspect of how intercultural connections happen in Los Angeles through the love of lowrider cars.

Lowriding is an art form and a "way of life" that continue to express vividly the intersections of race, class, and gender, along with respect and pride. These expressions are most salient in the generation of lowriders active from the 1960s through the 1970s, a period often considered the "cultural renaissance" of lowriding and an era in Los Angeles history in which lowriders often faced segregation and discrimination for their cruising activities on L.A. streets. This essay utilizes oral histories with Chicano and Black lowriders, in particular, the Ruelas brothers (Julio, Ernie, and Fernando), who founded the Dukes Car Club of Los Angeles, the oldest lowrider car club still in existence, and who are considered the "godfathers of lowriding." I also include their friendship with two African American lowriders: Terry Andersen and Ted Wells. The Ruelas family history begins in South Central Los Angeles, not the typical Chicano barrio experience of East Los Angeles, and provides an entry point for examining the sociohistorical interconnections between Chicano and Black cultural spaces in Los Angeles through the practice of lowriding. This essay grounds itself in the Chicano cultural space of lowriding in the key years of the 1960s through the 1970s, since Chicanos are the first group that organized car clubs in Los Angeles and also had the first magazine, *Lowrider,* beginning in 1977, and beyond that it examines, through the case study of the Dukes Car Club, how Chicano and Black lowriders interacted. The Chicano story of lowriding is central to L.A. history, as well as to lowrider history in general, since it has been one of the most documented and visualized aspects of that history. More important, the politics of bajito y suavecito/low and slow has been the mantra that has defined this cultural space and Chicano cultural identity.

The Politics of Bajito Y Suavecito

There is a conceptual framework for understanding the transformations and continuities of Chicano cultural identity within the urban landscape based on certain cultural knowledge of barrio life—a "barriology."[2] In *Barrio Logos: Space and Place in Urban Chicano Literature and Culture,* Raul Villa examines how within Los Angeles, working-class struggles and cultural movements of Mexican Americans can be mapped.[3] He labels these cultural movements and struggles "barriology," which is the documentation of the tensions based in "the practice of everyday life" for barrio residents of Los Angeles. Villa further explicates the importance of barrio life to cultural space and identity: "Manifesting alternative needs and interests of those of the dominant public sphere, the expressive practices of barrio social and cultural reproduction—from the mundane exercises of daily round and leisure activities to the formal articulation of community defensive goals in organizational forums and discursive media—reveal multiple possibilities for re-creating and re-imagining dominant urban space as community enabling place."[4]

Villa's analysis is helpful as a starting point for examining how car culture in Chicano and Black communities has involved a re-creation or a reimagining of the urban landscape of Los Angeles. As such, I would like to add to Villa's analysis of barriology the politics and practice of bajito y suavecito. Bajito y suavecito is not only a "leisure activity" but also a system of cultural knowledge grounded in the everyday practices of urban life. Lowriders, in choosing a particular aesthetics of car customizing, have created a subculture that has moved them beyond the barrios or neighborhoods of Los Angeles through the performance of mobility. Automobiles, especially in the 1950s and 1960s, allowed individuals or groups a means to transcend the limits of neighborhood. As lowriders cruised the boulevards of Los Angeles, they visualized their particular aesthetics to people outside their communities, who sometimes viewed them in the same manner they viewed the zoot-suiters, as juvenile delinquents or gang members. Many of these negative representations were due to the dominant media outlets like the *Los Angeles Times* newspaper. Luis Alvarez (2008) addresses how this racialization affected Black and Brown male bodies: "Popular discourse characterizing nonwhite youth as animal-like, hypersexual, and criminal marked their bodies as 'other' and, when coming from city officials and the press, served to help construct for the public a social meaning of African American and Mexican American youth. In these ways, the physical and discursive bodies of nonwhite youth were the sites upon which their dignity was denied."[5]

In an era in the 1940s, when ethnic minorities were expected to conform to Anglo-American styles of dress, the wearing of zoot suits enabled young Chicanos and Blacks to challenge the expectations of the dominant culture. It also meant that cultural identities were often fluid and multicultural. The pachuco/zoot-suiter, through his clothing (the suit originated in African American jazz/swing culture), language, and style, embodied resistance and cultural adaptation, just as a lowrider did in choosing to recustomize his American-manufactured automobile and drive it low to the ground.[6] In addition, both styles are visual and performative in calling on the white dominant society to see them. Unfortunately both styles were often seen in a negative light by the dominant society and even criminalized. In the 1940s, pachucos/zoot-suiters were seen by the dominant culture as juvenile delinquents, even people to be feared, as they were, for example, in the case of the Sleepy Lagoon murder in the summer of 1942, as well as in the Zoot Suit Riots of 1943.[7] Stuart Cosgrove explains the importance of the zoot suit within the American culture of the early 1940s: "The zoot suit was more than the drape-shape of the 1940s fashion, more than a colorful stage prop hanging from the shoulders of Cab Calloway, it was in the most direct and obvious ways, an emblem of ethnicity and a way of negotiating an identity. The zoot suit was a refusal: a sub-cultural gesture that refused to concede to the manners of subservience."[8]

The pachucos existed between both American and Mexican identities, creating their own space defined by the working-class roots of the barrio. To see and be seen, as a visible marker of difference, yet also of sameness by creating a community—of pachucos/zoot-suiters and eventually lowriders. Both subcultures within Mexican American communities were an expression of youth attempting to make a new identity for themselves, as well as incorporating the themes of pride, respect, brotherhood, and family. Over time, the pachuco and the lowrider became iconic symbols of a Chicano culture that is rooted in the process of adaptation through the forces of Americanization (Sánchez 1993). But the pachuco/zoot-suiter is also the beginning of a Chicano identity rooted in rebellion and resistance found in the philosophy of low and slow.

Therefore, the politics of low and slow has a long cultural legacy in Mexican American barrios in Los Angeles as a philosophy of cultural resistance and a way of life that requires *corazón*/pride, respect, *carnalismo*/brotherhood, and family or community. It is a cultural process that is both fluid and active, since at its core it is about being seen and visualizing a particular identity that is individual and collective as well as interethnic. The use of cars and boulevards is a tactic to create "community-enabling space." Lowriders become narratives or visual texts of working-class life—secondhand cars customized to be extravagant and luxurious—and of their owners' expressions of their individuality and communities. These cars establish links between consumer car culture, labor (skills), and gendered class and "race" positions. Low and slow is more than car aesthetics; it is also a cultural expression that is grounded in the urban sociohistorical experiences of Chicanos and African Americans in Los Angeles. Their cars, moving low and slow across the land of a thousand freeways, have helped to break down some of the barriers that separate the inhabitants of Los Angeles.

The History/*La Historia*

Lowriding in Los Angeles is a direct result of the post-World War II car culture boom when automobile manufacturing resumed and the demand for new cars increased. The rise of automobile culture in the United States has been discussed at length by Tom Wolfe (1965), James Flink (1975), and Cynthia Dettleback (1979), to name but a few. After World War II, the automobile industry quickly resumed producing new cars, which resulted in a surplus of used cars that could be bought by veterans, youth, working-class people, and ethnic minorities. Los Angeles was the perfect location for the explosion of car culture, since "in the 1950's Los Angeles' automobile industry was booming, with five factories in the county, it was the country's second-largest producer of cars and tires in the United States, after Detroit."[9] This situation, along with the affordability of used cars, was capitalized on by many working-class youth in Los Angeles. As Ernie Ruelas recalled, "You would buy a car in the 50s for fifteen dollars, it was easy to put dual pipes on it, you know, lower it and if you messed that one up you go get another one."[10] For African Americans, California in particular afforded economic opportunities, as well as freedom from Jim Crow segregation in the South, though they did face discrimination out West in the form of housing covenants and other racial restrictions in public accommodations. According to Flamming, "Restrictive covenants would be undone not by legislation but by the NAACP's dogged legal efforts, which finally resulted in favorable rulings in the U.S. Supreme Court during the late 1940s and early 1950s."[11] As housing opportunities for African Americans changed after the 1930s, automobile ownership flourished for this community. For instance, a survey of 12,142 African American households in Los Angeles in the 1930s found that 42 percent owned automobiles.[12] Also important to mention is the flourishing motorcycle culture within African American communities in California; in fact the formation of motorcycle clubs in the late 1940s and 1950s (Jimenez y West 2008) preceded the establishment of the lowrider car clubs in the late 1960s and 1970s (Penland 2003).

Another important aspect of the evolution of lowriding is its connection to American car culture in general. The surge in lowriding must also be framed within the proliferation of car leisure activities after World War II, such as hot-rodding, drag races, car shows, and demolition derbies. Cars were an extension of one's identity, becoming status symbols for working-class youth. Many car customizers used their vehicles to express resistance to the culture of conformity that existed in the 1950s. Historians trace the origins of lowriding to the birth of hot rod culture in the 1930s and 1940s in Southern California, an activity that was popular among many Anglo youth. This new "rebel culture," which transformed American popular culture after World War II, was captured in some notable Hollywood movies in the 1950s, such as *The Wild One* (1954), *Blackboard Jungle* (1955), and *Rebel without a Cause* (1955). Nora Donnelly elaborates further: "Hot rod culture evolved as an antidote to the cultural conformity of the 1950s. ... For the first time in American history, American teenagers were free to invent their own identities. How loud and fast your car roared became the external emblem of self for the postwar generation of teens. ... Working on your car became an acceptable craft and an artistic outlet."[13]

The various structural conditions inherent in the post-World War II economy created an environment that fostered a love affair between American males and their cars. Both hot-rodding and lowriding began as inherently masculine activities and remain so to this day. As an expressive form, lowriding was an affront to the (mostly Anglo-American) hot-rodders, who raised their cars off the ground and drove them fast. Lowriders practiced the opposite tactic: their cars were lowered to the ground and meant to go slow. Each car culture created a distinct aesthetics beckoning the viewer to look at the cars and pay respect to the cars' owners. For Chicano and African American lowriders this was particularly significant in a time period when they were often degraded in Los Angeles because of their race/ethnicity, class, and gender status. The cars represented a source of pride and quickly gained popularity in Chicano and Black communities. As Ted Wells recalls, "If you go down a street when I was growing up, your lowrider was the only car you had. You drove to school, to the store, on dates. ... Back then during the week, during the day, there were hundreds of lowriders on the streets."[14]

Lowriding had specific connections to life in the barrio for Mexican Americans, as Mexican American youth were also racially segregated within Los Angeles. Many Mexican American men had achieved recognition during World War II through their participation in the armed forces, yet their position within American society remained unchanged: Mexican Americans continued to be treated as second-class citizens. According to Acuna, "The de facto exclusion of Mexicans from public facilities, schools, trade unions, juries, and voting was common in many sections of the country."[15] In California, beginning in the early part of the twentieth century, Mexican American children were placed in schools and classrooms separate from their Anglo American peers. In 1946, this practice would be declared unconstitutional by the federal district Judge Paul J. McCormick in the *Mendez v. Westminster School District* case, a precursor to *Brown v. Board of Education* (1954). This reality was also shared by African American veterans, who also continued to face de facto and de jure segregation in public facilities and schools and also began to fight for their civil rights. In the everyday life of these working-class youth and men, automobiles then offered an avenue to transgress the limits of territory or their barrios or neighborhoods through the mobility of their cars. Michael Stone's analysis of the impact of car culture on Mexican Americans can also be applied to African Americans, since this cultural expression influenced perceptions of community and cultural identity: "Lowriding must be seen in light of changing self-perception of class and ethnic identity on part of Mexican American youth, as played against the broader context of American youth culture, the 'car culture,' the mass media, public education, military service, and the world of work."[16]

Furthermore many World War II veterans, especially among Mexican Americans and African Americans, gained mechanical skills through their work in shipyards, military motor pools, and airplane hangars. Many of these men were also part of the "52–20 club," in which the U.S. government paid them benefits of twenty dollars a month for one year after discharge for their military service. This extra income and the mechanical skills they acquired through their wartime service then made it possible for veterans to purchase and maintain a new or used car.[17] Manuel Cruz recalled how

Chicanos put their skills for car modifications to good use, and in the process they created a distinct car aesthetics:

> The cars were fixed this way—a '36 Chevy club coupe would get its front fender skirts off, no spot lights or skirts on it, usually a '34 Ford would get its front fenders and back fenders taken off. The best ones were the two door convertibles. Chicanos started fixing their cars. They would put dual pipes, rubber flaps with reflectors on them that went on the back of the rear flaps or license plates, skirts for their cars, one or two spot lights, white walls. If you wanted a lowrider, the only thing you could do then was put sand bags or cement sacks in the trunk to make them heavy ... that was before metal shocks. Those were the first lowriders in LA in the 40s.[18]

Automobiles allowed both economic and physical mobility. A car represented a middle-class American dream that was now available to working-class people; it also created a means for Chicano and Black lowriders to physically transgress the boundaries of racially segregated neighborhoods in Los Angeles.[19] Their participation in car leisure activities also formed a collectivity with other lowriders and maintained the link found in many popular cultural forms in which the individual uses popular culture to create a community with others. The cultural space that lowriders created in the 1950s initiated a community-enabling space within the barrios of Los Angeles, much as the pachucos and zoot-suiters of the 1940s did. Ruben Ortiz-Torres writes: "With the advent of lowrider culture, the individualistic American dream of driving away to escape it all has been replaced with the notion of driving together. Lowriders organize in car clubs and go cruising on the weekends on specific boulevards, updating the old Mexican practice of walking around a town plaza on Sundays in order to socialize and flirt with girls. They drive slowly, pumping their music and blocking traffic, messing with a social system that is not eager to accept them."[20]

Hydraulics marked the beginning of a new era of lowriding in Los Angeles. In 1958, Ron Aguirre, a Chicano from Los Angeles, installed the first hydraulic system in a 1957 Chevrolet Corvette. The setup allowed his car to be lowered or raised with a flip of a switch, an important innovation in the lowriding scene. The hydraulic parts, which consisted of hydro air pumps and dumps, were surplus parts from World War II fighter planes that assisted in lowering and raising the wing flaps. During the 1960s and 1970s, a large number of lowriders would purchase government surplus parts at Palley's Surplus in Vernon (a setup cost forty dollars in the 1960s) and have them installed at places such as the Ruelas's shop in South Los Angeles, Dick and Ron's in Hawthorne, Bill Hines's shop in Compton, and Al Sullivan's in Hyde Park. These surplus parts were a valuable asset to the lowriders, since they could ride as low as they wanted to on the boulevard, then return their cars to a legal ground clearance with the flip of a switch if they saw the police. Because the California vehicle code stipulated that no part of a car could be lower than the bottom portion of the wheel rim, the police often wrote tickets to owners of lowrider cars. Many lowriders felt they were targeted more than hot-rodders on L.A. streets. The official lowrider label began to be used in the 1960s, and according to *Lowrider* magazine, the term was first coined by the police after the 1965 Watts Riots. Jack Kennedy relates in *Lowrider: History, Pride, Culture,* "They [the police] were using the term 'lowrider' as a derogatory term for the young black kids that were causing all the trouble. ... They said that they were kids who drove cars with no springs and no seats so they could ride low."[21] The term *lowrider,* which began as an insult, took on new meaning as youth and young adults redefined it as a source of cultural pride.

The Dukes

Los Angeles is the birthplace of the oldest lowrider car club still in existence, the Dukes, which was founded by the Ruelas brothers. The Ruelas brothers are an example of the strength of the lowriding tradition based on *la familia* (brotherhood), respect, and pride. Within the Ruelas family, lowriding is a tradition that is passed on from one generation to the next, from father to son to grandson. The important legacy of the Dukes to lowrider history was celebrated in 2007 as its members welcomed their forty-fifth anniversary as a car club. The Ruelas brothers proudly call themselves pachucos and Chicanos. They are known for customizing '39 Chevys, a choice that made them stand out from the rest of the lowriders in the 1960s and 1970s, when most lowriders customized cars from the 1950s and 1960s.

The story of the Ruelas brothers reveals the cultural links between Chicanos and Blacks in Los Angeles through the practice of lowriding. During the 1950s and 1960s, the Ruelas brothers grew up in a South Los Angeles neighborhood that included pockets of Mexican American neighborhoods, like 41st Street and Alameda, but the schools they attended were in primarily African American neighborhoods. According to Flamming, by 1960 the area along Central Avenue was 95 percent black, and there was a "seven mile stretch of African American neighborhoods locked between Main Street and Alameda."[22] The high school that the Ruelas brothers attended, Jefferson, was within this Central Avenue district, and even though they were in the minority, they were respected by African Americans there. Ernie Ruelas once explained, "We were known as the 'black

Mexicans.' Our black brothers respected us for having courage."[23] Two African American friends of the Ruelas brothers, Terry Anderson and Ted Wells, remember meeting the Dukes in the early 1970s, an event about which Anderson remarked, "These guys had me at their home for *quinceañeras* (celebrations of teenage girls coming of age), funerals of car club members who died, and holidays. They took me into their family."[24] The politics of low and slow in South Central Los Angeles became a way to bridge the two divergent cultures of Mexican Americans and African Americans, and in the process life-long friendships would be formed. The story of the Dukes is not unlike other histories of lowriders in Los Angeles who live in multicultural communities, yet the story of the Ruelas brothers, the OGs (which abbreviates "original gangsters" but is used to mean veterans/*veteranos*) of the lowrider scene in Los Angeles, is a fascinating chapter that visualizes the interconnectedness of Blacks and Chicanos.

The Dukes' story begins south of downtown Los Angeles on 41st and Long Beach Avenue, in a time period in L.A. history when being Mexican was a reason to be seen as "inferior" to Anglo Americans.[25] In the mid-1950s Josefina Ruelas, a single mother, immigrated from Tijuana to Los Angeles with her four boys (Julio, Oscar, Fernando, and Ernie) and settled in with Uncle Tinker and Tia Chana. These relatives had settled in South Central Los Angeles in the mid-1930s and had an automotive shop. Uncle Tinker, who became a father figure to his nephews, introduced the boys to auto mechanics in an attempt to keep them off the streets, and in the process, he taught them about taking pride in their work. The most important lesson that he imparted to them was the positive influence of la familia working together. These would be lessons the Ruelas brothers passed on to their own sons. The love affair with cars began at a young age for Julio Ruelas, who is the oldest brother: "I got interested in lowriding through my family. Already our uncles were lowriding, and I was growing up seeing them. And around the neighborhood everybody had a low car with dual pipes. So that is when I took it from there, and I followed it ever since."[26]

When each of the brothers reached age thirteen, each had a car that he began to customize, and each became a "specialist" in certain areas of car customizing. For example, one brother specialized in bodywork, one in upholstery, and another in electrical wiring. Since each one possessed different talents, they built cars as a team. Even though they were not able to drive these cars legally, the brothers still took pleasure in their customizing work. Fernando recalls:

> Well, my first car was a 1949 Chevrolet four door; it was a deluxe. I bought it in 1963. And I bought from an individual that lived in Watts as a matter of fact. I paid fifty dollars for it, actually my brother

went and bought it for me, because I was only thirteen years old. I was too young, so my brother bought it for me. And fifty dollars was a lot of money back then; it was like per se thirty thousand to buy a car right now, or forty. So it was a lot of money. It was my first car, and the first thing I done on that car is I dropped it. And you know the methods back then to dropping a car if you didn't have any money, there was two, three methods to do that, so we would either heat the coils up in the front, put a lot of weight in the back. Cement rocks anything that's weighing and lowers it down. But the very early years of the lowriding, they would drop the front a little bit and leave it like in a slant like this, and they called it "Diego"—you know like baby Diego.[27]

The early style of low and slow (before hydraulics) captured the imagination of Fernando and his brothers. The process of building a car became a family effort as the brothers worked together. Family was a central tenet of life in the barrio, and one's neighborhood also became part of one's extended family. Carnalismo, or brotherhood, among men in the neighborhood produced barrio social clubs or gangs.[28] For the Ruelas brothers, having an uncle who was a mechanic afforded them the opportunity to learn about customizing firsthand at a very early age, as well keep them off the streets of South Los Angeles. One of the Ruelas brothers explained:

> He didn't want us in the street, hanging out with the guys. Very early age he would take us out to the junk yards to pick up bicycles, this was in the 50s, 1954, and we'll get the Schwinn cause that was a better looking bike … we done all kinds of crazy things to lowered Cadillac lights sticking out of the back with original blinkers, you know how they had back at that time. With raising the big handle bars, like they'd be sticking up like that, maybe we will be real creative. We'll even get that and make motor bikes out of them, we'll put lawn mower motors on them.[29]

Fernando learned the laborious process of "bodywork" at a young age, a process he labeled "the old-fashioned way." Early on, his uncle took the boys to scrap yards and taught them customizing skills. Fernando was just twelve years old when he started shooting his first metal flake (a method of painting a car). His brother Ernie meanwhile learned electrical wiring from Uncle Tinker by working on an old radio. Their mother also supported their activity, since it kept them off the streets and gave them something productive to do. As young boys, the Ruelas brothers were a part of the phase of lowriding in which car owners took pride in working on the cars themselves, as opposed to those in the present era, who take their cars to various shops around Los Angeles if they can afford to. The Dukes created a historic and classic lowriding standard that others have followed, and this standard also reflects the different generations of lowriders as well as the different customizing styles of each generation. Ernie Ruelas remarks,

> The early styles were historic, and you can't even find paint anymore to paint the cars that way. I believe that the ways that people install their hydraulics are also different. The old way, especially for old cars, there was only a small amount of people who knew how to do it that way. It was a professional installation, and now people do not cater to that installation so much; they just throw it in there and that's it. Before, people were very much into research—how it works right, how it rides right, and also how it changes. I think that hydraulics in our day were more for style symbol to keep your car low and to ride smooth and all that.[30]

These features also made the car stand out, especially to law enforcement. The police wrote tickets to those who violated the law that no part of a car could be lower than the bottom portion of the wheel rim, which made lowriders one of their favorite targets. Fernando Ruelas worked for thirty-five years on installing hydraulic setups, and he recalled the treatment lowriders received from police in the 1950s and 1960s.

> Back in the earlier days, per se the police department they didn't like low riders, and they just were out there just to knick pick, you see, … what they could find. In opposed to the Anglo they wouldn't bother them, but they would bother the Latino low rider a lot, because basically they probably figured "What is this guy doing in this nice looking car?" so there was a big feedback on the earlier years. In opposed to the late, like we are now, things have mellowed down. … it's still there, but it's not as exposed as it was back then.[31]

The Ruelas brothers readily admit that as boys in the late 1950s they joined the 38th Street gang out of a need for protection. The 38th Street club achieved mainstream recognition during the Sleepy Lagoon murder case of 1942, when twenty-two of their members were found guilty of crimes ranging from assault to first-degree murder through an unfair and racist trial. More important, living in South Central in the 1950s and 1960s required the Ruelas brothers to adapt to three cultures. As young members of the 38th Street, they proudly called themselves "pachucos" and had to interact with their pachuco brothers through music, language, and dress. They also had to interact with Mexican culture in their home, where their mother spoke to them in Spanish, and they were exposed to Mexican music. Then at school and in their mostly Black neighborhood, they had to interact with Black culture in order to be accepted. Brother Fernando explains this influence of three cultures on Chicanos living in South Los Angeles in this time period: "We had three cultures. We had our Mexican culture at home. Our mother spoke to us all in Spanish. Then we had our pachuco culture—we were pachucos. And we had our Black brothers out there. We had a variety and that was good."[32]

Jefferson High School historically produced many musical artists that the brothers were influenced by and some they knew personally. Artists like Etta James, Richard Berry, Arthur Lee May, and even Barry White all went to "Jeff." African American music was a cultural bridge to American culture for many Chicanos living in Los Angeles, who lived in the same neighborhoods as Blacks or in neighborhoods adjacent to Black communities, which often in turn encouraged intercultural exchanges (Lipsitz 1990; Macías 2008). Ernie Ruelas also explains the importance of that intercultural connection in shaping his identity and the car culture's lure for him: "My family went to school in South Central. We were the minority there. Nine Mexican boys and girls at Jefferson High School. Looking back at that, it made me what I am. We understood each other. We liked cars and that brought us together."[33]

The love of cars is what brought some Chicanos and Blacks together in the streets of Los Angeles in the late 1960s and early 1970s. The Ruelas brothers' reputation as good customizers earned them respect, and they were even invited into the homes of their Black neighbors and invited to cruise with the Black lowriders. As Terry Andersen explains, growing up on the West Side, he did not even know Latin lowriders, but "everyone heard about the Dukes because they came into the 'hood. They were accepted. They showed no prejudice."[34] Ernie Ruelas recalls that they would work on cars owned by African Americans, adding, "We treated them with respect." Yet there were spaces in Los Angeles where neither group was accepted or respected. For instance, Lynwood was called "Lynchwood" by Chicanos and African Americans, because if they drove into that neighborhood, they were quickly escorted out by the police. They learned early on that Lynwood was only for white people. As Ernie recalls, "Even when white people moved out, the police department maintained a 'keep it white attitude,' and a person could get hit with a flashlight by a cop."[35] Even in Huntington Park, a person could not be out on the streets after 10 p.m. These are areas that bordered the lowriders' own neighborhoods, but they learned early on the stigma of both being Black and Mexican in the streets of Los Angeles and driving the particular cars they owned. As Ernie says, "The police left the White hot-rodders alone; they did not get harassed."[36]

In 1962, the Ruelas brothers realized their passion for cars was enough to start their own car club, which also caused some tensions in their neighborhood. The Dukes car club became an alternative to gang life—or la vida loca. The car club initially was perceived as a threat to the control of the neighborhood by the 38th Street gang, and it caused some initial hard feelings between that gang and the Dukes. Yet, this tension would soon vanish as the Dukes soon brought honor and respect to their neighborhood. Fernando remembers those tensions:

> Well actually the first thing you had to do is you had to get out of the gang you were in. Because when you were in a gang and you were trying to start a club, your peers, your gang members, they didn't want a club, 'cause you got to understand when I grew up we were pachucos, and that's the hard thing there. You're going to do a club, you going to get individuals. It doesn't take one, two, three guys to start a club to begin with, and back then you had club members that per se it was a social club so it was cars. ... So we had to hassle there with our neighborhood guys to start this. So it was a big impact here; you know, you hassle with a society out there then if you are going to do a neighborhood club, and it was pretty hard, especially the neighborhood where I grew up—38th Street over there—its family history known with the Sleepy Lagoon murder and all this. So there's history there, so it was very hard to break away the pachuco image and to turn it into a car club thing.[37]

For the brothers, car clubs as social clubs provided an alternative option to gangs by creating a social environment that was considered respectable. So eventually the 38th Street gang agreed to let the brothers start a car club, since it would bring pride and respect to the neighborhood. In the 1970s Black car clubs like the Professionals, the Compton chapter of the Majestics, and the Individuals were established. As Ted Wells recalls, "When I turned sixteen and got a driver's license, you got a car, you were either a hot-rodder or a lowrider, and I chose a lowrider."[38] Black lowriders Ted Wells and Terry Anderson cite the Ruelas brothers as early innovators, and they often visited the brothers' shop in South Los Angeles. Yet, when the streets were turned into community-enabling space for Chicanos and Blacks, cruising locales were structured along lines of race/ethnicity. Chicanos cruised Whittier Boulevard in East Los Angeles, and Blacks cruised Crenshaw Boulevard. One reason these cruising spots were "racialized" in the development and transformation of Los Angeles neighborhoods is that historically East Los Angeles was a Mexican American neighborhood, and the neighborhood around Crenshaw Boulevard was primarily African American. So, if a Mexican American cruised Crenshaw in the early days of the late 1960s and early 1970s, they had to be invited by an African American car club. And if an African American cruised Whittier Boulevard in this same time period, they also had to be invited. Many of these protocols would disappear though by the late 1970s, as lowriding and cruising grew in popularity, and lowrider car shows became more well organized. For example, the first large-scale lowrider car show at the Los Angeles Convention Center occurred in 1979, and it was sponsored by *Lowrider* magazine.

Cruising has been an important aspect of lowrider culture and a popular pastime for American youth since the 1950s. The boulevards of Los Angeles became the perfect site to showcase their custom creations, and many lowriders have seen themselves as the "Picassos of the Boulevards." Until the end of the 1970s, one of the most popular cruising venues in the United States was Whittier Boulevard in East Los Angeles. At the height of its popularity in the 1960s and 1970s, Whittier Boulevard was the ideal place for working-class Chicanos to show off their cars, pick up dates, and have fun. According to many *veteranos* of that time, Whittier Boulevard had everything a young man desired: cars, music, and girls. Many labeled it "Chicano Disneyland," a playground for barrio youth. Whittier Boulevard was alive every weekend as the top cruising spot in Los Angeles, and the Dukes were an important part of that scene. Each lowrider club had its own spot on the boulevard, and the Dukes had the prime spot in the Huggie Boy car lot. As Fernando recalls, "Nobody parked in our lot; they knew it was ours. We filled it with '39s."[39] African Americans cruised Crenshaw, and by 1965, it was a happening spot. As Ted Wells recalls, "A friend of mine took me down to one of the all-time lowrider hangouts called Stop's Hamburgers, on the corner of Imperial and Central. Stop's was a place where on Sunday nights, in every direction, there were lowriders packing both sides of the streets."[40] And when Whittier Boulevard was shut down by law enforcement in the 1979, the traffic in South Central became more multicultural.

In 1974 Fernando Ruelas became president of the club (a position he held until his passing in 2010), and he was also responsible for the changes to come on the lowriding scene in the late 1970s. The Dukes, along with the Imperials and the Groupe car clubs, played a key role in the formation of the West Coast Association of Lowriders in 1978. The purpose of the association was to get car clubs to unite and do something positive within the Chicano community. Together these clubs put on the "Christmas Toys for

Kids" car show, and all the proceeds went to purchasing toys and Christmas stockings for underprivileged children. The Dukes, however, were influenced by the growing political activism in East Los Angeles during the Chicano movement of the late 1960s and 1970s, and the way they connected the clubs to political movements like this one separates them from the other car clubs. They organized car shows to benefit the broader Chicano community, from César Chávez and the United Farmworkers, to Mecha and other Chicano organizations, to even local prisons. They owned the "Dukes Bus," which they filled with club members and took to prisons to put on lowrider shows for the inmates. All of these activities reveal the importance of la familia and the community to lowriders, who do more than just cruise the streets. The Dukes believe in "giving back to the community," a motto that sustains *Chicanismo* in the barrios of Los Angeles, especially for the younger generations. As Fernando explains:

> I've done a lot of auditorium appearances back in those days, and talked to the kids. Where you had the first, second, third graders, I've got still their crayon drawings with "I love you Dukes thank you for the toys and stocking," and little cars all crooked with their kids you know. I got tons of that stuff put away, tons of it. And I would donate my time to do this with the kids, as well as you know I used to do car shows, I used to call it car night, but it was on Saturdays in the day where I would take kids from Jefferson High School, cause that's the school where I used to go, and I used to bring them there and teach them the mechanics, body work and the whole thing on lifts, hydraulics on a car. And I just got burned out, you know every Saturday. I just got burned out, we used to take a new group of people, and what I would do every month I would get a new group, and I'll do that. Hopefully some of those kids right now have cars like this.[41]

The brothers are acutely aware that lowriding is tied to the multicultural history of Los Angeles and is an avenue to build community with other lowriders. But more important, lowriding for them is something that people should take pride in. They want the customizing work that they do to have inspirational and motivational effects on the Chicano community and the broader L.A. community, especially the youth. The Ruelas brothers have applied lessons from the Chicano movement to their work as a car club. Fernando mentioned that the sole purpose in starting the club was not to get a thousand members but instead to capture the youth and give them an alternative to gangs.

The brothers also share their own stories of growing up in order to motivate youth to enter into activities in their communities. When asked what lowriding teaches youth, Ernie Ruelas responds: "I think that it is real positive, because it is bringing awareness, and it is bringing Mexican people or Chicano people to work together and to let them know that it is not about doing combat with one another, but loving one another in building something that is in our blood."[42]

According to the Dukes, their lowrider club is an extension of their family, and they believe that perspective is one of the main reasons for their longevity. In this manner, the car club is more than just cars; the Dukes believe they can use their love of cars to communicate stories to the younger generation, stories that will inspire them and teach them the lessons of pride, respect, carnalismo/brotherhood, and family. The politics of low and slow on the boulevards of Los Angeles not only links the past with the present but also speaks to lowriders' shared sense of community, Black and Chicano. This is illustrated best by the story of the Dukes, who have been innovators, artists, and "godfathers" on the scene for over forty years. Their lowrider stories of the 1960s and 1970s also demonstrate what authors writing on popular music in Los Angeles have revealed: interconnections of Black and Brown communities are at the heart of L.A. cultural history.

Conclusion: Black and Chicano Lowriders after the 1970s

The importance of family and fraternal relationships (carnalismo) among lowriders in the 1960s and 1970s is reflected in the formation of car clubs. Generally referred to by members as "second families," most clubs were originally established by small close-knit groups of custom-car enthusiasts comprising either blood relatives or individuals from the same neighborhoods. In addition to establishing a sense of solidarity among lowriders, these associations have also supported friendly competition among members who try to outdo one another in creating the "perfect" car. Furthermore, club membership provides an alternative to gang life (la vida loca) by replacing potentially dangerous or violent activities with positive and "respectable" social behaviors. In this sense, lowriding is keeping alive the carnalismo, just like the pachucos/zoot-suiters before them, as a source of community-enabling space.

There is a diversity of car club politics within the lowriding scene, but all the clubs share similar traits of family bonds, respect, and pride for their cars. In fact, their emphasis on these themes has resulted in the longevity of the car clubs. Despite the shared themes,

Chicanos have added a distinct style to lowriding that is all their own. Ernie Ruelas explains:

> I think that what we have added to lowriding has been our style. You see a Chicano car fixed up and all that, you know it is a Chicano car. You see a Black person's car and all that, and you know that it is a Black person's car. Their styles are different. I think what we have started here is using older cars with sun visors, with the hydraulics on older cars, and that kind of stuff. We started that. I think also we have brought some awareness all through this country that leads from the West Coast all the way to the East Coast.[43]

The story of the Dukes is in no way the ultimate story of Black and Brown interconnectedness within the lowriding scene, but it captures a particular moment in the 1960s and 1970s in which these communities shared a history of struggle and discrimination on the streets of Los Angeles and created a brotherhood through their mutual love of lowrider cars. The politics of low and slow provided a common ground of mutual recognition for some Chicano and Black lowriders. More important, as other scholarly work has shown, the Chicanos' struggle for a community-enabling space in Los Angeles has often meant creating new cultural identities that have borrowed and added to African American popular cultural modes of expression, like music, fashion, and dance. Although the importance of Chicanos' role as innovators and generators of lowrider culture in Los Angeles has been documented and visualized in many scholarly works and mainstream museum exhibitions, their elevation as such sometimes becomes a source of tension, because Black lowriders may feel that their stories and contributions are too minimized within lowrider history. Scholarly work is still needed to document and visualize the stories of Black lowriders in Los Angeles beyond the journalistic stories in *Lowrider* magazine and the content of hip-hop videos.

Finally, the demographic changes in the areas of South Los Angeles in the late 1980s and early 1990s, wherein African American communities became "Latino-cized" through immigration from Mexico and Central America, produced racial tensions between Black and Brown in the area's communities. Whereas earlier generations of immigrants like the Ruelas brothers were accepted by their African American peers in periods of intense "Americanization" of the 1950s and 1960s, these new generations of immigrants have often been labeled "illegal aliens" and "un-American" by some in the African American community who have viewed these people as taking their jobs.[44] Though exploring the issues born of demographic changes in South Los Angeles is out of the realm of this essay, these changes do point to the complicated patterns of community and identity in Los Angeles. For instance, in the various Latino communities here, recent immigrants and those who have been here for generations all have different connections to "American" culture, Latino immigrant culture, and Black culture. How this affects the politics of low and slow and the lowrider community remains to be documented and explored as the worlds of *Boulevard Nights* and *Boyz n the Hood* become less celebratory and more aligned with the current complicated cultural/racial politics of the City of Angels—Los Angeles.

Notes

1. *Lowrider* is used to describe a car that is customized primarily to be low to the ground, usually containing a hydraulic set-up, with a fantastic candy paint job, chrome features, and customized upholstery. Included among the categories of lowrider cars are "bombs" (American-made cars from the late 1930s to the early 1950s) and "Euros" (import cars such as Hondas and Acuras). Many lowriding purists believe that classic Chevrolets are the only cars that, once properly customized, can carry the lowrider label, yet today virtually any kind of vehicle can be transformed into a lowrider. There are now lowrider minitrucks, SUVs, motorcycles, bicycles, and even scaled-down model cars. Most important, the lowrider label is also used to describe people who participate in this car-culture phenomenon. Lowriding is a way of life for many of its participants, and its practice varies across the United States and abroad.

2. Raul Villa explains that the term was coined in "the late 1960s by the associated members of *Con Safos* magazine, an artist collective in East Los Angeles," and he paraphrases Tomas Ybarro-Frausto's definition of the term: "Barriology was a playful but serious promotion of the cultural knowledge and practices particular to the barrio." Raul Homero Villa, *Barrio Logos: Space and Place in Urban Chicano Literature and Culture* (Austin: University of Texas Press, 2000), 6–7.

3. Ibid., 6.

4. Ibid.

5. Luis Alvarez, *The Power of the Zoot: Youth Culture and Resistance during World War II* (Berkeley: University of California Press, 2008), 43.

6. Dressing in extravagantly garbed in high-waisted trousers, oversized coats, wide-brimmed hats, and long gold watch chains, the pachucos fashioned a new identity for themselves, one that made them stand out from people who were just trying to "fit in." In addition, they wore their hair a bit longer than was the style of the time, which was military crew cuts. Their defiance of the status quo was interpreted as an important act of cultural resistance and later became a source of inspiration for Chicanos during the Chicano movement, as well as for the other lowriders in the 1950s and 1960s.

7. The Zoot Suit Riots were fights between servicemen and zoot-suiters, in which the zoot-suiters were arrested and the servicemen were applauded by the media and even law enforcement. For a more detailed analysis of both the Zoot Suit Riots and the case of the Sleepy Lagoon murder, see, respectively, Mauricio Mazon, *The Zoot Suit Riots: The Psychology of Symbolic Annihilation* (Austin: University of Texas Press, 1984); and George Sanchez, *Becoming Mexican American: Ethnicity, Culture, and Identity in Chicano Los Angeles, 1900–1945* (New York: Oxford University Press, 1993).

8. Stuart Cosgrove, "The Zoot Suit and Style Warfare," *History Workshop Journal* 18 (Autumn 1984): 77.

9. Paige Penland, *Lowrider: History, Pride, Culture* (St. Paul, MN: Motor-books International, 2003), 13.

10. Ernie Ruelas in *Low and Slow* (South Padre Island, TX: Ritual Films, 1997), 16mm documentary, 27 minutes.

11. Douglas Flamming, *Bound for Freedom: Black Los Angeles in Jim Crow Era* (Berkeley: University of California Press, 2005), 350.

12. Ibid., 306.

13. Nora Donnelly, "Freedom, Style, Sex, Power and Motion—the Cult of Cars," in *Customized: Art Inspired by Hot Rods, Lowriders and American Car Culture,* edited by Nora Donnelly, 49–67 (Boston: Institute of Contemporary Art, 2000), 49.

14. Ted Wells, interview by author, digital recording, Altadena, CA, July 10, 2007.

15. Rodolfo Acuña, *Occupied America: A History of Chicanos,* 4th ed. (New York: Addison Wesley Longman, 2000), 279.

16. Michael Stone, "Bajito y Suavecito: Lowriding and the 'Class' of Class," *Journal of Latin American Popular Culture* 9 (1990): 87–88.

17. Ibid.

18. *Lowrider* 2, no. 2 (1977): 33.

19. Winslow Felix first opened his Chevrolet dealership in 1922 and is considered the first Mexican American car dealership owner in Southern California, according to numerous sources, including the Felix Chevrolet dealership owner Darryl Holter. Winslow Felix was a friend of filmmaker Pat Sullivan, whose animation studio created the Felix the Cat character, and Winslow was given special permission to use this image for his dealership. In an early time of consumer discrimination for many minorities in Los Angeles, this dealership provided opportunities for many first-time car owners. Winslow also created a "trial purchase plan," founded the Greater Los Angeles Motorcar Dealers, organized the annual Southern California auto shows, and staged midget-car races. The Felix the Cat image represents Los Angeles's love affair for Chevy cars. Even today, a sign of cultural authenticity is having a Felix the Cat sticker displayed in the window of a restored vintage GM vehicle. The beautiful neon sign of Felix the Car was erected in 1957 at the Felix Chevrolet dealership in Los Angeles on the corner of Jefferson and Figueroa.

20. Ruben Ortiz Torres, "Cathedral on Wheels," in *Customized,* 37.

21. Quoted in Penland, *Lowrider,* 26.

22. Flamming, *Bound for Freedom,* 378.

23. Ernie Ruelas, interview by author, digital recording, Los Angeles, CA, July 14, 2007.

24. Terry Andersen, interview by author, digital recording, Los Angeles, CA, July 14, 2007.

25. For a more detailed examination of this time period for Chicanos in Los Angeles, see Acuña, *Occupied America;* and Ricardo Romo, *East Los Angeles: History of a Barrio* (Austin: University of Texas Press, 1983).

26. Julio Ruelas, interview by author, tape recording, Los Angeles, CA, June 12, 1999.

27. Interview, Lowrider Oral History Project: Youth Voices, Los Angeles, March 15, 2008, Collection of Petersen Automotive Museum, Los Angeles (hereafter LOHP).

28. In the 1920s, most areas settled by Mexican Americans in Los Angeles began to organize their neighborhoods (barrios), such as happened in Maravilla, El Hoyo, Alpine, and Dogtown. Chicano youth would create social clubs connected to their barrios. In time these clubs were seen as gangs by the dominant culture, especially during World War II, when juvenile delinquency became a social problem for Los Angeles. By the 1950s, many of these social clubs had taken on the titles of gangs. For a more detailed look at the development of Chicano gangs in Los Angeles, see Joan Moore, *Homeboys: Gangs, Drugs and Prison in the Barrios of Los Angeles* (Philadelphia: Temple University Press, 1978); and James Diego Vigil, *Barrio Gangs: Street Life and Identity in Southern California* (Austin: University of Texas Press, 1988).

29. Interview, LOHP.

30. Ernie Ruelas, interview by author, tape recording, Los Angeles, June 12, 1999.

31. Interview, LOHP.

32. Ibid.

33. Interview, LOHP.

34. Terry Andersen, interview by author, digital recording, Los Angeles, July 14, 2007.

35. Ernie Ruelas, interview by author, digital recording, Los Angeles, July 14, 2007.

36. Ibid.

37. Interview, LOHP.

38. Ted Wells, interview by author, digital recording, Altadena, CA, July 10, 2007.

39. Fernando Ruelas, interview by author, tape recording, La Habra, CA, June 10, 1999.

40. Penland, *Lowrider,* 25.

41. Interview, LOHP.

42. Ernie Ruelas, interview by author, tape recording, Los Angeles, June 12, 1999.

43. Ibid.

44. A perfect example of this is friend and admirer of the Dukes, Terry Anderson, who spoke highly of their friendship and of other Chicano lowriders to me but also was involved in activism against Mexican immigration in Los Angeles and nationally until his death in July 2010. He hosted a weekly AM radio show on KRLA and spoke as a man who saw his

once African American community of South Los Angeles being "taken over by illegals" who took away jobs from his sons. I discovered this information after he had died and was therefore unable to do a follow-up interview with him for this essay.

References

Bright, Brenda Jo. 1995. "Re-mappings: Los Angeles Low Riders." In *Looking High and Low: Art and Cultural Identity*, ed. Brenda Jo Bright and Liza Blackwell, 89–123. Tucson: University of Arizona Press.

Dettleback, Cynthia. 1979. *In the Driver's Seat: The Automobile in American Literature and Popular Culture*. Westport, CT: Greenwood Press.

DeWitt, John. 2001. *Cool Cars, High Art: The Rise of Kustom Kulture*. Jackson: University Press of Mississippi.

Flink, James J. 1975. *The Car Culture*. Cambridge, MA: MIT Press.

Ganahl, Pat. 1996. *Hot Rods and Cool Customs*. New York: Artabras.

Geneat, Robert. 1998. *Hot Rod Nights: Boulevard Cruisin' in the USA*. Osceola, WI: Motorbooks International, 1998.

Jimenez y West, Christopher, curator. 2008. *Black Chrome* exhibit catalog. California African American Museum, Los Angeles, September 25, 2008, to April 12, 2009.

Lipsitz, George. 1990. *Time Passages: Collective Memory and American Popular Culture*. Minneapolis: University of Minnesota Press.

Macías, Anthony. 2008. *Mexican American Mojo: Popular Music, Dance, and Urban Culture in Los Angeles, 1935–1968*. Durham, NC: Duke University Press.

Mendoza, Ruben G. 2000. "Cruising Art and Culture in *Aztlán*: Lowriding in the Mexican American Southwest." In *U.S. Latino Literatures and Cultures: Transnational Perspectives*, ed. Francisco Lomeli and Karin Ikas, 3–35. Heidelberg, Germany: Carl Winter-Verlag.

Molina, Ruben. 2002. *The Old Barrio Guide to Low Rider Music, 1950–1970*. La Puente, CA: Mictlan.

Penland, Paige. 2003. *Lowrider: History, Pride, Culture*. St. Paul, MN: Motorbooks International.

Plascenia, Luis. 1983. "Lowriding in the Southwest: Cultural Symbols in the Mexican Community." In *History, Culture and Society: Chicano Studies in the 1980s*, ed. Mario Garcia, 141–75. Ypsilanti, MI: Bilingual Review Press.

Reyes, David, and Tom Waldman. 1998. *Land of a Thousand Dances: Chicano Rock 'n' Roll from Southern California*. Albuquerque: University of New Mexico Press.

Sánchez, George. 1993. *Becoming Mexican American: Ethnicity, Culture, and Identity in Chicano Los Angeles, 1900–1945*. New York: Oxford University Press.

Sandoval, Denise Michelle. 2003. "Cruising through Lowrider Culture: Chicana/o Identity in the Marketing of LowRider Magazine." In *Velvet Barrios: Popular Culture & Chicana/o Sexualities,* ed. Alicia Gaspar de Alba, 179–96. New York: Palgrave Macmillan.

Stone, Michael. 1990. "Bajito y Suavecito: Lowriding and the 'Class' of Class." *Journal of Latin American Popular Culture* 9: 87–88.

Trillin, Calvin. 1978. "Our Far-Flung Correspondents: Low and Slow, Mean and Clean." *New Yorker* 54: 70–74.

Wolfe, Tom. 1965. *The Kandy-Kolored Tangerine-Flake Streamline Baby.* New York: Noonday Press.

READING 8.1   POST-READING COMPREHENSION QUESTIONS

- Summarize the "Politics of Bajito y Suavecito."

- Describe the significance of visualizing and communicating cultural identity and community.

- Paraphrase the line: "… each of these communities, Black and Chicano, has shared a similar history of struggle in Los Angeles and that at moments cultural expressions, such as lowriding, have led to interconnections and the creation of multicultural spaces."

CHAPTER 8

Queer Aztlán: The Reformation of Chicano Tribe

In the following reading by Cherríe Moraga, she thoughtfully lays out an *historia* of her life and her experiences within the context of the Chicano Movement and the many ways in which Chicanos define struggle and resistance. Moraga is keen to highlight the significant connection to indigeneity within this narrative and points to moments of heartbreaking violence and destruction, but also seeks to underscore liberating philosophies of self-determination.

THINGS TO LOOK FOR AS YOU READ..

- Contradictions within the Chicano Movement
- Conceptions of Aztlán
- The significance of indigeneity

Queer Aztlán

The Reformation of Chicano Tribe

Cherríe Moraga

> How will our lands be free if our bodies aren't?
>
> —Ricardo Bracho

At the height of the Chicano Movement in 1968, I was a closeted, light-skinned, mixed-blood Mexican-American, disguised in my father's English last name. Since I seldom opened my mouth, few people questioned my Anglo credentials. But my eyes were open and thirsty and drank in images of students my age, of *vatos* and *viejitas,* who could have *primos,* or *tíos,* or *abuelitas* raising their collective fists into a smoggy East Los Angeles skyline. Although I could not express how at the time, I knew I had a place in that Movement that was spilling out of *barrio* high schools and onto police-barricaded streets just ten minutes from my tree-lined working class neighborhood in San Gabriel. What I didn't know then was that it would take me another ten years to fully traverse that ten-minute drive and to bring all the parts of me—Chicana, *lesbiana,* half-breed, and *poeta*—to the revolution, wherever it was.

My real politicization began, not through the Chicano Movement, but through the bold recognition of my lesbianism. Coming to terms with that fact meant the radical restructuring of everything I thought I held sacred. It meant acting on my woman-centered desire and against anything that stood in its way, including my Church, my family, and my "country." It meant acting in spite of the fact that I had learned from my Mexican culture and the dominant culture that my womanhood was, if not despised, certainly deficient and hardly worth the loving of another woman in bed. But act I did, because not acting would have meant my death by despair.

Cherríe Moraga, "Queer Aztlán: the Re-formation of Chicano Tribe," *Latino/a Thought: Culture, Politics, and Society, ed. Francisco H. Vazquez,* pp. 223-242. Copyright © 2009 by Rowman & Littlefield Publishing Group. Reprinted with permission.

That was twenty years ago. In those twenty years I traversed territory that extends well beyond the ten-minute trip between East Los Angeles and San Gabriel. In those twenty years, I experienced the racism of the Women's Movement, the elitism of the Gay and Lesbian Movement, the homophobia and sexism of the Chicano Movement, and the benign cultural imperialism of the Latin American Solidarity Movement. I also witnessed the emergence of national Chicana *feminista* consciousness and a literature, art, and activism to support it. I've seen the growth of a lesbian-of-color movement, the founding of an independent national Latino/a lesbian and gay men's organization, and the flourishing of Indigenous people's international campaigns for human and land rights.

A quarter of a century after those school walk-outs in 1968,1 can write, without reservation, that I have found a sense of place among *la Chicanada*. It is not always a safe place, but it is unequivocally the original familial place from which I am compelled to write, which I reach toward in my audiences, and which serves as my source of inspiration, voice, and *lucha*. How we Chicanos define that struggle has always been the subject of debate and is ultimately the subject of this essay.

"Queer Aztlán" had been forming in my mind for over three years and began to take concrete shape a year ago in a conversation with poet Ricardo Bracho. We discussed the limitations of "Queer Nation," whose leather-jacketed, shaved-headed white radicals and accompanying anglo-centricity were an "alien-nation" to most lesbians and gay men of color. We also spoke of Chicano Nationalism, which never accepted openly gay men and lesbians among its ranks. Ricardo half-jokingly concluded, "What we need, Cherríe, is a 'Queer Aztlán.'" Of course. A Chicano homeland that could embrace *all* its people, including its *jotería*.[1]

Everything I read these days tells me that the Chicano Movement is dead. In Earl Shorris' *Latinos,* the Anglo author insists that the Chicano *himself* is dead. He writes, "The Chicano generation began in the late 1960s and lasted about six or eight years, dying slowly through the seventies." He goes on to say that *Chicanismo* has been reduced to no more than a "handshake practiced by middle-aged men." Chicano sociologists seem to be suggesting the same when they tell us that by the third generation, the majority of Chicanos have lost their Spanish fluency, and nearly a third have married non-Chicanos and have moved out of the Chicano community. Were immigration from México to stop, they say, Chicanos could be virtually indistinguishable from the rest of the population within a few generations. My nieces and nephews are living testimony to these faceless facts.

I mourn the dissolution of an active Chicano Movement possibly more strongly than my generational counterparts because during its "classic period," I was unable to act publicly. But more deeply, I mourn it because its ghost haunts me daily in the blonde hair of my sister's children, the gradual hispanicization of Chicano students, the senselessness of barrio violence, and the poisoning of *la frontera* from Tijuana to Tejas. In 1992, we have no organized national movement to respond to our losses. For me, *"El Movimiento"* has never been a thing of the past, it has retreated into subterranean uncontaminated soils awaiting resurrection in a "queerer," more feminist generation.

What was right about Chicano Nationalism was its commitment to preserving the integrity of the Chicano people. A generation ago, there were cultural, economic, and political programs to develop Chicano consciousness, autonomy, and self-determination. What was wrong about Chicano Nationalism was its institutionalized heterosexism, its inbred *machismo,* and its lack of a cohesive national political strategy.[2]

Over the years, I have witnessed plenty of progressive nationalisms: Chicano nationalism, Black nationalism, Puerto Rican Independence (still viable as evidenced in the recent mass protest on the Island against the establishment of English as an official language), the "Lesbian Nation" and its lesbian separatist movement, and, of course, the most recent "Queer Nation." What I admired about each was its righteous radicalism, its unabashed anti-assimilationism, and its *rebeldía.* I recognize the dangers of nationalism as a strategy for political change. Its tendency toward separatism can run dangerously close to biological determinism and a kind of fascism. We are all horrified by the concentration and rape camps in Bosnia, falsely justified by the Serbian call for "ethnic cleansing." We are bitterly sobered by the nazism espoused by Pat Buchanan at the 1992 Republican Convention in which only heterosexual white middle-class voting Amerikans have the right to citizenship and heaven. Over and over again we are reminded that sex and race do not define a person's politics. Margaret Thatcher is a woman and enforces the policies of the Imperial whiteman and Clarence Thomas is Black and follows suit. But it is historically evident that the female body, like the Chicano people, has been colonized. And any movement to decolonize them must be culturally and sexually specific.

Chicanos are an occupied nation within a nation, and women and women's sexuality are occupied within Chicano nation. If women's bodies and those of men and women who transgress their gender roles have been historically regarded as territories to be conquered, they are also territories to be liberated. Feminism has taught us this. The nationalism I seek is one that decolonizes the brown and female body as it decolonizes the brown and female earth. It is a new nationalism in which *la Chicana Indígena* stands at the center, and heterosexism and homophobia are no longer the cultural order of the day. I cling to the word *"nation"* because without the specific naming of the nation, the nation will be lost (as when feminism is reduced to humanism, the woman is subsumed). Let us retain our radical naming but expand it to meet a broader and wiser revolution.

Tierra Sagrada: The Roots of a Revolution

Aztlán. I don't remember when I first heard the word, but I remember it took my heart by surprise to learn of that place—that "sacred landscape" wholly evident *en las playas, los llanos, y en las montañas* of the North American Southwest. A terrain that I did not completely comprehend at first, but that I continue to try, in my own small way, to fully inhabit and make habitable for its Chicano citizens.

Aztlán gave language to a nameless anhelo inside me. To me, it was never a masculine notion. It had nothing to do with the Aztecs and everything to do with Mexican birds, Mexican beaches, and Mexican babies right here in Califas. I remember once driving through Anza Borrego desert, just east of San Diego, my VW van whipping around corners, climbing. The tape deck set at full blast, every window open, bandana around my forehead. And I think, *this is México, Raza territory,* as I belt out the refrain ...

> *"Marieta, no seas coqueta*
> *porque los hombres son muy malos*
> *prometen muchos regalos*
> *y lo que dan son puro palos. ..."*

That day I claimed that land in the spin of the worn-out tape, the spin of my balding tires, and the spin of my mind. And just as I wrapped around a rubber-burning curve, I saw it: **"A-Z-T-L-A-N,"** in granite-sized letters etched into the face of the mountainside. Of course, I hadn't been the first. Some other Chicano came this way, too, saw what I saw, felt what I felt. Enough to put a name to it. *Aztlán. Tierra sagrada.*

A term Náhuatl in root, *Aztlán* was that historical/mythical land where one set of Indian forebears, the Aztecs, were said to have resided 1,000 years ago. Located in the U.S. Southwest, Aztlán fueled a nationalist struggle twenty years ago, which encompassed much of the pueblo Chicano from Chicago to the borders of Chihuahua. In the late sixties and early seventies, Chicano nationalism meant the right to control our own resources, language, and cultural traditions, rights guaranteed us by the Treaty of Guadalupe Hidalgo signed in 1848 when the Southwest was "annexed" to the United States at the end of the Mexican-American War. At its most radical, Chicano nationalism expressed itself in militant action. In the mid-1960s, Reies López Tijerina entered a campaign against the Department of the Interior to reclaim land grants for New Mexicans, resulting in his eventual imprisonment. In 1968, nearly 10,000 Chicano students walked out of their high schools to protest the lack of quality education in Los Angeles barrio schools. The same period also saw the rise of the Brown Berets, a para-military style youth organization regularly harassed by law enforcement agencies throughout the Southwest. These are highlights in Chicano Movement history. To most, however, El Movimiento, practically applied, simply meant fair and equitable representation on the city council, in the union halls, and on the school board.

I've often wondered why Chicano nationalism never really sustained the same level of militancy witnessed in the Puerto Rican, Black, and Native American Movements. Certainly violence, especially police violence, was visited upon Chicanos in response to our public protests, the murder of journalist Rubén Salazar during the National Chicano Moratorium of 1970 being the most noted instance. And like other liberation movements, the Chicano movement had its share of FBI infiltrators.

In 1969, El Plan de Aztlán was drawn up at the First Annual Chicano Youth Conference in Denver, Colorado, calling for a Chicano program of economic self-determination, self-defense, and land reclamation, and including an autonomous taxation and judicial system. By the mid-1970s, such radical plans had gradually eroded in the face of a formidable opponent—the United States government—and Chicano nationalism as a political strategy began to express itself more in the cultural arena than in direct militant confrontation with the government.

Another reason for the brevity of a unified militant movement may be the heterogeneity of the Chicano population. Chicanos are not easily organized as a racial/political entity. Is our land the México of today or the México of a century and a half ago, covering thousands of miles of what is now the Southwestern United States? Unlike the island of Puerto Rico whose "homeland" is clearly defined by ocean on all sides, Aztlán at times seems more *meta*physical than physical territory.

As a mestizo people living in the United States, our relationship to this country has been ambivalent at best. Our birth certificates since the invasion of Aztlán identify us as white. Our treatment by Anglo-Americans brand us "colored." In the history of African Americans, when the white slave owner raped a Black woman, the mixed-blood offspring inherited the mother's enslaved status. Over a century later, mixed-raced African Americans overwhelmingly identify as Black, not as mixed-blood. But the history of Mexicans/Chicanos follows a different pattern. The "Spanish-American" Conquest was secured through rape, intermarriage, the African slave trade, and the spread of Catholicism and disease. It gave birth to a third "mestizo" race that included Indian, African, and European blood. During colonial times, "Spanish-America" maintained a rigid and elaborate caste system that privileged the pure-blood Spaniard and his children over the mestizo. The pure blood *indio* and *africano* remained on the bottom rungs of society. The remnants of such class/race stratification are still evident throughout Latin America.

Chicano Nation is a mestizo nation conceived in a double-rape: first, by the Spanish and then by the Gringo. In the mid-19th century, Anglo-America took possession of one-third of México's territory. A new English-speaking oppressor assumed control over the Spanish, Mestizo, and Indian people inhabiting those lands. There was no denying that the United States had stolen Aztlán from México, but it had been initially stolen from the Indians by the Spanish some 300 years earlier. To make alliances with other nationalist struggles taking place throughout the country in the late sixties, there was no room for Chicano ambivalence about being Indians, for it was our Indian blood and history of resistance against both Spanish and Anglo invaders that made us rightful inheritors of Aztlán. After centuries of discrimination against our Indian-ness, which forced mestizos into denial, many Mexican-Americans found the sudden affirmation of our indigenismo difficult to accept. And yet the Chicano Indigenous movement was not without historical precedence. Little more than fifty years earlier, México witnessed a *campesino-* and Indian-led agrarian and labor movement spreading into the Southwest that had the potential of eclipsing the Russian Revolution in its vision. Political corruption, of course, followed. Today, the pending Free Trade Agreement with the United States and Canada marks the ultimate betrayal of the Mexican revolution: the final surrender of the Mexican people's sovereign rights to land and livelihood.

Radicalization among people of Mexican ancestry in this country most often occurs when the Mexican ceases to be a Mexican and becomes a Chicano. I have observed this in my Chicano Studies students (first, second, and third generation, some of whose families are indigenous to Aztlán) from the barrios of East Los Angeles, Fresno, and all the neighboring Central Valley towns of California—Selma, Visalia, Sanger, the barrios of Oakland, Sanjo, etc. They are the ones most often in protest, draping their bodies in front of freeway on-ramps and trans-bay bridges, blocking entrances to University administration buildings. They are the ones who, like their Black, Asian, and Native American counterparts, doubt the "American dream" because even if *they* got to UC Berkeley, their brother is still on crack in Boyle Heights, their sister had three kids before she's twenty, and *sorry but they can't finish the last week of the semester cuz Tío Ignacio just got shot in front of a liquor store.* My working-class and middle-class Mexican immigrant students,[3] on the other hand, have not yet had their self-esteem nor that of their parents and grandparents worn away by North American racism. For them, the "American dream" still looms as a possibility on the horizon. Their Mexican pride sustains them through the daily assaults on their intelligence, integrity, and humanity. They maintain a determined individualism and their families still dream of returning home one day.

A new generation of future Chicanos arrives every day with every Mexican immigrant. Some may find their American dream and forget their origins, but the majority of México's descendants soon comprehend the political meaning of the disparity between their lives and those of the gringo. Certainly the Mexican women cannery workers of Watsonville who maintained a two-year victorious strike against Green Giant in the mid-eighties, and farm workers organized by César Chávez's UFW in the late sixties and early seventies are testimony to the political militancy of the Mexican immigrant worker. More recently, there are the examples of the Mothers of East Los Angeles and the women of Kettleman City who have organized against the toxic contamination proposed for their communities. In the process, the Mexicana becomes a Chicana (or at least a *Mechicana); that is, she becomes a citizen of this country, not by virtue of a green card, but by virtue of the collective voice she assumes in staking her claim to this land and its resources.

Plumas Planchadas: The De-Formation of the Movement

> With our heart in our hands and our hands in the soil, we declare the independence of our mestizo nation.
> —*"El Plan Espiritual de Aztlán"*

El Movimiento did not die out in the seventies, as most of its critics claim; it was only deformed by the machismo and homophobia of that era and co-opted by "hispanicization" of the eighties.[4] In reaction against Anglo-America's emasculation of Chicano men, the male-dominated Chicano Movement embraced the most patriarchal aspects of its Mexican heritage. For a generation, nationalist leaders used a kind of "selective memory," drawing exclusively from those aspects of Mexican and Native cultures that served the interests of male heterosexuals. At times, they took the worst of Mexican machismo and Aztec warrior bravado, combined it with some of the most oppressive male-conceived idealizations of "traditional" Mexican womanhood and called that cultural integrity. They subscribed to a *machista* view of women, based on the centuries-old virgin-whore paradigm of *la Virgen de Guadalupe* and *Malintzin Tenepal.* Guadalupe represented the Mexican ideal of *"la madre sufrida,"* the long-suffering desexualized Indian mother, and *Malinche* was *"la chingada,"* sexually stigmatized by her transgression of "sleeping with the enemy," Hernán Cortez. Deemed traitor by Mexican tradition, the figure of Malinche was invoked to keep Movimiento women silent, sexually passive, and "Indian" in the colonial sense of the word.

The preservation of the Chicano *familia* became the Movimiento's mandate and within this constricted "familia" structure, Chicano politicos ensured that the patriarchal father figure remained in charge both in their private and political lives.[5] Women were, at most, allowed to serve as modern-day *"Adelitas,"* performing the "three fs" as a Chicana colleague calls them: "feeding, fighting, and fucking." In the name of this "culturally correct" familia, certain topics were censored both in cultural and political spheres as not "socially relevant" to Chicanos and typically not sanctioned in the Mexican household. These issues included female sexuality generally and male homosexuality and lesbianism specifically, as well as incest and violence against women—all of which are still relevant between the sheets and within the walls of many Chicano families. In the process, the Chicano Movement forfeited the participation and vision of some very significant female and gay leaders and never achieved the kind of harmonious Chicano "familia" they ostensibly sought.

To this day, although lip service is given to "gender issues" in academic and political circles, no serious examination of male supremacy within the Chicano community has taken place among heterosexual men. *Veteranos* of Chicano nationalism are some of the worst offenders. Twenty years later, they move into "elderhood" without having seriously grappled with the fact that their leadership in El Movimiento was made possible by all those women who kept their "plumas planchadas"[6] at every political event.

A Divided Nation: *A Chicana Lésbica* Critique

> We are free and sovereign to determine those tasks which are justly called for by our house, our land, the sweat of our brows, and by our hearts. Aztlán belongs to those who plant the seeds, water the fields, and gather the crops and not to the foreign Europeans. We do not recognize capricious frontiers on the bronze continent.
> —From *"El Plan Espiritual de Aztlán"*

When "El Plan Espiritual de Aztlán" was conceived a generation ago, lesbians and gay men were not envisioned as members of the "house"; we were not recognized as the sister planting the seeds, the brother gathering the crops. We were not counted as members of the "bronze continent."

In the last decade, through the efforts of Chicana feministas, Chicanismo has undergone a serious critique. Feminist critics are committed to the preservation of Chicano culture, but we know that our culture will not survive marital rape, battering, incest, drug and alcohol abuse, AIDS, and the marginalization of lesbian daughters and gay sons. Some of the most outspoken criticism of the Chicano Movement's sexism and some of the most impassioned activism in the area of Chicana liberation (including work on sexual abuse, domestic violence, immigrant rights, Indigenous women's issues, health care, etc.) have been advanced by lesbians.

Since lesbians and gay men have often been forced out of our blood families, and since our love and sexual desire are not housed within the traditional family, we are in a critical position to address those areas within our cultural family that need to change. Further, in order to understand and defend our lovers and our same-sex loving, lesbians and gay men must come to terms with how homophobia, gender roles, and sexuality are learned and expressed in Chicano culture. As Ricardo Bracho writes: "To speak of my desire, to find voice in my brown flesh, I needed to confront my male mirror." As a lesbian, I don't pretend to understand the intricacies or intimacies of Chicano gay desire, but we do share the fact that our "homosexuality"—our feelings about sex, sexual power and domination, femininity and masculinity, family, loyalty, and morality—has been shaped by heterosexist culture and society. As such, we have plenty to tell heterosexuals about themselves.

When we are moved sexually toward someone, there is a profound opportunity to observe the microcosm of all human relations, to understand power dynamics both obvious and subtle, and to meditate on the core creative impulse of all desire. Desire is never politically correct. In sex, gender roles, race relations, and our collective histories of oppression and human connection are enacted. Since the early 1980s, Chicana lesbian feminists have explored these traditionally "dangerous" topics in both critical and creative writings. Chicana lesbian-identified writers such as Ana Castillo, Gloria Anzaldúa, and Naomi Littlebear Moreno were among the first to articulate a Chicana feminism, which included a radical woman-centered critique of sexism *and sexuality* from which both lesbian and heterosexual women benefited.

In the last few years, Chicano gay men have also begun to openly examine Chicano sexuality. I suspect heterosexual Chicanos will have the world to learn from their gay brothers about their shared masculinity, but they will have the most to learn from the "queens," the *"maricones."* Because they are deemed "inferior" for not fulfilling the traditional role of men, they are more marginalized from mainstream heterosexual society than other gay men and are especially vulnerable to male violence. Over the years, I have been shocked to discover how many femme gay men have grown up regularly experiencing rape and sexual abuse. The rapist is always heterosexual and usually Chicano like themselves. What has the Gay Movement done for these brothers? What has the Chicano Movement done? What do these young and once-young men have to tell us about misogyny and male violence? Like women, they see the macho's desire to dominate the feminine, but even more intimately because they both desire men and share manhood with their oppressors. They may be *jotos,* but they are still men, and are bound by their racial and sexual identification to men (Bracho's "male mirror").

Until recently, Chicano gay men have been silent over the Chicano Movement's male heterosexual hegemony. As much as I see a potential alliance with gay men in our shared experience of homophobia, the majority of gay men still cling to what privileges they can. I have often been severely disappointed and hurt by the misogyny of gay Chicanos. Separation from one's brothers is a painful thing. Being gay does not preclude gay men from harboring the same sexism evident in heterosexual men. It's like white people and racism, sexism goes with the (male) territory.

On some level our brothers—gay and straight—have got to give up being "men." I don't mean give up their genitals, their unique expression of desire, or the rich and intimate manner in which men can bond together. Men have to give up their subscription to male superiority. I remember during the Civil Rights Movement seeing newsreel footage of young Black men carrying protest signs reading, "I AM A MAN." It was a powerful statement, publicly declaring their humanness in a society that daily told them otherwise. But they didn't write "I AM HUMAN," they wrote "MAN." Conceiving of their liberation in male terms, they were unwittingly demanding the right to share the whiteman's position of male dominance. This demand would become consciously articulated with the emergence of the male-dominated Black Nationalist Movement. The liberation of Black women per se was not part of the program, except to the extent that better conditions for the race in general might benefit Black women as well. How differently Sojourner Truth's "Ain't I a Woman" speech resonates for me. Unable to choose between suffrage and abolition, between her womanhood and her Blackness, Truth's 19th-century call for a free Black womanhood in a Black- and woman-hating society required the freedom of all enslaved land disenfranchised peoples. As the Black feminist Combahee River Collective stated in 1977, "If Black women were free, it would mean that everyone else would have to be free since our freedom would necessitate the destruction of all the systems of oppression." No progressive movement can succeed while any member of the population remains in submission.

Chicano gay men have been reluctant to recognize and acknowledge that their freedom is intricately connected to the freedom of women. As long as they insist on remaining "men" in the socially and culturally constructed sense of the word, they will never achieve the full liberation they desire. There will always be jotos getting raped and beaten. Within people of color communities, violence against women, gay bashing, sterilization abuse, AIDS and AIDS discrimination, gay substance abuse, and gay teen suicide emerge from the same source—a racist and misogynist social and economic system that dominates, punishes, and abuses all things colored, female, or perceived as female-like. By openly confronting Chicano sexuality and sexism, gay men can do their own part to unravel how both men *and* women have been formed and deformed by racist Amerika and our misogynist/catholic/colonized *mechicanidad;* and we can come that much closer to healing those fissures that have divided us as a people.

The AIDS epidemic has seriously shaken the foundation of the Chicano gay community, and gay men seem more willing than ever to explore those areas of political change that will ensure their survival. In their fight against AIDS, they have been rejected and neglected by both the white gay male establishment and the Latino heterosexual health-care community. They also have witnessed direct support by Latina lesbians.[7] Unlike the "queens" who have always been open about their sexuality, "passing" gay men have learned in a visceral way that being in "the closet" and preserving their "manly" image will not protect them, it will only make their dying more secret. I remember my friend Arturo Islas, the novelist. I think of how his writing begged to boldly announce his gayness. Instead, we learned it through vague references about "sinners" and tortured alcoholic characters who wanted nothing more than to "die dancing" beneath a lightning-charged sky just before a thunderstorm. Islas died of AIDS-related illness in 1990, having barely begun to examine the complexity of Chicano sexuality in his writing. I also think of essayist Richard Rodriguez, who, with so much death surrounding him, has recently begun to publicly address the subject of homosexuality; and yet, even ten years ago we all knew "Mr. Secrets" was gay from his assimilationist *Hunger of Memory.*[8] Had he "come out" in 1982, the white establishment would have been far less willing to promote him as the "Hispanic" anti-affirmative action spokesperson. He would have lost a lot of validity ... and opportunity. But how many lives are lost each time we cling to privileges that make other people's lives more vulnerable to violence?

At this point in history, lesbians and gay men can make a significant contribution to the creation of a new Chicano movement, one passionately committed to saving lives. As we are forced to struggle for our right to love free of disease and discrimination, "Aztlán" as our imagined homeland begins to take on renewed importance. Without the dream of a free world, a free world will never be realized. Chicana lesbians and gay men do not merely seek inclusion in the Chicano nation; we seek a nation strong enough to embrace a full range of racial diversities, human sexualities, and expressions of gender. We seek a culture that can allow for the natural expression of our femaleness and maleness and our love without prejudice or punishment. In a "queer" Aztlán, there would be no freaks, no "others" to point one's finger at. My Native American friends tell me that in some Native American tribes, gay men and lesbians were traditionally regarded as "two-spirited" people. Displaying both masculine and feminine aspects, they were highly respected members of their community, and were thought to possess a higher spiritual development.[9] Hearing of such traditions gives historical validation for what Chicana lesbians and gay men have always recognized—that lesbians and gay men play a significant spiritual, cultural, and political role within the Chicano community. *Somos activistas, académicos y artistas, parteras y políticos, curanderas y campesinos.* With or without heterosexual acknowledgement, lesbians and gay men have continued to actively redefine familia, *cultura,* and *comunidad.* We have formed circles of support and survival, often drawing from the more egalitarian models of Indigenous communities.

Indigenismo: The Re-Tribalization of Our People

In recent years, for gay and straight Chicanos alike, our indigenismo has increased in importance as we witness the ultimate failure of Anglo-Americanism to bring harmony to our lives. In Ward Churchill's *Struggle for the Land,* he describes an "Indigenist" as someone who "takes the rights of indigenous peoples as the highest priority," and who "draws upon the traditions ... of native peoples the world over." Many Chicanos would by this definition consider themselves Indigenists, subscribing to an indigenismo that is derived specifically from the traditions of *mechicano indio* peoples. Since the early seventies, Chicanos have worked in coalition with other Native American tribes and have participated in inter-tribal gatherings, political-prisoner campaigns, land-rights struggles, and religious ceremonies. Chicano Nation has been varyingly accepted as a tribe by other Native American peoples, usually more in the honorary sense than in any official capacity. The Indigenous Women's Network, for example, has included Chicanas since its inception in 1984.

Most Chicanos can claim, through physical traits alone, that we are of Native blood (we often joke that Chicanos are usually the most Indian-looking people in a room full of "skins"). The majority of us, however, has been denied direct information regarding our tribal affiliations. Since our origins are usually in the Southwest and México, Chicanos' Indian roots encompass a range of nations including Apache, Yaqui, Papago, Navajo, and Tarahumara from the border regions, as well as dozens of Native tribes throughout México. Regardless of verifiable genealogy, many Chicanos have recently begun to experience a kind of collective longing to return to our culture's traditional indigenous beliefs and ways of constructing community in order to find concrete solutions for the myriad problems confronting us, from the toxic dump sites in our neighborhoods to rape.

"Tribe," based on the traditional models of Native Americans, is an alternative socio-economic structure that holds considerable appeal for those of us who recognize the weaknesses of the isolated patriarchal capitalist family structure. This is not to say that all Native Americans subscribe to the sametribal structures or that contemporary Indians fully practice traditional tribal ways. Few Native peoples today are allowed real political autonomy and self-determination. Tribal governments are corrupted by U.S. interference through the Bureau of Indian Affairs, the U.S. military, the FBI, and the U.S. Department of Energy. In essence, however, the tribal model is a form of community-building that can accommodate socialism, feminism, and environmental protection. In an ideal world, tribal members are responsive and responsible to one another and the natural environment. Cooperation is rewarded over competition. Acts of violence against women and children do not occur in secret and perpetrators are held accountable to the rest of the community. "Familia" is not dependent upon male-dominance or heterosexual coupling. Elders are respected and women's leadership is fostered, not feared.

But it is not an ideal world. Any Indian on or off the reservation can tell you about the obstacles to following traditional ways. The reservation is not indigenous to Native Americans; it is a colonial model invented to disempower Native peoples. The rates of alcoholism, suicide, and domestic violence are testimony to the effectiveness of that system. Chicanos, living in the colony of the U.S. barrio, have the same scars: AIDS, drugs, brown-on-brown murder, poverty, and environmental contamination. Nevertheless, the present-day values and organized struggles of traditional Native communities throughout the Americas represent real hope for halting the quickly accelerating level of destruction affecting all life on this continent.

Madre Tierra/Madre Mujer: The Struggle for Land[10]

Journal Entry

I sit in a hotel room. A fancy hotel room with two walls of pure glass and pure Vancouver night skyline filling them. I sit on top of the bed and eat Japanese take-out. The Canadian t.v. news takes us east to the province of Quebec, to some desolate area with no plumbing or sewage, no running water, where a group of Inuit people have been displaced. To some desolate area where Inuit children stick their faces into bags and sniff gas fumes for the high, the rush, the trip, for the escape out of this hell-hole that is their life. One young boy gives the finger to the t.v. camera. "They're angry," an Inuit leader states. "I'm angry, too." At thirty, he is already an old man. And I hate this Canada as much as I hate these dis-United States.

But I go on eating my Japanese meal that has somehow turned rotten on my tongue and my bloody culpability mixes with the texture of dead fish flesh and no wonder I stand on the very edge of the balcony on the 26th floor of this hotel looking down on restaurant-row Vancouver and imagine how easy and impossible it would be to leap in protest for the gas-guzzling Inuit children.

The primary struggle for Native peoples across the globe is the struggle for land. In 1992, 500 years after the arrival of Columbus, on the heels of the Gulf War and the dissolution of the Soviet Union, the entire world is reconstructing itself. No longer frozen into the Soviet/Yanqui paradigm of a "Cold" and invented "War," Indigenous peoples are responding en masse to the threat of a global capitalist "mono-culture" defended by the "hired guns" of the U.S. military. Five hundred years after Columbus' arrival, they are spearheading an international movement with the goal of sovereignty for all Indigenous nations.

Increasingly, the struggles on this planet are not for "nation-states," but for nations of people, bound together by spirit, land, language, history, and blood.[11] This is evident from the intifada of the Palestinians residing within Israel's stolen borders and the resistance of the Cree and Inuit Indians in northern Quebec. The Kurds of the Persian Gulf region understand this, as do the Ukrainians of what was once the Soviet Union. Chicanos are also a nation of people, internally colonized within the borders of the U.S. nation-state.

Few Chicanos really believe we can wrest Aztlán away from Anglo-America. And yet, residing in those Southwestern territories, especially those areas not completely appropriated by *gringolandia*, we instinctively remember it as Mexican Indian land and can still imagine it as a distinct nation. In our most private moments, we ask ourselves, *If the Soviet Union could dissolve, why can't the United States?*

Dreams of the disintegration of the United States as we know it are not so private among North American Indians. The dissolution of the Soviet Union has given renewed impetus to seccessionist thinking by Indians here in the United States. One plan, the "North American Union of Indigenous Nations," described in Ward Churchill's book, calls for the reunification of Indian peoples and territories to comprise a full third of continental United States, including much of Aztlán. Not surprisingly, Chicano Nation is not mentioned as part of this new confederacy, which speaks to the still tenuous alliance between Chicano and Native American peoples. Nevertheless, the spirit of the plan is very much in accord with Chicano nationalists' most revolutionary dreams of reclaiming a homeland, side by side with other Indian Nations.

If the material basis of every nationalist movement is land, then the reacquisition, defense, and protection of Native land and its natural resources are the basis for rebuilding Chicano nation. Without the sovereignty of Native peoples, including Chicanos, and support for our land-based struggles, the world will be lost to North American greed, and our culturas lost with it. The "last frontier" for Northern capitalists lies buried in coal and uranium-rich reservation lands and in the remaining rainforests of the Amazon. The inhabitants of these territories—the Diné, the North Cheyenne, the Kayapó, etc.—are the very people who in 1992 offer the world community "living models" of ways to live in balance with nature and safeguard the earth as we know it. The great historical irony is that 500 years after the Conquest, the conqueror must now turn to the conquered for salvation.

We are speaking of bottom-line considerations. I can't understand when in 1992 with 100 acres of rainforest disappearing every minute, with global warming, with babies being born without brains in South *Tejas,* with street kids in Río sniffing glue to stifle their hunger, with Mohawk women's breast milk being contaminated by the poisoned waters of the Great Lakes Basin, how we as people of color, as people of Indian blood, as people with the same last names as our Latin American counterparts, are not alarmed by the destruction of Indigenous and mestizo peoples. How is it Chicanos cannot see ourselves as victims of the same destruction, already in its advanced stages? Why do we not collectively experience the urgency for alternatives based not on what our oppressors advise, but on the advice of elders and ancestors who may now speak to us only in dreams?

What they are telling us is very clear. The road to the future is the road from our past. Traditional Indigenous communities (our Indian "past" that too many Chicanos have rejected) provide practical answers for our survival. At the Earth Summit in Río de Janeiro in June 1992, representatives from "developing countries," and grassroots, Indigenous, and people-of-color organizations joined together to demand the economic programs necessary to create their own sustainable ecologically sound communities. In a world where eighty-five percent of all the income, largely generated from the natural resources of Indigenous lands and "Third World" countries, goes to twenty-three percent of the people, Fidel Castro said it best: "Let the ecological debt be paid, not the foreign debt."

And here all the connecting concerns begin to coalesce. Here the Marxist meets the ecologist. We need look no further than the North American Free Trade Agreement (NAFTA) to understand the connection between global ecological devastation and the United States' relentless drive to expand its markets. NAFTA is no more than a 21st-century plot to continue the North's exploitation of the cheap labor, lax environmental policies, and the natural resources of the South. The United States has no intention of responding to the environmental crisis. George Bush's decision to "stand alone on principle" and refuse to sign the Bio-Diversity Treaty said it all. Profit over people. Profit over protection. No sustainable development is possible in the Americas if the United States continues to demand hamburgers, Chrysler automobiles, and refrigerators from hungry, barefoot, and energy-starved nations. There is simply not enough to go around, no new burial ground for toxic waste that isn't sacred, no untapped energy source that doesn't suck the earth dry. Except for the sun ... except for the wind, which are infinite in their generosity and virtually ignored.

The earth is female. Whether myth, metaphor, or memory, she is called "Mother" by all peoples of all times. *Madre Tierra.* Like woman, Madre Tierra has been raped, exploited for her resources, rendered inert, passive, and speechless. Her cries manifested in earthquakes, tidal waves, hurricanes, volcanic eruptions are not heeded. But the Indians take note and so do the women, the women with the capacity to remember.

Native religions have traditionally honored the female alongside the male. Religions that grow exclusively from the patriarchal capitalist imagination, instead of the requirements of nature, enslave the female body. The only religion we need is one based on the good sense of living in harmony with nature. Religion should serve as a justification against greed, not for it. Bring back the rain gods, corn gods, father sun, and mother moon and keep those gods happy. Whether we recognize it or not, those gods are today, this day, punishing us for our excess. What humankind has destroyed will wreak havoc on the destroyer. Fried skin from holes in the ozone is only one example.

The earth is female. It is no accident then that the main grassroots activists defending the earth, along with Native peoples, are women of all races and cultures. Regardless of the so-called "advances" of Western "civilization," women remain the chief caretakers, nurturers, and providers for our children and our elders. These are the mothers of East Los Angeles, McFarland, and Kettleman City, fighting toxic dumps, local incinerators and pesticide poisoning, women who experience the earth's contamination in the deformation and death occurring within their very wombs. We do not have to be mothers to know this. Most women know what it is to be seen as the Earth is seen—a receptacle for male violence and greed. Over half the agricultural workers in the world are women who receive less training and less protection than their male counterparts. We do not control how we produce and reproduce, how we labor and love. And *how will our lands be free if our bodies aren't?*

Land remains the common ground for all radical action. But land is more than the rocks and trees, the animal and plant life that make up the territory of Aztlán or Navajo Nation or Maya Mesoamerica. For immigrant and native alike, land is also the factories where we work, the water our children drink, and the housing project where we live. For women, lesbians, and gay men, land is that physical mass called our bodies. Throughout *las Américas,* all these "lands" remain under occupation by an Anglocentric, patriarchal, imperialist United States.

La Causa Chicana: Entering the Next Millennium

As a Chicana lesbian, I know that the struggle I share with all Chicanos and Indigenous peoples is truly one of sovereignty, the sovereign right to wholly inhabit oneself (*cuerpo y alma*) and one's territory *(pan y tierra)*. I don't know if we can ever take back Aztlán from Anglo-America, but in the name of a new Chicano nationalism we can work to defend remaining Indian territories. We can work to teach one another that our freedom as a people is mutually dependent and cannot be parceled out—class before race before sex before sexuality. A new Chicano nationalism calls for the integration of both the traditional and the revolutionary, the ancient and the contemporary. It requires a serious reckoning with the weaknesses in our mestizo culture, and a reaffirmation of what has preserved and sustained us as a people. I am clear about one thing: fear has not sustained us. Fear of action, fear of speaking, fear of women, fear of queers.

As these 500 years come to a close, I look forward to a new América, where the only "discovery" to be made is the rediscovery of ourselves as members of the global community. Nature will be our teacher, for she alone knows no prejudice. Possibly as we ask men to give up being "men," we must ask humans to give up being "human," or at least to give up the human capacity for greed. Simply, we must give back to the earth what we take from it. We must submit to a higher "natural" authority, as we invent new ways of making culture, making tribe, to survive and flourish as members of the world community in the next millennium.

Notes

An earlier version of this essay was first presented at the First National LLEGO (Latino/a Lesbian and Gay Organization) Conference in Houston, Texas, on May 22, 1992. A later version was presented at a Quincentenary Conference at the University of Texas in Austin on October 31, 1992.

1. Chicano term for "queer" folk.
2. To this day, there are still pockets of Chicano nationalists—mostly artists, poets, and cultural workers—who continue to work on a local and regional level.
3. UC Berkeley's Chicano/Latino immigrant students have not generally encountered the same degree of poverty and exploitation experienced by undocumented Mexican and Central American immigrants.
4. Further discussion of the "hispanicization" of the U.S. Latino can be found in Cherríe Moraga, "Art in *América con Acento*" in *The Last Generation,* (Cambridge, MA: South End Press).
5. The twenty-five-year-old Chicano *Teatro* Movement is an apt example. Initiated by Luis Valdez' *Teatro Campesino,* the teatro movement has been notorious for its male dominance even within its so-called collective structures. Over eighty percent of the Chicano Theatres across the country are directed by men. No affirmative-action policies have been instituted to encourage the development of Chicana playwrights, technicians, or directors. In recent years, however, there has been some progress in this area with the production of a handful

of Chicana playwrights, including Josefina López, Evelina Fernández, Edit Villareal, and this author. To this day, gay and lesbian images and feminist criticism are considered taboo in most Chicano theatres.

6. The image alludes to Chicano cultural nationalists who during the seventies neoindigenist period sometimes wore feathers *(plumas)* and other Indian attire at cultural events.

7. In contrast to the overwhelming response by lesbians to the AIDS crisis, breast cancer, which has disproportionately affected the lesbian community, has received little attention from the gay men's community in particular, and the public at large. And yet, the statistics are devastating. One out of every nine women in the United States will get breast cancer: 44,500 U.S. women will die of breast cancer this year *(Boston Globe,* November 5, 1991).

8. See Rodríguez' essay "Late Victorians" in his most recent collection, *Days of Obligation: An Argument with My Mexican Father.*

9. This was not the case among all tribes nor is homosexuality generally condoned in contemporary Indian societies. See Ramón A. Gutiérrez "Must We Deracinate Indians to Find Gay Roots?" *Outlook: National Lesbian and Gay Quarterly,* Winter 1989.

10. I wish to thank Marsha Gómez, the Indigenous Women's Network, and the *Alma de Mujer* Center for Social Change in Austin, Texas, for providing me with statistical and other current information about Indigenous peoples' struggles for environmental safety and sovereignty, as well as published materials on the '92 Earth Summit in Brazil.

11. The dissolution of what was heretofore the nation-state of Yugoslavia, composed of Serbs, Slovenes, Croats, Albanians, and Macedonians, including the Muslim and Orthodox religions, represents the rise of bitter nationalist sentiment gone awry. It is a horror story of ethnic and cultural nationalism turned into nazism and serves as a painful warning against fascist extremism in nationalist campaigns.

READING 8.2 POST-READING COMPREHENSION QUESTIONS

- Summarize how *El Movimiento* was "de-formed."

- Describe what "Queer Aztlán" is.

- Paraphrase the quote: "I'm clear about one thing: fear has not sustained us. Fear of action, fear of speaking, fear of women, fear of queers."

End-of-Chapter Critical Thinking Questions

Directions: Respond to each of the questions about the readings. Refer to these sources to support your answers.

- How can we link struggles for social and political rights to notions of identity and culture?

- How can we understand Lowriders as narratives or visual texts of working-class life?

- According to Moraga, how can we invent new ways of making culture that are sustainable for Chicana and Chicano communities in the future?

Further Readings

Barnet-Sanchez, Holly, and Tim Drescher. *Give Me Life: Iconography and Identity in East LA Murals.* Albuquerque, NM.: University of New Mexico Press, 2016.

Cockcroft, Eva Sperling, and Holly Barnet-Sánchez. *Signs From The Heart: California Chicano Murals.* Venice, LA. and Albuquerque, NM.: SPARC and UNM Press, 1990.

Gaspar de Alba, Alicia. *Velvet Barrios: Popular Culture & Chicana/o Sexualities.* New York, NY.: Palgrave Macmillan, 2003.

Gómez-Quiñones, Juan. "On Culture," *Revista Chicano-Riqueña* 5, no. 2 (1977): 29–47.

Johnson, Gaye Theresa. *Spaces of Conflict, Sounds of Solidarity: Music, Race, and Spatial Entitlement in Los Angeles.* Berkeley, CA.: University of California Press, 2013.

Kelley, Robin D.G. *Race Rebels: Culture, Politics, and the Black Working Class. Reprint ed.* New York, NY.: Free Press, 1996.

Kun, Josh, and Laura Pulido. *Black and Brown in Los Angeles: Beyond Conflict and Coalition.* Berkeley, CA.: University of California Press, 2013.

Latorre, Guisela. *Walls of Empowerment: Chicana/o Indigenist Murals of California.* Austin, TX.: University of Texas Press, 2008.

Lipsitz, George. *Rainbow at Midnight: Labor and Culture in the 1940s.* Urbana and Chicago, IL.: University of Illinois Press, 1981.

Moraga, Cherríe. *The Last Generation: Prose and Poetry.* Boston, MA.: South End Press, 1993.

Moraga, Cherríe, and Gloria E. Anzaldúa. *This Bridge Called My Back: Writings by Radical Women of Color.* Berkeley, CA.: Third Women Press, 2002.

Montoya, Malaquias, and Lezlie Salkowitz-Montoya. "A Critical Perspective on the State of Chicano Art." *Metamorfosis: The Journal of Northwest Art and Culture* 3, no. 1 (1980).

Ontiveros, Randy J. *In the Spirit of a New People: The Cultural Politics of the Chicano movement.* New York, NY. and London, UK.: NYU Press, 2014.

Bright, Brenda Jo, and Elizabeth Bakewell eds. *Looking High and Low: Art and Cultural Identity.* Tucson, AZ.: University of Arizona Press, 1995.

Epilogue

W hile the sources in this volume bring together a cross section of ideas and historical circumstances, one important theme that is common to the body of readings is that of class consciousness. It is true that cultural and ethnic ties serve to bind many of the *voces* featured in the book, yet a broader case can be made that a collective consciousness of class emerges and supports the struggle for self-determination throughout these narratives. Whether it was *Las Gorras Blancas* using notions of race and class to organize and respond to oppressive land dispossession, or the Wobblies (IWW) seeking to create "One Big Union" across racial lines to ward off violence aimed at migratory laborers, or the collaboration between Chicano and manong farmworkers during the 1960s and 1970s to create more equitable working conditions, class consciousness clearly played a critical role in the struggle for autonomy.

Without question, the initial duty of Chicano history was to recapture and recover narratives that all too often had been omitted, obscured, and distorted by traditional historians. The rejection of the idea that Mexicans and Mexican Americans were an ahistorical people fueled a cadre of researchers and writers to begin the development of this field, and this volume is evidence of that academic charge. According to historian Natalia Molina, this generation of scholars "... provided ways to think about the relationship among race and power, institutionalized racism, segmented labor markets, community formation, segregation in the urban landscape, and civil rights outside of a black-white binary."[1] With time and with introspection Chicana/o history emerged as an attempt to develop a more expansive, more complete, and more inclusive form of history. The sources included in this volume demonstrate the trajectory and maturation of Chicana/o history, and how that history has been used to advocate for change.

---

1 Natalia Molina, "Examining Chicana/o History through a Relational Lens," *Pacific Historical Review* 82, no. 4 (2013): 520–41.

CPSIA information can be obtained
at www.ICGtesting.com
Printed in the USA
LVHW061237200123
737508LV00011B/805